EYEWITNESS TRAVEL

BRITTANY

EYEWITNESS TRAVEL

BRITTANY

LONDON, NEW YORK,
MELBOURNE, MUNICH AND DELHI
www.dk.com

Produced By Hachette Tourisme, Paris, France

Editorial Director Cécile Boyer
Project Editor Catherine Laussucq
Art Director Jad-Hersienne
Designers Maogani
Cartography Fabrice Le Goff

Contributors
Gaëtan du Chatenet, Jean-Philippe Follet,
Jean-Yves Gendillard, Éric Gibory, Renée Grimaud,
Georges Minois

Dorling Kindersley Limited
Publishing Managers Jane Ewart, Fay Franklin
English Translation & Editor Lucilla Watson
DTP Jason Little, Conrad van Dyk
Production Sarah Dodd

Printed and bound in China.

First Published in Great Britain in 2003
by Dorling Kindersley Limited,
80 Strand, London WC2R 0RL

15 16 17 18 10 9 8 7 6 5 4 3 2 1

Reprinted with revisions 2005, 2007, 2009, 2011, 2013, 2015

Copyright © 2003, 2015 Dorling Kindersley Limited, London
A Penguin Random House Company

MIX
Paper from
responsible sources
FSC
www.fsc.org   FSC™ C018179

Front cover main image: Côtes Sauvage, Morbihan

◀ Castel Meur House in Côtes d'Armor

Contents

Painting of Louis XII and Anne of
Brittany, Musée Thomas Dobrée

The Tour de l'Horloge, offering a wide view
over Dinan

Portsall in Côte des Abers *(see pp132–3)*

Basilique Notre-Dame, in Folgoët

Travellers' Needs

Bagpipe-player at Festival Interceltique in Lorient

Faïencerie Henriot retail outlet in Quimper

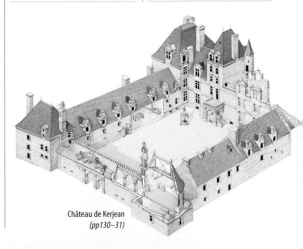
Château de Kerjean
(pp130–31)

HOW TO USE THIS GUIDE

This Eyewitness Travel Guide helps you to get the most from your stay in Brittany. It provides detailed practical information and expert recommendations. *Introducing Brittany* maps the entire region, sets it in its historical and cultural context. The six regional chapters describe important sights with the help of maps, photographs and illustrations. The *Travellers' Needs* section gives detailed information about hotels, restaurants, shops and markets, entertainment and sports. The *Survival Guide*, provides practical advice on everything from transport to personal safety.

Brittany Region by Region

This region has been divided into six colour-coded areas for easy reference. Each chapter opens with an introduction to the area. This is followed by a regional map showing the most interesting towns, villages and places. Finding your way around the chapter is made simple by the numbering system used throughout. The most important sights and towns are covered in detail in two or more full pages.

1 Introduction
The landscape, history and character of each region is described here, showing how the area has developed over the centuries and what it has to offer the visitor today.

A locator map shows the region in relation to the whole of Brittany.

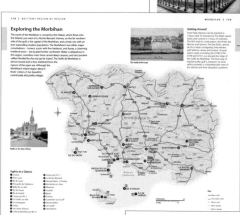

Each area of Brittany can be quickly identified by its colour coding.

2 Regional Map
This gives an illustrated overview of the whole region. All the sights are numbered and there are also useful tips on getting around the area by car and public transport.

Story boxes highlight special or unique aspects of a particular sight.

3 Detailed information on each sight
All the important towns and other places to visit are described individually. They are listed in order, following the numbering on the Regional Map. Within each town or city, there is detailed information on important buildings and other major sights.

4 **Major Towns**
An introduction covers the history, character and geography of the town. The main sights are described individually and plotted on a Town Map.

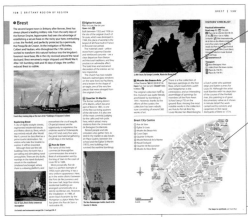

Practical Information lists all the information you need to visit every sight such as address, telephone number, open and closed dates.

The Town Map shows all main through roads as well as minor streets of interest to visitors. All the sights are plotted, along with the bus and train stations, parking, tourist offices and churches.

5 **Street-by-Street Map**
Towns or districts of special interest to visitors are shown in detailed 3D, with photographs of the most important sights. This gives a bird's-eye view of towns or districts of special interest.

A suggested route for a walk covers the most interesting streets in the area.

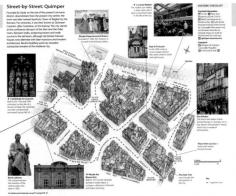

A Visitors' Checklist gives contact points for tourist and transport information, plus details of market days and local festival dates.

6 **The top sights**
These are given two or more pages. Important buildings are dissected to reveal their interiors; museums have colour-coded floorplans to help you locate the most interesting exhibits.

Key indicate the features no visitor should miss.

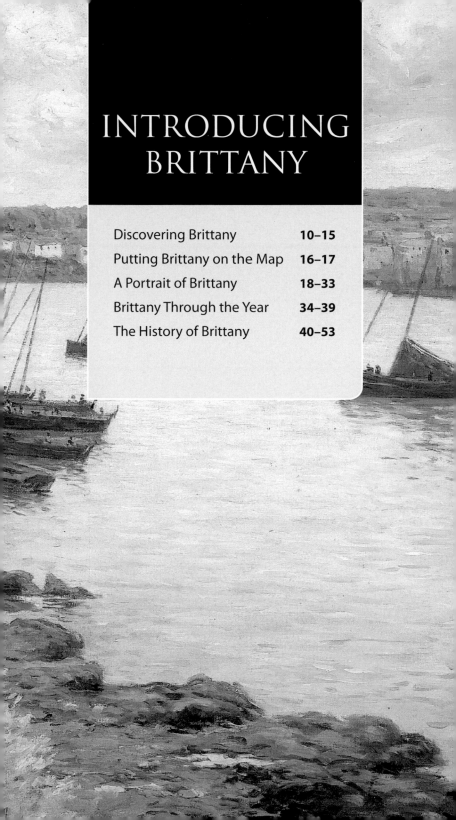

INTRODUCING BRITTANY

DISCOVERING BRITTANY

The following itineraries have been designed to take in the highlights of Brittany with a minimum of driving. The first itinerary outlined here is a week's tour of southwestern Brittany that takes in some of the region's most beautiful towns and cities, coastal resorts and the megalithic wonders around the Golfe du Morbihan. Next is a week in southern Brittany based around the lively city of Nantes – a tour with a number of

family-friendly activities. Finally, there is a two-week itinerary that covers the attractions of northern Brittany between Rennes and Brest, including the two cities and encompassing the stunning Côte de Granite Rose, Mont-St-Michel and St-Malo. Additional suggestions are included for visitors who wish to extend the stay for one or more days. Split, combine and follow your favourite tours or simply be inspired.

A Week in Southwestern Brittany

- Admire the magnificent altarpiece of the Ten Thousand Martyrs in **Crozon**.

- Discover the secrets of **Quimper**'s colourful glazed pottery.

- Hike along the scenic Pointe du Cabellou promontory, just south of the evocative walled port of **Concarneau**.

- Wander through the pretty lanes and art galleries of **Pont-Aven**.

- Explore some of Brittany's most breathtaking coasts and beaches, along the **Presqu'île de Quiberon**.

- Marvel at **Carnac**'s extraordinary megalithic alignements, and the **Cairn de Gavrinis**, France's largest dolmen.

The dock at Concarneau
Yachts, trawlers and sardine boats dot the dock of Concarneau, one of France's leading fishing ports. The Musée de la Pêche, at the entrance to the *ville close*, offers an insight into the town's maritime history.

Two Weeks in Northern Brittany

- Explore Brittany's largest market at the Place des Lices in **Rennes**.
- Tour the mighty medieval castles in **Vitré** and **Fougères**.
- Visit spectacular **Mont-St-Michel** and its abbey, majestically isolated in a sweeping tidal bay.
- Imagine the lives of the *corsairs* in the granite walled port of **St-Malo**.

- Identify the curious eroded shapes in the Côte de Granite Rose around **Perros-Guirec**.
- Descend in a glass-lined lift into a pod of sharks at the remarkable Océanopolis in **Brest**.
- Admire the scenery of cliffs and beaches at **Le Conquet**, and sail to France's westernmost point, the **Île d'Ouessant**.

Château de Vitré
Perched on a rocky outcrop, the imposing Château de Vitré houses an excellent museum that contains medieval and Renaissance sculpture, Breton paintings as well as 16th- and 17th-century tapestries.

A Week in Southern Brittany

- Ride a giant mechanical elephant at Les Machines d'Île in **Nantes**.
- Seek out the Tomb of Merlin and the Fountain of Youth in the **Forêt de Paimpont**.
- Watch the colourful exotic bird show in the **Parc Zoologique de Branféré**.
- Take a boat ride past thatched cottages in the **Parc Naturel Régional de la Grande Brière**.
- Relax on the sandy beaches of **La Baule**, and encounter creatures from the deep at the **Océarium du Croisic**.
- Discover the history of the great Transatlantic ocean liners at Escal-Atlantique in **St-Nazaire**.

Key

— Two Weeks in Northern Brittany
— A Week in Southwestern Brittany
— A Week in Southern Brittany

A Week in Southwestern Brittany

- **Airport** Arrive at the Brest-Bretagne Airport.
- **Transport** A car is essential for the trip.
- **Moving on** Depart from Rennes by train or bus.

Day 1: Landévennec to Quimper
Head southeast from the Brest-Bretagne airport to take the scenic Corniche de Térénez to **Landévennec** *(p152)* to see the ruins of the abbey and explore the Musée de l'Ancienne Abbaye. Drive on to **Crozon** *(p152)* to swim in its turquoise lagoons and relax on its sandy beaches. While here, visit the Église St-Pierre to marvel at the extraordinary 16th-century altarpiece of the Ten Thousand Martyrs, with its 24 sculpted wooden, painted panels. Carry on to **Camaret** *(pp152–3)* for a tour of Vauban's fortifications; on the outskirts are the 142 menhirs of the Alignements de Lagatjar *(p153)*. End the day at **Pleyben** *(pp156–7)*, renowned for its unique dark granite "Gospel in Stone" calvary.

Day 2: Quimper
Spend a day in the historical, faïence-manufacturing town of **Quimper** *(pp164–71)*. Start at the covered market and walk along Rue Kéréon and its surrounding streets to see Quimper's traditional corbelled houses. Next, visit the **Cathédrale St-Corentin** *(pp168–9)*, a Romanesque Gothic masterpiece dating back to 1239

and illuminated by 15th-century stained glass windows. Take time to explore the nearby **Musée des Beaux-Arts** *(p167)*, with works by the Pont-Aven school, and the **Musée Départemental Breton d'Art et de Traditions Populaires** *(pp166–7)*, covering 3,000 years of Breton history and traditional costumes. If time allows, head for the **Musée de la Faïence** *(p168)* in the historic Locmaria district, which explains why Quimper makes faïence, along with a display of historic pottery. Top it all off with a factory tour of **Faïencerie HB-Henriot** *(p168)*.

Day 3: Concarneau
Known as the "Blue Town" after the blue fishing nets used in the early 20th century, the walled **Concarneau** *(pp172–4)* is the sixth-largest fishing port in France. Visit the Musée de la Pêche *(p174)* which houses maritime exhibits as well as an aquarium containing Atlantic fish species. A short walk southwest is the Marinarium *(p174)*, one of Europe's first marine research stations. After a seafood lunch, take a walk around the nearby Pointe du Cabellou *(p174)*, a beautiful promontory lined with sandy coves.

Day 4: Pont-Aven and Quimperlé
Drive to the famous 19th-century artists' colony of **Pont-Aven** *(p175)*, where Paul Gauguin painted many of his early masterpieces. Spend time exploring the town's various art galleries housing works by contemporary artists. The Musée de Pont-Aven provides

A cluster of half-timbered medieval houses in Vannes

an insight into the town's history. From here, take the highway east to **Quimperlé** *(p175)*, an impressive town of noble residences and churches.

Day 5: Kernascléden, Pontivy and Josselin
Delve inland to **Kernascléden** *(p201)* to see eerie frescoes depicting the Dance of Death in the village's 15th-century church. Carry on to **Pontivy** *(p200)* for a stroll around the medieval town that sprawls out around the imposing Château des Rohans. Round off the day in **Josselin** *(p197)* with a tour of its impressive Flamboyant-Gothic chateau and the Basilique Notre-Dame-du-Roncier, which shelters a miraculous statue of the Virgin.

Day 6–7: Vannes and the Golfe du Morbihan
A 45-minute drive from Josselin, **Vannes** *(pp192–5)* is a beautiful medieval city. Begin at the splendid Cathédrale St-Pierre *(p194)*, and then head to the nearby Musée de la Cohue *(p194)* to explore its fine collection of works, including Delacroix's celebrated *Crucifixion*. Later, visit the Musée d'Histoire *(p195)*, filled with intriguing prehistoric relics. Vannes makes a superb base for exploring the **Golfe du Morbihan** *(pp188–91)*. The main attraction here is the **Cairn de Gavrinis** *(p190)* – the largest dolmen in France. Around 30 km (19 miles) west of the town

View of the 17th-century cloisters at Ste-Anne-d'Auray

are the astonishing alignments of **Carnac** (pp184–5). Don't miss the enormous broken menhir and tumulus at Locmariaquer (p186), a short distance east of Carnac. Take in the breathtaking scenery along the **Presqu'île de Quiberon** (p181) on the way to **Auray** (pp186–7), which boasts the great pilgrimage church, **Ste-Anne d'Auray** (p187), then head to the train station at Rennes.

To extend your trip...
Spend a couple of days exploring the islands in the Golfe du Morbihan: **Belle-Île-en-Mer** (pp182–3), the **Île de Houat** (p182), and the **Île de Hoëdic** (p183).

A Week in Southern Brittany

- **Airport** Arrive and depart from the Nantes-Atlantique Airport.
- **Transport** A car is essential for this trip.
- **Moving on** Depart Nantes by train or bus.

Day 1–2: Nantes
Begin with a tour of the pedestrianized **Place du Bouffay** (p210), and then walk northeast to the **Cathédrale St-Pierre-et-St-Paul** (p212). Set aside plenty of time to explore the history museum in the Renaissance **Château des Ducs de Bretagne** (pp214–15). Afterwards, go to the **Musée des Beaux-Arts** (p212) which houses works by Monet, Rubens and Courbet.
Start the next day at the Neo-Classical **Quartier Graslin** (p210), and then head for the **Musée Thomas Dobrée** (p211) nearby to see his excellent private collection of paintings, tapestries and armour. While away the afternoon in the 19th-century **Passage Pommeraye** shopping arcade (pp210–11), before visiting the **Musée Jules-Verne** (p213). Don't miss the **Les Machines de l'Île** (p213), where artist-engineers create delightful handcrafted steam punk rides and installations.

Outdoor café in the walled old town of Guérande

Day 3: Redon and Paimpont
Drive to **Redon** (p70) to see the 9th-century Benedictine abbey of St-Sauveur, with a triple-tiered Romanesque belfry. From there, carry on north to **Paimpont** (p68), which serves as the starting point for hikes in the **Forêt de Paimpont** (p68) – the magical Forêt de Brocéliande of Arthurian legend. Browse exhibits at the Centre de l'Imaginaire Arthurien that occupies the Château de Comper, which is said to have been the home of the fabled fairy Vivian. Later, follow the D31 to seek out Merlin's Tomb and the Fountain of Youth.

Day 4: Ploërmel to La Roche-Bernard
Proceed west to **Ploërmel** (p197) to admire the striking reliefs on the Église St-Armel and the Maison des Marmousets. Make a stopover at **Questembert** (p196) to see its remarkable covered market, before heading to **La Roche-Bernard** (p196) on the Vilaine estuary. Here, visit the Musée de la Vilaine Maritime, then spend the rest of the day in the colourful botanical gardens of the Parc Zoologique de Branféré.

Day 5: Parc Regionale de la Grande Brière and Guérande
Take a boat tour of the **Parc Régionale de la Grande Brière** (pp208–209) past thatched cottages and fascinating Neolithic monuments, including the impressive La Barbière dolmen. Afterwards, drive to

charming **Guérande** (p206), the Renaissance walled town synonymous with France's gourmet table salt. Soak up some of the local history at the Musée Château du Pays de Guérande, before visiting the Musée de la Poupée et du Jouet Ancien, famous for its historic toy collection.

Day 6: Le Croisic and La Baule
Drive west to the tip of the Presqu'île de Guérande for a morning at the fishing port of **Le Croisic** (p206). Stop by the Océarium du Croisic (p206) to observe marine life from the Atlantic, and then head to the nearby Musée des Marais Salants (p206), dedicated to the history of the local salt marshes and salt pans. In the afternoon, relax on the long sandy beaches of **La Baule** (p207) or **Pornichet** (p207).

Day 7: St-Nazaire and Pornic
In the great ship-building port of **St-Nazaire** (p207), learn all about the various aspects of its main industry at the STX Chantiers de l'Atlantique, where cruise liners are built. Next, check out the Escal-Atlantic's exhibition on historic ocean liners. After lunch, explore the Écomusée devoted to the natural history of the Loire estuary. While here, take a tour of the French submarine L'Espadon. Spend the afternoon exploring the lavish 19th-century resort village of **Pornic** (p216) before returning to Nantes.

Exquisitely carved exterior of the Hôtel de Ville, Rennes

Two Weeks in Northern Brittany

- **Airports** International as well as domestic flights serve both Rennes-St-Jacques and Brest-Bretagne.
- **Transport** A car is essential for this trip.

Day 1: Rennes

The regional capital of Brittany, **Rennes** (pp62–7) is dotted with handsome timber-framed houses and Neo-Classical public buildings. Start with a stroll around the **Place des Lices** (p64), and then walk south to **Cathédrale St-Pierre** (p64) to see its 16th-century Flemish altarpiece. Next, visit the Neo-Classical **Hôtel de Ville** (p64) and **theatre** (p64), before checking out the nearby **Parlement de Bretagne** (pp66–7). Later, head to the **Musée des Beaux-Arts** (p65) that houses works by Leonardo da Vinci and Botticelli. After lunch, drive out to the medieval town of **La Guerche-en-Bretagne** (p71) to appreciate the carvings depicting the Seven Deadly Sins on the choir stalls of its Flamboyant-Gothic church. Round off the day at the enigmatic La Roche aux Fées (p71), one of the region's most spectacular Megalithic marvels with four chambers constructed from 41 enormous stones.

Day 2: Vitré and Fougères

Head for the elegant **Château des Rochers-Sévigné** (p72), which was once home to the

Marquise de Sévigné. From here, drive 8 km (5 miles) northwest to the picturesque fortified town of **Vitré**. Spend time exploring the impressive chateau-museum that displays the precious 16th-century triptych of Limoges enamels. Afterwards, visit the majestic Église Notre-Dame (p72). In the afternoon, carry on north to **Fougères** (p73) to explore the ramparts of its great medieval military castle set with 13 towers. End the day at the Musée Emmanuel-de-La Villéon (p73) filled with Impressionist paintings of Breton landscapes and scenes of daily life.

Day 3–4: Mont-St-Michel and around

Travel northwest to the rocky islet of **Mont-St-Michel** (pp78–81), one of France's best-known landmarks, with its pyramid-shaped pile of abbey and town majestically rising out of the tidal bay. Devote the first day to exploring the abbey. Marvel at its towering spire, before heading to the beautiful Abbey Church. Pause awhile to admire the Norman Gothic cloister, and then make your way to the abbey's 13th-century Gothic masterpiece, Le Merveille, built directly into the rock face.

Allow a day to explore the fascinating **Baie du Mont-St-Michel** (p77) and its environs. Begin at the **Menhir de Camp Dolent** (p76), the tallest and finest of Brittany's standing stones. A short drive northwest lies **Dol-de-Bretagne** (p76), site of the colossal and splendid Cathédrale St-Samson (p79),

crowned with a lofty dome and full of artistic treasures, including 13th-century stained glass windows and one of the region's oldest Renaissance tombs. Afterwards, make your way up the granite outcrop of **Mont-Dol** (p77), which was once an island like Mont-St-Michel and famous for its breathtaking views over the surrounding area.

Day 5–6: St-Malo and around

Famous for its bold corsairs and long sandy beaches, **St-Malo** (pp84–9) is worth a day's exploration. Arrive at the imposing **Porte St-Vincente** (p84), the main entrance into the city, and head straight to the **Cathédrale St-Vincent** (p86) to see its magnificent interiors. From here, head to the **Musée d'Histoire** (p88), devoted to St-Malo's fascinating history. Afterwards, check out the aristocratic **Hôtel Magon-d'Asfeld** (p87) to see how the city's wealthy corsairs once lived.

Next day, visit the nearby oyster farms in **Cancale** (p83), and pack a picnic lunch for a hike along the coastal cliffs overlooking the English Channel; be sure to arrange a taxi for a ride back. Drive across the Rance to spend some time in **Dinard** (pp90–91), home to grand 19th-century mansions. See the 11th-century church of **St-Lunaire** (p91), before going for a stroll along the Chemin des Peintres in **St-Briac** (p91), where Renoir and Signac once set up their easels.

Day 7: Dinan

Drive south along the Rance River to picturesque **Dinan** (pp 114–17), renowned for its fine

Spectacular view of Mont-St-Michel

The imposing Fort La Latte looking out over the sea

half-timbered houses, notably around Place des Merciers *(p115)*. Explore the historic walled town and its harbour, before heading to the splendid Romanesque-Gothic St-Sauveur *(pp116–17)*, founded by a crusader, and then, Église St-Malo *(p116)* that boasts a fine Renaissance doorway. Climb up to the platform at the top of the castle keep to soak in gorgeous views over the town.

Day 8: Cap Fréhel and Pléneuf-Val-André
Head to the coastal resort of **St-Cast-Le Guildo** *(p113)* to take an hour-long boat trip on the old sailing boat, the *Dragous*, to the mighty **Fort La Latte** *(p113)*, which was the scene of battles during the Hundred Years' War. The trip also affords views of one of the most beautiful landscapes in all of Brittany: the majestic, sheer pink cliffs and promontory of **Cap Fréhel** *(p113)*. After the boating excursion, drive west to **Sables-d'Or-Les-Pins** *(p112)*, for a swim or walk along the beautiful Cap d'Erquy, before travelling to the chic holiday resort of **Pléneuf-Val-André** *(p112)*.

> **To extend your trip...**
> Take a short boat ride from Pointe de l'Arcouest *(p105)* to spend a day walking or cycling along the paths of the beautiful **Île de Bréhat** *(p104)*, or "Island of Flowers", with its charming town, Mediterranean flora, and lighthouses.

Day 9: St-Brieuc to Perros-Guirec
In the morning, drive to **St-Brieuc** *(p108)* for a walk around its historic centre, and a visit to the Cathédrale St-Étienne to admire its glorious Rococo altarpiece. Then, follow the coast west to the old fishing port of **Paimpol** *(p105)* for a wander among the romantic ruins of the Abbaye de Beauport. After lunch, go to **Tréguier** *(p106)* to see the impressive Cathédrale St-Tugdual *(pp106–107)*. End the day with a tour of the pink granite coast around **Perros-Guirec** *(p101)*; spend the night in **Lannion** *(p99)*.

Day 10: Morlaix to Carantec
Visit **Morlaix** *(pp122–5)*, once a major shipping port on the English Channel; today, its harbour hosts a flotilla of pleasure boats. Take a walk around town to see its fine historic houses and church buildings. Spend time exploring the Musée de Morlaix *(p123–24)*, with a beautifully carved granite spiral staircase and fireplace. From here, walk to the Église St-Matthieu to see a rare 14th-century statue of the Virgin and Holy Trinity. After lunch, drive over to the **Cairn de Barnenez** *(p125)*, Europe's largest and oldest burial mound dating from 4,500 BC. Later, go to **Carantec** *(p126)* to explore the Château du Taureau, built by the locals to defend themselves from English pirates.

Day 11: St-Thégonnec to Goulven
Travel south to see the magnificent Renaissance-era parish closes at **St-Thégonnec** *(pp144–5)* and **Guimiliau** *(p144)*, followed by the exquisite 16th-century church at **Bodilis** *(p143)*, with a beautiful porch and richly painted beams. In the afternoon, take a tour of the **Château de Kerjean** *(p130–31)*, which boasts features of a classic French chateau as well as a traditional Breton manor. Afterwards, take a leisurely stroll among the scenic dunes at Keremma *(p129)*, just east of **Goulven** *(pp128–9)*.

Day 12: Lesneven to Brest
Start in **Lesneven** *(p129)* at the Musée du Léon, which documents the local history. Next, visit the 15th-century pilgrimage church Basilique Notre-Dame in **Le Folgoët** *(p129)*, before heading to **Brest** *(pp138–41)* to get up close to the sharks and other marine creatures inhabiting the tanks of Océanopolis *(p141)*. Afterwards, stroll amidst the fascinating botanical wonders of the Conservatoire Botanique *(p141)*.

Day 13–14: Brest and around
Begin the day with an exploration of the Musée du Vieux Brest *(p140)*, before heading to the Musée des Beaux-Arts *(p139)*. Devote the rest of the day to touring westernmost Finistère. Drive out to visit the remarkable church at **La Martyre** *(p143)*, then head a short distance west to see the attractive riverbank houses and habitable bridge at **Landerneau** *(pp142–3)*. Travel south to **Daoulas** *(p142)* to see the beautiful cloisters and gardens of the abbey. Next day, visit **St-Renan** *(p134)* to explore the Musée du Patrimoine, dedicated to the town's markets. Wind off the day with a tour of the stunning cliffs and beaches at **Le Conquet**.

> **To extend your trip...**
> Spend a few days exploring France's westernmost point: the unspoiled **Île Ouessant** *(p135)*, with its lighthouses, beaches, and the ancient cromlech at the Presqu'île de Pen ar Lan *(p137)*.

Putting Brittany on the Map

Surrounded by 2,863 km (1,779 miles) of coastline, Brittany covers an area of 34,000 sq km (13,125 sq miles), or 6 per cent of French territory. It has over 4 million inhabitants (7 per cent of the French population) including Loire-Atlantique, and a population density of 119 per sq km (308 per sq mile). Over the last 25 years, Brittany's population has increased faster than the national average. The westernmost point of France, Brittany has become an economic hub of international importance. Its growing prosperity is paralleled by a strong cultural identity.

Key

- ☐ Area covered in this guide
- ▬ Motorway
- ▬ Major road
- ▬ International border
- ┄ Ferry route
- ─ Railway

0 km   100
0 miles   100

A PORTRAIT OF BRITTANY

With its eventful history, contrasting landscapes, diverse economy and exceptionally rich cultural heritage, Brittany is a multifaceted region. While Breton traditions are very much alive, and while the region is famous for its menhirs, Brittany has also embraced the technological revolutions of the modern age. It is, for example, a major centre of the electronics industry.

Brittany consists of two distinct areas: a coastal region and an inland area. This is reflected in the Celtic names Armor, meaning "country by the sea", and Argoat, "wooded country". The coastline consists of a succession of cliffs, dunes, estuaries, mud flats and marsh land. The westernmost point of France, Brittany sinks beneath the sea, extended by a continental shelf. To the north, this shelf rises to form the British Isles. To the south, it extends along the coast of Brittany.

Since ancient times, this maritime region has provided rich fishing grounds. Today, the abundant fish stocks here are still a mainstay of the Breton economy. Another is the seaweed that grows along the coast and that is used by the food, pharmaceuticals and cosmetics industries.

Bordered by the English Channel and the Atlantic Ocean, Brittany is closely associated with seafaring. From the monks that sailed from Britain in their makeshift boats to evangelize Armorica (the old name for western Brittany), to the international yachtsmen of today, and including some great explorers and notorious privateers, Brittany's seamen have an illustrious place in the annals of European seafaring. It was shipbuilding and metalworking that stripped the Argoat region of most of its trees,

Stately ships at the Fête Internationale de la Mer et des Marins, a major event held in Brest every four years

◀ Procession with parish banners and traditional costume, at the Grand Pardon in Quimper

Breton lace for sale at a market in Ste-Anne-d'Auray, in the Morbihan

which had already been heavily exploited since Roman times. Only 10 per cent of Brittany's primeval forest remains today.

A Diverse Economy

Bretons have never been daunted by harsh natural elements. They went as far as Newfoundland and Iceland during the peak deep-sea fishing years of the 19th century, then, following the collapse of that trade, turned to factory ships, which concentrated on the Atlantic coastlines of Africa, Morocco, Mauritania, Senegal and South America. Local coastal

Old advertising poster for Béghin-Say sugar

fishing, by contrast, has proved more resistant to economic instability. However, while the industry still involves three-quarters of Breton fishing vessels, it has to contend with foreign imports, falling prices, dwindling fish stocks, industrial pollution, periodic oil spillages and competition from fish farming. The industry is now undergoing reorganization in order to strengthen its infrastructure.

While fishing has been under threat for some 50 years, agriculture, food crops and tourism underpin the region's economy. Brittany is the foremost milk producer in France. It also provides a quarter of the country's livestock and is a prime producer of fruit and vegetables. Breton produce is marketed under such well-known brand names as Saupiquet, Béghin-Say, Petit Navire, Paysans Bretons, Père Dodu and Hénaff (a famous pâté). Manufacturing and the service industry are also well developed. One Breton in five works in manufacturing or the building trade, while one in two works in retailing, the service industry or

Plage du Casino, one of the beautiful beaches at St-Quay-Portrieux, on the Côtes d'Armor

administration. High-tech industries have multiplied and many technological innovations have been developed in the region. Brittany is also one of the most popular tourist destinations in France.

A Culture Revived

Traditional Breton music underwent a major revival in the 1960s thanks to Alan Stivell, Kristen Noguès, Gilles Servat and Tri Yann, who, with others, have been prominent among the *bagadou*, as Breton musical groups are known. For several years now, a second wave in the revival of Breton music has turned certain recordings into bestsellers. Denez Prigent, the pioneer of this generation, has also played a major role in the revival of traditional Breton dance and *festou-noz*, or popular Breton dance festivals.

However, the music scene in Brittany goes well beyond traditional forms. In terms of their importance, rock festivals such as the Les Trans Musicales in Rennes, the Route du Rock in St-Malo, and the Festival des Vieilles Charrues in Carhaix, are on a par with the great Festival Interceltique in Lorient.

In parallel with the Breton cultural revival of the 1960s and 1970s, the Breton language has also been reinvigorated, thanks most notably to the establishment of bilingual schools (known as Diwan). Although only a minority of Bretons support this revival, the whole population is aware of Armorica's great literary heritage.

Breton woman at the Festival Interceltique in Lorient

The growth of high-tech establishments can seem incongruous in this land of menhirs, Romanesque chapels, Gothic churches, fortified castles, coastal forts and 18th-century manor houses. Since Neolithic times, when menhirs were raised, and cairns, megalithic monuments and other passage graves were built, religion has imbued local culture. Romanesque churches appeared in the 11th and 12th centuries, but the golden age of religious architecture came in the 13th century, with the Gothic period.

If religion has left its mark on the landscape of Brittany, so has secular life. Throughout the Middle Ages, local noblemen, engaged in wars with France and England, built fortresses and citadels. Indeed, Brittany is one of the regions of France with the greatest number of historic monuments. These, with the local traditions of furniture-making, textiles, gastronomy and painting, contribute to Brittany's fabulously rich cultural heritage.

Street sign in Quimper

The Roche aux Fées, one of Brittany's finest megalithic monuments, in the Ille-et-Vilaine

Landscape and Birds of Brittany

Brittany attracts more sea birds than any other coastal region of France. At the end of the summer, birds that have nested in northern Europe begin to appear on the coast of Brittany. While some species continue on their southern migrations to spend the winter in warmer climates, many stay in Brittany until the early spring, when, together with birds newly returned from the south, they fly north once again to breed.

Male and female razorbills

Flat, Sandy Coastline

Plants growing on beaches and dunes can withstand saline conditions. Sea rocket and several species of orach grow on the beaches. Among the grasses that take root on the dunes and prevent them from being eroded by wind, are spurge, sea holly, convolvulus and gillyflowers.

Bays and Marshy Coasts

Sandy, muddy coastal areas are covered with greyish, low-growing vegetation such as glasswort, salt-wort and obione, and sometimes with the purple-flowering sea lavender. These plants thrive in saline, waterlogged ground, which is washed by the tide twice a day.

The ringed plover patrols sandy beaches, where it feeds on marine worms, sandhoppers and small molluscs.

The European bee-eater is seen in Brittany from April to September. It overwinters south of the Sahara.

The sanderling, which breeds in northern Europe, arrives in Brittany in August. It will either spend the winter there or fly south to Africa.

Sandpipers move about in large flocks, constantly probing the mud with their beaks.

Herring gulls nest in northern Europe. At the end of August, they arrive in Brittany, where they spend the winter.

The pied oystercatcher can be seen in Brittany all year round. It feeds mostly on mussels, cockles and winkles.

The Guillemot

This diving sea bird, with black and white plumage, a short neck and slender wings, spends the winter on the coasts of the English Channel and Atlantic Ocean. It nests in colonies on cliffs at Cap Fréhel and Cap Sizun, at Camaret and on the Sept-Îles, laying a single egg on a rocky ledge. It can also be seen on isolated rocks, often with penguins and kittiwakes. During the breeding season, its cry is a strident cawing. The young bird takes to the water 20 days after hatching, but begins to fly only at two months of age. It feeds mainly on fish, which it catches out at sea by diving to depths of more than 50 m (165 ft).

A colony of guillemots

Cliffs and Rocky Coasts

Particular types of plants grow on the cliffs. They include sea pinks, the pink-flowering campion, golden rod and the yellow-flowering broom, as well as sea squill, small species of fern and many varieties of different-coloured lichen.

The fulmar spends most of its time at sea. It nests on the ledges of sheer cliffs.

The puffin feeds on fish that it catches far out at sea. In spring, it excavates deep burrows where the female lays a single white egg.

The sheerwater's only nesting grounds in France are in Brittany – on the Sept-Îles and in the archipelagos of Ouessant and Houat.

Heathlands of the Interior

For much of the year, various species of heathers cover Brittany's heathlands with a carpet of pink, which contrasts with the yellow flowers of the gorse and broom. The heathlands are also dotted with thickets of bramble and dog-rose.

The hen-harrier preys on voles and small birds, which it finds in open land.

The curlew migrates from June onwards to the Atlantic coast, where large numbers spend the winter.

The warbler feeds all year round on small insects and spiders.

Rural Architecture

The scenic appeal of the Breton countryside owes much to its picturesque old houses, which seem to be fixed in time. Their appearance varies markedly according to topography, available materials and local traditions. In Upper Brittany, houses were built in rows, standing gable to gable so as to form rectangular groups *(longères)*. Typical of Lower Brittany is the *pennti*, a more compact house, with contiguous outbuildings, such as byres and coach houses surrounding the yard and providing shelter from the prevailing wind. Until the mid-19th century, these modest houses rarely had an upper floor. Thatched and asymmetrical, they blend harmoniously with the surrounding fields, heath and woodland.

Windows, which are narrow and relatively few, are usually framed by dressed stones. They were once closed from within by wooden shutters.

Chimneys are built into the gable wall.

The coping stone, sometimes decoratively carved, crowns the apex of the gable.

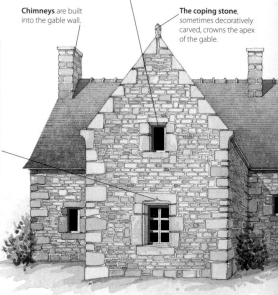

Lintels above older windows are bevelled and sometimes have an ogee arch, a legacy of the Gothic style. Such windows are typical of manor houses.

Exterior Stairways

Several types of exterior staircase can be seen on Breton country houses. Many houses in the Léon and Vannes areas have a stairway parallel to the façade. The stairway, covered with an awning, led up to the loft, where hay and other provisions might be stored. The space beneath the steps was sometimes occupied by a pigsty. In plainer houses, the stairway, which often had no awning, was set in the angle of two buildings.

Steps parallel to the façade

Steps set between buildings, with no awning

Around the House

Certain integral features of the rural Breton house are to be found not inside its walls but outside. One is the bread oven, the style of which has remained almost unchanged since the Middle Ages. Because of the danger of fire, the oven was often located away from the house. The granite trough, a traditional piece of equipment in Lower Brittany, served as a drinking trough for animals and was also used as a mortar in which fodder was ground before it was given to horses.

Granite drinking-trough or mortar

Bread oven with small recess

The ridge of the roof was sometimes finished with a row of slates – known as *kribenn* in Breton. The slates may be carved into shapes such as cats or birds, or into dates or initials.

Houses with Extensions

Many houses in Finistère have an extension – known as apoteiz *or* kuz taol *in Breton – that protrudes 4 to 5 m (13 to 16 ft) from the façade. This additional space was used to store the table, benches and sometimes a box-bed, so as to create more space around the hearth.*

Blocks of hewn stone were used as cornerstones in both houses and enclosure walls.

The granite doorway, with a lintel consisting of three voussoirs (blocks of curved stone), is one of the most typical of Brittany.

Dormer windows are a relatively late feature of rural Breton houses. They did not appear until the 1870s.

Religious Architecture

Brittany boasts several abbeys, nine cathedrals, some 20 large churches, about 100 parish closes and thousands of country chapels. This rich heritage is proof not only of the strength of religious faith but also of the skill of local builders. The golden age of religious architecture in Brittany occurred in the 16th and 17th centuries, when buildings were profusely decorated. Porches and rood screens sprouted motifs carved in oak, limestone or *kersanton*, a fine-grained granite almost impervious to the passage of time.

Calvary at Notre-Dame-de Tronoën *(see p160)*

Crypt of the Église St-Mélar in Lanmeur

Pre-Romanesque and Romanesque (6th–8th C.)

The Romanesque style reached Brittany after it had become established in Anjou and Normandy, reaching its peak in about 1100 with the building of abbeys, priories and modest churches. A distinctive feature of these buildings is the stylized carvings on the capitals of columns.

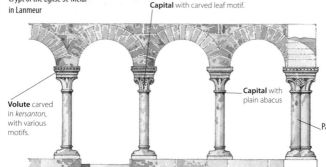

Capital with carved leaf motif.

The cloister of the Abbaye de Daoulas, restored in 1880, is one of the finest examples of Romanesque architecture in Brittany.

Capital with plain abacus

Volute carved in *kersanton*, with various motifs.

Paired columns

Early Gothic (13th–14th C.)

At a time when buildings in the Romanesque style were still being constructed, the Gothic style and the art of the stained-glass window took root in Brittany. Buildings in this new, restrained style, shaped by Norman and English influences, were based on a rectangular or T-shaped plan, and had a tall steeple.

Stained glass, Cathédrale St-Samson, Dol-de-Bretagne

Statue of a bishop

North tower, left unfinished.

West front, built in the 12th century

Buttresses

Foliate architrave

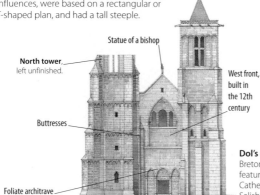

Dol's cathedral, a fine example of Breton Gothic architecture, shares features in common with Coutances Cathedral in Normandy and with Salisbury Cathedral in England.

Flamboyant Gothic (14th–15th C.)

As an expression of their political power, the dukes and noblemen of Brittany funded the decoration of Gothic churches. These buildings thus acquired elegant chapels and finial belfries, carved doorways, wall paintings and beautiful rose windows.

The Porche du Peuple of the Cathédrale St-Tugdual in Tréguier features some fine examples of 14th-century decorative carving.

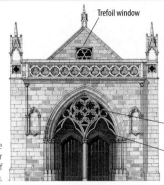

Trefoil window

Rood screen in the Basilique du Folgoët

Quatrefoil tracery framed by two trefoils.

Tierce-point arch divided into two trilobe arches.

Breton Renaissance (16th C.)

The Flamboyant Gothic style was gradually superseded by a new, markedly purer style. Adopted by architects, metalworkers and sculptors, the Breton Renaissance style combined that of the Loire and that of Italy. In Lower Brittany, the fashion for parish closes and open belfries became established.

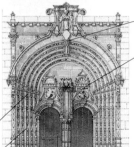

Arches decorated with secular motifs.

Bust of François I set within a scallop shell.

Figures of the 12 apostles.

Pilaster with lozenge decoration.

West door of the Basilique Notre-Dame-du-Bon-Secours in Guingamp (1537–90).

Pediment, in the Baroque style, over the archway.

Stone wall, designed to prevent farm animals from entering the sacred enclosure.

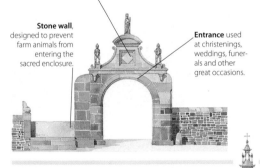

Entrance used at christenings, weddings, funerals and other great occasions.

Detail of the rood screen of the church at La Roche Maurice

The ceremonial entrance to the parish close of the Église St-Miliau in Guimiliau, one of the most important in northern Finistère.

Baroque (17th C.)

The Counter-Reformation brought out a taste for extravagant church decoration. This took the form of statues of apostles, dramatic depictions of the Pietà, highly ornate pulpits, Baroque altarpieces and garlanded columns. There are around 1,300 churches with such Baroque decoration in Brittany.

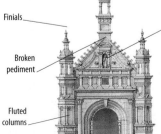

Finials

Broken pediment

Fluted columns

Statue of St Derrien flanked by the heads of two angels.

The great porch (1645–55) of the church at Commana, whose interior furnishings are in an extravagant Baroque style, still has many Renaissance features.

Breton Music

As it continues to grow in popularity, Breton music goes from strength to strength. In the 1990s, *L'Héritage des Celtes* and *Again*, two of Alan Stivell's albums, sold in their thousands, the instrumentalist Dan Ar Braz has twice been awarded the prestigious Victoire de la Musique, and the techno specialist Denez Prigent has won critical acclaim. In Brittany, music is a central aspect of popular culture. Almost 70 per cent of French traditional musicians are Bretons, and in Brittany new music venues open at a faster rate than anywhere else in France. Celtic heritage lives on.

Poster advertising a music festival in Brest in 1932.

Traditional Instruments

The bagpipes and the bombard are the only two specifically Breton musical instruments. Although others are played by Breton musicians, the bagpipes and bombard, sometimes accompanied by a drum or tambourine, are the traditional combination.

Drum

The bombard, a wind instrument similar to the oboe, is made of ebony or fruitwood.

The Breton bagpipe is increasingly neglected in favour of the larger Scottish bagpipes.

Bagpipes are known as *biniou* in Brittany. In the Guérande region and in the Breton fenlands of the Vendée they are known as *veuze*.

Irish transverse flute

The Celtic harp, sacred instrument of bards and druids, captivated audiences throughout antiquity and the Middle Ages.

The diatonic accordion, known as *bouëze* in Brittany, has gradually replaced the old concertina that was once seen mostly in rural areas.

Sonneurs are players of Breton and Scottish bagpipes who traditionally perform together. In the early 20th century, some *sonneurs* learned to play the clarinet – popularly known as "tronc de choux" (cabbage stalk) – the accordion and later the saxophone. *Sonneurs* once made their living from music.

Alan Stivell has recorded over 20 albums since his *Reflets* was released in 1970.

Tri Yann, a band that celebrated its 40th anniversary in 2011, practises the Breton musical tradition of extemporization. For the second time since the band came into existence, a woman has replaced one of its founders.

Gilles Servat gave a fresh boost to Breton music during the 1970s.

Scottish bagpipes

Dan Ar Braz, from Quimper, has twice won the Victoire de la Musique. He has represented France at the Eurovision Song Contest and he now attracts a large audience. Describing the music that he plays, he prefers to call it the music of Brittany rather than traditional Breton music.

Breton Orchestras

Bagadou, *or Breton orchestras, feature bombards, bagpipes and drums. It is these orchestras that are responsible for keeping alive Breton musical tradition. Among the most famous* bagadou *are those of Landerneau and Lann Bihoué.*

The Contemporary Scene

The young generation understands that it is new kinds of music that will help Breton traditions survive, by mixing the traditional with the contemporary to create new styles. Erik Marchand, who was born in Paris, learned Breton songs and then went on to join forces with gypsy and Oriental musicians. Kristen Nikolas gave Breton music a techno flavour. His band, Angel IK, freely mixed wild guitar-playing with Breton songs. Yann-Fanch Kemener, who began his career as a singer of Breton songs, now performs with jazz musicians. Nolwenn Leroy popularised Breton music with cover versions of traditional Celtic songs. One of the most outstanding talents is Denez Prigent. After specializing in *gwerzou* (ballads) and *kan ha diskan* (songs with descant), he has been exploring techno.

Denez Prigent

Breton Literature

Perhaps because of its melancholy mists and secret woodlands, or because of the peculiar light that bathes its windswept coastline, Brittany is a strangely inspirational land. How else to account for the unique alchemy that encourages the imagination to take wing and that instills an innate penchant for the mystical, the mysterious and the marvellous? All those Bretons who figure in the history of regional as well as French literature, have this characteristic, the inevitable consequence of life lived on the edge of the world.

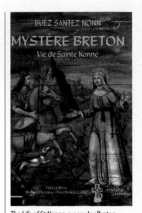

The Life of St Nonne, a popular Breton mystery play

Literature in Breton

Relatively little is known about medieval Breton literature. Besides a few glimpses gained from the charters compiled in abbeys and a single page from an obscure treatise on medicine dating from the late 8th century, no single Breton text survives to this day.

There is every evidence, however, that Armorican poets enjoyed a certain prestige in courtly circles and that their lays – ballads or poems set to music and accompanied on the harp – played an important part in the development of the chivalrous epics of the Middle Ages. It was, indeed, this Breton tradition that provided French minstrels with tales of the valour of Lancelot, the adventures of Merlin and other wonders of the Forêt de Paimpont (see p68), the legendary Forêt de Brocéliande.

Barzhaz Breizh

Mystery Plays

The earliest surviving evidence of a true literary tradition dates from the 15th century, in the manuscripts of mystery plays. In these plays, religious scenes, such as *Buez Santez Nonn*, which tells the story of the life of a saint, were enacted. Performed in the open air, they were extremely popular, especially in the Trégor. The actors, who might be clog-makers or weavers by trade, knew by heart entire tracts of the most dramatic plays, such as *Ar pevar mab Hemon (The Four Sons of Aymon)*, which was still being performed in about 1880.

Contemporary with this popular repertoire, a handful of long, erudite poems with sophisticated internal rhyming has survived, as well as a considerable body of literature (such as missals and books of hours) written by clergymen in imperfect Breton. For hundreds of years, the latter was ordinary people's only reading matter.

Stories and Legends

The literary genre in which Bretons excelled was that of stories and legends. During long winter evenings and at country gatherings, woodcutters, beggars and spinners would weave stories of make-believe filled with fairytale princesses and such legendary figures as giants in glass castles. It was by listening to these imaginative storytellers that Théodore Hersart de la Villemarqué (1815–95), whose Breton name was Kervarker, and François-Marie Luzel, or Fañch An Uhel (1821–95), compiled collections of Breton literature. The stories are, however, too good to be true: it is now known that neither man set them down as he heard them but that they polished and rounded off the stories.

At the end of the 19th century, Lan Inizan (1826–91) published *Emgann Kergidu*, an historic account of events that occurred in the Léon district during the Terror (see p52). Anatole Le Braz

Théodore Hersart de la Villemarqué, a great 19th-century recorder of Breton tales and legends

Per-Jakez Hélias, author of the novel *Le Cheval d'Orgueil*

The Breton Language

Brezoneg, an ancient Celtic language that is related to Welsh, is spoken west of a line running from Plouha to Vannes. Although this linguistic frontier has hardly changed since the 12th century, over recent generations Brezoneg has become much less widely spoken. In 1914, 90 per cent of the population of that part of Brittany spoke Brezoneg. After 1945, parents were encouraged to have their children speak French and, until 1951, Brezoneg was surpressed in schools. It was thus no longer passed down from parent to child. Today, although it is increasingly rare to hear Brezoneg spoken (only 240,000 Bretons over 60 know it well), it is attracting fresh interest. There are now bilingual schools (Diwan), an official Breton institute, and a Breton television channel (TV Breizh), all of which contribute to keeping Brezoneg alive.

Breton grammar books used in Diwan schools

(1859–1926), meanwhile, explored Breton legends that are concerned with death.

Breton Classics

During the 1930s, three accomplished novelists – Youenn Drezen, Yeun ar Gow and Jakez Riou – demonstrated that Breton literature was not limited to the description of life in the countryside in times gone by. While their novels had only a small readership, those of Tanguy Malmanche enjoyed wider renown. Two poets also emerged: Yann-Ber Kalloc'h (1888–1917), a native of Vannes, with his moving *Ar en deulin (Kneeling)*, and Anjela Duval (1905–81), of the Trégor.

The most widely read Breton writer is Per-Jakez Hélias, who came to the notice of the general public in 1975 with *Le Cheval d'Orgueil (Horse of Pride)*, which was subsequently translated into 20 languages.

Ernest Renan, noted for his writing on science and religion

Literature in French

Although not part of the Breton literary canon, three of the greatest

19th-century French authors were of Breton stock. Two were natives of St-Malo. One of these was the statesman, traveller and memoir-writer François René de Chateaubriand *(see p75)*, author of *Génie du Christianisme* and *Mémoires d'Outre-Tombe*. Describing his attachment to the region, he once said "It was in the woods near Combourg that I became what I am". The other was Félicité de Lamennais, whose social ideals included harnessing political liberalism to Roman Catholicism. At his manor house at St-Pierre-de-Plesguen, near Dinan, he entertained a coterie of disciples. The third, Ernest Renan, author of *Vie de Jésus (Life of Jesus)*, often returned to his native Trégor, where,

he said, "you can feel a strong opposition to all that is dull and flat".

In the 20th century, too, Breton soil spawned many writers of renown: they include the poets René-Guy Cadou, Eugène Guillevic and Xavier Grall, the essayist Jean Guéhenno, of Fougères, and the novelist Louis Guilloux, of St-Brieuc, whose *Le Sang Noir (Black Blood*, 1935) and *Ma Bretagne (My Brittany*, 1973) were hailed by critics as works of major importance.

Louis Guilloux, author of *Le Sang Noir* and *Ma Bretagne*

Traditional Breton Costume

There were once 66 different types of traditional Breton costume and around 1,200 variations. Breton clothing differed from one small area to the next. In the 19th century, it was possible to tell at a glance the precise geographical origins of any Breton. Colours also indicated an individual's age and status: in Plougastel-Daoulas, young women wore a small flowery shawl, married women a shawl with squares, widows a white shawl, and, when they had lost a close relative, a winged headdress. Unmarried men wore green waistcoats, and married men, blue jackets.

Femmes de Plougastel au Pardon de Sainte-Anne by Charles Cottet (1903)

Bigouden Costume

In the area of Pont-l'Abbé, capital of the Bigouden region, traditional costume is very uniform. Women were still wearing it as everyday dress in the early 20th century. According to their wealth, they either wore richly decorated, layered bodices or modest embroidered cuffs.

Shirt

Embroidered sleeve

Lace gloves

Chupenn, a man's coat

Embroidered waistcoat

Child's bonnet

Jewellery
In Cornouaille and western Brittany, the most popular pieces of jewellery were "pardon pins", brooches made of silver, copper or blown glass.

Lace and Embroidery

Aprons worn on feast days, women's bodices and men's waistcoats are richly embroidered with silk, metallic thread, and steel or glass beads. Executed in chain stitch, motifs include floral patterns featuring palmettes and fleur-de-lys, and stylized elements such as sun discs and concentric circles. They are always very bright, like the orange and yellow *plum paon* motifs that are typical of the Bigouden.

Lace-makers from Tréboul, in Finistère

Embroidery from Pont-l'Abbé

Embroidery from Quimper

Detail of a beaded costume

Newborn children, represented here by dolls, were once all customarily dressed in a bonnet, gown and apron. Not until the age of five or six did boys swap their infant clothes for adult male clothing. Girls would start to wear a headdress from the time of their first communion.

Headwear

Traditional Breton headwear is extraordinarily diverse. This can be appreciated today only thanks to René-Yves Creston (1898–1964), an ethnologist who recorded its range before it ceased to be worn on a daily basis. Some headdresses had back-swept wings, others were tied at the chin with ribbons, and still others had "aircraft" or "lobster-tail" wings. Many women possessed two *koef*, or, in French, *coiffes* (headdresses), a small one made of lace netting that covered the hair, and a tall one, which was worn over the smaller one, though only on ceremonial occasions. The most spectacular headdresses are those of the Bigouden, which are almost 33 cm (13 in) high and which older women wear on Sundays. Men's hats are decorated with long velvet ribbons and sometimes with an oval buckle.

Small lace *coiffe*

Women's headdress

Apron

Brooch

Chain

Belt buckles, like this heart-shaped example, were part of a man's costume. The waistcoat and trousers, which replaced the traditional baggy trousers in the mid-19th century, are tied at the waist by a belt.

The back of the bodice was decorated with flowers whose size indicated the wearer's status. A married woman's bodice featured gold thread, spangles and tinsel.

Men's waistcoats were eye-catchingly sumptuous. In Plougastel, young men wore a green waistcoat under a purple jacket, and adult men a blue waistcoat, the hue being darker or paler according to their age. Men wore a purple waistcoat on their wedding day and at the christening of their first child.

Aprons, worn to keep a woman's skirt clean, were originally plain rather than decorated. These voluminous working garments were made of ordinary fabric and were tied at the waist with a ribbon. Aprons were usually worn with a bib – a rectangular piece of fabric that covered the chest.

BRITTANY THROUGH THE YEAR

In Brittany, every season has something to offer. In spring, towns and villages reawaken from their winter slumber: feast days in honour of patron saints and popular festivals mark this renewal. As the sun shines more brightly, heath and woodland come to life. Through the summer, the tourist season is in full swing, and every community holds its own *fest-noz* or pardon. The high point is the Festival Interceltique de Lorient, the greatest Celtic festival in France. By the autumn, the number of tourists begins to dwindle and festivals are fewer. Bretons ward off the rigours of winter by meeting in bistros or holding such events as the Trans Musicales de Rennes.

Spring

In Brittany, spring is a time of joyfulness. From March, watered by gentle showers, gorse blooms cover the landscape in a carpet of golden yellow. In May, broom comes into flower, with its lighter yellow blooms. Fruit and vegetables – including Brittany's famous artichokes – are piled high in the markets. The region is reborn, and welcomes the return of warm, sunny days.

Advertisement for Étonnants Voyageurs, a festival held in St-Malo

April
Salon du Livre *(mid-Apr)*, Bécherel, Ille-et-Vilaine. An antiquarian book festival held in a medieval town. Bookbinders, booksellers and second-hand dealers hold open house.

May
Festival En Arwen *(early May)*, Cléguérec, Morbihan. A festival of traditional Breton music, drawing many performers and enthusiasts.

Fields of gorse, thickly carpeted in flowers from March

Festival Étonnants Voyageurs *(three days, late May/early Jun)*, St-Malo. The focus of this festival *(Amazing Explorers)*, held in the historic port of St-Malo, is travel writing and accounts of exploration. It features exhibitions, lectures and book signing sessions. Organized by a group of enthusiasts, it has become a major cultural event, and is now taken to other countries.

Summer

As one of the most popular tourist regions of France, Brittany receives a large number of visitors during the summer. Coastal resorts are busy, and bars and nightclubs are filled to capacity. Besides swimming in the sea or relaxing on the beach, going hiking or cycling, or taking a boat trip round the coast, there are many other activities for visitors to enjoy *(see pp250–3)*.

June
Festival Art Rock *(May–Jun)*, St-Brieuc, Côtes d'Armor. Concerts, exhibitions, shows and contemporary dance.

July
Festival Tombées de la Nuit *(early Jul)*, Rennes, Ille-et-Vilaine. Filled with musicians, comedians, mime artists and storytellers from all over the world, Rennes, the capital of Brittany, becomes a gigantic stage.
Festival des Pierres qui Parlent *(mid-Jul to Aug)*, at megalithic sites at Locronan, Crozon, Concarneau, Loctudy, Arzon, Carnac and Ploemeur. Held at sunset, a storyteller weaves beguiling Celtic tales. **Art dans les Chapelles** *(early Jul to mid-Sep)*, Pontivy and environs, Morbihan. About 15 chapels in and around Pontivy, and dating from the 15th and 16th centuries, host exhibitions

Average Daily Hours of Sunshine

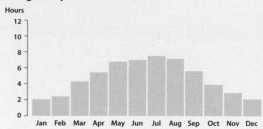

Hours

12
10
8
6
4
2
0

Jan Feb Mar Apr May Jun Jul Aug Sep Oct Nov Dec

Sunshine Chart
High pressure from the Azores gives southern Brittany more than 2,200 hours of sunshine per year. The north, by contrast, has only 1,700 hours per year. Coastal areas, where rainfall is lighter than in the interior, sometimes suffer from drought during the summer.

of contemporary painting, sculpture and photography.
Troménie (second Sun in Jul), Locronan, southern Finistère. One of the largest and most elaborate pardons in Brittany.
Festival Médiéval (14 Jul, every two years), Josselin, Morbihan. A day of medieval entertainment centred around the old market square, with troubadours and tumblers.
Festival des Vieilles Charrues (mid-Jul), Carhaix-Plouguer, southern Finistère. Rock festival featuring both international stars and local bands. James Brown, Massive Attack and numerous others have performed in front of large audiences here.
Fête Internationale de la Mer et des Marins (mid-Jul, every four years), Brest, northern Finistère. The largest tall ships regatta in the world, first held in 1992.
Fête de la Crèpe (third weekend in Jul), Tronjoly-Gourin, southern Finistère. Pancake-tastings and lessons in how to made pancakes, held in the municipal park.

Fête des Remparts (third weekend in Jul, every two years), Dinan, Côtes d'Armor. Historical reconstructions, theatrical farce, dancing, games, concerts, jousts and a procession in costume.
Grand Pardon (26 Jul), Ste-Anne-d'Auray, Morbihan. Brittany's greatest pilgrimage has a million followers.
Festival de Jazz (last week of Jul), Vannes, Morbihan. Blues and jazz played by professional and amateur musicians are the festival's main attractions.

August
Fête des Fleurs d'Ajoncs (first Sun in Aug), Pont-Aven, southern Finistère. A picturesque procession in honour of flowering gorse, dating back to 1905.
Festival Interceltique (first two weeks in Aug), Lorient, Morbihan. Musicians and other performers from Scotland, Ireland, the Isle of Man, Wales and Cornwall, Galicia and Asturia (in Spain), and, of course, Brittany gather for the largest Celtic festival in the world.

Fête internationale de la Mer et des Marins in Brest

Route du Rock (mid-Aug), St-Malo, Ille-et-Vilaine. Held in the Fort de St-Père, a rock festival at the cutting edge of the genre.
Festival des Hortensias (late Jul to early Aug), Perros-Guirec, Côtes d'Armor. Accompanied by traditional music, festivities in honour of the hydrangea, whose deep blue flowers are prized and which thrives in Brittany's acid soil.
Fête des Filets Bleus (mid-Aug), Concarneau, southern Finistère. Traditional Breton bands parade through the streets of the town, and a festival queen is chosen. The programme also includes concerts, shows and fishing competitions.
Fête de l'Andouille (fourth Sun in Aug), Guémené-sur-Scorff, Morbihan. The Confrérie des Goustiers de l'Andouille (sausage-makers' guild) celebrate this prized Breton delicacy.

Rock group at the Festival des Vieilles Charrues at Carhaix-Plouguer

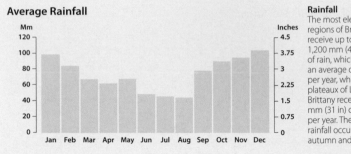

Average Rainfall

| Mm | | Inches |

Rainfall
The most elevated regions of Brittany receive up to 1,200 mm (47 in) of rain, which falls over an average of 200 days per year, while the plateaux of Lower Brittany receive 800 mm (31 in) of rainfall per year. The heaviest rainfall occurs in autumn and winter.

Autumn

Those of a romantic disposition who love open spaces will find this season particularly appealing. There are still many fine days. The equinox on 21/22 September marks the beginning of the great autumn tides, when large expanses of the seabed are exposed. Rapidly changing weather and the dramatic ebb and flow of the sea also make for a landscape whose appearance alters by the hour. Inland, the leaves on the trees start to turn, catching the sunlight between scudding clouds. As tourists become fewer, Bretons return to their daily lives, anticipating winter.

September
Championnat de Bretagne de Musique Traditionelle *(first weekend in Sep)*, Gourin, southern Finistère. The finest performers of traditional Breton music gather at the Domaine de Tronjoly to take part in marching, music and dancing competitions; these are held in two categories: *kozh* (with Breton pipes and bombards) and *bras* (with Scottish bagpipes and bombards). A *fest-noz* also takes place.

October
Festival du Film Britannique *(early Oct)*, Dinard, Ille-et-Vilaine. The British film industry's producers and distributors come here to promote British cinema in France. The event attracts around 15,000 people.
Festival de Lanvallec *(second half of Oct)*, in the Trégor, Côtes d'Armor. The leading exponents of Baroque music perform in various churches in the region, particularly in Lanvallec, which has one of the oldest organs in Brittany.

Fête du Marron *(end of Oct)*, Redon, Ille-et-Vilaine. The town hosts a chestnut festival with a traditional fair, chestnut tastings and, most prominently, the largest *fest-noz* in Brittany. The Bogue d'Or, a musical contest in which the best traditional Breton musicians compete, takes place in the morning. In the evening, the winners give a performance, along with other traditional Breton music groups.
Quai des Bulles *(mid-Oct)*, St-Malo, Ille-et-Vilaine. An annual gathering attended by around 400 strip-cartoonists and animated cartoon producers, together with a following of enthusiasts. Showings of cartoon films and exhibitions also form part of the event. In the year 2000, when the festival marked its 20th year, the world's leading cartoonists and animators attended.

November
Festival des Chanteurs de Rue et Foire St-Martin *(early Nov)*, Quintin, Côtes d'Armor. Since 1993, the St Martin's Fair, which dates back to the 15th century, has been held at the same time as this festival of street singers. Hawkers, entertainers and comedians re-enact historical scenes of daily life and singers perform time-honoured songs, with the audience joining in the chorus. Traditional Breton food is also on offer, such as crêpes and moules marinière.

A signing session during the Quai des Bulles in St-Malo

Average Monthly Temperature

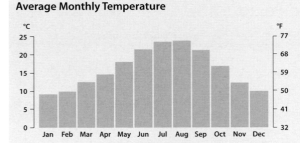

Temperature
The chart shows the average minimum and maximum temperatures for each month. Average winter temperatures are between 6 and 8° C (43 and 46° F). Average summer temperatures are between 16 and 18° C (61 to 64° F).

Winter

Winter brings periods of inclement weather, which become progressively more severe as the season advances. However, warm, moist air from the tropics can cause temperatures to rise to as much as 12° C (54° F), even in mid-January. Warm rainfall allows camellias to thrive, flowering in sheltered areas. In winter, the prevailing wind is from the northwest. Cold and strong, it batters the region in squally gusts. As an antidote to such tempestuous weather, Bretons hold rumbustuous weekend festivals.

A still winter seascape in Brittany

December
Les Trans Musicales *(early Dec)*, Rennes, Ille-et-Vilaine. The buzzing rock scene has spawned such artistes as Étienne Daho, Niagara, Marquis de Sade and a long list of bands that are well-known in France. Since 1979, this key festival has launched the careers of many British and American bands, as well as that of other musicians, such as the Icelandic singer Björk, who has performed in France since the start of her career.

February
Travelling *(end of Feb)*, Rennes, Ille-et-Vilaine. This is a festival that focuses on international filmmaking. Each year a different country is represented and around 200 films are screened at different venues in the city. There are master classes, cine-concerts, short and feature films.
Flambée Musicales *(early Feb)* Fougères. An international dance and music festival that takes place over several days. The theme changes every year, and ranges from Baroque to Andalusian gypsy music.

Public Holidays

New Year's Day (1 Jan)
Easter Sunday and Easter Monday
Ascension (sixth Thu after Easter)
Pentecost (second Mon after Ascension)
Labour Day (1 May)
Victory Day (8 May)
Bastille Day (14 Jul)
Assumption (15 Aug)
All Saints' Day (1 Nov)
Armistice Day (11 Nov)
Christmas Day (25 Dec)

A stall at the Christmas market in Brest

Pardons and Festou-noz

The term *pardon* dates from the Middle Ages, when popes granted indulgences (remissions of punishment for sin) to worshippers who came to church. The annual pardon later became a day of worship honouring a local patron saint, with a procession and pilgrimage. In rural areas, a large number of saints were venerated, and here, minor pardons have evolved into occasions when communities join together to celebrate. After mass, the confession of penitents and procession of banners, the secular *fest-noz*, with singing and dancing, begins.

Celtic cultural clubs, which give displays at pardons, still perform dances that are specific to particular areas of Brittany.

The bagad is a group of musicians playing bombards, bagpipes and drums, while touring the streets. They provide dance music for the *fest-noz*.

Gwenn ha du, the Breton flag

Sonneurs, bagpipe and bombard players, have always been an integral part of Breton festivities. Seated on a table or a large barrel, they took it in turns to play popular tunes both to accompany dancing and as entertainment during the outdoor banquet that traditionally followed a pardon.

Gouel an Eost

In several parishes, pardons are also occasions when older people can relive the sights and sounds of a traditional harvest. Activities include threshing by traditional methods: threshers, truss-carriers and sheaf-binders set up the chaff-cutter and the winnowing machine, which separates the grain from the chaff, and harness horses to the circular enclosure where the grain is milled. A hearty buffet rounds off this *gouel an eost*.

Harvest festival

Traditional dancing is not the exclusive preserve of Celtic cultural clubs. Far from sitting on the sidelines, local people and holiday-makers both eagerly join in, accompanied by the *sonneurs* and singers of *kan ha diskan* (songs with descant).

Banners, made of embroidered silk, are carried in procession during pardons. Each parish has its own banner, behind which the parishioners walk. This one belongs to the Chapelle Notre-Dame de Lambader, in Haut-Léon.

The Troménie at Locronan is not only a major pilgrimage but also a test of physical endurance for those who carry the banners. Dressed in traditional costume, for five hours they continuously circle a hill in the heat of July, holding aloft banners, statues and relics.

Banner with the image of the patron saint of a parish.

Tro Breiz

Held in honour of the seven saints – Samson, Malo, Brieuc, Paul Aurélien, Patern, Corentin and Tugdual – who established Christianity in Brittany, the Tro Breiz is not a modest parish pardon but a lengthy pilgrimage covering about 650 km (400 miles) and linking the towns of the seven saints. Pilgrims from all over the world have attended this event.

Modern banner, carried in honour of the well-known preacher Mikael an Nobletz *(see p133)*.

Blessing the Sea takes place during pardons in villages around the coast of the Golfe du Morbihan. The clergy boards a boat and blesses all the vessels in the harbour following a custom that dates from the 19th century.

The pardon of Ste-Anne-d'Auray has become a spectacular event over the centuries, with a long procession of priests and pilgrims. After mass, they fervently sing Hail Marys and Breton hymns.

THE HISTORY OF BRITTANY

Brittany's long history, no less than its geography, has made it one of the most distinctive regions of France. It has a strong cultural identity, and, at the westernmost point of France, it has benefited from its location at the centre of Europe's Atlantic seaboard – between land and sea, and between Britain and France.

The borders of Brittany have altered often since ancient times. During the prehistoric period, the coastline was very different from what it is today. Many sites of human occupation, some of which date back 500,000 years, have been discovered in places that are now beneath the sea. During the glaciations of the early Quaternary period, the sea level was about 30 m (100 ft) lower than it is today.

When the glaciers melted, about 10,000 years ago, the sea level rose dramatically. Large areas of land were flooded, creating the present coastline, which is indented by long narrow inlets – or rias – ancient river valleys flooded by the sea. It may be some remote memory of this cataclysmic event that gave rise to legends about submerged cities, like the town of Ys.

Megalith-Builders

Traces of human occupation become more numerous at the beginning of the Neolithic period, around 5000 BC, when local populations adopted agriculture and a settled way of life. They made axes of polished granite, which were traded in the Rhône valley, in southeastern France, and in

Britain. This was also a time of stable social organization, when impressive megalithic monuments were built. Skeletons and pottery were placed in megalithic tombs (dolmens), some in the form of burial chambers approached by a long corridor, consisting of huge blocks of stone covered by an earth mound. The oldest and most impressive of these megalithic monuments, the cairn at Barnenez (see p125), dates from 4600 BC. No less spectacular are the menhirs, that were standing stones probably connected to a religion involving astronomy. The most important menhirs are those at Carnac (see pp184–5). Some, like the Giant of Locmariaquer (see p186), are as much as 20 m (65 ft) high.

The Celts

In about 500 BC, the peninsula, which was then known as Armorica, or "country near the sea", was invaded by Celts. Five tribes settled there: the Osismes (in present-day Finistère), the Veneti (in the Morbihan), the Coriosolites (in the Côtes d'Armor), the Riedones (in the Ille-et-Vilaine), and the Namnetes (in the Loire-Atlantique). The Celts, who lived in villages and fortified

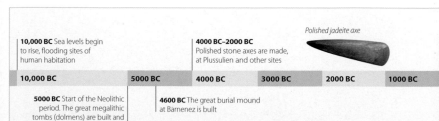

10,000 BC Sea levels begin to rise, flooding sites of human habitation		4000 BC–2000 BC Polished stone axes are made, at Plussulien and other sites			*Polished jadeite axe*	
10,000 BC	**5000 BC**	**4000 BC**	**3000 BC**	**2000 BC**	**1000 BC**	
5000 BC Start of the Neolithic period. The great megalithic tombs (dolmens) are built and menhirs erected		**4600 BC** The great burial mound at Barnenez is built				

◀ The mythical origins of the kingdom of Armorica, from Le Baud's *Chroniques de Bretagne* (1480–82)

settlements, were agriculturalists who also worked iron, minted coins and engaged in overseas trade. They were ruled by a warrior aristocracy and a priesthood, the druids, at the head of a religion whose deities represented the forces of nature. Bards (poet-musicians) sang of the exploits of mythical heroes. Armorica gradually entered the annals of recorded history. Explorers from the Mediterranean, among them the Carthaginian Himilco (c. 500 BC) and the Greek merchant-explorer Pytheas (c. 320 BC), arrived on its shores.

Bronze figure of an ox, from a Roman villa at Carnac

Roman Armorica

In 57 BC, the Romans occupied Armorica, as well as the rest of Gaul. However, in 56 BC, the Veneti rebelled and held the Romans at bay by taking refuge on the rocky promontories of the Atlantic coast. With difficulty, Julius Caesar routed them in a sea battle outside the Golfe du Morbihan. For 400 years, Armorica, incorporated into the province of Lugdunensis, was under Roman domination. The province was divided into five areas (pagi), corresponding to Celtic tribal territory. A network of roads was built and a few small towns estab-lished, which aided the process of Romanization. Among them were Condate (now Rennes), Fanum

Roman Venus from Crucuny, Carnac

Martis (Corseul), Condevincum (Nantes) and Darioritum (Vannes). While baths, amphitheatres and villas marked the influence of Roman civilization, Celtic and Roman gods were amalgamated. Rural areas, however, were less affected by the Roman presence. From AD 250–300, as the Roman Empire began to decline, instability set in. Raids by Frankish and Saxon pirates led to the desertion of towns. The coastline was ineffectually defended by forts, such as Alet (near St-Malo) and Le Yaudet (in Ploulec'h). As the 5th century dawned, Armorica was abandoned to its fate.

Arrival of the Britons

During the 6th century, large numbers of Britons from Wales and Cornwall crossed the English Channel to settle in Armorica, which they named "Little Britain", or "Brittany". This peaceful invasion continued for 200 years. Among the newcomers were many Christian monks, who introduced a Celtic variant of Christianity, distinct from Roman Christianity. Many isolated hermitages were built on small offshore islands. The monasteries were headed by an abbot who also acted as itinerant bishop. Among them were Brieuc, Malo, Tugdual (in Tréguier) and Samson (in Dol); with Gildas, Guénolé, Méen and Jacut, whose lives and miracles became the subject of hagiographies from the 8th century onwards. They inspired the religious traditions that survive today, marked by pilgrimages and pardons, such as the Troménie in Locronan (see p159). It was these

c. 500 BC The Celts reach Brittany

57 BC The Romans conquer Armorica

1st and 2nd centuries Armorica is Romanized

3rd century Saxon raids become more frequent

| 500 BC | 0 | 100 | 200 | 300 |

56 BC Julius Caesar defeats the Veneti in a naval battle

Coins minted by the Veneti

4th century The Romans withdraw from Armorica

St Corentin laying the foundation stone of Quimper Cathedral in front of Cornouaille's King Gradlon

immigrants from Britain who introduced the typically Breton place names consisting of the prefix *plou*, or its derivatives *plo*, *plu*, *plé*, followed by a proper name or other word (as in Plougastel and Ploufragan). *Plou*, from the Latin *plebs* (the common people), refers to a community of Christians. *Lan* (as in Lannion and Lannilis) refers to a monastery. *Tré* (as in Trégastel), from the ancient British word *treb*, refers to a place of habitation.

The concentration of these place names in western Brittany, and the frequency of those ending in *ac* in the eastern part of the region, from the Latin *acum* (as in Trignac and Sévignac), indicates a cultural duality. This is backed up by the coexistence of two languages: French, which is derived from Latin, east of a line running from La Baule to Plouha, and Breton to the west.

The Breton Kingdom

From the 6th to the 10th century, the peninsula, now known as Britannia, fought off the attempts of Frankish kings who now controlled Gaul to dominate the region.

Several times, Brittany was invaded by the Merovingians. Their influence was short-lived, however, and the Bretons kept their independence – ruled by warlike local chiefs or petty kings.

The powerful Carolingian dynasty could do no more than establish a buffer zone, the Marches, which extended from the Baie du Mont-St-Michel to the Loire estuary. From about 770, this was controlled by Roland, "nephew" of Charlemagne. In the 9th century, the Bretons established an independent kingdom, whose frontiers stretched to Angers in the east, Laval in the south and Cherbourg in the northwest. The kingdom was founded by Nominoë, who overcame Charles the Bald at the Battle of Ballon in 845. His son, Erispoë, succeeded him but was murdered in 857 by his cousin Salomon, whose reign, until 874, marked the peak of the short-lived Breton monarchy.

Brittany's political independence was strengthened by the clergy, who resisted the jurisdiction of the see of Tours. This was the great age of the Benedictine abbeys, rich centres of culture. Fine illuminated manuscripts were produced (*see p153*), and the historic Cartulaire de Redon compiled.

The Cartulaire de Redon, a charter in which statutes were recorded from the 9th century

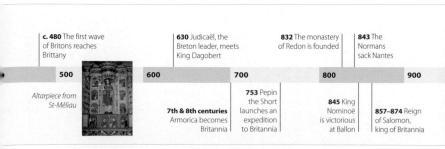

c. 480 The first wave of Britons reaches Brittany

630 Judicaël, the Breton leader, meets King Dagobert

832 The monastery of Redon is founded

843 The Normans sack Nantes

| 500 | 600 | 700 | 800 | 900 |

Altarpiece from St-Méliau

7th & 8th centuries Armorica becomes Britannia

753 Pepin the Short launches an expedition to Britannia

845 King Nominoë is victorious at Ballon

857–874 Reign of Salomon, king of Britannia

William the Conqueror takes Dinan, a scene from the Bayeux Tapestry

The Norman Invasions

From the end of the 8th century, the raids led by the Normans, from Scandinavia, became more frequent. Sailing up Brittany's coastal inlets and estuaries, they ransacked towns and monasteries, bringing terror to the land. Nantes was sacked in 843. Entire monastic communuties fled east, taking with them the relics of saints. After the murder of Salomon in 874, Brittany descended into chaos. From around 930–40, a semblance of order returned when King Alain Barbetorte regained Nantes in 937 and defeated the Normans at Trans in 939. Settling in neighbouring Normandy, the invaders gradually ceased their raiding activities, although they remained a dangerous presence.

Feudal Brittany

From the mid-10th century to the mid-14th, Brittany slowly evolved into a feudal state, maintaining a fragile independence from the kings of France and of England, both of whom had designs on Brittany.

In the 12th century, Brittany, now a county, narrowly avoided being absorbed into the Anglo-Angevin kingdom of the Plantagenets. Victorious at the Battle of Hastings in 1066, William the Conqueror had unified Normandy and England. His successor, Henry Plantagenet, was also Count of Anjou. In 1156, he took Conan IV, Count of Brittany, under his protection; Conan's daughter Constance was to marry Geoffrey, son of the king of England and brother of Richard the Lionheart and John Lackland. In 1203, the latter murdered Geoffrey's son, Arthur, and Brittany fell under the rule of the king of England. Philippe Auguste, king of France, then forced Alix, Arthur's half-sister, to marry a French prince, Pierre de Dreux, (Pierre Mauclerc). As a royal fiefdom, Brittany then came under the direct control of the French Crown. The Count of Brittany paid obeisance to the king of France, pledging his loyalty and aid. Despite these vicissitudes, a Breton state was forming. In 1297, Philip the Fair, king of France, made the fiefdom a vassal-duchy, and a ducal government was set up.

Henry II Plantagenet

William the Conqueror

c. 900 The Norman invasion. Monks flee Brittany

c. 1000 The feudal system is established

1066 Led by William the Conqueror, many Bretons take part in the Norman Conquest of England

| 900 | 950 | 1000 | 1050 |

937 Alain Barbetorte reconquers Brittany, expelling the Normans

11th century Many castles are built and small towns established

Château de Vitré

Although tied to the king of France through his vassal status, by the 13th century the count (then the duke) of Brittany was in a sufficiently strong position to move towards independence. As Count of Richmond, in Yorkshire, he was also a vassal of the Plantagenet king, and was thus able to steer a political course between the two monarchs.

In Brittany, however, his authority was limited by the power of his vassals, who controlled extensive fiefdoms from the safety of impregnable castles. These included the barons of Vitré and Fougères, on the border with Normandy; the Viscount of Porhoët, who ruled over 140 parishes and 400,000 ha (990,000 acres) of land from the Château de Josselin; and the Viscount of Léon, who, with the Count of Penthièvre, controlled part of the northern coast around Lamballe.

Life in Town and Country During the Middle Ages

Breton country-dwellers seem to have led more peaceful lives than those of their counterparts in France. In the west of the peninsula, there existed an unusual type of land tenure that persisted until the French Revolution. Every piece of farmland was owned by two people, one owning the land and the other the buildings and crops. Neither could be forced out without being paid for the value of what he owned. The towns, all of them small, enjoyed no administrative autonomy. Almost all were fortified, and many stood at the head of an inlet. Town-dwellers lived from the linen trade.

The seven saints who founded the Breton sees

Feudal Brittany was intensely religious. In areas of population growth, the number of parishes increased as new hamlets sprung up, their names prefixed with *loc* (as in Locmaria) or *ker* (as in Kermaria). Ancient pagan beliefs melded with the cult of old Breton saints, whose relics were the focus of pardons and pilgrimages. The best-known is the Tro Breiz, a tour of Brittany, about 650 km (400 miles) long, taking in shrines in St-Malo, Dol, Vannes, Quimper, St-Pol, Tréguier and St-Brieuc.

War of the Breton Succession

From 1341 to 1364, Brittany was ravaged by the warring of two families who claimed

St Yves

Born at the Manoir de Kermartin, near Tréguier, in 1248, St Yves was a magistrate at the bishop's tribunal in Rennes, then in Tréguier. He was also the parish priest at Trédrez and then at Louannec, in the Trégor. He preached, led an ascetic life, and ensured justice for the poor, all of which brought him favourable renown. He died in 1303 and was canonized in 1347. He is the patron saint of Bretons and barristers. His skull is paraded in a procession at Tréguier that takes place on the third Sunday of May *(see pp106–7)*.

St Yves, between a rich and a poor man

	1166 With Henry Plantagenet, Brittany is under English rule	**1203** Arthur, Count of Brittany, is murdered by John Lackland	**c. 1250** Dominican and Franciscan monasteries are founded	**1297** Brittany becomes a vassal-duchy
1100	1150	1200	1250	1300
12th century Cistercian abbeys are founded	**1185** Geoffrey Plantagenet gives Brittany its own government	**1203** With Pierre de Dreux, Brittany comes under the control of France	**1270** Jean I sets off on a Crusade with St Louis	**1303** Death of St Yves

St Louis

The Battle of Thirty, 1351, in which 30 Bretons, led by Beaumanoir, fought 30 Englishmen

the dukedom. This conflict became part of the Hundred Years' War (1337–1453) fought between the kings of France and England. While the former supported Charles of Blois and his wife, Joan of Penthièvre, the latter aided Jean of Montfort and his wife, Joan of Flanders. This war, in which both women were closely involved, gave rise to such isolated incidents as the Battle of Thirty (1351).

The war ended in victory for the Montforts and their English allies: Charles of Blois was killed at the Battle of Auray (1364) and Bertrand du Guesclin was taken prisoner. Jean IV of Montfort's victory was ratified by the Treaty of Guérande and, for over a century, his dynasty held power in an almost independent Brittany, which could rely on English support to foil the ambitions of the king of France.

Apogee of the Breton State

The Breton state reached the peak of its power in the 15th century. The Duke of Brittany, who enjoyed the status of ruler

and who was crowned in Rennes Cathedral, took up residence in Nantes. Surrounded by courtiers, he inaugurated a new age, patronizing artists and encouraging an interpretation of history that exalted Breton culture.

Government (the council, chancellery, court of exchequer, parliament and law court) was shared between Nantes, Vannes and Rennes. Every year, the States of Brittany held a meeting at which they voted on taxes. Complex and burdensome, these taxes were not sufficient to finance the duke's ever more extravagant tastes, nor to cover the upkeep of fortresses and the maintenance of an army. But, raising the necessary funds himself, the duke managed to keep his distance from the king of France.

During the reign of Jean V (1399–1442), Brittany remained relatively neutral in the Hundred Years' War. This allowed Bretons to enjoy a certain prosperity: maritime trade developed, with Breton seamen acting as

The Battle of Auray (1364), at which the Montforts and their English allies overcame the French

1341 Start of the War of the Breton Succession	**1364** Death of Charles of Blois at the Battle of Auray	**1378** Charles V attempts to secure the dukedom of Brittany	**15th century** The duchy of Brittany reaches its peak. Flowering of the Breton Gothic style

1340   **1360**   **1380**   **1400**   **1420**

1351 Battle of Thirty	**1365** Treaty of Guérande: the Montforts are victorious	**1380** Death of famous mercenary Bertrand du Guesclin	**1399–1442** Reign of Jean V. Shifting allegiance between France and England

Equestrian statue of Breton mercenary Olivier de Clisson

middlemen between Bordeaux and England, and exporting salt from Guérande and linen cloth from Vitré, Locronan and Léon. The population of Brittany, less seriously affected by the great plagues than that of France, reached 800,000. Refugees from Normandy settled in the east, while many impoverished petty noblemen left to seek their fortune in France. During the Hundred Years' War, Breton mercenaries fighting on both sides won renown for their prowess. Three of them – Bertrand du Guesclin, Olivier de Clisson and Arthur de Richemont – became constables (chief military officers) of France.

Noblemen enlarged their castles, turning them into impressive residences. There was a lack of morality, however, and this reached its nadir in the depraved treatment of children and their cruel murder, in a satanic ritual, committed by Gilles de Rais, companion-at-arms of Joan of Arc, at the Château de Tiffauges, near Nantes.

In the 15th century, a typically Breton variant of the Gothic architectural style developed, combining the delicacy of the

Bertrand du Guesclin

A minor nobleman born in about 1320 near Broons, Bertrand du Guesclin showed his prowess as a warrior during the War of the Breton Succession. He was also victorious at some famous jousts and duels, such as the one he fought in Dinan with Sir Thomas Canterbury. In the service of Charles V, he retook part of France from the English, and defeated the king of Navarre at Cocherel in 1364. He led *compagnies* (bands of mercenaries) to Spain. He was taken prisoner by the Black Prince at Najera in 1367, but returned to the battlefield. He was made a constable of France, and died during a siege in 1380.

Du Guesclin kneeling before Charles V

Flamboyant Gothic with the austerity of granite, the local building material. The first texts in Breton appeared and, with the advent of printing in 1484, printed books were produced; one of the first was *Catholicon*, a Breton-French-Latin lexicon. A university was founded in Nantes in 1460.

The End of Independence

François II (1458–88), the incapable and debauched Duke of Brittany, was powerless to prevent the increasing use of royal power in France, where Louis XI abolished the last great vassals in 1477. The king then turned his attention to Brittany, the only major fiefdom that still remained to be sub-jugated. Forced into a war, François II was defeated in 1488. By the Treaty of Le Verger, the duke was forced to submit to the king if his successor was to rule Brittany. He died soon after. His daughter and successor, Anne of Brittany, was not yet 12 years old.

The execution of Gilles de Rais in 1440

Dance of Death (late 15th century)

1460 Foundation of the University of Nantes

1488 Battle of St-Aubin-du-Cormier. Treaty of Le Verger

1514 Death of Anne of Brittany

40   1460   1480   1500   1520

140 Execution of child-murderer lles de Rais

1491 Anne of Brittany marries Charles VIII of France

1499 Anne of Brittany marries Louis XII of France

Anne of Brittany

Anne of Brittany

A central figure in the history of Brittany, Anne stood both for the duchy's independence and, through her marriage first to Charles VIII and then to Louis XII – both of them kings of France – for its integration with France. The vissicitudes of her short and eventful life also made her popular. She became a duchess at the age of 11, a queen at 13, a mother at 16, and a widow at 21. She died at the age of 37, having lost seven of her nine children. Even today, some Bretons revere her almost as a saint. A patron of the arts, she aided the development of Breton culture by supporting artists and historians.

Anne of Brittany's coat of arms feature a Franciscan nun, an ermine and the motto "To my Life."

Jean de Rely, bishop of Angers.

The Marriage of Charles VIII and Anne of Brittany

On the death of François II, Duke of Brittany, Charles VIII, the young king of France, resumed war with his successor Anne and forced her to marry him. The ceremony took place in Langeais on 6 December 1491. This early 19th-century painting shows the couple making their marriage vows.

Pierre de Baud, canon of Vitré, wrote a *History of Brittany* in 1505, at Anne's behest. The first account of its kind, it gave Breton identity a historical perspective.

Anne of Brittany at the age of 13.

Anne of Brittany's Residences

The castle in Nantes *(see pp214–15)* was Anne's main residence. She was born there, in the part known as the "old building", and she undertook the work that gives the castle its present appearance. As a young girl, she regularly stayed in Vannes, in the Château de l'Hermine and the Manoir de Plaisance, which now no longer exists, and in the Château de Suscinio, in the Morbihan, and the Château de Clisson, in the Loire-Atlantique. In Rennes, she lived in what is known as the Logis des Ducs, in the old town. During her tour of Brittany in 1505, she stayed in private houses, many of which are difficult to identify today. In Hennebont, Quimper, Locronan, Morlaix, Guingamp, St-Brieuc and Dinan, houses reverently known as "the Duchess Anne's houses" keep alive the memory of her visit. She also stayed for a few days in the castles at Hunaudaye, Vitré and Blain.

Château des Ducs de Bretagne, Nantes, Anne of Brittany's main residence

Louis XII, who succeeded Charles VIII, married Anne according to an agreement made at the time of her marriage to Charles.

Charles VIII

As patroness of the arts and a woman of the Renaissance, Anne supported artists and writers. Here, the Dominican friar Antoine Dufour presents to her his *Lives of Illustrious Women*.

Claude of Brittany, Anne's daughter, was born in 1499 and married François of Angoulême, the future François I. As king, he acquired through Claude the duchy of Brittany. Their son became François III, Duke of Brittany.

Burial of Anne of Brittany took place at the Château de Blois, on 9 January 1514. She was 37 years old.

This gold reliquary contains the heart of Anne of Brittany. According to her last wish, Anne's heart was brought from Blois to her native land, "the place that she loved more than any other in the world, so that it might be interred there". It was placed in the tomb that she had built for her parents in Nantes.

Map of Brittany in 1595, at the time of the wars of the Holy League

Brittany Joins France

Brittany's integration into the kingdom of France made no fundamental difference to the lives of Bretons. The Treaty of Union of 1532 ensured that their "rights, freedoms and privileges" would be respected. The province was ruled on behalf of the king by a governor, who usually had connections with the great Breton families. The interests of the population were, in principle, defended by the States of Brittany, an assembly that was, however, unrepresentative, since the rural population had no delegate. The nobility and high clergy played the most prominent role. Every year, the

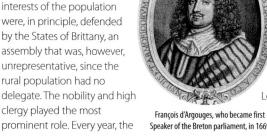
François d'Argouges, who became first Speaker of the Breton parliament, in 1669

delegates agreed with the king the level of taxation to be levied on the province. Brittany paid lower taxes than the rest of the kingdom and was exempt from the salt tax.

Parliament, restored in 1554, was housed in a suitably imposing building in Rennes dating from 1618–55 *(see pp66–7)*. Parliament was the supreme court of Breton law and was also a court in which royal decrees became statute. Brittany was thus able to retain its own legal system.

In the 16th century, Brittany was largely unaffected by the Wars of Religion fought between Catholics and Protestants. Strongly Catholic, it contained only a small number of Calvinists. However, under Henri IV, king of France and governor of Brittany, was the ambitious Philippe-Emmanuel de Lorraine, Duke of Mercœur. One of the mainstays of the Holy League – a group of Catholic extremists – he attempted to harness the loyalty of Bretons to Rome so as to draw them into a war against the heretical king, and lured them with thoughts of independence. After ten years of conflict, from 1589 to 1598, Mercœur was forced to withdraw, and, in Nantes, Henri IV signed the Edict of Nantes, ending the Wars of Religion.

Resistance to the Monarchy

In the 17th century, royal power became absolute, and the monarchy in France developed centralized rule. Local autonomy was curtailed and taxes rose. New taxes on tobacco and on

Parish close at La Martyre

1532 Treaty of Union signed by Brittany and France	1554 Creation of the Breton parliament		1589–1598 Wars of Religion			
1530	**1550**	**1570**	**1590**	**1610**	**1630**	**165**
1534–1542 Jacques Cartier explores Canada			1598 Edict of Nantes		c. 1600–1650 Parish closes are built	

Jacques Cartier

printed paper used for legal documents caused a revolt in Lower Brittany in 1675. The harsh repression that followed was described by Madame de Sévigné (see p73).

In 1689, so that his decisions might be more effectively implemented, Louis XIV placed the province under the control of an intendant, whose remit was to impose law and order and collect taxes. These measures caused a resurgence of Breton nationalism, most strongly among the petty nobility, that continued until the end of the Ancien Régime.

Much more troublesome for royal rule was legal opposition mounted against the intendant and the governor led by the States of Brittany and the Breton parliament. While the States claimed to defend Breton autonomy, they in fact supported the interests of the nobility. From 1759 to 1770, tensions ran high, reaching a climax in the conflict between Louis-René de Caradeuc de La Chalotais, the Breton parliament's ambitious and popular procurator-general, and the Duke of Aiguillon, the authoritarian and efficient

Henri IV on a military campaign against partisans of the Holy League, a group of Catholic extremists, in Brittany in 1598

commander-in-chief of Brittany. The "Breton question" enflamed the province and did not die down until the death of Louis XV, in 1774.

Brittany's Thriving Ports

Under the Ancien Régime, Brittany experienced vigorous economic growth. Port activity prospered as a result both of Brittany's integration with France and of the opening of sea routes across the Atlantic. Brittany played its part in voyages of discovery with the expedition to Canada undertaken by Jacques Cartier, of St-Malo, (1534–42). The three busiest French seaports were St-Malo, Nantes and Lorient, built in 1666 as a base for the French East India Company. Conflict between France and England interfered with economic activity on the coasts, as the English launched attacks on St-Malo, Belle-Île and St-Cast. Naval warfare also led to Colbert's building an arsenal at Brest (c. 1680), while Vauban increased coastal defences.

St-Malo, France's major port at the end of the 17th century, used for trade and for fitting out the ships of privateers

1675 Revolt against taxes on tobacco and printed paper; the Bonnets Rouges

1711 Rio de Janeiro taken by Duguay-Trouin

René Duguay-Trouin

1758 The Duke of Aiguillon repulses an attempted English invasion at St-Cast

| 1670 | 1690 | 1710 | 1730 | 1750 | 1770 |

1689 The administration of Brittany is set up

1693 The English attack St-Malo

1720 Pontcallec's conspiracy

1764–74 The Breton Question (La Chalotais and the Duke d'Aiguillon)

The Chouans and the Revolution

During the French Revolution, Brittany was divided between *"les bleus"*, who were in favour of new ideas, and *"les blancs"*, supporters of the Ancien Régime. *"Les bleus"* consisted of the liberal bourgeoisie and of country-dwellers of those cantons of Lower Brittany that were opposed to the clergy and nobility; *"les blancs"*, consisting mostly of nobility and unruly clergy, predominated in southern and eastern Brittany.

Jean Cottereau, known as Jean Chouan

In 1792, a few aristocrats led by La Rouërie hatched an unsuccessful counter-revolutionary plot, but in 1793, when the National Convention ordered that 300,000 men should be levied to fight in the war, the Loire-Atlantique, Morbihan and Ille- et-Vilaine rebelled. The Chouans, led by Cadoudal, Guillemot, Boishardy and Jean Chouan, fought a guerrilla war in the countryside. The Republicans responded by launching the Terror: in Nantes, 10,000 people were beheaded or drowned.

"Les blancs" had been dealt a blow. The army of Catholics and royalists was defeated at Savenay in 1793; attempts by émigré nobles to land in Brittany, with British aid, were quashed. At Quiberon, in June 1795, 6,000 of them were taken prisoner by Hoche's republican army and 750 executed.

Stability was not restored until the advent of Napoleon Bonaparte, who reconciled Church and State, appointed prefects, and ensured military control by building roads and establishing garrison towns, such as Napoléonville in Pontivy. Because of the Napoleonic Wars, during which the British ruled the seas, Brittany's fortunes were in decline, despite the exploits of privateers such as Robert Surcouf of St-Malo.

The 19th Century

During the 19th century and until the 1950s, Brittany, isolated from the centres of the industrial revolution, became a rural backwater, although it supported a thriving canning industry. Fishing off Iceland and Newfoundland was another key activity.

Awareness of Brittany's Celtic heritage gathered strength as poets, ethnologists and folklorists documented and recorded Breton

Mass drownings in the Loire at Nantes, ordered by Jean-Baptiste Carrier during the French Revolution

1789 Riots in Rennes	**1793–1802** Chouan uprising	*Nantes is attacked by the Vendéens*	**1865** The Paris-Brest railway is completed	**1886** Paul Gauguin arrives in Pont-Aven	**189** The URB founde
1780	**1800**	**1820** **1840**	**1860**	**1880**	
1792 La Rouërie's plot	**1795** The landing of royalist émigrés in Quiberon ends in failure	**1839** La Villemarqué publishes *Barzaz Breiz*	**1848** F. de Lamennais is elected people's delegate at the Constituent Assembly	**1896** La Borderie starts his *History of Brittany*	

De Lamennais

traditions and ancient tales. The Breton language, strongly discouraged in undenominational schools during the Third Republic (1870–1940), found ardent supporters among the clergy, while regional history became the object of renewed interest, culminating in La Borderie's monumental *History of Brittany*. Strong cultural regionalism asserted itself around 1900, with the Union Régionaliste Bretonne, followed by the formation of the Parti National Breton, which was supported by the occupying Germans in 1940–44.

Poster for the inauguration of the Paris-Brest railway

In the 19th century, continuing high birth rates and the absence of industry caused large-scale rural emigration to Paris, where a vigorous Breton community became established. Bretons became prominent on the national stage. Among them were Chateaubriand, politician and writer of the Romantic age; René Pléven, a minister during the Fourth Republic; Félicité de Lamennais, a founder of social Catholicism; and the religious sceptic Ernest Renan. With the arrival of the railway in the mid-19th century, Brittany began to attract writers and artists, drawn by the wild beauty of its countryside and the exotic nature of its Celtic traditions.

Brittany suffered greatly during the two world wars: in 1914–18, the proportion of Breton soldiers killed was twice the national average. In 1940–45, the region was occupied by Nazi Germany, and several ports, including St-Nazaire, Lorient, Brest and St-Malo, were razed by fighting during the Liberation.

Brittany in the Modern World

Brittany made a remarkable recovery after World War II. Since 1950, the Comité d'Étude et de Liaison des Intérêts Bretons has attracted investment and such decentralized operations as that of PSA in Rennes and telecommunications in Lannion. Toll-free highways, high-speed train services and the installation of airports have ended Brittany's isolation. Cross-channel links and a strong hotel industry make it the second-most popular tourist destination in France.

Brittany is also France's foremost producer of fruit and vegetables, and a leading producer of pigs and chickens. Such success has its price: farmers are crippled by the cost of modern equipment and soil is overloaded with nitrate. The region's problems are now being addressed: the need to preserve places of historic interest and natural beauty is seen as a priority, as is the importance of keeping alive Brittany's links with other Celtic regions in Europe.

Naval dockyards at St-Nazaire, where cruise liners are now built

1925 Morvan Marchal designs the *Gwenn-ha-du*, the Breton flag

1944 End of the German occupation. Many ports are destroyed

1978 Oil spill from the *Amoco Cadiz*

1989 High-speed-train link to Rennes

2003 The RMS *Queen Mary 2*, the world's largest ocean liner, built in St-Nazaire shipyards

00   1920   1940   1960   1980   2000   2020

Breton flag

1932 The PNB is founded

1950 The CELIB is founded

1992 The terms of the Maastricht Treaty concerning the European Union are supported by 60 per cent of Bretons

2017 New LGV fast train line due to be finished

2000 The aircraft carrier *Charles de Gaulle* is launched at Brest naval arsenal

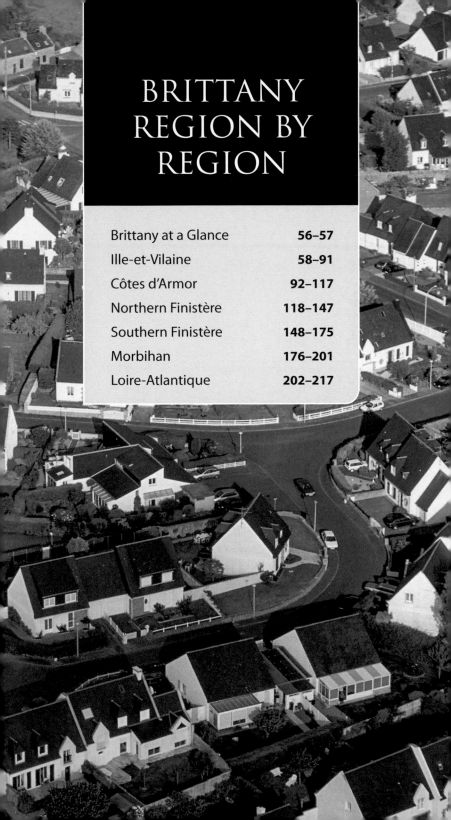

BRITTANY REGION BY REGION

Brittany at a Glance

Brittany's beaches, like those on the Côte d'Émeraude and Côte de Granit Rose, the Golfe du Morbihan and Belle-Île, are very popular with holiday-makers. Brittany is also a land of history, with a rich heritage of ancient monuments. The timber-framed houses in Vannes and Dinan conjure up the Middle Ages, while in Nantes and St-Malo the town houses of shipowners reflect the fortunes that were made in the 17th and 18th centuries. Coastal forts such as that in St-Malo and castles in the Breton marches have fiercely defended Brittany from attack from land and sea throughout the centuries.

Château de Kerouzéré is one of many fortified castles in the region *(see p128).*

Logis de Rohan, a tower in Quimper, houses the Musée Départemental Breton *(see p166).*

Perros-Guirec

Roscoff
Lannion

Île d'Ouessant

Morlaix

NORTHERN FINISTÈRE
(See pp118–147)

Brest
Guingamp

Châteaulin

SOUTHERN FINISTÈRE
(See pp148–175)

Quimper
Pontivy

Concarneau

MORBIH.
(See pp176–2

Lorient
Île de Groix
Van

Atlantic Ocean

Belle-Île

Porte Poterne in Vannes, not far from the Château de l'Hermine, leads through to pleasant gardens beneath the city walls *(see pp192–3).*

0 kilometres 20

0 miles 20

◀ Aerial view of houses between St-Malo and Le Minihic, Ille-et-Vilaine

The timber-framed houses in St-Brieuc *(see pp108–9)* surround the city's impressive cathedral.

The famous Mont-St-Michel is one of the most remarkable sights on the coast of Brittany *(see pp76–81)*.

Dinard
St-Malo
Dinan
Mont-St-Michel

-Brieuc

TES D'ARMOR
(See pp92–117)

udéac

Fougères

ILLE-ET-VILAINE
(See pp58–91)

Rennes

Ploërmel

Châteaubriant

Cathédrale St-Pierre in Rennes *(see pp62–3)* has a magnificent 19th-century interior.

LOIRE-ATLANTIQUE
(See pp202–217)

rande

St-Nazaire

Nantes

Pornic

Théâtre de Nantes is notable for its Neo-Classical interior *(see pp210–11)*.

ILLE-ET-VILAINE

In the north, the Côte d'Émeraude and Mont-St-Michel face onto the English Channel. Further south, at the confluence of the Ille and the Vilaine rivers, lies Rennes, the regional capital, which is famous for its elegant parliament building. To the east, the proud fortresses of the Breton marches, which once protected the duchy of Brittany, face neighbouring Normandy.

The beaches of the Côte d'Émeraude are lined by a succession of resorts. But well before this part of Brittany was discovered by tourists, Pierre-Auguste Renoir, Paul Signac and other artists had already been struck by its beauty when they came to paint in St-Briac.

Whether they are drawn to the megalithic Roche-aux-Fées or to the fortified castle in Fougères, lovers of ancient monuments will be spoiled for choice. On the coast, Mont-St-Michel stands as a jewel of Gothic religious architecture, while the citadel in St-Malo encloses within its ramparts several luxury hotels. Inland, noblemen built a multitude of manor houses, symbols of social standing, during the 16th and 17th centuries. In the towns, a prosperous and influential middle class developed; the medieval houses in Vitré and Dol, as well as the town houses in Rennes, are proof of this opulence. As acts of piety, tradesmen's guilds commissioned the artists of Laval to create rich altarpieces.

From Celtic mythology to French Romanticism, the *département* of the Ille-et-Vilaine also has two emblems of Breton literary heritage: one is the the Forêt de Paimpont, the legendary Forêt de Brocéliande where Merlin fell under the spell of the fairy Vivian; the other is the lugubrious Château de Combourg, haunted by the ghost of the 19th-century writer and statesman the Vicomte de Chateaubriand.

Slender stone columns that form the cloisters of Mont-St-Michel Abbey

◀ View of the waterfront town of Cancale, the oyster capital of Brittany

Exploring the Ille-et-Vilaine

This *département*, which covers an area of 6,758 sq km (2,608 sq miles), is named after the two rivers that flow through it: the Ille and the Vilaine. In the north, a hilly area culminating in Mont-Dol overlooks the coast. East of Cancale, the marshlands of Dol have been converted into polders, sunken areas of land reclaimed from the sea. The coastline then descends to trace a bay out of which rises Mont-St-Michel. From the Pointe du Grouin, the Côte d'Émeraude (Emerald Coast) is marked by alternating jagged cliffs and soft sandy beaches. Rennes, in the centre of the *département*, is the administrative capital. On the eastern border of the Ille-et-Vilaine, the fortresses of Fougères and Vitré face neighbouring Normandy. Occupying a corner of the Morbihan and of the Ille-et-Vilaine, the Forêt de Paimpont is a vestige of Argoat, the woodland that once covered the whole of inland Brittany.

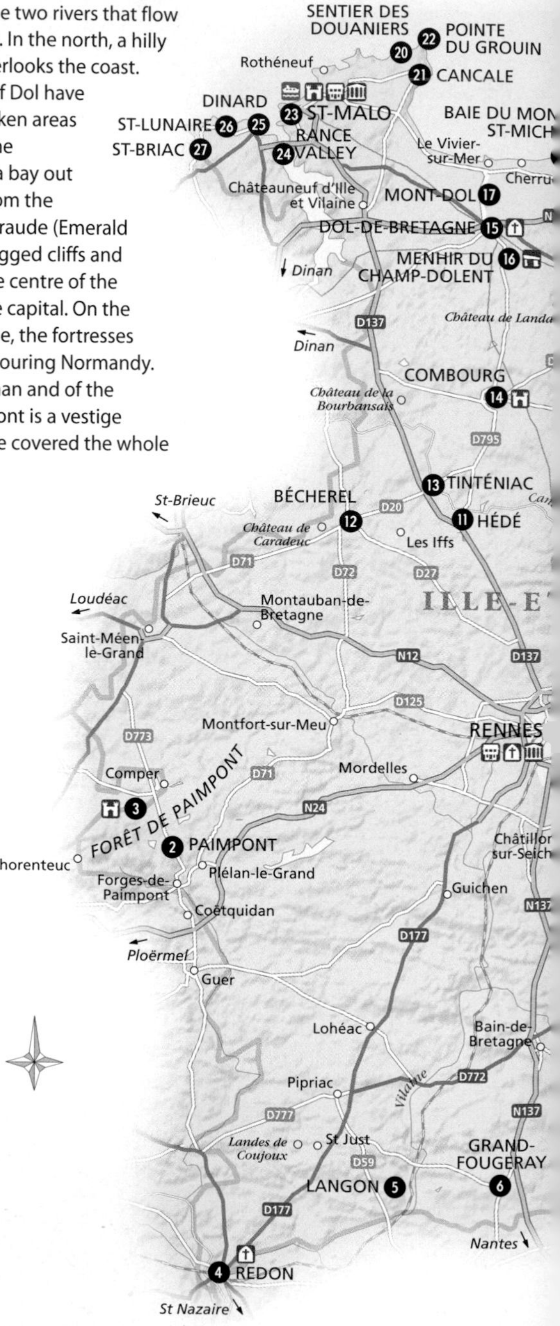

Sights at a Glance

1. *Rennes pp62–7*
2. Paimpont
3. Forêt de Paimpont
4. Redon
5. Langon
6. Grand-Fougeray
7. La Guerche-de-Bretagne
8. Vitré
9. Château des Rochers-Sévigné
10. Fougères
11. Hédé
12. Bécherel
13. Tinténiac
14. Combourg
15. Dol-de-Bretagne
16. Menhir du Champ-Dolent
17. Mont-Dol
18. Baie du Mont-St-Michel
19. *Mont-St-Michel pp78–81*
21. Cancale
22. Pointe du Grouin
23. *St-Malo pp84–9*
24. Rance Valley
25. Dinard
26. St-Lunaire
27. St-Briac

Hike

20. Sentier des Douaniers

0 kilometres   20

0 miles   20

Agricultural land near Bain-de-Bretagne

Getting Around

Rennes is linked to Paris by the A11 motorway to Le Mans, then the A81 to Laval, then by the N157-E50. Two major roads – the N137 and N24 – run through the Ille-et-Vilaine. The D137 links St-Malo and Rennes, and continues southwards to Nantes. From Rennes, the N24 runs west to Lorient, passing through Ploërmel. Also from Rennes, the N12-E50 runs to St-Brieuc. The marches of Brittany can be reached by following any of the minor roads leading to the region's eastern border: these are the D177 from Redon to Pipriac, the D772 from Pipriac to Bain-de-Bretagne, the D777 from Bain-de-Bretagne to Vitré, and the D178 from Châteaubriant to Fougères. The Ille-et-Vilaine's major towns are served by rail and bus links from Rennes.

Key

▬▬▬	Motorway
▬▬▬	Major road
▬▬▬	Secondary road
▭▭▭	Minor road
▬▪▬▪	Main railway
----	Minor railway
▬▬▬	Regional border

Timber-framed houses on the Place des Lices in Rennes

For keys to symbols *see back flap*

❶ Street-by-Street: Rennes

Around the cathedral, narrow streets wind
between timber-framed houses that conceal
courtyards. On Saturdays, the Place des Lices
throngs with the colourful stalls of one of the
liveliest markets in Brittany. During the week,
the district's many bars and restaurants are filled
with the animated babble of students. Neo-
Classical buildings by the architect Jacques
Gabriel (1667–1742) line Place de la Mairie. Rue Le
Bastard, leading off the square, is a pedestrianized
zone and the main link between the Vilaine and
the northern part of the city.

★ **Place du Champ-Jacquet**
Tall timber-framed houses dating from the
17th century back onto the old city walls.

★ **Hôtel de Blossac**
This is one of the finest
mansions in Rennes. The
building, in the Neo-Classical
style, was designed by a
follower of Jacques Gabriel.

Hôtel de Robien

Hôtel Hay de Tizé

Basilique St-Sauveur

★ **Cathédrale St-Pierre**
The building stands on the site of an
ancient place of worship. Although it
retains its 16th-century façade, the
cathedral was rebuilt from 1784.

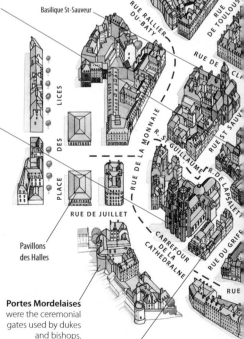

Pavillons
des Halles

Portes Mordelaises
were the ceremonial
gates used by dukes
and bishops.

Rue de la Psalette is lined
with medieval houses.

0 metres	100
0 yards	100

Key

— Suggested route

Parlement de Bretagne
Now housing the law courts, this building's sumptuous decoration and paintings have been restored to their original splendour following a fire in 1994 *(see pp66–7)*.

Église St-Germain reflects the opulence of the haberdashers' parish in the 16th century.

VISITORS' CHECKLIST

Practical Information
Road map E3. ⚠ 212,500.
🚌 Sat am; Place des Lices. ℹ 11 Rue St-Yves, (02) 99 67 11 11.
🎭 Les Tombées de la Nuit (theatre & concerts; Jul), Les Trans Musicales (rock and electro; first week in Dec), Film Festival (Feb).
🅦 **tourisme-rennes.com**

Transport
🚊 🚌 ✈ Rennes Metropolitan.

Theatre
In designing the theatre, which consists of a rotunda with arcades and covered alleyways, the architect Millardet wished to create a meeting place and centre of trade. He also designed the neighbouring residential buildings.

RUE HOCHE
RUE VICTOR HUGO
ALOMON
RUE SAINT GEORGES
PLACE DU PARLEMENT
DE BRETAGNE
RUE NATIONALE
RUE E. CAVELL
RUE DU VAU SAINT GERMAIN
RUE D'ESTRÉES
RUE DE BRILHAC
RUE DE CO ETQUEN
PLACE DE LA MAIRIE
RUE DE L'HERMINE
RUE D'ORLEANS
CLIN
RUE DE L'HORLOGE
RUE F. BUISSON
RUE DE ROHAN
RUE BEAUMANOR
ONTFORT
PLACE DU CALVAIRE
RUE DU CARTAGE
APITRE
RUE SAINT-YVES
G.
N
RUE LE BOUTEILLER

Hôtel de Ville
Built by Jacques Gabriel after the great fire of 1720, the town hall consists of two wings framing the clock tower, with a belfry in the Italian style. Sculptures by Jacques Verberckt decorate the main entrance.

Chapelle St-Yves houses the tourist office.

Head of an Angel by Botticelli, in the Robien Collection

Robien's Cabinet of Curiosities

Built at the beginning of the 17th century, the mansion known as the Hôtel de Robien was acquired in 1699 by Christophe Paul de Robien. Filled not only with paintings and statues but also with plants and minerals, it became a true cabinet of curiosities. Robien bequeathed the collection to his son in 1756, but it was confiscated by the Revolutionaries in 1792. It was stored in the Church of the Visitation, then in the Carmelite convent in Rennes. The Robien Collection now forms part of the city's Musée des Beaux Arts.

Exploring Rennes

Despite the fire that devastated the city centre in 1720, Rennes still has some fine medieval houses. It also has many delightful mansions and a remarkable 17th-century palace. The city has stood at a strategic crossroads since Roman times. In the 10th century, it withstood Norman invaders and became a symbol of Breton resistance. In the 15th century, new fortifications were built to strengthen the existing Gallo-Roman ramparts. When Brittany became part of France in 1532 and the parliament of Brittany was created (*see pp66–7*), Rennes became the regional capital. After the fire of 1720, a Neo-Classical city centre with rigidly straight streets was built. This layout, and the buildings dating from the same period, give Rennes a somewhat austere appearance. A university town, Rennes has a conspicuously lively population of students.

Timber-framed houses around Place des Lices

Old Town

Between the Vilaine in the south and Place des Lices in the north, the medieval centre of Rennes is full of timber-framed houses. **Place des Lices** (Square of the Lists) takes its name from the lists where jousting tournaments where once held. It was here that Bertrand du Guesclin (*see p47*) first entered the lists. Around the square, three mansions – the Hôtel du Molant, Hôtel de la Noue and Hôtel Racapée de la Feuillée – all built before the fire of 1720 – stand as symbols of the power of the Breton parliamentary nobility.

Wooden statue in Impasse de la Psalette

The **Portes Mordelaises**, at the end of Rue de la Monnaie, were the main gateway through which dukes and bishops entered the city. Behind the **Cathédrale St-Pierre**, in Rue du Chapitre, the Hôtel de Brie and **Hôtel de Blossac**, with a monumental stairway, are among the finest residences.

Place de la Mairie is a large Neo-Classical square designed by Jacques Gabriel. The most prominent feature of the **Hôtel de Ville**, overlooking the square, is the clocktower, which replaced the old belfry. The sculptures on the doors are by Jacques Verberckt, who worked on the decoration of Versailles for Louis XV. The **theatre** and

arcaded residential buildings opposite were designed by Millardet in 1836.

The 17th–18th century **Basilique St-Sauveur**, in Rue de Clisson, is associated with the composer Gabriel Fauré, who was organist there. Rue St-Georges, lined with old houses, leads to the **Église St-Germain**, whose transept is a fine example of Breton Romanesque architecture. Behind the Église Notre-Dame is the **Jardin du Thabor**, a masterpiece by the Bühler brothers (*see p65*).

Cathédrale St-Pierre

Between the Portes Mordelaises and Rue de la Psalette.

The cathedral stands on the site of an ancient shrine in front of which a trove of Gallo-Roman artifacts was discovered. Work on the building began in the 16th century, and the façade was completed in the 17th century. The rest was built from 1784 to plans by the architect Crucy. The 19th-century stuccowork and gilding within give the interior an opulence worthy of Roman basilicas. The gilt wood altarpiece, dating from 1520 and by the Flemish School, is of particular note.

Marine Bleue, by G. Lacombe, in the Musée des Beaux-Arts, Rennes

The Bühler Brothers

Although little-known today, Denis (1811–90) and Eugène (1822–1907) Bühler revolutionized the art of garden design. Giving imagination free reign, they rejected the strictures of the classic formal gardens in the French style. The Bühler brothers designed some 100 gardens. About 20 of these are in Brittany, and they include the gardens of the Château de Kervenez in St-Pol-de-Léon and of

The Jardin du Thabor, laid out by the Bühler brothers

the Château de la Briantais in St-Malo. But it was in Rennes that they designed their finest garden, the Jardin du Thabor. Laid out in the style of a 19th-century park, the garden follows the contours of the land and incorporates greenhouses, pavilions and an aviary. Exotic and indigenous trees frame the garden's perspectives.

🏛 Musée des Beaux-Arts

20 Quai Émile-Zola. **Tel** (02) 23 62 17 45. **Open** Tue–Sun. 🗷

The Robien Collection (see p63) contains drawings by Leonardo da Vinci, Botticelli, Donatello and Dürer. There is also a strong focus on the 17th-century, with works by Le Brun and Philippe de Champaigne, Rubens' *Tiger Hunt* and the star of the museum, *Nouveau-né* by Georges de La Tour. The museum has expanded its collection with an additional space for modern and contemporary art. Modern art is represented by such painters as Corot, Denis, Gauguin, Lacombe, Caillebotte and Sisley. The contemporary collection includes works by Poliakoff, Nicolas de Staël, Raymond Hains and Dufrêne.

🏛 Les Champs Libres

10 Cours des Alliés. **Tel** (02) 23 40 66 00. **Open** Tue–Sun pm only. 🗷

This cultural centre has a museum on Brittany, a science centre, a public library and a conference hall. Exhibitions address subjects such as literature, history, physics and astronomy.

🏛 Écomusée de la Bintinais

On the road to Châtillon-sur-Seiche, via the D82, 4 km (3 miles) south of Rennes. **Tel** (02) 99 51 38 15. **Open** Tue–Fri, Sat–Sun pm. **Closed** Mon and public holidays. 🗷

La Bintinais is one of the largest old farms in the countryside around Rennes. Converted into a living museum, it illustrates the history of rural life.

Fields have been planted to show various farming practices of the past, and a conservation orchard has been created to preserve varieties of cider apples that have become rare.

Rennes City Centre

① Portes Mordelaises
② Cathédrale St-Pierre
③ Basilique St-Sauveur
④ Hôtel de Ville
⑤ Theatre
⑥ Parlement de Bretagne
⑦ Jardin du Thabor
⑧ Église St-Germain
⑨ Musée des Beaux-Arts

Key

See pp62–3

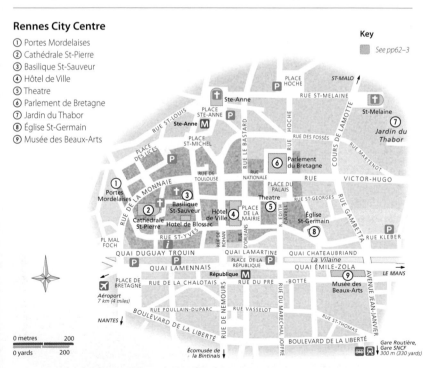

Parlement de Bretagne

The Breton parliament, dating from 1618–55, is a major landmark in the city of Rennes. Salomon de Brosse, the architect of the Palais du Luxembourg in Paris, designed the façade in the Italian style. The interior courtyard, by contrast, is built in brick and stone in the French style. The interior decoration of the building emphasizes the hallowed importance of Brittany's independent political power: the sumptuous Salle des Pas-Perdus, with the coat of arms of Brittany and France, and the ceiling of the Grand'Chambre, designed by Louis XIV's foremost painter, amply express this. Gutted by fire in February 1994, the building took ten years to restore.

★ **Court of Assises**
The tables and benches in the audience chambers are made of oak. The room is lit by antique and modern chandeliers.

★ **Salle des Pas-Perdus**
The door to the Salle des Pas-Perdus (the lobby) features windows decorated with metalwork. The room has an ornate wooden coffered ceiling.

Salle Jobbé-Duval
The allegories painted by Félix Jobbé-Duval in 1866 were the last decorative elements to be added. The allegory seen here is *Eloquence*.

KEY

① Pediment

② Former Court of Criminal Justice

③ Slate roof, covering 5,200 sq m (18,660 sq ft)

④ The ground-floor rooms were used for religious and official ceremonies.

Salle des Piliers
This is the grand entrance hall to the parliament building. Like the rest of the interior, it is built of stone, a traditionally French construction that contrasts with Jacques Gabriel's classical façade.

Upper Gallery
The audience chambers on the upper level are arranged in a gallery running around the court.

★ **Grand'Chambre**
Charles Errard, in charge of the building's decoration, experimented here before starting the decoration of Versailles. For the Grand'Chambre, he called on his pupil Noël Coypel, and, for the First Chamber, on Jean-Baptiste Jouvenet. Both decorated the rooms with allegorical paintings.

Allegorical Figures
Four allegorical figures, representing Eloquence, Fortitude, Law and Justice, once decorated the roof of the south lodges. Cast in lead and covered in gold leaf, the figures were made by Dolivet in the 19th century and restored by Jean-Loup Bouvier.

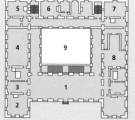

Parlement de Bretagne

Key to Floorplan

1 Salle des Pas-Perdus (lobby)
2 Salle Jobbé-Duval
3 Chapel
4 Court of Assises
5 Salle Nicolas-Gosse
6 Salle Ferdinand-Elle
7 Salle Jean-Jouvenet
8 Grand'Chambre (upper house)
9 Courtyard and galleries

The Château de Trécesson, built in the late 14th century and surrounded by a moat

❷ Paimpont

Road map E3. 30 km (18.5 miles) south of Rennes via the N24 then the D38. 🚉 Rennes. 🏠 1,385. 🛈 Place du Roi Judicaël, Paimpont; (02) 99 07 84 23. 🎭 Pardon (Whitsun).

The village grew up around an abbey founded in the 7th century. Of this, only the 13th-century abbey church and a 17th-century building, now the village hall, survive. The abbey church features Romanesque elements, a Gothic rose window and some 17th-century woodcarvings. The village is the starting point for hikes in the Forêt de Brocéliande, with its many oaks and beeches.

Environs
Industrial buildings at **Forges-de-Paimpont**, 6 km (4 miles) southeast of Paimpont on the

Forêt de Paimpont, vestige of the legendary Forêt de Brocéliande

D773, are vestiges of the village's former iron and steel industry, which began in 1663. The metal foundries declined after the rise of the iron and steel industry in northern and eastern France.

❸ Forêt de Paimpont

Road map E3. Around Paimpont. 🛈 Place du Roi Judicaël, Paimpont; (02) 99 07 84 23.

This woodland, the Forêt de Brocéliande of Celtic legend, was originally the extensive forest that once covered almost all of inland Brittany. Today, the woodland around Paimpont is all that remains and it is peppered with sites that have kept Arthurian legends alive. The Château de Comper, where the fairy Vivian is supposed to have lived, houses the **Centre de l'Imaginaire Arthurien**, where exhibitions and shows take place, and from which walks are organized. Rebuilt in the 18th century in Renaissance style, the building features three 14th-century towers.

The D31 leads northeast to Merlin's Tomb and the Fountain of Youth. The tree above the tomb is filled with strange offerings. From the hamlet of Folle Pensée, a short walk leads to the Fontaine de Barenton, into which young women once cast pins in order to find a husband. Here, druids are

supposed to have nursed people suffering from foolish thoughts. Take the interactive trail from the Paimpont tourist office through the forest.

Environs
At Coëtquidan is the École de St-Cyr, a military academy. The **Musée des Souvenirs des Écoles** here displays gifts from prominent alumni, such as the statesman General de Gaulle (1890–1970). The unusual Chapelle de Tréhorenteuc, 14 km (9 miles) west of Paimpont, contains mosaics and stained-glass windows on the theme of the Round Table. This is the starting point for the Promenade du Val-sans-Retour (Valley of No Return), dwelling place of Morgan le Fay, Arthur's half-sister, who trapped unfaithful men here. Passing the lake known as the Étang du Miroir-aux-Fées, the path leads up onto moorland and then on through the valley. Further south is the 14th-century red schist **Château de Trécesson**.

🏠 **Centre de l'Imaginaire Arthurien**
Château de Comper. **Tel** (02) 97 22 79 96. **Open** Mar–Jun, Sep: Thu–Mon; Jul–Aug: Thu–Tue. 🎨

🏠 **Château de Trécesson**
Tel (02) 97 74 02 70 (Plouermel Tourist Office). **Open** Jul–mid-Aug. 🎨

🏛 **Musée des Souvenirs des Écoles**
Coëtquidan, Guer. **Tel** (02) 97 70 77 52. **Open** Tue–Sun. 🎨

Romances of the Round Table

A large number of romances (medieval vernacular tales) make up the cycle of Arthurian literature. From that of Chrétien de Troyes, writing in the 12th century, to that of Sir Thomas Malory, in the 15th, there are almost 100 separate accounts. While the earliest are in verse, later ones are in prose, and they are written either in French, English or German. They tell of the adventures of Gawain, of the love of Tristan and Iseult (the queen with the milk-white hands), of Arthur's unstoppable rise, of Merlin's tragic fate, of the creation of the Round Table, of magic and sorcery in Brittany, of the quest for the Holy Grail and of the epic Battle of Salesbières. A conflation of several different ideologies, Arthurian literature contains pagan Celtic and Indo-European elements, and Christian dialectic, giving an insight into the multifaceted culture of the late Middle Ages. Long neglected, Arthurian literature was rediscovered at the beginning of the 20th century. It has inspired not only literature but also music (Wagner's *Parsifal*, for example), and film (John Borman's *Excalibur*, for instance).

The conception of Merlin the wizard took place between the Devil and a pious mortal.

Angels support the Holy Grail, an aspect of Christianity incorporated into Arthurian legend.

Sir Galahad, destined to find the Holy Grail.

The Holy Grail, symbol of the mystery of the Eucharist.

The Holy Grail
The vessel used by Christ and his disciples at the Last Supper appeared before the Knights of the Round Table. In The Quest of the Holy Grail, it is said to have floated in mid-air, giving the knights divine sustenance while a heavenly voice invited them to go in search of it.

King Arthur and the Knights of the Round Table are shown in this fresco by Eugène Viollet-le-Duc. The knights are dressed in their familiar colours.

Merlin's passion for Vivian led the wizard to reveal to his pupil the secrets that were to lead him to his unhappy fate. He was imprisoned forever in a tree.

The cloister of the Abbaye de St-Sauveur in Redon, dating from the 17th century

❹ Redon

Road map E3. 🚉 10,500. 🚌
ℹ️ Place de la République, (02) 99 71 06 04. 🗓️ Mon, Fri & Sat. 🎭 Mois du Marron, Oct. 🌐 **tourisme-pays-redon.com**

This town is located on the borders of three *départements*: the Ille-et-Vilaine, the Loire-Atlantique and the Morbihan. From the 9th century, it was renowned for its Benedictine abbey, which was the most important in Brittany. The Cartulaire de Redon *(see p43)*, the earliest document in the history of Brittany, was written here. At the hub of roads and railways, and near the confluence of two rivers, Redon developed a diverse economy and became an industrial centre.

In the 20th century, several important companies chose it as their base.

In the historic centre, timber-framed houses dating from the 15th, 16th and 17th centuries can be seen around Grande-Rue. In the harbour, houses with overhanging upper storeys alternate with 17th- and 18th-century shipowners' mansions. In Rue du Port, three 17th-century salt warehouses, now restored, can be seen at Nos. 32, 36 and 40. The **Musée de la Batellerie**, on Quai Jean-Bart, illustrates the history of river navigation in Brittany through models and documents.

The **Abbaye de St-Sauveur**, the most important abbey in Brittany during the Middle Ages, is a monument to the power of the Benedictine order. Its Romanesque belfry, built in limestone and granite and set apart from the abbey itself, rises in three open tiers. It is unique in Brittany. The Romanesque nave with wooden ceiling contrasts with the choir, which has quatrefoil columns and Gothic chapels. The cloister was rebuilt in the 17th century. In 1622, Richelieu was an abbot here.

Environs

Some 10 km (6 miles) north of Redon, the perfume manufacturer Yves Rocher and the Muséum National d'Histoire Naturelle have joined forces to create the **Végétarium de La Gacilly**. In this botanical garden, over 1,000 species of plants are grown in their appropriate habitat, and their uses explained.

St Just, 20 km (12 miles) north of Redon, is at the centre of an area rich in megaliths, including the galleried grave at **Tréal** and the **Landes de Coujoux**, a long narrow ridge with many megaliths. At Lohéac, 15 km (9 miles) north of St Just, the **Manoir de l'Automobile** contains a display of over 400 collectors' cars, including Rolls-Royces, Ferraris, Lamborghinis, Cadillacs and pre-war models. There is also a go-karting circuit.

🏛 **Musée de la Batellerie**
Quai Jean-Bart. **Tel** (02) 99 72 30 95. **Open** Apr–mid-Jun & mid-Sep–mid-Nov: Sat–Mon & Wed pm; mid-Jun–mid-Sep: daily. **Closed** mid-Nov–Mar. 🅿️

🏰 **Abbaye de St-Sauveur**
Place St-Sauveur. **Tel** (02) 99 71 06 04. 🎫 Jul–Aug: Mon, Tue, Fri.

🌿 **Végétarium de La Gacilly**
La Croix-des-Archers. **Tel** (02) 99 08 35 84. **Open** daily. 🎫 Jul–Aug: Mon–Fri.

🗿 **Tréal Archaeological Site and Landes de Coujoux**
Open all year. **Tel** (02) 99 72 69 25. 🎫 Jul–Aug: Fri & Sun *(phone for details).* 🅿️

🏛 **Manoir de l'Automobile**
Lohéac, on the D177. **Tel** (02) 99 34 02 32. **Open** Jul–Aug: daily; Sep–Jun: Tue–Sun. 🅿️

Church Altarpieces

Detail of altarpiece at Domalain

Reacting against Protestant austerity, the Counter-Reformation in Brittany extolled the Catholic faith through magnificent church ornament. Altarpieces carved in wood or stone in an extravagant Baroque style graced the region's churches. The town of La Guerche-de-Bretagne is located in the heart of a region in which artists from Laval excelled in this field. Working with marble from Laval and Le Mans, and with tufa from the Loire, the sculptors Houdault, Corbineau and Langlois created consoles, pyramids, putti, foliate scrolls and garlands of fruit.

Exhibits at the Manoir de l'Automobile in Lohéac

The Chapelle Ste-Agathe, dedicated to Venus, in Langon

➎ Langon

Road map E3. 20 km (13 miles) northeast of Redon via the D177 then the D55. ▦ 1,300.

This small town is separated from the Vilaine river by marshland known as the Marais de l'Étier. The **Chapelle Ste-Agathe** is a rare survival from the Gallo-Roman period. It is dedicated to Venus and, behind the altar, there is a fresco depicting Venus rising from the waves and Eros astride a dolphin. The **Église St-Pierre** is worth a visit for its unusual bell tower, which features 12 bell-turrets.

On the Lande du Moulin stands an alignment of menhirs known as the **Demoiselles de Langon**. According to legend, young girls who chose to dance on the heath rather than attend vespers were punished by being turned to stone.

➏ Grand-Fougeray

Road map E3. 30 km (18.5 miles) northeast of Redon, via the D177 then the D54. ▦ 4,125.

The Tour du Guesclin is all that remains of the medieval castle that once stood in Grand-Fougeray. The fortress belonged to the Rieux family, allies of Jean IV, Duke of Brittany, against the constable (chief military officer) Olivier de Clisson. In 1350, an English sea captain took the castle. Bertrand du Guesclin *(see p47)* and his men later recaptured it for France and ever since it has borne his name.

➐ La Guerche-de-Bretagne

Road map F3. 20 km (12.5 miles) south of Vitré via the D178. ▦ 4,090. **🛈** Centre Culturel, La Salorge; (02) 99 96 30 78. 🚌 Tue.

On the border with Normandy, La Guerche-de-Bretagne is one of the fortified towns that once defended the borders of Brittany. Its geographical location also made it an important centre of commerce, and it was especially renowned for its linen trade *(see p110)*. The market that takes place here each week was first held in 1121 and is one of the oldest in France.

Half-timbered houses that date from the 16th and 17th centuries line the main square. The many gables on the **Collégiale Notre-Dame** are fine examples of the Flamboyant Gothic style of Upper Brittany *(see p27)*.

The church, built in the 15th and 16th centuries, has unusual Renaissance choir stalls (1525) with carvings depicting the Seven Deadly Sins. The dark blue barrel-vaulted ceiling and 15th-century stained-glass windows are also notable.

Environs
La Roche-aux-Fées stands 15 km (9 miles) west of La Guerche-de-Bretagne. It was built during the third millenium BC and is one of the most important dolmens in France. It consists of 41 stones, some of which weigh 45 tonnes, and is 19.5 m (64 ft) long and 4 m (13 ft) high. The interior contains four chambers. How and why it was built has still not been determined.

The ponds and wood around Martigné-Ferchaud, 15 km (9 miles) south of La Roche-aux-Fées, have become a sanctuary for migratory birds. The Étang de la Forge is a haven for ducks, coots and small waders. The pond is named after the ironworks, dating from 1672, that are to be found nearby.

🏛 Collégiale Notre-Dame
Place Charles-de-Gaulle.
Tel (02) 99 96 30 78. **Open** daily. 🗝 by request, phone the tourist office.

🗿 La Roche-aux-Fées
From La Guerche-de-Bretagne, take the D178 towards Chateaubriant then the D47 towards Retiers and the D41 towards Janzé. The site is 2 km (1 mile) from Retiers. **Open** daily. Open access.

La Roche-aux-Fées, one of Brittany's mysterious megalithic monuments

8 Vitré

Road map F3. 15,910.
Place Général de Gaulle; (02) 99 75 04 46. Mon & Sat. **ot-vitre.fr**

Unusually well preserved, this fortified town has a wealth of picturesque houses. Until the end of the 17th century, it owed its prosperity to the trade in linen cloth, which was exported all over Europe and as far away as South America. In 1472, the Brotherhood of the Annunciation became the organizational force behind this international trade.

A succession of powerful lords – Laval, Montmorency and Montfort – were prominent in the region's history. In the 16th century, Guy XVI established what amounted to a court in Vitré. **Château de Vitré**, perched on a rocky outcrop, is one of the great fortresses that defended the marches of Brittany. It was enlarged from the 13th century onwards. The entrance is defended by a small castle flanked by machicolated towers. A triangular wall set with towers encloses the complex.

The museum within the castle contains a remarkable 16th-century triptych decorated with 32 Limoges enamels. Also on display are medieval and Renaissance sculpture, 16th- and 17th-century tapestries, and Breton paintings. The top of the Tour Montafilant commands a superb panorama over the town.

The **Église Notre-Dame**, in Rue Montafilant, was rebuilt from 1420 to 1550, and is in the Flamboyant Gothic style, this can be seen clearly on its southern side, which bristles with finials. Inside are altar pieces *(see p70)* and a beautiful Renaissance stained-glass window. A plaque commemorates Field-marshal Gilles de Rais *(see p47)*, lord of Vitré and companion-at-arms of Joan of Arc. He was, however, executed for having murdered children.

Around the church, in Rue d'Embas, Rue Baudrairie, Rue St-Louis and Rue de Paris, the finest medieval and Renaissance houses in Vitré can be seen.

Environs
The 15th-century **Collégiale de Champeaux**, 9 km (6 miles) west of Vitré, recalls the former power of the lords of Espinay. It contains canopied Renaissance choir stalls with notable carvings, as well as 16th-century stained glass by the Fleming Jehan Adrian.

🏰 Château de Vitré
Place du Château. **Tel** (02) 99 75 04 54. **Open** Apr–Sep: daily; Oct–Mar: Mon, Wed–Sat, Sun pm.

⛪ Collégiale de Champeaux
On the D29. **Tel** (02) 99 49 82 99 (information from the mairie). **Closed** for restoration.

The Breton coat of arms in the Église Notre-Dame in Vitré

9 Château des Rochers-Sévigné

Road map F3. 8 km (5 miles) southeast of Vitré via the D88. **Tel** (02) 99 75 04 54. **Open** Apr–Sep: daily; Oct–Mar: Sun pm. obligatory.

This castle, located 8 km (5 miles) southeast of Vitré, was built in the 15th century and later remodelled. It consists of two wings set at right angles. At the intersection is a polygonal turret, which contains a staircase. The circular tower on the opposite side predates the 15th century. The 17th-century chapel has a hull-shaped roof and is crowned by a lantern.

On the ground floor of the north tower, visitors can see a plan of the castle as it was in 1763, and, on the first floor, a portrait of Madame de Sévigné. The castle overlooks an elegant garden, laid out in the 17th century by Charles de Sévigné, son of the *marquise*.

The Château de Vitré, once defending the marches of Brittany and now containing a museum

Timber-framed houses in the Marchix quarter of Fougères

❿ Fougères

Road map F2. 🏰 22,800. 🚂
🚌 Place de la République. 🛈 2 Rue
Nationale; (02) 99 94 12 20. 🚢 Sat.
🎭 Voix des Pays (Jul). Fêtes des
Angevines (early Sep).
Ⓦ ot-fougeres.fr

A major town in the marches
of Brittany, Fougères (the name
derives from the Old French
word for "ferns") has had a
chequered history over the
centuries. The French invasion
of 1488 *(see p47)* began here,
and the defeat of the Bretons
at the Battle of St-Aubin-du-
Cormier sounded the death-
knell for their independence.

The imposing **Château de
Fougères** is a superb example of
medieval military architecture. It
was built between the 12th and
15th centuries, and its ramparts,
set with 13 towers, enclose an
area of 2 ha (5 acres).

It is built to a concentric
plan that is typical of
12th-century fortresses. In
the 15th century, with the
development of artillery,
the walls were strengthened
and the embrasures widened
so as to accommodate the
barrels of canons. The five
towers that defend the walls –
the Châtelet de l'Avancée, de
Coëtlogon, du Cadran, de Guibé
and de Coigny – also date from
this period. The rampart walk
offers a fine view over the town.

The **Église St-Sulpice**, with a
slender spire, was built between
the 15th and 18th centuries in
the Flamboyant Gothic style.
The two 15th-century granite
altarpieces in the transept
contrast with the monumental
18th-century altarpiece in the
choir. Also of note is a fine
14th-century *Virgin and Child* in
painted limestone.

The old town (Bourg Vieil), at
the foot of the castle, is filled
with old timber-framed houses,
particularly in **Place du Marchix**
and Rue de Lusignan. The new
town (Bourg Neuf) overlooks the
castle. Gutted by fire on several
occasions, it was rebuilt in the
18th century.

A timber-framed building in
Rue Nationale, with a porch and
corbelling typical of 15th–16th-
century houses in Upper Brittany,
contains the **Musée Emmanuel-
de-La-Villéon**. As well as 70
paintings dating from the 17th
and 18th centuries, the museum
contains 18 works by Emmanuel
de La Villéon (1858–1944), an
Impressionist who was born in
Fougères, and whose work
depicts Breton landscapes and
scenes of daily life.

Château de Fougères, a masterpiece of
military architecture

Environs
The **Parc Floral de Haute-
Bretagne**, 20 km (13 miles)
northwest of Fougères, was laid
out in the 19th century as an
English landscaped park.

🏰 **Château de Fougères**
Place Pierre-Symon. **Tel** (02) 99 99 79
59. **Open** Jun–Sep: daily; Oct–May:
Tue–Sun. **Closed** Jan. 🖼

🏛 **Musée Emmanuel- de-
La-Villéon**
Rue Nationale. **Open** May: Sat & Sun
pm; Jun–Sep: Tue–Sun pm.
Closed Mon. 🖼

🌷 **Parc Floral de Haute-Bretagne**
La Foltière, Le Châtellier. **Tel** (02) 99 95
48 32. **Open** Mar–Nov: daily. 🖼

Letters of the Marquise de Sévigné

The walls of the Château des Rochers-
Sévigné seem still to breathe the finely
honed prose of Madame de Sévigné.
In 1644, Marie de Rabutin-Chantal
married the Marquis Henri de
Sévigné, a spendthrift and libertine.
After his death in a duel, the
marquise withdrew to the chateau.
She filled her days by writing long
and frequent letters to her daughter
– to whom she addressed almost 300
– as well as to the Countess of Grignan,
who was living in the Drôme, in
southern France. The immediacy
of this correspondence is still
compelling today.

Marie de Rabutin-Chantal,
Marquise de Sévigné

The locks at Hédé, still manually operated

⑪ Hédé-Bazouges

Road map E2. 14 km (9 miles) south of Combourg on the D795. 🏛 1,930. 🛈 Town Hall; (02) 99 45 46 18. 🚌 Tue.

Gustave Flaubert described the valley in which Hédé is located as "wide, beautiful and fertile, broad vista of greenery and trees". Of Hédé's castle, only a part of the walls and one side of the keep remain. The church, built in the 11th century, is in the early Romanesque style.

La Madeleine, 1 km (0.5 mile) north of Hédé, is the starting point of the **Promenade des Onze-Écluses**, a delectably bucolic walk along the Ille-et-Rance canal, which has a flight of 11 locks with a 27-m (88-ft) rise.

⑫ Bécherel

Road map E2. 17 km (10.5 miles) north of Monfort via the D72, D70 and D20. 🏛 670. 🛈 4 Route de Montfort; (02) 99 66 65 65. 🎭 Fête du Livre Ancien (Easter weekend). 🌐 becherel.com

With a wealth of antiquarian booksellers, second-hand book dealers, bookbinders and bookshops, Bécherel has both a literary and a medieval atmosphere. The castle, built in 1124 and now in ruins, was wrested from the English by Bertrand du Guesclin in 1374 after a 15-month siege. In the 17th and 18th centuries, the town prospered from the linen and hemp trade, exporting cloth

throughout Europe. This former wealth can be seen in the houses of the town's historical middle class – handsome granite buildings of uniform design.

Environs

The **Château de Caradeuc**, 1 km (0.5 mile) west of Bécherel, once belonged to L. R. de Caradeuc La Chalotais (1701–85), Attorney-General of the Breton parliament and a heroic figure in Breton resistance to centralized French government. Built in the 18th century, the chateau has an elegant Regency façade and is set in a lovely park.

Les Iffs, 6 km (4 miles) east of Bécherel, is named after the 100-year-old yew trees (ifs) in its parish close. The church here, built in Flamboyant Gothic style, has nine beautiful stained-glass windows. The Fontaine St-Fiacre, just outside Les Iffs on its northern side, is a spring that was enclosed in the 15th century. In time of drought, pilgrims would come here to pray for rain.

The **Château de Montmuran**, on the road to Tinténiac, has associations with Bertrand du Guesclin, who was knighted in its chapel in 1354. The gatehouse, with original portcullis, is 14th-century, while

Clogs, Musée de l'Outil et des Métiers, Tinténiac

the main building is mostly 18th-century, with 13th-century towers.

🏰 **Château de Caradeuc**
Tel (02) 99 66 81 10. **Open** Park only: Jul Aug: pm daily. 🚫

🏰 **Château de Montmuran**
Tel (02) 99 45 88 88. **Open** Jun–Sep: Sun–Fri pm. 📷 obligatory. 🚫

⑬ Tinténiac

Road map E2. 30 km (19 miles) north of Rennes via the D137 then the D20. 🏛 2,500. 🚌 Wed.

This small town is associated with the Chevalier de Tinténiac, who fought alongside the Chouans (see p52). The **Musée de l'Outil et des Métiers**, located on the canalside, contains collections of tools used for rope-making, harness-making, blacksmithing, barrel-making and other rural crafts. The church was completely rebuilt in the Byzantine style at the beginning of the 20th century.

Environs

The **Château de La Motte-Beaumanoir**, 12 km (8 miles) north of Tinténiac, has been rebuilt many times and is now a hotel. The façade gives an idea of its appearance in the 15th century: the main part of the castle is a two-storey building with a corner tower

Le Seanachi, one of many antiquarian bookshops in Bécherel

For hotels and restaurants see pp224–5 and pp234–5

The Château de Combourg, now inhabited by a descendant of Chateaubriand's elder brother

containing a staircase. In 1776, the naval captain Jean Thomas de Lorgeril, who had prospered as a privateer, acquired the manor, adding two wings to it.

About 12 km (8 miles) north of Tinténiac, towards Dinan, is the **Château de la Bourbansais**, built in the 16th century and enlarged in the 18th. On the ground floor are 18th-century furniture, Aubusson tapestries and Oriental porcelain imported by the French East India Company. The surrounding park contains a zoo.

Musée de l'Outil et des Métiers
Magasin à Grain, Quai de la Donac. **Tel** (02) 99 23 09 30. **Open** Jul–Sep: daily.

Château de la Bourbansais and Zoo
Pleugueneuc. **Tel** (02) 99 69 40 07. Chateau: Apr–Sep: daily. Zoo: **Open** daily.

⑭ Combourg

Road map E2. 4,843. Maison de la Lanterne, 23 Place Albert-Parent; (02) 99 73 13 93. Mon. Foire de l'Angevine, first Mon in Sep.

This town is closely associated with the French Romantic writer François René de Chateaubriand, who lived in the **Château de Combourg**, an imposing building with pepperpot towers. The castle, whose origins go back to the 11th century, was rebuilt in the late Gothic style in the 14th and 15th centuries.

In 1761, it was acquired by Chateaubriand's father, a rich shipowner from St-Malo. As a child, Chateaubriand spent much time here, as described in *Mémoires d'Outre-Tombe*.

Inside the castle, the writer's desk, armchair and deathbed, and a bust of him by David d'Angers, can be seen in the archive room. The rest of the interior was entirely restored in 1875. The landscaped park was designed by the Bühler brothers *(see p65)*.

Environs
The **Château de Landal**, 15 km (9 miles) northeast of Combourg, has an impressive location, within ramparts. Two of its corner towers date from the 15th century. Before it was acquired by Joseph de France, in 1696, it belonged to some of the greatest Breton families. It was left to ruin for over ten years but since 2013, the new owners have been restoring it.

Château de Combourg
Tel (02) 99 73 22 95. Park: **Open** Apr–Jun & Sep–mid Oct: Sun pm–Fri; mid-Oct–mid-Nov: Mon–Fri, Sat & Sun pm; Jul–Aug: daily. Chateau: **Closed** mid-Nov–Mar. obligatory.

Château de Landal
3 km (2 miles) north of Broualan, on the Aigles de Bretagne route. **Closed** Jul–Aug.

François René de Chateaubriand

"It was in the woods around Combourg that I became what I am," stated Chateaubriand (1768–1848) in his *Mémoires d'Outre-Tombe (Memoirs from Beyond the Grave;* 1830–41). Born in St-Malo, this great Romantic writer spent periods of time in the family castle. He later studied in Dol-de-Bretagne, Rennes, then Dinan, and regularly stayed with his sisters in Fougères until 1791. He came to fame with *Atala* (1801). *Le Génie du Christianisme (The Genius of Christianity;* 1802) established his reputation. The biographical *Mémoires* are considered to be his masterpiece.

François René de Chateaubriand

⓯ Dol-de-Bretagne

Road map E2. 🚠 5,020. 🚌 ℹ️ 5
Place de la Cathédrale; (02) 99 48 15
37. 🚌 Sat. 🎭 Folk festival (last Sun in
Jul); Christmas market.
🌐 **pays-de-dol.com**

The religious capital of
Nominoë, king of Brittany
during the 9th century, Dol
owes its prestige and prosperity
to its cathedral, which is one of
the finest examples of Gothic
architecture in Brittany.

In about 548, St Samson,
one of the seven monks who
established Christianity in
Brittany, arrived from England
and founded a monastery. A
town grew up around it and,
despite suffering repeated
attacks by English-controlled
Normandy and from the kings
of France, it flourished and
enjoyed great prestige until
1801. In 1793, it was the scene
of bloody conflict between
Chouan royalists and
Republicans *(see p52)*.

The **Cathédrale St-Samson**
stands on the site of a
Romanesque church that was
burned down by Jean sans Terre
in 1203. The great 14th-century
doorway on the south side is
finely decorated. The north side,
by contrast, faces the open
countryside and has the
appearance of a fortified wall.
The interior is impressive through
its sheer size. In the nave, 93 m
(305 ft) long, seven spans of
arches rise through three tiers
(an arcade, triforium arches and
a clerestory), and the crossing is
crowned by a 20-m (65-ft) high
dome. The columns, arches and
stylized motifs with which
they are decorated

are in the Anglo-Norman
Gothic style, and are similar to
those in Salisbury Cathedral.

A very expressive *Scourging of
Christ* can be seen in the north
aisle, and in the north transept
lies the splendid tomb of Thomas
James, bishop of Dol from 1482
to 1504. Dating from the 16th
century, with figures of classical
inspiration, this tomb is one
of the earliest signs of the
Renaissance in Brittany. It was
carved in the workshop of the
Florentine sculptor Jean Juste,
who also made the tomb of
Louis XII in St-Denis, near Paris.
The 77 choir stalls are lit by an
outstanding 13th-century
stained-glass window with
medallion-shaped panels. Some
of the stained-glass windows
here are among the oldest
in Brittany.

Using the most up-to-date
techniques, **Medièvalys**, in the
former bishop's palace on Place
de la Cathédrale, gives a history
of the cathedral's construction
and the work of the craftsmen
involved, from building
techniques and skills used, to the
symbolism of the decoration on
the façade and the making of
the stained-glass windows.

The Promenade des Douves
(Moat Walk), which passes
behind the cathedral's apse,
follows the ramparts on the
northern side of the town, from
where there is a view of the
marshes and of Mont Dol.
Grande-Rue-des-Stuart, with
houses with pillared porches,
offers a glimpse of Dol as it
appeared in the Middle Ages.
At No. 17, the Maison des Petits-
Palets, with carved
Romanesque arcades,

is a rare example of French
12th-century town architecture.
Opposite, a porch leads to the
Cour aux Chartiers, a
15th-century courtyard.

The Logis de la Croix Verte,
at No. 18, also dating from the
12th century, was once an inn
run by the Knights Templar.
The Maison de la Guillotière, at
No. 27, has a porch supported
on polygonal columns with
carved capitals.

🏛️ Cathédrale St-Samson
Place de la Cathédrale. **Open** daily.
🔔 Jul–Aug: daily. Concerts: Jul–Aug:
Tue & Thu eve.

🏛️ Medièvalys
Place de la Cathédrale. **Tel** (02) 99 48
35 30. **Open** Apr–Sep: daily; Oct–mid-
Nov: Sat & Sun pm. **Closed** mid-Nov–
Mar. ♿

The Menhir du Champ-Dolent, in the
"Field of Sorrow"

⓰ Menhir du Champ-Dolent

Road map E2. About 2 km (1 mile)
south of Dol-de-Bretagne on the
D795. **Open** daily. Open access.

Consisting of a single block
of granite 9.5 m (31 ft) high,
the Menhir du Champ-Dolent
is the tallest – and some
would say also the finest –
of Brittany's standing stones.
According to legend, it fell
from the sky, separating
two warring brothers who
were locked in deadly battle.
It is this legend that accounts
for the name "Champ
Dolent", meaning "Field
of Sorrow".

Arch of the porch of the Cathédrale St-Samson in Dol-de-Bretagne

Sand yachts on wide, flat beaches near Cherrueix

conditions. It is, apparently, possible to predict the weather accordingly, and every bit as accurately as the official forecast.

Oak stakes, known as *bouchots*, can be seen all along the bay. Driven into the sea bed, they are used for mussel-breeding, a practice that goes back as far as the 13th century. A quarter of all mussels farmed in France are raised in this bay, where the yield reaches 10,000 tonnes per year.

Windmills and low thatched houses line the coast as far as Cancale. At Le Vivier-sur-Mer, the **Maison de la Baie** houses an exhibition on mussel-farming and on the area's plants and animals. Visits to the *bouchots*, which are reachable on foot or by tractor-drawn transport, also start from here. Beware of fast-rising tides and quicksand. At Cherrueix, there is a sand-yachting centre, where this sport *(see p253)* is taught on the beaches.

⊠ Maison de la Baie
Le Vivier-sur-Mer.
Tel (02) 99 48 84 38.
Open Mon–Sat (Jul–Aug: daily).
🖼 for exhibitions and guided walks.

🟦 Mont Dol

Road map E2. 2 km (1 mile) north of Dol-de-Bretagne on the D155.

This outcrop of granite, 65 m (213 ft) high, commands a breathtaking view over an expanse of polders (reclaimed land). Like neighbouring Mont-St-Michel and Mont Tombelaine, Mont Dol was once an island. During the Palaeolithic period, the region was covered in steppe and fenland. Finds of animal bones and stone tools prove that hunter-gatherers lived on the meat of reindeer, mammoth, lion, woolly rhino, horse, aurochs (a type of 17th-century wild cattle), bear and wolf. Much later, Mont Dol became a sacred place where druids worshipped.

A legend tells how St Michael and the Devil fought a battle on Mont Dol. Supposed traces of this can be seen on the rock: the Devil's claw marks, a hole for the Devil dug by St Michael, and footprints left by the Archangel Michael when he leaped across to Mont-St-Michel.

South of Mont Dol lies the small town of the same name. Frescoes dating from the 12th and 14th centuries, depicting scenes from the life of Christ, have been discovered in the nave of the church here.

🟦 Baie du Mont-St-Michel

Road map E-F1. 🅸 Dol-de-Bretagne; (02) 99 48 15 37. 🏄 Fête des Moules (Aug); Pardon de Ste-Anne in Roz-sur-Couesnon (Aug).

The coastline here flattens out into a wide expanse of sand from which, almost magically, Mont-St-Michel rises. The appearance of its silhouette subtly changes with atmospheric

Polders – Land Reclaimed From the Sea

As glaciers began to melt at the end of the Ice Age, 10,000 years ago, the sea level rose, flooding coastal Brittany. The marshland around Mont Dol was eventually invaded by the sea. Work to reclaim the land began in the Middle Ages, when dykes were built. Crops were grown on these areas of fertile land, known as polders. However, since a dyke was built between Mont Dol and the mainland, sediment is no longer flushed out to sea on the ebbing tides, so that the bay is silting up. A solution under consideration is to remove part of the dyke, allowing Mont Dol to become an island again.

Cultivation on the polders in Baie du Mont-St-Michel

⑲ Mont-St-Michel

Wreathed in mist and surrounded by water, Mont-St-Michel, which stands at the Couesnon estuary, between Brittany and Normandy, is one of the most extraordinary sights on the French coast. The rocky islet was originally known as Mont-Tombe, and a small oratory was built here in the 8th century. Work on the abbey began in the 10th century, and by the 16th century it had increased the height of the mount almost two-fold. The mount drew many pilgrims, particularly during medieval times. During the French Revolution it became a prison. In 1874 its upkeep was entrusted to the Service des Monuments Historiques. Austrian architect Dietmar Feichtinger designed the Passerelle Mont-Saint-Michel to replace the old causeway that first connected the island to the mainland. For the first time in 134 years, the Mont becomes an island again in 2015.

The abbey in the 10th century

The abbey in the 11th century

The abbey in the mid-17th century

Chapelle St-Aubert
Built on the rock in the 15th century, the chapel is dedicated to St Aubert, who founded Mont-St-Michel in AD 708.

★ **Ramparts**
The town was fortified during the Hundred Years' War, to protect it from attack by the English.

Entrance

700	1000	1300	1600	1900	2015
966 A Benedictine abbey is founded	**1211–1228** Gothic buildings of La Merveille are completed	**1434** Final attack by the English. Ramparts are built	**1877–1879** The dyke is built **1789** During the Revolution, the mount is used as a prison for political dissidents	**1895–1897** The tower, spire and statue of St Michael Archangel are added **1922** Church services resume	
708 St Aubert builds an oratory on Mont-Tombe **1017** Work starts on the building of the abbey	**1067–1070** Mont-St-Michel is depicted in the Bayeux Tapestry *Detail of the Bayeux Tapestry*	**1516** The abbey declines	**1874** Upkeep of the mount is entrusted to Monuments Historiques	**1969** Benedictine monks return to the mount **2007** The Benedictine monks leave once more	**2015** Mont-St-Michel becomes an island again

Tides in Baie de Mont St-Michel
The bay is washed by unusually long tides, which flow unimpeded over the smooth quicksand. The strong spring tides can move at speeds of up to 10 kmh (6 mph).

VISITORS' CHECKLIST

Practical Information
Road map F1 ℹ️ Corps de Garde des Bourgeois, at entrance to Mont-St-Michel (02) 33 60 14 30. Abbey: **Tel** (02) 33 89 80 00. **Open** May–Aug: 9am–7pm daily; Sep–Apr: 9:30am–6pm daily. **Closed** 1 Jan, 1 May, 25 Dec. 🎫 free 1st Sun of month from Nov–Mar. ⛪ noon Tue–Sat, 11:15am Sun. 📧 🌐 mont-saint-michel.monuments-nationaux.fr, ot-montsaintmichel.com

Transport
🚌 as far as Pontorson, then by bus. 🅿️ near the dam.

Sault Gauthier
This vantage point at the top of the Grand Degré commands a magnificent view over the south side of the bay.

KEY

① **Tour Gabriel**

② **Abbey** Enclosed within high walls, the abbey and its church occupy an impregnable position.

③ **Église St-Pierre**

④ **Tour de la Liberté**

⑤ **Tour de l'Arcade**, where the guards were accommodated.

⑥ **Tour du Roy**

★ **Grande-Rue**
The route once taken by pilgrims as they made their way to the abbey, but now filled with tourists and souvenir shops, passes the Église St-Pierre.

Abbaye du Mont-St-Michel

The history of Mont-St-Michel can be read in its architecture. The abbey, the most prominent building, has served several different purposes; once attached to the Benedictine monastery, it later became a prison for political dissidents. The original abbey church was built in 1017, on the site of a 10th-century, pre-Romanesque building, the Notre-Dame-Sous-Terre. In the early 13th century, La Merveille, an imposing three-storey building, was added to the north side of the church, built directly onto the rockface.

★ Abbey Church
Only four of the original seven bays in the nave survive. The other three collapsed in 1776.

Monks' Refectory
This large room is bathed in soft light entering through windows in the end wall and through high, narrow niches.

Salle des Chevaliers
The vaulting and capitals in the Knight's Hall are in a pure Gothic style.

Upper Level (Church)

Intermediate Level

Lower Level

KEY

① **Crypte Notre-Dame-des-Trente-Cierges** (Our Lady of the Thirty Candles) is one of two crypts beneath the transept.

② **La Merveille** This masterpiece of Gothic architecture took 16 years to complete.

③ **Crypte St-Martin,** a barrel-vaulted chapel, gives an idea of the austere appearance of the original abbey church.

④ **The abbatial buildings,** near the square in front of the church, allowed the abbot to entertain important visitors in suitable comfort. Lesser pilgrims were received at the almshouse.

★ Cloisters
With slender pudding-stone columns in an off-set alignment, the cloister is a perfect example of Anglo-Norman Gothic.

Abbey Guide

The three levels on which the abbey is built reflect the hierarchy of the monastery. The monks' cells were on the upper level, where the church, cloister and refectory were also located. Important guests were entertained by the abbot on the intermediate level. On the lower level was accommodation for the guards, as well as for humbler pilgrims. The customary route for pilgrims was from the almshouse (which is now a shop), where the poor were given alms, to the church via the grand staircase.

Church

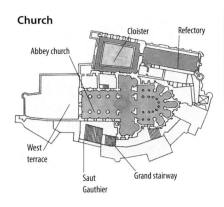

Cloister · Refectory · Abbey church · West terrace · Saut Gauthier · Grand stairway

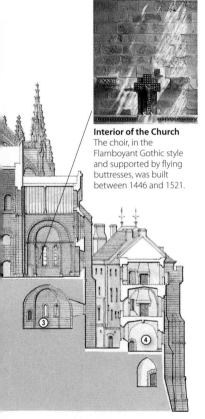

Interior of the Church
The choir, in the Flamboyant Gothic style and supported by flying buttresses, was built between 1446 and 1521.

Intermediate Level

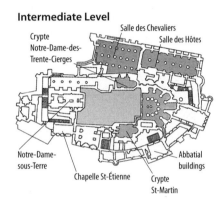

Crypte Notre-Dame-des-Trente-Cierges · Salle des Chevaliers · Salle des Hôtes · Notre-Dame-sous-Terre · Chapelle St-Étienne · Crypte St-Martin · Abbatial buildings

Lower Level

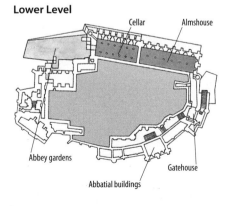

Cellar · Almshouse · Abbey gardens · Abbatial buildings · Gatehouse

Benedictines
The small community of Benedictine monks left the abbey in 2007. Now the Fraternité de Jérusalem inhabit the abbey instead.

⑳ Sentier des Douaniers

This stretch of the GR34 (a *grande randonnée*, or long-distance path) starts at Cancale, follows the Pointe du Grouin along the edge of cliffs 40 m (130 ft) high, and ends at Les Daules. On one side is the English Channel and on the other a residential area with well-designed modern houses.

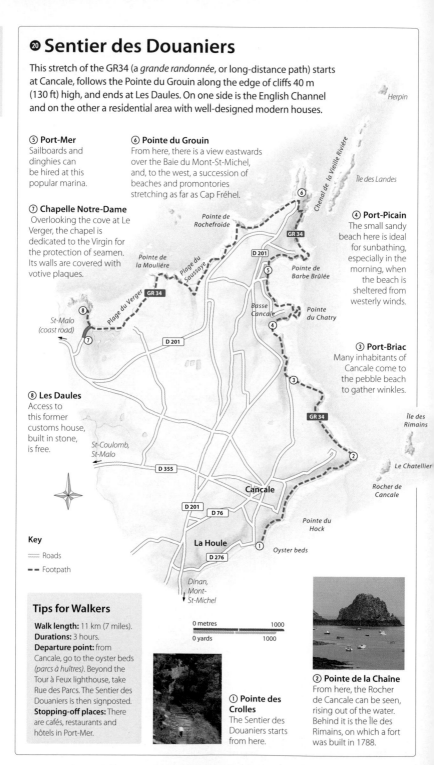

⑤ Port-Mer
Sailboards and dinghies can be hired at this popular marina.

⑥ Pointe du Grouin
From here, there is a view eastwards over the Baie du Mont-St-Michel, and, to the west, a succession of beaches and promontories stretching as far as Cap Fréhel.

⑦ Chapelle Notre-Dame
Overlooking the cove at Le Verger, the chapel is dedicated to the Virgin for the protection of seamen. Its walls are covered with votive plaques.

④ Port-Picain
The small sandy beach here is ideal for sunbathing, especially in the morning, when the beach is sheltered from westerly winds.

③ Port-Briac
Many inhabitants of Cancale come to the pebble beach to gather winkles.

⑧ Les Daules
Access to this former customs house, built in stone, is free.

Herpin

Île des Landes

Pointe de Rochefroide

GR 34

D 201

Pointe de Barbe Brûlée

Pointe de la Mouliére

Plage du Saussaye

Plage du Verger

GR 34

St-Malo (coast road)

Basse Cancale

Pointe du Chatry

D 201

Chenal de la Vieille Rivière

GR 34

Île des Rimains

St-Coulomb, St-Malo

D 355

Cancale

Le Chatellier

Rocher de Cancale

D 201

D 76

Pointe du Hock

Key
— Roads
- - Footpath

La Houle

D 276

Oyster beds

Dinan, Mont-St-Michel

Tips for Walkers

Walk length: 11 km (7 miles).
Durations: 3 hours.
Departure point: from Cancale, go to the oyster beds (*parcs à huîtres*). Beyond the Tour à Feux lighthouse, take Rue des Parcs. The Sentier des Douaniers is then signposted.
Stopping-off places: There are cafés, restaurants and hôtels in Port-Mer.

0 metres   1000
0 yards   1000

① Pointe des Crolles
The Sentier des Douaniers starts from here.

② Pointe de la Chaîne
From here, the Rocher de Cancale can be seen, rising out of the water. Behind it is the Île des Rimains, on which a fort was built in 1788.

❷ Cancale

Road map E1.  5,350. 🚌 **i** 44
Rue du Port; (02) 99 89 63 72. 🎉 Fêtes
des Reposoirs (15 Aug); Fêtes de la
Confrérie des Huîtres (third Sat in Sep).
🚐 Sun. **w** cancale-tourisme.fr

This centre of oyster-farming
has kept its distinctive identity.
The flat oysters *(belons)* that are
farmed here today are famed
for their large size. Along
the harbour at La Houle,
fishermen's houses have been
converted into restaurants,
cafés and shops.

When the cod-fishing
industry collapsed in the 19th
century, Cancale's fishermen
turned to oyster-farming, using
their boats – the *bisquines* – to
harvest the oysters in the bay.
Visitors can take a trip out to sea
in one of them, La Cancalaise.

The **Musée des Arts et
Traditions Populaires de
Cancale et sa région**, laid out
in a deconsecrated church, the
18th-century Église St-Méen,
describes the history of oyster-
farming. It also looks at the
lives of the seamen who once
sailed to Newfoundland to fish
for cod and those of their
wives, whose legendary
outspokenness goes back to
the time when they would
hawk fish on the quayside.

Port-Mer, Cancale's residential
quarter, has an excellent sailing
school. The terraces above the
beach are an inviting place to
stop and rest before walking
around the Pointe du Grouin on
the coast path, the Sentier
des Douaniers.

🏛 **Musée des Arts et Traditions
Populaires de Cancale et
sa région**
Place St-Méen. **Tel** (02) 99 89 79 32.
Open May–Jun & mid-Sep: Wed–Mon
pm; Jul–Aug: daily. 🖼

Île des Landes Bird Sanctuary

Declared a bird sanctuary in 1961, the Île des Landes is separated
from the Pointe du Grouin by a narrow channel, the Chenal de la
Vieille Rivière. The island attracts the largest colony of cormorants in
Brittany. Other species include the crested cormorant, herring gull
and various other species of gull, and pied oystercatchers as well as
the Belon sheldrake, the only sea duck
native to Brittany. From August through
to October, puffins, gannets and other
sea birds flock to the island. Visitors
can watch the birds through a fixed
telescope and, every day throughout
the summer, Bretagne Vivante (Living
Brittany) organizes interesting nature
walks on the island.

Pied oystercatchers on the Île
des Landes

🚢 **La Cancalaise**
Boat trips. **Tel** (02) 99 89 77 87.
Open Apr–Oct: call for times. 🖼
w lacancalaise.org

Pointe du Grouin, halfway along the Sentier
des Douaniers

❷ Pointe du Grouin

Road map E1. **i** (02) 99 89 63 72
(Cancale); (02) 98 49 07 18 (Bretagne
Vivante).

The longest promontory
in the Ille-et-Vilaine, Pointe
du Grouin is covered with
heath and coastal grassland
that are typical of Brittany's
rocky coast.

Having suffered degradation
caused by excessive numbers
of visitors, the area, which
covers 21 ha (52 acres), is
now under environmental
protection. Soil erosion, the
degradation of the chalky
grassland and damage to
protected species of plants
by walkers have led the local
council to lay out official paths
and close off areas in order to
allow grasses and wildflowers
to recover. This plan of action
has borne fruit, although the
area is still vulnerable.

During World War II, German
forces built *blockhausen*
(blockhouses, or fortified gun
positions) here to defend
the strategically important
headland. Most have survived
intact, and one has been
converted into a visitor centre.
The greater horseshoe bat,
one of the most endangered
animals in France, nests in
the abandoned blockhouses.

The lighthouse west of the
promontory, built in 1861 and
modernized in 1972, was
decommissioned in 1999.

Environs
The Chapelle du Verger, which
has been rebuilt on several
occasions, nestles in an inlet
known as the Cul-du-Chien
(Dog's Bottom Cove). The
belfry, at the foot of which
many votive offerings have
been laid, overlooks Cancale's
largest sandy beach.

Flat-bottomed boats are used to harvest the oysters in the bay at Cancale

For hotels and restaurants see pp224–5 and pp234–5

㉓ Street-by-Street: St-Malo's Walled City

At the end of the 17th century, St-Malo was France's foremost port, and shipowners who held a monopoly over trade with the East Indies amassed huge fortunes. Following attacks by the English in 1693 and 1695, plans were made to build a new fortified town, and the architect was Siméon de Garangeau. From 1708 to 1742, St-Malo grew rapidly, expanding by over one third. Tragically, during fighting at the end of World War II, in August 1944, 80 per cent of the port city was destroyed. It was, however, rebuilt in a style in keeping with its historic character, using granite-clad concrete. Immediately after the war, some buildings were reconstructed using their original stones.

The best view of St-Malo, from Dinard

Grande Porte
A niche inside the gate contains a 15th-century statue of Notre-Dame-de-Bon-Secours.

Porte St-Vincent
The main entrance to the city is through a gateway in the walls, which are 7 m (23 ft) thick. From the gateway, a stairway leads up to the rampart walk.

Cathédrale St-Vincent

QUAI SAINT VINCENT

ESPLANADE SAINT VINCENT

The castle's four towers were built by François II of Brittany and his daughter, Anne.

PLACE CHATEAUBRIAND

RUE SAINT VINCENT

RUE DU CERF

RUE SAINTE BARBE

RUE SAINT THOMAS

RUE CHATEAUBRIAND

RUE DE LA CORNE DU CERF

R. DU PÉLICOT

RUE DU COLLEGE

GRANDE RUE

PLACE DU POIDS DU ROI

PORCON LA BAR

PL. J. CHAT

RUE TOUILLER

R. DE LA VICTOIRE

L'ÉVENTAIL

PLACE VAUBAN

Rue du Pélicot

RUE DU CHATEAU GAILLARD

PLAGE MALO

★ **Château**
Built by Jean V, Duke of Brittany, and enlarged by Anne of Brittany, the castle now houses the local council offices and the Musée d'Histoire de St-Malo. The museum is in the castle's keep.

Église St-Benoît
The doorway of the former Église St-Benoît was built by the architect Jean Poulier in 1705, to a design by Garangeau. It consists of a pair of granite columns supporting a curved pediment.

★ **Hôtel d'Asfeld**
This mansion, once the residence of Auguste Magon de La Lande, head of the French East India Company in 1715, is fronted by a courtyard and a gateway. It was used as a prison during the Revolution. Chateaubriand's mother was incarcerated here.

VISITORS' CHECKLIST

Practical Information
Road map E1. 49,100.
Esplanade St-Vincent; 0825 135 200. Tue & Fri in the old town. Étonnants Voyageurs (Book Fair, Whitsun); Folklore du Monde (Jul); Festival de Musique Sacrée (Jul–mid-Aug); Route du Rock (mid-Aug); Quai des Bulles (Oct/Nov); Route du Rhum (transatlantic race; Nov, every four years from 2018). **W** saint-malo-tourisme.com

Transport
Dinard-Pleurtuit-St-Malo.
Brittany ferries: 08 25 82 88 28.
Avenue Anita Conti

Hôtel André-Désilles

Porte de Dinan

QUAI DE DINAN

CHARTRES

RUE D'ASFELD

RUE DE

RUE FEYDEAU D'ORLEANS

RUE DE LA FOSSE

TOULUSE

RUE DES VIEUX REMPARTS

RUE DES FORGEURS

RUE DE DINAN

RUE SAINT PHILIPPE

RUE DE TOULOUSE

BOREL

Bastion St-Philippe

DE L'ORME

RUE

RUE D'ESTÉES

R. VAU

RUE GUY LOUVEL

PLACE BREVET

RUE SAINT SAUVEUR

PLAGE DU MÔLE

RUE BROUSSAIS

RUE DE LA PIE QUI BOIT

RUE DE LA CROSSE

RUE DU BOYER

NNAIS

Statue of Jacques Cartier

PLACE DU BON SECOURS

Église St-Sauveur
Completed in 1743 by the architect Michel Marion to plans by Garangeau, the church is now used as a venue for temporary exhibitions. The west front, which faces the street, is plain to the point of being austere.

| 0 metres | 100 |
| 0 yards | 100 |

Key
— Suggested route

★ **Ramparts**
Many stages of the city's history can be seen from the rampart walk. Among the oldest parts are the Cavalier des Champs-Vauverts and the Tour Bidouane, built around the late 16th-century arsenal that predates the 17th-century fortified town.

Exploring St-Malo

Throughout its history, this port city, sheltered from battering winds by its ramparts, has maintained a fierce spirit of independence. This is reflected in the motto "Foremost a native of St-Malo, a Breton perhaps, and a Frenchman last". Its indomitable seamen have sailed the high seas in search of undiscovered lands and of exotic goods that could be traded for a high return in Europe. Both privateers and shipowners made their fortunes here, and, in the 17th and 18th centuries, the kings of France as well as St-Malo itself also profited handsomely. The private residences and *malouinières* (grand country residences) that can be seen today are proof of this fabulous success.

Garangeau

The civil and naval architect Siméon de Garangeau (1647–1741) had worked in Marseille and in Brest before he took charge of building St-Malo's fortifications. The great military engineer Vauban considered that the coastal fort of La Conchée, which Garangeau built, was the best building in France. As a civil architect, Garangeau was also responsible for much of St-Malo's unique architectural character.

Fortifications of St-Malo

An Eventful History

As early as 1308, the inhabitants of St-Malo showed their mettle by establishing the first free town in Brittany, and, in 1395, rebelling against the Duke of Brittany, they obtained leave to answer only to Charles VI, king of France. St-Malo was then granted the status of an independent port, and for the next 300 years its economic success was assured. In 1415, Jean V, Duke of Brittany, attempted to regain authority over St-Malo and began to build the castle here. In 1436, the English described the seamen of St-Malo in these terms: "The people of St-Malo are the greatest thieves …that ever sailed the seas… These pilferers who sail under false colours … have no respect for their dukes." Neither did they have respect for France, as, in 1590, they formed an

Cathedral gargoyle

independent, albeit shortlived, republic in defiance of Henri IV's royal authority. By the end of the 15th century, having grown prosperous through trade and from fishing off Newfoundland, St-Malo had become a port of international renown. From 1698 to 1720, cargo ships sailing from St-Malo exported linen cloth, lace and other everyday goods to America, returning laden with gold and precious stones. The immensely rich shipowners were "invited" to lend the king half of the cargo brought back by their ships, thus saving France from bankruptcy.

🏛 St-Malo's Walled City

The main entrance into the walled city of St-Malo is **Porte St-Vincent**, built in 1709 and standing on its northeastern side. Inside the pedestrians' entrance is a map of the city showing the main stages in its

construction and identifying the most important buildings. A stairway leads up to the rampart walk, which offers a wide view of the city. Further north, in front of Place du Poids-du-Roi, is **Grande Porte**, a 15th-century gateway with machicolated towers.

Cathédrale St-Vincent, on Place de Châtillon, was begun in the 12th century and completed in the 18th. Grimacing gargoyles stare down from the heights of the outer walls. Inside, the high, delicate Gothic choir contrasts with the nave, in the Angevin Romanesque style. It is an example of the influence of

The Quai St-Louis and Quai St-Vincent, on the western side of St-Malo

For hotels and restaurants see pp224–5 and pp234–5

Anglo-Norman architecture on the design of churches in northern Brittany. The great rose window is filled with modern, brightly coloured glass. The tomb of Jacques Cartier, the 16th-century explorer from St-Malo, can be seen in the north chapel.

At No. 3 Cour de la Houssaye, near Rue Chateaubriand, is the **Maison de la Duchesse Anne** *(see p48)*. With its outer tower, it is a typical example of a late Medieval urban manor house. Destroyed during World War II, it was rebuilt on the basis of old engravings.

Rue du Pélicot, which runs across Rue Chateaubriand, has some unusual "glass houses" – early 16th-century wooden houses with glazed galleries. At the end of Rue Mac-Law stands the Chapelle St-Aaron (1621), perched on the summit of the rock and facing the law courts. The evangelizing monk Aaron,

St-Malo's original inhabitant, chose this spot for his hermitage.

The rampart walk on the eastern side of the walled city, near Porte de Dinan, offers a bird's-eye view of several 18th-century shipowners' houses that either escaped war damage or were reconstructed. Built in a restrained and uniform style, they have an aristocratic elegance, and reflect both the personal wealth and social standing of their owners, who used them as a base for trading activities. The ramparts also afford fine views as far as Dinard and the Côte d'Emeraude.

🏠 Hôtel Magon-d'Asfeld Demeure de Corsaire

5 Rue d'Asfeld. **Tel** (02) 99 56 09 40.
🕐 Jul–Aug: Mon–Sat, Sun pm; Feb–Jun & Sep–Nov: Tue–Sun (only guided tour at 3pm). **Closed** Dec–Jan. 🎫

This fine building was once the residence of Auguste Magon de

Maison de la Duchesse Anne, a typical urban manor house

La Lande, one of the wealthiest shipowners in St-Malo and the head of the French East India Company in 1715.

With guided tours, it offers the opportunity to see inside one of these aristocratic houses, with their vaulted cellars.

St-Malo City Centre

① St-Malo Walled City
② Château
③ Fort National
④ St-Servan
⑤ Musée du Long Cours
　 Cap-Hornier
⑥ Corniche d'Alet
⑦ Paramé
⑧ Grand Aquarium

Key

🔲 See pp84–5

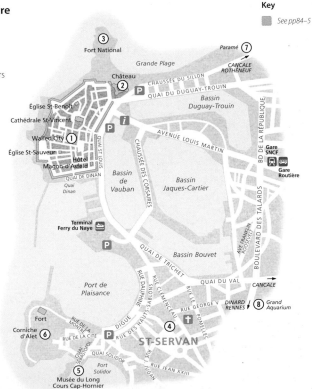

0 metres 400
0 yards 400

🏠 Château

Place Chateaubriand, in the Citadel.
Built in the 15th and 16th
centuries, the castle was used
by Jean V, Duke of Brittany
(1399–1442), mainly as a base
from which to keep watch over
the infamously rebellious
people of St-Malo. Jean's
daughter Anne *(see pp48–9)*,
who became queen of France
through her marriage to Charles
VIII, enlarged the castle, with the
same purpose in mind. Knowing
the dissenting character of the
townspeople, she had these
words engraved in the wall of a
tower in the castle's east wing:
*"Quic en groigne, ainsi sera, car tel
est mon plaisir"* (Thus will it be,
whoever complains, for this is
my will.) The people of St-Malo
defiantly christened the castle
Quic-en-Groigne.

🏛 Musée d'Histoire de St-Malo

In the castle keep. **Tel** (02) 99 40 71 57.
Open Apr–Sep: daily; Nov–Mar: Tue–
Sun. **Closed** public holidays. 🅿

This museum, dedicated to the
history of St-Malo, occupies
the keep, which stands at the
entrance to the castle. With
granite walls and high chimney-
pieces, it provides a sumptuous
setting for the exhibits.

The collection consists of
paintings, sculpture, figure-
heads, models of ships and
topographical models illustrating
the city's history and its seafaring
traditions. Prominent citizens,
such as the corsair Robert Surcouf,
the explorer Jacques Cartier, and
men of letters Chateaubriand
(see p75) and Lamennais *(see
p31)* are also honoured.

Lee Miller's Wartime Scoop

In October 1944, an eight-page report on the siege of St-
Malo appeared in the pages of American *Vogue*. The report and
accompanying photographs were by-lined Lee Miller, Man Ray's
companion, a friend of Paul Éluard and Pablo Picasso, and a
model and fashion photographer. The only journalist in the city

during the bombings, she
recorded the destruction of
St-Malo. "My heel sank into
a disembodied hand, and I
cursed the Germans for the
horrible destruction that
they had inflicted on this
once-splendid city," she
wrote at the time. Antony
Penrose, Lee Miller's son
and the author of her
biography, relates that the
photographs taken by his
mother were such a scoop
that they were confiscated
by the British censors: it
was during the liberation of
St-Malo that napalm had
first been used.

Place Chateaubriand in 1944

🏠 Fort du Petit-Bé

Tel 06 08 27 51 20. **Open** depends on
the weather; phone ahead. 🅿 🍽

Facing the Bidouane Tower
and Champs-Vauverts gate,
this fort, which was designed
by Vauban *(see p173)* in the
17th century, is accessible
either by foot at low tide or
by boat. It was owned by the
French army until 1885, then
decommissioned and restored
to the city of Saint-Malo. It
was classified as a historic
monument in 1921.

Reproductions of 17th- and
18th-century military plans
illustrate the history of the
defence of St-Malo. An ancient
mareographe, used to calcu-
late the tides, is also on display.

🏠 Fort National

Northeast of the castle. **Tel** (06) 72 46
66 26. *Accessible on foot at low tide.
When the French flag flies over the fort,
it is open to the public.* 🎫 Jun–Sep:
Wed–Mon (mid-Jul–mid-Aug: daily. 🅿

In the 18th century, five coastal
forts – La Varde, Le Petit-Bé, La
Conchée, Harbour and the Fort
National – defended the Baie
de St-Malo. The Fort National
was designed by the military
engineer Vauban in 1689. It was
built by Garangeau *(see p86)* on
the Rocher de l'Islet, where
criminals were once executed.
From here, there is a splendid
view of the ramparts, the Rance
estuary and the Îles Chausey.

🏢 St-Servan

This residential district to the
south of the walled city of
St-Malo contains some fine
houses. Numerous sailing ships
are berthed in the Les Bas-
Sablons harbour. From here, a
road leads to Alet.

🏛 Musée du Long Cours Cap-Hornier

In the Tour Solidor. **Tel** (02) 99 40 71
58. **Open** Apr–Sep: daily; Nov–Mar:
Tue–Sun. **Closed** public holidays. 🅿

The tower now houses a
museum devoted to those who,
following trade routes, sailed

The Fort National, designed by Vauban and built by Garangeau

Notre-Dame-des-Flots, an oratory on the cliffs near Rothéneuf

round Cape Horn in the 19th and 20th centuries. Items on display include navigational instruments, models of ships, sails, sperm whales' teeth and canoe paddles from New Caledonia. The tower, which is some 30 m (33 ft) high, was built on the orders of Jean V, Duke of Brittany, between 1364 and 1382. It commands a fine view of the estuary.

Corniche d'Alet

Alet, inhabited by Celts in 80–70 BC, was settled before St-Malo was founded. Around 270, the peninsula was enclosed by walls and then, in about 350, a castellum (small fort) was built here, on a site now covered by the gardens of the Château de Solidor. In about 380, Alet became the capital of the Coriosolites, a Gaulish tribe inhabiting what is now the Côtes d'Armor. In the mid-12th century, the see of St-Malo was transferred to Alet, causing the city to decline. The walls, cathedral and castle were razed on the orders of St Louis, although a few ruins can still be seen.

The coast walk offers a breathtaking view of the walled city, the Île du Petit-Bé and Île du Grand-Bé, where Chateaubriand was laid to rest.

Paramé

On the road north out of St-Malo. Paramé and Rothéneuf have formed part of St-Malo since 1967. The coastal resort of Paramé was established at the end of the 19th century, when developers built the dyke and holiday villas here. Two

beaches, the Plage du Sillon and Plage Rochebonne, stretch for 4 km (2 miles).

Rothéneuf

Northeast of Paramé, via the D201. A long-distance footpath (GR34) follows the coast to Rothéneuf from Pointe de la Varde, from where the view stretches from the Baie de St-Malo right round to Cap Fréhel (see p113). This is a quiet village with two beaches, one of which lines a cove.

Grand Aquarium

La Ville-Jouan, Avenue du Général-Patton. Tel (02) 99 21 19 00. Open daily. Closed Jan, 2 weeks in Nov.

This fascinating aquarium offers the opportunity to view almost 500 different species of cold-water and warm-water marine life. The route through the aquarium corresponds to that taken by the great navigators, from the North Atlantic to the Caribbean Sea. With a circular tank containing sharks, a tropical room, tanks where visitors can touch the fish, and the reconstruction of the wreck of a galleon, the aquarium has much to interest people of all ages.

Havre du Lupin

On the road north out of Rothéneuf. Also known as Havre de Rothéneuf, this cove is a saltwater lake at high tide and an expanse of sand at low tide. It is connected to the sea by a 300-m (985-ft) wide channel running between the coast and a peninsula, the Presqu'île Benard.

Carved Rocks

Chemin des Rochers-Sculptés. From the walled city of St-Malo, take the track in the direction of Rothéneuf. Tel (02) 99 56 23 95. Open daily.

Between 1870 and 1895, the Abbé Fourré, a partly paralysed country priest, produced a masterpiece of naive art. He carved about 300 figures – a fantastic assemblage of grimacing monsters, animals and humans – out of the granite rockface.

From here, a path leads to the Oratoire Notre-Dame-des-Flots, in a converted coastguard's house. The simplicity of this chapel, on the cliff edge, gives the spot a special atmosphere.

One of the figures carved out of the living rock by the Abbé Fourré

Musée Jacques-Cartier

Manoir du Limoëlou. Accessible via Rue David-Mac-Donald-Stewart. Tel (02) 99 40 97 73. Open Jun–Sep; Oct–May: Mon–Sat

The museum is housed in a farmstead built in the 15th and 16th centuries and enlarged in the 19th century. It is devoted to the explorer Jacques Cartier, who discovered Canada in 1534 and lived here between 1541 and 1557. There is also an excellent section illustrating daily life in the region during the 16th century.

The Manoir de Limoëlou, housing the Musée Jacques-Cartier

St Sauliac, Rance Valley

㉔ Rance Valley

Road map E1. 2.5 km (3 miles) south of St-Malo via the N137. 🚗 🚌
ℹ 2 Boulevard Féart, Dinard; (02) 99 46 94 12.

The Rance river, which runs for 25 km (16 miles) from Dinan to the coast, was once a busy trading route. Traditional *chalands* (barges) transported cereal and wood from Dinan to St-Malo; on the return trip they were charged with coal. Since the early 19th century, tourists have outnumbered the barges, and the river is navigated by pleasure boats steering past the tidal mills, fishermen's houses, mariners' chapels and fortifications that line the banks.

A tidal power station *(usine marémotrice)* is located on the bridge over the Rance estuary, on the Dinard side. Harnessing the energy of the tides, which are among the strongest in the world here, the power station generates enough electricity to supply a town of 250,000 inhabitants for a year, or a quarter of what a nuclear power station would produce. It has no negative environmental impact. Built on the principle of tidal mills, it was inaugurated in 1966, after 25 years' research and six years' building work. It consists of a dam, a lock and an embankment, which contains the power station and a discovery centre.

Just south of the dam, **Atelier Manoli** – home to sculptor Pierre Manoli for more than 25 years – is regarded as one of Brittany's main art centres. Over 300 of his works are displayed here, distributed between eight rooms of the traditional granite buildings and throughout the grounds. Among Manoli's major works are *La grande voile* at the Gare Montparnasse in Paris, and the altar and liturgical furniture at the Cathédrale St-Corentin in Quimper *(see pp168–9)*.

On the right bank of the Rance is the picturesque village of **St Sauliac**, a fishing port many of whose houses date from the 14th and 15th centuries. The 13th-century church is one of the few examples of an *enclos paroissial* (parish close) in this part of Brittany. Many lovely walks start from here, including one that leads to the ancient Moulin de Beauchet, one of the oldest tide mills in the region.

🏛 **Atelier Manoli**
9 Rue du Suet. **Tel** (02) 99 88 55 53.
Open Jul–Aug: daily; Apr–Jun & Sep: Wed–Mon, pm only. ♿

Dinard, a fashionable and elegant resort since the 19th century

㉕ Dinard

Road map E1. 🏠 11,000. ✈ Dinard-Pleurtuit-St-Malo; (02) 99 46 18 46.
🚗 🚌 ℹ 2 Boulevard Féart; 0821 235 500. 🛒 Tue, Fri & Sat.
🎭 International Festival de Musique Classique (Aug); Festival du Film Britannique (end Aug–beginning Oct).
🌐 ot-dinard.com

At the beginning of the 19th century, Dinard was no more than a small fishing village. That

Malouinières

Second residences of the wealthy shipowners of St-Malo, *malouinières* were built in the 17th and 18th centuries, a time when this port city of privateers was expanding. Their design being influenced by military architecture, *malouinières* typically have simple outlines, harmonious proportions and a certain austerity. Further characteristics are a steeply pitched roof and high chimneys with lead or terracotta stacks, emblems of the new élite. Bands of dressed Chausey granite surround window frames and mark the angles of the walls. The emphasis on symmetry and ordered perspective is in keeping with the Neo-Classical style of the period.

Part of the façade of a *malouinière* in Puits-Sauvage

was before a small group of British and Americans created the fashion for comfortable mansions in coastal resorts. In 1873, the Lebanese aristocrat Joseph Rochaïd Dahda purchased land on which to build. English-style manor houses then appeared, along with Louis XIII-style chateaux, colonial houses and mock-Breton villas. British and European aristocrats flocked to Dinard's palatial residences. The attraction, albeit slightly antiquated, is still alive today, and the smart young set continues to come here. Walks in either direction along the coast pass ostentatious villas typical of Dinard in its fashionable heyday. The **Promenade de la Malouine** leads to the west, while the **Promenade Robert-Surcouf** leads eastwards to the Pointe du Moulinet, from where there is a spectacular view.

Environs
Located at Pleurtuit, 7 km (4 miles) south of Dinard, is the **Domaine de Montmarin**. This is a fine example of a *malouinière* (sea captain's manor house), and the only one to be found on the left bank of the Rance. It was built in 1760 by the Magons, an important ship-owning family. Although the house isn't open to the public, the gardens are well worth visiting. There is a series of terraces which slope down to the river's edge, a formal French garden, a romantic garden planted with rare species, and a vast collection of hydrangeas.

The harbour at St-Briac, depicted by many 19th-century painters

Domaine de Montmarin
D114, Le Montmarin. **Tel** (02) 99 88 58 79. **Open** Apr–Oct: Sun–Fri pm.

㉖ St-Lunaire
Road map E1. 2 km (1 mile) west of Dinard, via the D786. 🚐 2,200. 🚉 *i* Blvd Générale de Gaulle; (02) 99 46 31 09. 🔲 saint-lunaire.com

This small resort, which, like Dinard, came into being at the end of the 19th century, is named after an Irish monk who settled here in the 6th century. The 11th-century **church** is one of the oldest in Brittany. It contains the tomb of St Lunaire, with a 14th-century recumbent figure.

Pointe du Décollé, north of St-Lunaire, is worth the detour for the panorama of the Côte d'Émeraude that it commands. The point is

connected to the mainland by a natural bridge spanning a chasm known as the Trou du Chat (Cat's Hole).

㉗ St-Briac
Road map E1. 5 km (3 miles) southwest of Dinard, via the D786. 🚐 1,825. *i* 🚉 49 Grande-Rue; (02) 99 88 32 47. 🔲 tourisme-saint-briac.fr

Like Pont-Aven, in Finistère, this former fishing village, located on the right bank of the Frémur, attracted many painters at the end of the 19th century, among them Auguste Renoir, Henri Rivière, Émile Bernard and Paul Signac. The **Chemin des Peintres** is a path that leads out of the village where various artists set up their easels to paint the landscape. There are also two other marked trails: Chemin des Moulins, which takes you along the Frémur River, and the Promenade du Vieux St-Briac. A map in English can be found in the tourist office.

The stained-glass windows in the 19th-century church show scenes from the life of St Briac, who, it is said, looked after the insane. Members of the Habsburg and Hohenzollern families used to visit. The Grand Duke of Russia himself, pretender to the Russian throne, would come to stay here too.

The pleasingly simple 11th-century church in St-Lunaire

CÔTES D'ARMOR

It is on the Côtes d'Armor that the most timeless aspects of Brittany are preserved. While jewel-like churches and chapels hidden in remote hamlets express a profound piety, a wealth of fine buildings stands as ample proof of material riches derived from the linen trade. Here, also, are gentle landscapes and thriving crops, as well as fishing harbours and pirates' nests that are now picturesque holiday resorts.

Majestic Cap Fréhel, on the Côte d'Émeraude, marks the eastern boundary of the Côtes d'Armor, where pink limestone cliffs and windswept heathland create a striking landscape, and the coast is lined with beaches.

The hinterland south of St-Brieuc is the border between the Celtic, western part of Brittany and Lower Brittany. Lamballe, east of St-Brieuc, marks a later boundary. It was once the capital of the duchy of Penthièvre, enemy of the house of Brittany, and several fortresses were built near here.

While the historic towns of Quintin and Moncontour owe their rich heritage to the manufacture of linen cloth in the 17th and 18th centuries, Paimpol, on the Côte du Goëlo, looks back to an illustrious past, when courageous seamen left from here to sail for Iceland: 2,000 of Paimpol's fishermen never returned.

For nature-lovers, the Île de Bréhat, which has an almost Mediterranean microclimate, offers the opportunity to enjoy scenic walks, while the Sept-Îles archipelago is home to 15 species of sea birds. On the Côte de Granit Rose, outcrops of warm-toned granite eroded by wind and rain create a striking sight.

With their attractive settings and many beaches, resorts such as Perros-Guirec and Trégastel throng with holiday-makers during the summer. Inland, the heaths of the Trégor give way to the fields and wooded valleys of ancient Argoat, whose churches and calvaries reflect centuries of religious faith. Tréguier, with a delicately ornamented Gothic cathedral, is one of the finest cities in Brittany.

Aerial view of sea mist on Brehat in the Côtes d'Armor

◄ Overview of the old town of Dinan in the Côtes d'Armor

Exploring the Côtes d'Armor

The name "Côtes d'Armor", meaning "coasts of the sea country", comes from the area's deeply indented coastline formed by rias (ancient river valleys flooded by the sea). Jutting headlands, like the Trégor, alternate with wide inlets, such as the Baie de St-Brieuc. The highest point of the Côtes d'Armor are the Monts d'Arrée and the heathland of Le Méné, in the south. Coastal resorts such as Val-André, St-Cast and Perros-Guirec are the region's main tourist spots, and fishing harbours and islands, particularly the Sept-Îles archipelago and Île de Bréhat, are popular with holiday-makers. Inland are such picturesque medieval towns as Dinan, Quintin and Moncontour, and many impressive religious buildings, such as Tréguier's great Gothic cathedral.

Cloister of the Cathédrale St-Tugdual, Tréguier

Sights at a Glance

1. Mûr-de-Bretagne
2. Lac de Guerlédan and Forêt de Quénécan
3. Gorges de Daoulas
4. Guingamp
5. Bulat-Pestivien
6. Belle-Isle-en-Terre
7. Plestin-les-Grèves
8. Ploubezre
9. Lannion
10. Trébeurden
11. Pleumeur-Bodou
12. Trégastel-Plage
13. Ploumanac'h
14. Perros-Guirec
15. La Roche-Derrien
16. Port-Blanc
17. Plougrescant
18. Sillon de Talbert
20. Paimpol
21. Tréguier
22. Chapelle Kermaria-an-Iskuit
23. St-Quay-Portrieux
24. *St-Brieuc pp108–9*
25. Quintin
26. Moncontour
27. Lamballe
28. Pléneuf-Val-André
29. Sables-d'Or-les-Pins
30. Cap Fréhel
31. Fort La Latte
32. St-Cast-Le-Guildo
33. *Dinan pp114–17*

Tour
19. Île de Bréhat

Getting Around

The N12, a major road, runs through the heart of the Côtes d'Armor. St-Brieuc is the hub of the region's road network. From here, the D786 runs along the Côte de Granit Rose to Plestin, and, heading southwards, the D790 and D700 link St-Brieuc with the heart of the region. From Rennes, the N12 leads to Montauban and the N164 to Loudéac, Mûr-de-Bretagne, Gouarec and Rostrenen. There is a bus service from St-Brieuc to Vannes every two hours. From Guingamp, a train service runs five times a day both to Carhaix and to Paimpol.

The coast path between Perros-Guirec and Ploumanac'h

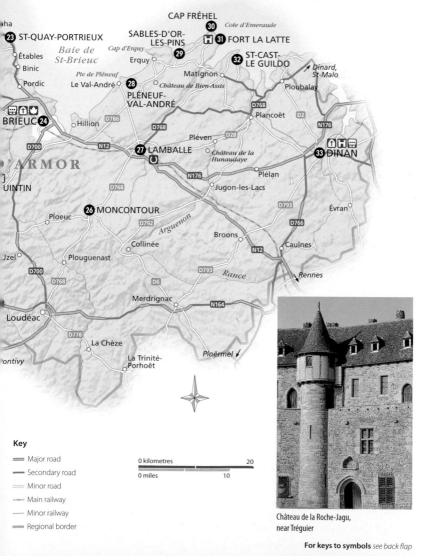

CAP FRÉHEL

30 Cote d'Emeraude

23 ST-QUAY-PORTRIEUX

SABLES-D'OR-LES-PINS

31 FORT LA LATTE

Baie de St-Brieuc

Cap d'Erquy

Étables

Erquy **29**

32 ST-CAST-LE GUILDO

Binic

Pte de Pléneuf

Matignon

Dinard, St-Malo

Pordic

Le Val-André **28**

Château de Bien-Assis

Ploubalay

PLÉNEUF-VAL-ANDRÉ

BRIEUC **24**

Hillion

D786

D768

Plancoët

D768

D2

N176

D700

N12

Pléven

D28

33 DINAN

'ARMOR

27 LAMBALLE

Château de la Hunaudaye

UINTIN

D768

N176

Plélan

Jugon-les-Lacs

Ploeuc

26 MONCONTOUR

D792

Arguenon

D793

Évran

Collinée

Broons

D766

Jzel

Plouguenast

D700

D768

D793

Rance

Caulnes

N12

Rennes

D6

Merdrignac

N164

Loudéac

D778

La Chèze

ontivy

La Trinité-Porhoët

Ploërmel

Key

━━━ Major road

━━━ Secondary road

═══ Minor road

╍╍ Main railway

──── Minor railway

━━━ Regional border

0 kilometres   20

0 miles   10

Château de la Roche-Jagu, near Tréguier

For keys to symbols *see back flap*

❶ Mûr-de-Bretagne

Road map D2. 17 km (11 miles) west of Loudéac via the N164. 🚗 2,140. 🛈 Place de l'Église; (02) 96 28 51 41. 🚆 Jul–Aug: Fri. 🌐 **guerledan.fr**

The town of Mûr-de-Bretagne marks the linguistic boundary between the Celtic, western part of Brittany and the eastern part.

The menhirs in the vicinity, especially the Neolithic **Menhir de Botrain** and the privately-owned **Menhir de Boconnaire**, as well as the numerous burial mounds, show that the region was quite densely populated in prehistoric times.

The **Chapelle Ste-Suzanne**, north of Mûr, in a stand of oak trees, was painted by Corot (1796–1875). It was built in 1496, although the choir (1694) and belfry (1752–64) are later.

❷ Lac de Guerlédan and Forêt de Quénécan

Road map D2. 22 km (14 miles) west of Loudéac via the N164. Watersports centre: **Tel** (02) 96 67 12 22. Holiday village: **Tel** (02) 96 28 50 01. 🛈 (02) 96 28 51 41. 🎉 Fête du Lac (15 Aug).

Filling a valley that was flooded when a hydroelectric dam was built in 1930, the Lac de Guerlédan, just west of Mûr-de-Bretagne, stretches for 12 km (8 miles). A watersports centre, a camp site and a holiday village, it attracts lovers of the great outdoors. From the banks of the Blavet, there is a stunning view of the Barrage de Guerlédan, which is not open to the public. The power station is open to visitors however. The **Musée de l'Électricité** nearby illustrates the history of electricity production, and the ways in which electricity is used.

Southwest of the lake is the 3,000-ha (7,400-acre) Forêt de Quénécan, with beech, spruce and pine. Like the Forêt de Paimpont, it is a vestige of the Forêt de Brocéliande *(see p68)*.

🏛 Musée de l'Électricité

St-Aignan. **Tel** (02) 97 27 51 39. **Open** mid-Jun–mid-Sep: Mon–Sat, Sun pm; for other times phone ahead. 🅿️ 📷 obligatory

❸ Gorges de Daoulas

Road map D2. 30 km (18.5 miles) west of Loudéac via the N164.

The high escarpments and the plant life of the Gorges de Daoulas give this gorge the appearance of an Alpine defile. The river here has eroded the schist, and the water flows swiftly between high cliffs that have a wild beauty.

The partially ruined **Abbaye Cistercienne de Bon-Repos**, just off the N164, was built in the 12th century. The monastic buildings and cloister both date from the 18th century. An exhibition hall holds contemporary art exhibition. There is also a *son et lumière* show in early August.

Abbaye Cistercienne de Bon-Repos, founded in the 12th century and now partly in ruins

🏰 Abbaye Cistercienne de Bon-Repos

St-Gelven. Via the N164. **Tel** (02) 96 24 82 20. **Open** Mar–Jun & Sep–Nov: Mon–Fri, Sun pm; Jul–Aug: daily. 🅿️

❹ Guingamp

Road map C2. 🚗 8,830. 🛈 2 Place au Champ-au-Roy; (02) 96 43 73 89. 🚉 🚌 St-Brieuc. 🚆 Fri & Sat. 🎭 Bugale Breizh (Breton dancing and Pardon de Notre-Dame, early Jul); Fête de la St-Loup (mid-Aug). 🌐 **ot-guingamp.fr**

Standing at a crossroads and once fortified, Guingamp is an attractive town with fine timber-framed houses, particularly on Place du Centre.

The **Basilique Notre-Dame**, in Rue Notre-Dame, was built in several stages between the 13th and 16th centuries, and therefore exhibits several different styles. While the columns at the crossing, which are decorated with grotesque figures, are typically Romanesque, both the west door and the triforium are in an accomplished Renaissance style. The apse is Gothic.

The **Hôtel de Ville**, on Place Verdun, occupies the former Monastère des Hospitalières, dating from the early 17th century. The Baroque chapel here contains paintings by the Pont-Aven group *(see p175)*. Ramparts on Place du Petit-Vally are all that remains of the 15th-century castle, which was demolished in 1626.

Environs
Some 10 km (6 miles) west of Guingamp is the holy mountain of **Menez-Bré**. From the summit, there are spectacular views of the Trégor. The 17th-century chapel here is dedicated to St Hervé, healer, exorcist and

The Lac de Guerlédan, offering many watersports activities

patron of bards. The fountain 300 m (330 yds) from the chapel is said to have sprung at his command. Sick children were dipped in its miraculous waters in the hope of curing them.

Châtelaudren, 13 km (8 miles) east of Guingamp via the N12-E50 then the D7, is well worth the detour for the Chapelle Notre-Dame-du-Tertre, which contains 132 remarkable 15th-century frescoes on biblical themes.

The nave of the Basilique Notre-Dame in Guingamp

❺ Bulat-Pestivien

Road map C2. 18 km (11 miles) southwest of Guingamp via the D787 then the D31. 🚏 440. 🎭 Pardon (early Sep).

This small village (famous, rather quirkily, as a centre for the breeding of the Breton spaniel) boasts a magnificent 14th-century church, **Eglise de Notre Dame**. Its tower is the earliest example of Renaissance architecture in Brittany. Like those of the church at Loc-Envel *(see below)*, the exterior walls are covered in gargoyles, monsters and grimacing *ankous* (skeletons). Both the porch and the main entrance dazzle with their elaborate decoration. According to legend, this church was built by a lord in thanks to the Virgin Mary, who restored his son to him when the child was snatched by a monkey. This strange scene is depicted in the sacristy.

Environs
About one km (0.5 mile) to the north is a charming **parish close** with a calvary dating from 1550. The **Gorges du Corong**, 10 km (6 miles) south of Bulat-Pestivien, are wreathed in ferns and have a wild and dramatic beauty. According to legend, the great rocks beneath which the river flows are the stones that a giant shook out of his clogs.

❻ Belle-Isle-en-Terre

Road map C2. 18 km (11 miles) west of Guingamp via the N12. 🚏 1,110. 🛈 15 Rue de Crec'h-Ugen; (02) 96 43 01 71. 🚆 Guingamp. 🛒 Wed. 🎭 Les Fêtes de Belle-Isle (end Jul). 🌐 ot-belle-isle-en-terre.com

This town lies between the rivers Guer and Guic, which join to form the Léguer, the river that flows into the Baie de Lannion. It is a popular area for fishing, and the meadows and woods round about are ideal walking country.

Tradition dictates that the origins of Belle-Isle-en-Terre go back to the 9th century and its name is probably from the monks of Belle-Isle, an island off the western coast of Brittany, who founded a monastery in nearby Locmaria.

Just north of the village is the Chapelle de Locmaria, which has a 15th-century rood screen.

The castle here houses the **Centre Régional d'Initiation à la Rivière**, which is dedicated to environmental protection.

The church at Bulat-Pestivien, in the Renaissance style

Environs
The village of **Loc-Envel**, 4 km (3 miles) southwest of Belle-Isle via the D33, stands on the edge of the **Forêt de Coat-an-Noz**.

Loc-Envel is well worth a visit for its 16th-century church. The belfry, with gargoyles, is in the Gothic style, but it is the interior that is particularly fascinating. The rood screen, richly decorated in the Flamboyant Gothic style, and the vaulting of the nave, from which hosts of carved monsters stare down, are remarkable.

The forest, with age-old trees whose branches are covered with moss, lichen and ferns, is a magical place in which to stroll. The forest's undulating terrain, and the paths that wind between clumps of box-tree dating from Roman times, make it interesting walking country.

The Flamboyant Gothic rood screen in the church at Loc-Envel

The Château de Rosanbo, owned by the same family for 600 years

❼ Plestin-les-Grèves

Road map C1. 15 km (9 miles) southwest of Lannion via the D786. 🚂 3,300. 🚌 Morlaix, Lannion and Plouaret. 🛈 Place 19 Mars 1962; (02) 96 35 61 93. 🚌 Sun.

The jewel in the area around Plestin (*Plistin* in Breton) is a wide, soft sandy beach known as **Lieue de Grève**. This beach, which stretches for miles when the tide is out, has held a strong appeal for holiday-makers since the 1930s. Several holiday residences, including the Villa Trenkler (House of the Eagle) and Villa Lady Mond at the coastal village of St-Efflam, date from this period.

Unfortunately, since 1970, the water on this small stretch of coastline has been regularly infested with prolific, foul-smelling green algae. However, if taking the sea air is out of the question, it is possible to climb up to the Grand Rocher, which, 80 m (262 ft) high, overlooks the beach, or to follow the coast road, the Corniche de l'Armorique (D42), for a view of the Baie de Locquirec. Several species of birds, including sheldrake and sandpiper, can also be seen here.

Environs

The **Château de Rosanbo**, which has been in the same family for 600 years, is located just 6 km (4 miles) from Plestin-les-Grèves. This fine residence was restored in the Neo-Gothic style in 1895. The chateau's formal garden, with hedgerows and bowers, was designed by Duchêne, the landscape gardener who laid out the gardens at Vaux-le-Vicomte. The architect Lafargue designed the library for the 8,000-book collection of Claude Le Pelletier, who was to succeed Colbert as Louis XIV's finance minister. The dining room was reconstructed on the basis of 18th-century inventories.

The church in the village of **Lanvellec** is also worth a visit. It contains a fine organ built by Robert Dallam in 1653.

Altarpiece in the Chapelle de Notre-Dame de Kerfons

🏠 Château de Rosanbo

Lanvellec (D22). **Tel** (02) 96 35 18 77. **Open** Apr–Jun & Sep–Oct: daily pm; Jul–Aug: daily. 🚫 📷

❽ Ploubezre

Road map C1. 3 km (2 miles) south of Lannion via the D11. 🚂 2,700. 🛈 Mairie; (02) 96 47 15 51.

To discover so fine a chapel in a remote location such as this is always a pleasant surprise. **Notre-Dame de Kerfons**, in Ploubezre, is one of the most exquisite examples of religious architecture in Brittany.

The chapel was built in the Flamboyant Gothic style, probably under the aegis of a powerful local lord. When it was remodelled in the Renaissance style, its builders took the trouble to use stones from the same quarry, the better to blend the new style with the old.

The detailed and elaborate decoration of the interior culminates in the rood screen, a tracery of painted and gilt wood, with reliefs depicting Christ, the 12 Apostles, St Barbara and St Mary Magdalen.

The **Château de Kergrist**, built in 1537 by Jean de Kergrist and remodelled in the 17th and 18th centuries, is characteristic of the great Renaissance residences built by the Breton aristocracy. The Huon de Penanster family, which has owned the castle since 1860, has opened to visitors the gardens and one of the three blocks that frame the main courtyard. The interior is filled with interesting traditional Breton furniture, including a decorated wardrobe, and tapestry door screens.

🏠 Notre-Dame de Kerfons

Kerfons (D31b). **Open** Jul–Aug: daily. 🚫 📷

🏠 Château de Kergrist

Ploubezre (D11). **Tel** 06 11 52 26 57. **Open** Jun–Aug: daily. 📷 obligatory. Garden: **Open** Apr–Oct: daily. 🚫 ♿ Garden & ground floor only.

Lieue de Grève, a wide sandy beach north of Plestin-les-Grèves

The ruined 13th-century Château de Tonquédec

Environs

About 2 km (1 mile) from the Château de Kergist stand the impressive ruins of the **Château de Tonquédec**, built in the 13th century. During the Wars of the Holy League, the castle had become a Huguenot stronghold. Because of this, it was partly demolished in 1626 on the orders of Cardinal Richelieu, principal minister to Louis XIII. The fortifications consist of 11 towers and a courtyard in which attackers could easily be trapped. From the rampart walk there is a panoramic view of the wooded valley of the Léguer.

Château de Tonquédec
Tonquédec (D31b). **Tel** (02) 96 54 60 70. **Open** Apr–mid-Jun & mid-Sep–end Sep: daily pm; mid-Jun–mid-Sep: daily; Oct: Sat & Sun pm.
W tonquedec.com

❾ Lannion

Road map C1. 19,400.
i Quai d'Aiguillon; (02) 96 05 60 70.
Fêtes Vocales (late Jul); Estivales de la Photographie (Jul–Oct). Thu.
W bretagne–cotedegranitrose.com

The bustling town of Lannion (*Lannuon* in Breton) has profited handsomely from the installation of the Centre National d'Études des Télécommunications in 1960, and from the TGV (high-speed-train) link. The nexus between the telecommunications centre at Pleumeur-Bodou (*see p100*) and the optical industries, Lannion has attracted thousands of researchers and students of engineering specializing in state-of-the-art technology.

Such dynamism might have altered the town's picturesque character and identity, but nothing could be further from the truth. Breton is still spoken in the busy market square. The heart of the old town has ancient paved alleyways and some charming timber-framed, granite and cob houses, such as those at Nos. 1–3 Rue des Chapeliers, which escaped destruction during the Wars of Religion (1591), and Nos. 29–31 Place du Général-Leclerc, which were rebuilt after 1630. These houses are clad in slate and decorated with human figures, animals, crosses and lozenges. Some of them have overhanging windows.

Of all the religious buildings in Lannion, the most appealing is the **Église de Brélévenez**. It is reached via a flight of steps lined with small, attractive houses decorated with statues of patron saints or ceramic friezes. The church was founded in the 12th century by a branch of the order of the Knights Templar, the Trinitarians of St John. The choice of materials used in its construction reflects the importance of this church: pink and yellow granite for the south porch, large ashlars for the apse, black marble and tufa for the high altar, and painted wood for the altarpiece (1630) in the north transept – a slightly macabre reminder of the impending Day of Judgment.

Église de Brélévenez
i (02) 96 46 41 00. **Open** daily. Jun–Aug: Mon–Fri, Sun pm.

Le Yaudet, in a beautiful setting on the Léguer estuary

Environs

About 3 km (2 miles) west of Lannion, on the left bank of the Léguer, is **Loguivy-lès-Lannion** (*Logivi* in Breton), whose parish close has a notable portal and a Renaissance fountain. The oak altarpiece inside features a wealth of carvings.

The coast road leads on to the scenic hamlet of **Le Yaudet** (*Ar Yeoded* in Breton), whose granite houses cling to the hillside. Uniquely in Brittany, the village chapel contains a depiction of a recumbent Virgin next to the figure of Christ.

Set on a promontory, with a stunning view of the Léguer estuary, Le Yaudet has one of the most beautiful natural settings in the Trégor. Excavations led by archaeologists from Brest and Oxford have uncovered a Gallo-Roman fishing village on the promontory.

Le Yaudet
Le Yaudet (D88). **Tel** (02) 96 05 60 70. Jul–Aug: Mon.

Half-timbered houses in the historic centre of Lannion

A beach at the popular coastal resort of Trébeurden

⑩ Trébeurden

Road map C1. 7 km (4 miles) northwest of Lannion via the D65. 🚉 Lannion. 🚍 3,540. 🛈 Place de Crec'h-Héry; (02) 96 23 51 64. 🚌 Tue. 🎪 Fest-noz (Jul); concerts (Wed in summer). 🆆 tourisme-trebeurden.com

A popular coastal resort, Trébeurden has several beautiful beaches either side of Le Castel, a rugged peninsula with pink granite rocks. The **Île Milliau**, opposite the peninsula, is accessible at low tide. More than 270 species of plants grow there. The island was inhabited 7,000 years ago; evidence of human habitation is a Neolithic passage grave, the **Allée Couverte de Prajou-Menhir**, 14 m (46 ft) long and with carvings on its stones. The **Marais du Kellen**, behind Plage de Goas-Trez, attracts snipe, teal grebe and other birds.

⑪ Pleumeur-Bodou

Road map C1. 6 km (4 miles) northwest of Lannion via the D65 then the D21. 🚉 Lannion. 🚍 4,000. 🛈 11 Rue des Chardons; (02) 96 23 91 47. 🚌 Sat. 🆆 pleumeur-bodou.com

Bristling with giant antennae that provide worldwide communication, Pleumeur-Bodou is well known as the site of the telecommunications centre where the first satellite link between the United States and Europe was made, in 1962. The radar dome, a gigantic sphere 50 m (160 ft) high, is open to visitors. In the **Cité des Télécoms,** there's a museum tracing the 150-year history of telecommunications from

their earliest days to the age of digital communications, and a **Planetarium**, with a screen measuring 600 sq m (6,460 sq ft).

Opposite the planetarium is the reconstruction of a Gaulish settlement, the **Le Village Gaulois**. This whole complex goes under the name Cosmopolis.

🏛 Cité des Télécoms
Tel (02) 96 46 63 80. **Open** Apr–Jun & Sep: Mon–Fri, Sat–Sun pm; Jul–Aug: daily; Oct–Mar: Mon–Fri, Sun pm during school holidays. **Closed** Jan. 🎪

🏛 Planetarium
Tel (02) 96 15 80 32. **Open** Jul–Aug: daily; during school holidays. **Closed** Jan. 🎪 🆆 planetarium-bretagne.fr

🏛 Le Village Gaulois
Tel (02) 96 91 83 95. **Open** Easter–Jun & Sep: Mon–Fri, Sun pm; Jul–Aug: daily. 🎪 🆆 levillagegaulois.org

Environs
The **Île Grande**, north of Trébeurden, is accessible via a bridge on the D788. As well as beaches and footpaths, the island has an ornithological centre. The **Maison LPO**, a centre set up by an organization for the protection of birds, highlights the rich flora and fauna of the Sept-Îles archipelago. Tours are also organized from here. The **Menhir de St-Uzec**, 2 km (1 mile) from Penvern, is a standing stone 8 m (26 ft) high, one of the finest in Brittany. In the 17th century, a cross and a depiction of the

Board for Aquarium Marin, Trégastel

Passion of Christ were carved on it to convert it into a Christian monument.

📷 Maison LPO
Île Grande. **Tel** (02) 96 91 91 40. **Open** Jun, Sep & school holidays: daily pm; Jul–Aug: Mon–Fri, Sat & Sun pm; other times: Sat–Sun pm. 🎪

⑫ Trégastel-Plage

Road map C1. 6 km (4 miles) west of Perros-Guirec via the D788. 🚉 Lannion. 🚍 2,290. 🛈 Place Ste-Anne; (02) 96 15 38 38. 🚌 Mon. 🎪 Fest-noz (Jun); 24 Heures de la Voile (mid-Aug).

This resort is famous for the blocks of pink granite that rise up behind its beaches, Plage du Coz-Pors and Plage de Grève-Blanche. The orientation table between these two beaches offers a splendid panorama of the coast and of the countryside inland.

At the **Aquarium Marin**, housed in a cave, visitors can see fish and other marine life of the waters around Brittany. **Kerguntuil**, 2 km (1 mile) south, on the D788 towards Trebeurden, is of interest for its Neolithic passage grave and dolmen.

📷 Aquarium Marin
Boulevard de Coz-Pors. **Tel** (02) 96 23 48 58. **Open** Jul–Aug: daily; rest of year: times vary, check website. 🎪 🆆 aquarium-tregastel.com

The reconstructed village of Le Gaulois, Pleumeur-Bodou

⓭ Ploumanac'h

On account of its spectacular rocks, this former fishing village, now a district of Perros-Guirec, is one of the greatest tourist attractions in Brittany. **Pointe de Squewel**, one hour's walk along the coast path from Plage St-Guirec, north of Ploumanac'h, is a promontory with gigantic piles of rocks that suggest such incongruous shapes as tortoises, rabbits and tricorn hats. The **Maison du Littoral**, level with the lighthouse, contains displays explaining how the rocks were formed, and describing local flora and fauna.

The **Chapelle Notre-Dame-de-la-Clarté** (1445), midway between Ploumanac'h and Perros-Guirec, is the focus of a very lively annual pardon. The chapel has an interesting porch with relief decoration, and, inside, a stoup (1931) decorated with heads of Moors and the Stations of the Cross. It was made by Maurice Denis, a founder of the group of painters known as the Nabis.

The **Vallée des Traouïéros**, between Ploumanac'h and Trégastel, runs between blocks of granite and lush vegetation. The restored tidal mill here dates from the 14th century.

✖ Maison du Littoral

Opposite lighthouse. **Tel** (02) 96 91 62 77. **Open** Mid-Jun–mid-Sep: Mon–Sat; school holidays: Mon–Fri pm.

Plage de Trestraou, one of several beaches at Perros-Guirec

⓮ Perros-Guirec

Road map C1. 🚉 Lannion. 🚗 7,890. 🛈 21 Place de l'Hôtel-de-Ville; (02) 96 23 21 15. 🗓 Fri. 🎭 Festival de la Bande Dessinée (Apr); Fête des Hortensias (Jul); Ploumanac'h Regatta (Aug); Pardon de Notre-Dame-de-la-Clarté (15 Aug). 🌐 **perros-guirec.com**

With about a dozen beaches and many hotels, this coastal resort attracts large numbers of visitors in summer. As at Ploumanac'h, the coast here has extraordinary rock formations shaped by the erosion of wind and rain.

The coast path, running the 6 km (4 miles) between Plage de Trestraou and the famous rocks at Ploumanac'h, offers stunning views.

Environs

From Perros-Guirec there is a boat service to the **Sept-Îles Archipelago**, one of the best places to see sea birds. One of the islands, the **Île aux Moines**, is named after the Franciscan friars who settled there in the Middle Ages. Also on the island is a lighthouse and a small fort built by Garangeau, the architect responsible for St-Malo's fortifications (*see pp84–9*).

🛥 Embarcadère des Sept-Îles

(boarding point for boat service), Plage de Trestraou. **Tel** (02) 96 91 10 00. **Open** Mar–Nov: daily; rest of the year: by arrangement.

Sept-Îles Bird Sanctuary

Although the islands' best-known inhabitant is the puffin, the Sept-Îles archipelago, a protected area, is also home to fulmars, kittiwakes, pied oystercatchers, gulls, crested cormorants and other sea birds. Twenty thousand pairs breed in this protected area. Only one island, the Île aux Moines, is accessible to the public, although the birds on the other islands can be observed from motorboats. On the Île de Roizic, 15,130 pairs of gannets and 248 pairs of puffins nest in the craggy rocks. Grey seals can sometimes be seen at the foot of the cliffs in the islands' secluded creeks.

The puffin, emblematic inhabitant of the Sept-Îles

Granite rocks at Pointe de Squewel, a major tourist attraction

Stained-glass window in the Église Ste-Catherine in La Roche-Derrien

richly decorated façade and the south porch, with a pointed arch, has some notable reliefs. While the lintel is carved with a scene of the Annunciation and with a Pietà, the side panels feature a host of carved figures, four of whom stick out their tongues at the viewer. In front of the church is a rare 15th-century outdoor pulpit.

⑮ La Roche-Derrien

Road map C1. 15 km (9 miles) northeast of Lannion via the D786 then the D6. 🚊 Guingamp or Lannion. 🚌 1,100. 🅸 10 Place du Martray; (02) 96 91 59 40. 🚌 Fri. 🅆 larochederrien.fr

In the middle ages, La Roche Derrien (*Ker Roc'h* in Breton, meaning Town of the Rock), was a fortified town over which many battles were fought. The castle, overlooking the Jaudy valley, was besieged during the War of the Breton Succession, a conflict between the English, the French and the Bretons *(see p46)*. In the 14th century, it passed into the hands of Bertrand du Guesclin *(see p47)*, who is said to have planted the yew tree that still stands in the close of the 18th-century Chapelle de Notre-Dame-de-la-Pitié, on the road to Kermezen.

Today, La Roche-Derrien offers pleasant walks on the banks of the Jaudy. In the town, several timber-framed houses line Place du Martray. The Église Ste-Catherine, built in the 12th and 15th centuries, contains an elaborate 17th-century altarpiece. The modern stained-glass window in the transept depicts the battle between supporters of Charles of Blois and the English.

Altarpiece in the chapel at Confort

Environs

The 16th-century chapel at **Confort**, 13 km (8 miles) southwest of La Roche-Derrien on the D33, is built in a combination of the Flamboyant Gothic and Renaissance styles. The bell tower, in the style of Lannion belfries, incorporates a stair turret. The chapel contains an altarpiece in which the Virgin is depicted in the likeness of Anne of Brittany and the Angel Gabriel in that of Louis XII, king of France *(see pp48–9)*.

About 6 km (4 miles) southeast of La Roche-Derrien on the D8, the church at **Runan**, dating from the 14th–16th centuries, was once owned by the Knights Templar, then by the Knights of St John of Jerusalem. It has a

⑯ Port-Blanc

Road map C1. 8 km (5 miles) northwest of Tréguier via the D70a, the D70 then the D74. 🚊 Lannion. 🚌 2,500. 🅸 12 Place de l'Église, Penvenan; (02) 96 92 81 09. 🚌 Sat. 🎺 Pardons (Whitsun & 15 Aug).

Lying west of Plougrescant and sheltered by a barrier of dunes, the coastal village of Port-Blanc is a pleasant holiday resort. The highly picturesque 16th-century chapel, which nestles among rocks, is the focal point of the village. The chapel's roof is unusual in that it reaches almost to the ground. The 17th-century calvary in the close depicts St Yves, St Joachim, St Peter and St Francis. The chapel contains several old statues, including the traditional group depicting St Yves between a rich and a poor man.

From the harbour, trips out to sea are offered in an old sardine boat, the **Ausquémé**. The coast path from Port-Blanc to Buguélès commands some magnificent views.

🚤 **Ausquémé**
Tel 06 07 59 04 03.
Open Jul–Sep: daily. 🎣

The 16th-century chapel at Port-Blanc

The Sillon de Talbert, a natural spit of land with the Héaux lighthouse in the distance

⑰ Plougrescant

Road map C1. 6 km (4 miles) north of Tréguier on the D8. 🚍 Guingamp or Lannion. 🚶 1,430. 🛈 42 Hent St Gonéry, Plougrescant; (02) 96 92 56 83. 🌐 tregor-cotedajoncs-tourisme. com

The most prominent feature of Plougrescant is its chapel, the Chapelle St-Gonéry, which has an eyecatchingly crooked belfry. The church consists of two sections, the first of which is Romanesque, dating from the 10th century. From this section rises the belfry, built in 1612. The other part is the nave, which was built in the 15th century. The chapel is of interest chiefly for its remarkable 15th-century frescoes. Covering the barrel-vaulted ceiling, they loosely depict scenes from the Old and New Testaments. These scenes, which are painted on an ochre background dotted with stars, are in a naive style. The contrasting colours, and areas of black and white, emphasize outlines and accentuate perspective. The strikingly fine monuments inside the chapel include the tomb of Guillaume du Halgouët, bishop of Tréguier, and an alabaster statue of the Virgin, both of which date from the 16th century. Also notable is a reliquary with finely carved panels. During the summer, trips out to sea in an old sailing boat, the **Marie-Georgette**, depart from the harbour.

🚢 **Marie-Georgette**
Tel (02) 96 92 58 83.
Open Apr–Sep.

⑱ Sillon de Talbert

This natural spit of land extends for 3 km (2 miles) from the tip of the Presqu'île Sauvage, the peninsula between Tréguier and Paimpol. Made up of sand and pebbles, the spit was created by the opposing currents of two rivers, the Trieux and the Jaudy. It is now called Réserve Naturelle Régionale, a protected site, as, were it to disappear, the two inlets on each side of the peninsula would be at the mercy of tidal currents. The Héaux lighthouse can also be seen from here.

Famous Names in Port-Blanc

Théodore Botrel

Port-Blanc has appealed to a variety of different people, from authors and songwriters to scientists and pioneers of aviation. In 1898, the writer Anatole Le Braz bought the property known as Kerstellic. He recorded Breton stories and legends that he heard told by the inhabitants of the Trégor. *La Légende de la Mort* (1893), is considered by Armorican Bretons to be his best work. Le Braz's friend and neighbour was the writer Ernest Renan *(see p107)*, who lived at Rosmapamon. The songwriter Théodore Botrel, who wrote *La Paimpolaise*, bought land at Port-Blanc on which he built a house that he named *Ty Chansonniou* (House of Songs). He later left to live in Pont-Aven. In 1922, Alexis Carrel, winner of the Nobel Prize for Medicine, purchased the Île St-Gildas, where he was buried in 1944. His friend Charles Lindbergh was a frequent visitor. In 1938, after his pioneering flight across the Atlantic, Lindbergh acquired the Île d'Illiec, where he briefly lived before returning to the United States.

⑩ Île de Bréhat

Because of the luxuriant vegetation that thrives in its gentle climate, the Île de Bréhat is also known as the Island of Flowers. Bréhat, a paradise for walkers and a haven for artists, actually consists of two large islands linked by a bridge. In the north, heathland predominates and the indented coastline is reminiscent of Ireland. In the south, the landscape is softer, with pine trees, pink pebble beaches and Mediterranean plants. There is no motorized transport, but it is easy to walk or cycle along the island's sunken paths.

④ **Phare du Paon**
Destroyed by German forces during World War II, the lighthouse was rebuilt in red porphyry in 1947. Stairs lead up to the platform, from which there is a view of the open sea.

⑥ **Chapelle St-Michel**
Perched on a rise 26 m (85 ft) high, the Chapelle St-Michel overlooks the whole island. It was rebuilt in 1852, and has long served as a landmark for shipping. The path leads straight down to an old tidal mill.

⑤ **Phare du Rosédo**
The 19th-century lighthouse overlooks the heathland of the northwest of the island. Ernest Renan (see p107) came here to enjoy the beauty of the surroundings.

⑦ **Le Goareva**
This fort is a fine example of 18th-century military architecture.

① **Port-Clos**
In 1770, Charles Cornic built this harbour, a port of call for ships from the mainland.

Key
— Suggested route
-- Footpaths
═ Other routes

③ **Chaussée Vauban**
A bridge built by Vauban links the south and north islands. The harbour in the Anse de la Corderie, west of the bridge, was once Bréhat's port.

Map labels: Chaise de Renan, Pointe du Rosedo, Signal Station, Île Nord, Chapelle St-Rion, Île ar-Morbic, Anse de la Corderie, la Croix de Maudez, Île Séhérès, Étang de Birlot, Moulin de Crec'h Tarek, Île Sud, Île Lavrec, Raguénès Meur, Île Logodec, Plage de Guerzido, Pointe de l'Arcouest

0 metres 1000
0 yards 1000

Tips for Drivers

Tour : about 9 km (5.5 miles).

Access :15 minutes from Pointe de l'Arcouest; information **Tel** (02) 96 20 04 15. Bicycles can be hired in Port-Clos.

Stopping-off places :La Potinière, on Plage du Guerzido offers oysters and mussels; Le Paradis Rose, in the north, serves crêpes.

Bréhat, the flower-filled island

② **The town**
Bréhat consists of houses clustered around a 12th-century church with 17th–19th-century alterations.

⑳ Paimpol

Road map D1. ⚡ 8,420.
🚉 Avenue Général-de-Gaulle. 🚌
ℹ️ Place de la République; (02) 96 20
83 16. 🏪 Tue. 🎪 Fête des Terre-
Neuvas et des Islandais (third Sun in
Jul); Songs of the sea (every 2 years in
Aug from 2013); Fest-noz (14 Jul).
🌐 **paimpol-goelo.com**

Although pleasure boats have
now replaced the schooners that
once filled the harbour, this is
still the heart of Paimpol, with
coasters and trawlers tied up
alongside the quais. As Pierre Loti,
in his novel *Pêcheurs d'Islande (An
Iceland Fisherman)*, so eloquently
described, the sea has exacted a
heavy price from Paimpol: 100
schooners and 2,000 men were
lost in the fishing expeditions
that left Paimpol for Iceland.

The first left in 1852 and, in
1895, 82 schooners of 400
tonnes burden set sail for the
North Sea. Each was crewed by
about 20 seamen, who for six
months endured not only cold
and great physical strain, but also
separation from their families.
Their wives, the famous
Paimpolaises immortalized by
Théodore Botrel, would scour
the horizon for their return at
the Croix des Veuves-en-
Ploubazlanec, north of the town.
When the ships came in, there
were either joyful reunions or
scenes of mourning. The last
expedition to Iceland left
Paimpol in 1935.

The Place du Martray, in
the town centre, is lined with
16th-century houses. On the
corner of Rue de l'Église is a
shipowner's house in the
Renaissance style, with a turret.
The house was used as a hunting

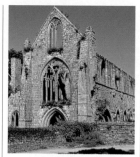

The 13th-century Abbaye de Beauport, in Paimpol, now in ruins

lodge by the Rohans, a powerful
Breton dynasty. The **Musée du
Costume**, on Place du Pont Neuf,
contains displays of *coiffes*
and costumes from the Trégor
and Goëlo. Through photographs,
models, ships' logs, nautical
equipment and votive offerings,
the **Musée de la Mer**, in a
building once used for drying cod,
describes the fishing expeditions
to Newfoundland and Iceland.

From Paimpol, visitors can take
a **boat trip** out to sea or a ride on
a **steam train** up the Trieux
valley to Pontrieux.

🏛 **Musée du Costume**
Place du Pont Neuf. **Tel** (02) 96 55 04
61. **Open** mid-Jul–Aug: Tue–Sun pm.
📷

🏛 **Musée de la Mer**
Rue Labenne. **Tel** (02) 96 22 02 19.
Open mid-Apr–mid-Jun & Sep: daily
pm; mid-Jun–Aug: daily. 📷

🚢 **Boat Trips**
Tel (02) 96 55 44 33.
🌐 **voilestraditions.fr**
Sardine Boat Trips
Tel (02) 96 55 99 99.
Open Apr–Nov.
🌐 **eulalie-paimpol.com**
Steam Train: Vapeur du Trieux
Tel (02) 96 20 52 06.
Open mid-May–mid-Sep.

Environs
The ruined Romanesque
Abbaye de Beauport,
2 km (1 mile) south of Paimpol
via the D786, is one of the
most beautiful abbeys in
Brittany. Built in the Anglo-
Norman style in the early 13th
century, it was an important
religious centre. Visitors can
see the chapterhouse,
cloisters, refectory and
storerooms. Concerts and
son et lumière spectaculars
are staged here during the
summer. From the abbey, a
road leads to the **Chapelle
Ste-Barbe**, the starting point
of a coastal path.

The **Pointe de l'Arcouest**,
reached via the D789
from Paimpol, is the main
boarding point for the Île
de Bréhat.

🏠 **Abbaye de Beauport**
On the D786. **Tel** (02) 96 55 18 58.
Open daily. 📷

🚢 **Pointe de l'Arcouest**
Les Vedettes de Bréhat.
Tel (02) 96 55 79 50.

Artists on Bréhat

Between the late 19th and early 20th centuries, many writers and
artists came to Bréhat. Writers included Ernest Renan, the Goncourt
brothers, Pierre Loti and Théodore Botrel, and the artists Henri
Rivière, Paul Gauguin, Henry Matisse, Tsugouharu Foujita, Henri
Dabadie and many others. All found inspiration in the island's
landscapes, but they also frequented the town's cafés. Mme Guéré,
the fearsome landlady of a certain café, once threatened to behead
a customer if he failed
to settle his slate. Taking
her at her word, the
miscreant painted his
face on the side of his
glass. Ever since, artists
have customarily
painted their portraits
on glasses at the Café
des Pêcheurs, which
now has a collection of
over 200 glasses.

Une Rue à Bréhat, a painting by Henri Dabadie

Vintage steam train in the station
at Pontrieux

For hotels and restaurants see pp225–6 and pp235–7

㉑ Tréguier

The capital of the Trégor and an ancient bishopric, Tréguier is today a quiet city. The narrow streets around the splendid cathedral are lined with timber-framed houses and grander granite residences. The 16th-century timber-framed house in Rue Renan that is the birthplace of the writer Ernest Renan is now a museum, and visitors can see the nursery, Renan's studio and various other exhibits relating to his life and work. The Flamboyant Gothic Cathédrale St-Tugdual, one of the finest examples of Breton religious architecture, dominates Tréguier. The Pardon de St-Yves, in May, honours the cathedral's patron saint, who is also that of lawyers.

Cathédrale St-Tugdual

A masterpiece of Breton Gothic religious architecture, the cathedral was built in the 14th–15th centuries.

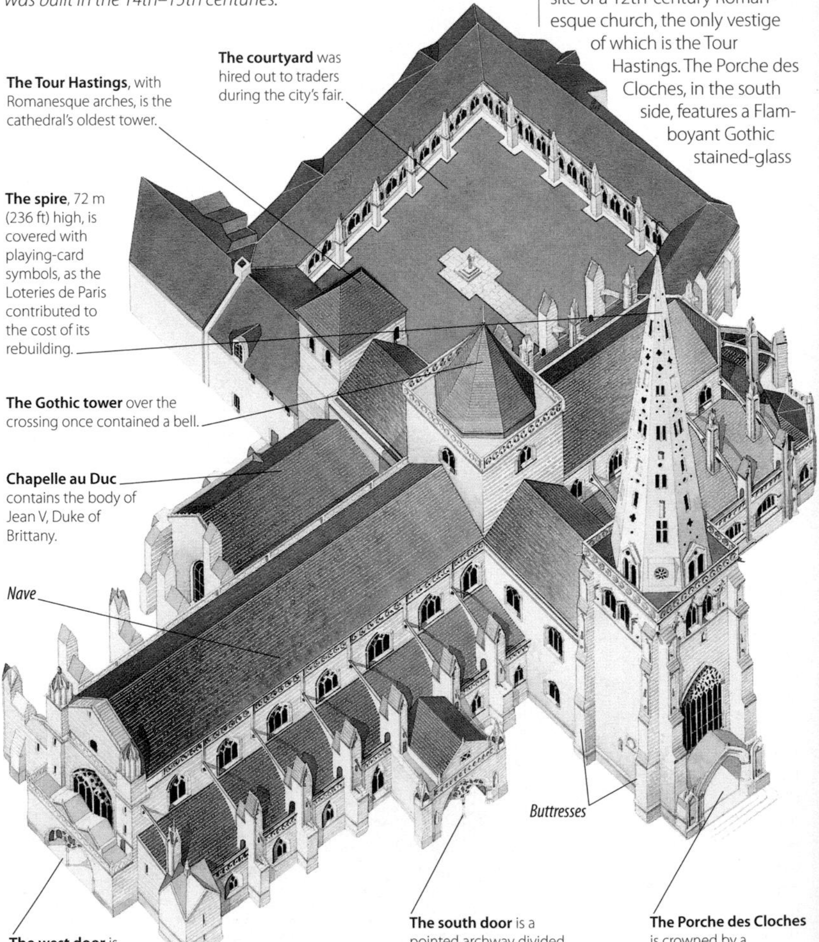

The Tour Hastings, with Romanesque arches, is the cathedral's oldest tower.

The courtyard was hired out to traders during the city's fair.

The spire, 72 m (236 ft) high, is covered with playing-card symbols, as the Loteries de Paris contributed to the cost of its rebuilding.

The Gothic tower over the crossing once contained a bell.

Chapelle au Duc contains the body of Jean V, Duke of Brittany.

Nave

Buttresses

The west door is framed by an arch with a terrace above.

The south door is a pointed archway divided by a column. Above is a rose window.

The Porche des Cloches is crowned by a Flamboyant Gothic stained-glass window.

VISITORS' CHECKLIST

Practical Information
Road map C1. 2,950. 13 Place de l'Église, Penvénan; (02) 96 92 81 09. Wed. Pardon de St-Yves (third Sun in May); Beg Chopin music festival: mid-Jul.

Transport
Paimpol or Lannion.

Cathédrale St-Tugdual

Place du Martray. **Open** Jun–Sep: 9am–7pm daily; Oct–May: 9am–noon & 2–6pm daily. **Closed** to visitors during services. to cloisters & treasury (Mar–Oct).

The cathedral was built on the site of a 12th-century Romanesque church, the only vestige of which is the Tour Hastings. The Porche des Cloches, in the south side, features a Flamboyant Gothic stained-glass

For hotels and restaurants see pp225–6 and pp235–7

window. An 18th-century spire rises from the tower. The south-side outer wall is covered in Gothic tracery. The arches inside rise in three tiers to a height of 18 m (59 ft) above the nave, and grotesques stare down from the base of some of the arches. The choir, in the Anglo-Norman style, has 46 Renaissance stalls with strikingly realistic decoration. The cathedral also contains the tomb of Jean V, Duke of Brittany, the tomb of St Yves (1890), and the saint's reliquary. The 15th-century cloisters north of the choir are the best-preserved in Brittany. The ambulatory is filled with sculptures of recumbent figures.

🏛 **Maison Natale d'Ernest-Renan**
20 Rue Ernest-Renan. **Tel** (02) 96 92 45 63. **Open** Apr–Jun: Wed–Sun; Jul–Aug: daily; Sep: Wed–Sun. **Closed** Oct–Mar. 🏷

Environs
The village of **Minihy-Tréguier**, 1 km (0.5 mile) south of

Ernest Renan

Born in Tréguier, Ernest Renan (1823–92) intended to join the priesthood, but his reading of the philosopher Hegel turned him against this vocation. A philologist who specialized in Semitic languages, he published writings that were thought to be scandalous because they proposed a rational, analytical approach to Christianity. Renan's *Vie de Jésus* (Life of Jesus) had particularly dramatic repercussions. When his statue was unveiled in 1903, the police were forced to act to prevent its desecration.

Ernest Renan, a native of Tréguier

Tréguier, is famously associated with Yves Helory de Kermartin, who was canonized in 1347. A member of the local nobility, he became a protector of the poor, and turned the village into a refuge *(minihy)*. An annual pardon (third Sun in May) is held in his honour. The 15th-century church contains painted wooden statues of St Yves, shown, as usual, between a rich and a poor man. The **Château de La Roche-Jagu**, 14 km (9 miles) southeast of Tréguier, was built in the 15th century, on the site of one of the ten forts that, from the 11th century, defended the Trieux valley.

🏰 **Château de La Roche-Jagu**
Tel (02) 96 95 62 35. **Open** mid-May–mid-Oct; Nov & Christmas hols: daily pm. 🏷 Jul–Aug: fêtes and music. 🏷

Fresco of the Dance of Death in the Chapelle de Kermaria-an-Iskuit

❷ Chapelle de Kermaria-an-Iskuit

Road map D1. 11 km (7 miles) north-west of St-Quay-Portrieux via the D786 then D21. 🏷 Pardon (third Sun in Sep).

About 3 km (2 miles) from Plouha, via the D21, stands the Chapelle Kermaria-an-Iskuit, "Chapel of Mary Restorer of Health". Founded in the 13th century by a former Crusader, it contains some extremely rare frescoes. One of them (1501) depicts the Dance of Death; the fear of death was widespread in late medieval

Europe. Regardless of their rank, the *Ankou* (skeletal figure) leads men, from pope and king to knight and peasant, in a macabre dance.

❷❸ St-Quay-Portrieux

Road map D1. 🚉 St-Brieuc. 🚗 3,430. 🚢 Motorboat service to Île de Bréhat Apr–mid-Sep. 🛈 17 bis Rue Jeanne-d'Arc; (02) 96 70 40 64. 🍽 Mon & Fri. 🌐 **saintquayportrieux. com**

The pleasant coastal resort of St-Quay-Portrieux, north of St-Brieuc, once relied for its livelihood on fishing off Newfoundland. Uniquely for a

town of this size, the deep-water harbour here can berth 1,000 boats. A coast path leads to a signal station.

Environs
The resort of **Binic**, 7 km (4 miles) south of St-Quay-Portrieux, was a large port in the 19th century. The **Musée d'Arts et Traditions Populaires** is devoted to local history, especially the Newfoundland fishing industry. Breton headdresses are on display.

🏛 **Musée d'Arts et Traditions Populaires**
Avenue du Général-de-Gaulle, Binic. **Open** Sep: Wed–Mon pm; Jul–Aug: pm (phone first).

The bay at St-Quay-Portrieux, a coastal resort with beautiful beaches

㉔ St-Brieuc

The history of St-Brieuc is closely linked to its evolution as a centre of religion. In the 5th century, Brieuc, a Gaulish monk, founded an oratory on the site of the present Fontaine St-Brieuc, in Rue Notre-Dame. The city was sacked in the late 16th century, during the Wars of the Holy League *(see p50)*, although stability returned in the 17th and 18th centuries. Lying between the valleys of the Gouédic and the Gouët, St-Brieuc, capital of the Côtes d'Armor, is a pleasant city. Also a dynamic centre of culture, it has spawned cultural organizations and hosts events such as Art Rock *(see p34)*. It also has associations with several great French writers.

Timber-framed house in Rue Fardel, in the old town of St-Brieuc

One of the towers on the fortified Cathédrale St-Étienne

🏛 Old Town
Built in the 14th and 15th centuries, the **Cathédrale St-Étienne**, located on Place du Général de Gaulle, has the appearance of a fortress. Its central porch is flanked by two sturdy towers: the 14th-century Tour Brieuc, 28 m (92 ft) high, and the 15th-century Tour Marie, 33 m (108 ft) high. Both are pierced with openings that allowed defensive weapons of many kinds to be used.

The large Chapelle de l'Annonciation, dating from the 15th century, has a notable altarpiece made by Yves Corlaix in 1745. With rocaille decoration, gilt polychrome and curves and counter-curves, it is a masterpiece of Baroque art. In the choir, some of the capitals are carved with grotesques or foliage. The organ was built by Cavaillé-Coll, who also built the organ in St-Sulpice in Paris.

Rue Pohel, Rue Fardel and Rue Quinquaine, in the vicinity of the cathedral, are lined with many timber-framed houses dating from the 15th and 16th centuries.

The 15th-century building in Rue Fardel known as **Maison Ribault** is the oldest house in St-Brieuc. In Rue Quinquaine, the Hôtel des Ducs de Bretagne, the ducal residence built in 1572, is also of interest for its elegant Renaissance façade with grotesque masks and figures carved in relief. On Place du Chai, modern buildings stand alongside restored wine warehouses. A covered passageway links the square with Rue Houvenagle, which is lined with ancient timber-framed houses faced with pilasters and featuring overhanging upper storeys. Three pedestrianized streets, Rue St-Gouéno, Rue Charbonnerie and Rue St-Guillaume run through the city's main shopping area are worth seeing.

🏛 Musée d'Art et d'Histoire
Cours Francis-Renaud. **Tel** (02) 96 62 55 20. **Open** Tue–Sat, Sun pm.

Through models, paintings, objects from everyday life and digital works of art, this museum presents the history of the *département* of the Côtes d'Armor from its origins in the 18th century up until the 20th century. The displays illustrate several themes, including fishing, shipbuilding, the cloth and linen trade, and agriculture and land reclamation, as well as popular traditions.

Literary life in St-Brieuc

Jean Grenier

Growing up in St-Brieuc in the early 20th century, Jean Grenier and Louis Guilloux formed a strong friendship. While the latter spent his life in St-Brieuc, Grenier left in 1930 to teach at the *lycée* in Algiers, where one of his pupils was the young Albert Camus. As a teacher, Grenier influenced Camus' later work. Camus, the author of *L'homme Révolté* and winner of the Nobel Prize for Literature in 1957, was steeped in the writings of both Grenier and Guilloux, and of Georges Palante, another philosopher who was a native of St-Brieuc. Guilloux came to the attention of the publisher Gaston Gallimard, winning the Prix Renaudot with *Le Jeu de Patience* (1949). Gide and Malraux judged his novel *Le Sang Noir* (1935) to be a work of major importance.

Anse d'Yffiniac, seen from the Maison de la Baie

Parc des Promenades

These walks circle the law courts. East of Rue St-Guillaume, the municipal garden, decorated with sculptures, follows the outline of the old city walls. On the right of the law courts stands a bust of the writer Villiers de l'Isle-Adam, who was born in St-Brieuc, by Elie Le Goff, and a sculpture entitled *La Forme se Dégageant de la Matière* (Form Emerging from Matter) by Paul Le Goff. There is a also a monument dedicated to Paul Le Goff on Boulevard de La Chalotais.

Environs

Lying some 3 km (2 miles) inland, St-Brieuc is linked to the sea by the port of **Légué**, on the Gouët estuary. Here, shipowners' houses evoke the great age of the 19th-century Newfoundland cod-fishing industry, which has been replaced by the scallop industry. A footpath runs around the Pointe du Roselier. From the point, there is a view of the whole bay, from Cap d'Erquy in the east to the Île de Bréhat in the northwest. After passing an 18th-century cannon-ball foundry, the long-distance footpath GR34 leads to Martin-Plage. The Anse d'Yffiniac, an inlet behind the bay, is a sea-bird sanctuary: 50,000 birds of various species nest in this protected site. They arrive from northern Europe at the end of summer. Most spend the winter here. The **Maison de la Baie**, north of Hillion, has displays documenting the bay's flora and fauna and describing its seafaring economy.

Near Hillion, long paths leading far into the Dunes de Bon-Abri allow walkers to have a closer look at the plant life of the protected site.

Maison de la Baie

Rue de l'Etoile. **Tel** (02) 96 32 27 98. **Open** Oct–May: Wed, Fri pm, Sun pm; Jun, Sep: Wed–Fri pm, Sun pm; Jul–Aug: Mon–Fri, Sat & Sun pm.

VISITORS' CHECKLIST

Practical Information
Road map: D2. 48,900.
7 Rue St-Gouéno; 02 96 33 32 50. Wed & Sat. Art Rock (Whitsun); Festival du Tambour de St-Brieuc (early Jul); Fête de la Moule (Aug); Les Nocturnes (Jul–Aug). **W** baiedesaintbrieuc.com

Transport
Boulevard Charner.
Rue du 71 ème Regiment d'Infanterie.

St-Brieuc City Centre

① Cathédrale St-Étienne
② Maison Ribault
③ Musée d'Art et d'Histoire
④ Parc des Promenades

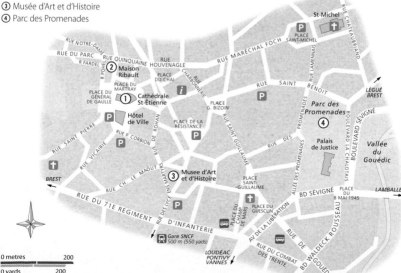

The elegant Château de Quintin, built in the 17th century

❷❺ Quintin

Road map D2. 18 km (11 miles) southwest of St-Brieuc via the D700, the D790 and the D7. 🚉 St-Brieuc. 🚍 2,930. 🚺 6 Place 1830; (02) 96 74 01 51. 🌄 Jul–Aug: Mon. 🚌 Tue. 🎭 Pardon de Notre-Dame (second Sun in May); Festival St Martin (Nov); Fête des Tisserands (mid-Aug).

During the 17th and 18th centuries, Quintin was an important centre of the linen cloth industry. This age of prosperity gave the town its chateau as well as the timber-framed houses and fine granite-built residences that line Place 1830, Place du Martray and Grande Rue. The Maison du Tisserand in Rue des Degrés houses the **Musée-Atelier des Toiles** which documents this period of the town's history.

The 19th-century Neo-Gothic **Basilique Notre-Dame**, in Rue de la Basilique, is dedicated to the patroness of spinners. A relic reputed to be a piece of the Virgin's girdle is kept in the basilica. It is particularly venerated by pregnant women.

Opposite the tourist office, the **Château de Quintin,** built in the 17th–18th centuries, houses a unique collection of over 280 pieces of porcelain.

🏠 **Château de Quintin**
Entrance on Place 1830. **Tel** (02) 96 74 94 79. **Open** Apr–Jun & Sep–Oct: daily pm; Jul–Aug: daily. 🎨

🏛 **Musée-Atelier des Toiles**
Rue des Degrés. **Tel** (02) 90 03 24 02. **Open** Jun–Sep: Tue–Sat. 🎨

❷❻ Moncontour

Road map D2. 15 km (9 miles) southwest of Lamballe via the D768. 🚉 Lamballe. 🚍 900. 🚺 4 Place de la Carrière; (02) 96 73 49 57. 🚌 Tue. 🎭 Fête Médiévale (every 2 years; early Aug); Festival de Musique Ancienne (Sep).

This medieval walled town stands on a promontory at the point where two valleys meet. Fine 16th- and 18th-century residences and half-timbered houses line Rue des Dames and Place de Penthièvre, where a linen market was once held. The **Église St-Mathurin**, dating from the 16th–18th centuries, is well worth a visit for its 16th-century stained-glass windows. Those showing scenes from the life of St Yves, on the left of the nave, exhibit traces of Flemish influence.

Pietà in the Église St-Mathurin

❷❼ Lamballe

Road map D2. 🚉 Boulevard Jobert. 🚍 🚍 11,200. 🚺 Place du Champ du Foire; (02) 96 31 05 38. 🚌 Thu. 🎭 Foire des Potiers (May); Pardon de Notre-Dame (Sep); National de Cheval Breton (Sep). 🌐 **lamballe-tourisme.com**

Founded in the sixth century, Lamballe began to develop in the 11th century. Capital of the duchy of Penthièvre, the region was one of the most important strongholds of Brittany. Until the 18th century, Penthièvre was in repeated conflict with its rival, the house of Brittany.

The **Musée d'Art Populaire du Pays de Lamballe**, on Place du Martray, has exhibits dating from prehistory, as well as local costumes, headdresses and tools. The collections illustrate the daily life in Lamballe and its environs in historical times. The **Musée Mathurin-Méheut**, housed in the charming half-timbered Maison du Bourreau, has a large collection relating to this local painter, who was also a leading exponent of Art Nouveau. About 4,000 of his works are exhibited in rotation, illustrating a different theme each year.

The **Collégiale Notre-Dame-de-Grande-Puissance** in Rue Notre-Dame, has the appearance of a fortified church. It is built in a combination of Romanesque

Linen Cloth

The linen cloth industry brought prosperity to Brittany in the 17th and 18th centuries. St-Brieuc, Quintin, Uzel, Loudéac and Moncontour – which, between them, had more than 8,000 weavers – were the main centres of production. In 1676, a statute was passed regulating the standards of quality of the linen cloth woven in western Europe. That produced in Brittany was then acknowledged to be the best in France. Loaded onto ships in St-Malo and Nantes, it was exported worldwide.

A loom on which linen cloth was once woven

Mathurin Méheut

Painter, interior decorator, illustrator, designer of jewellery and wallpaper, Mathurin Méheut (1888–1958) was a multi-talented artist. One of the earliest exponents of Art Nouveau, Méheut was commissioned to design the interior decoration of 27 liners. This included producing four oil paintings for the *Normandie*. After World War II, he was appointed painter to the French Navy and produced many fishing scenes. In 1923, a retrospective exhibition of his work was held in San Francisco.

Mathurin Méheut, a pioneering exponent of Art Nouveau

and Gothic styles. The north door, dating from the 12th century, has capitals carved with foliage. The thick columns and floral motifs in the nave show Norman influence, while the Flamboyant Gothic rood screen (1415) is perfectly counterbalanced by the Louis XIII organ loft of 1741. Near the church, a walking path has been laid out on the site of a castle that was destroyed in 1626.

The **Haras National**, in Place du Champ-de-Foire, in the west of Lamballe, is the second-largest national stud in France. Set up in 1825, it was well regarded in the early 20th century, and is still important today. It has capacity for 400 animals, and the horses bred here include Breton post-horses, thoroughbreds and Connemaras, thus helping to preserve these breeds.

 Haras National
Place du Champ-de-Foire. **Tel** (02) 96 50 06 98. Jul–Aug: daily; other times: 3pm daily.

Environs
Northeast of Lamballe, not far from Pléven, are the ruins of the restored **Château de La Hunaudaye**. Of particular interest are the 15th-century keep, pierced by arrowslits; the seigneurial quarters, which have a fine Renaissance staircase; and two 13th-century towers. In summer, actors in costume recreate a

The Maison du Bourreau, in Lamballe, which houses the Musée Mathurin-Méheut

sense of the château's history for visitors.

 Château de La Hunaudaye
On the D28. **Tel** (02) 96 34 82 10. Apr–Jun & mid-Sep–Oct: daily, pm; Jul–mid-Sep: daily. **W** la-hunaudaye.com

 Musée d'Art Populaire du Pays de Lamballe
Hosté du Pilori. **Tel** (02) 96 34 77 63. **Open** Sep: Tue–Sat. **W** alp22400.net

 Musée Mathurin-Méheut
Maison du Bourreau. **Tel** (02) 96 31 19 99. **Open** Apr–Jun & Sep: Tue–Sat; Jul–Aug: Tue–Sat, Sun pm; Oct–Dec: Tue–Sat pm. **Closed** Jan–Mar.

 Collégiale Notre-Dame-de-Grande-Puissance
Rue Notre-Dame. **Open** call tourist office for information. early Jul–late Aug: Mon–Fri, Sun pm.

The charming medieval village of Moncontour, perched on a promontory

The Château de Bienassis, near Pléneuf-Val-André

❷❽ Pléneuf-Val-André

Road map: D1. ➔ 🚉 Lamballe.
🏔 3,770. ℹ️ Cours Winston-Churchill;
(02) 96 72 20 55. 🛒 Tue in Pléneuf;
Fri in Val-André. 🎿 Fête du Nautisme
& regatta (Jul); jazz (Jul–Aug: every
Tue); Pardon de Notre-Dame-de-la-
Garde (Aug); Fête de la Mer (mid-Aug).

Originally no more than a
quiet fishing harbour, Pléneuf-
Val-André was transformed
in the late 19th century,
when developers turned it
into one of Brittany's most
sophisticated holiday resorts.
With a beautiful sandy beach
2 km (1 mile) long, it soon
became very popular.

From the 16th century,
fishermen from the neigh-
bouring village of Dahouët
came to Pléneuf-Val-André to
prepare for cod-fishing expeditions off Newfoundland. In
those days, ships' captains
would call at local inns to enlist
sailors, whose drunkenness
would guarantee that they
signed up without protest.

From Pléneuf-Val-André, two
walks, to Pointe de la Guette
and to Pointe de Pléneuf, offer
spectacular views. The **Îlot du
Verdelet**, opposite Pointe de
Pléneuf, is a bird sanctuary,
accessible at low tide. Trips out
to sea on the sailing boat
Pauline are organized during
the holiday season.

🚤 **Pauline**
Port de Dahouët. **Tel** (02) 96 63 10 99.
Open Jun–Sep: daily; Oct–May: by
arrangement.

Environs

The **Château de Bienassis**,
4 km (3 miles) east of Pléneuf-
Val-André, was built in 1400
and has been remodelled
several times since. The only
surviving original part is a
tower behind the chateau.
Destroyed during the Wars
of the Holy League (see p50),
the chateau was rebuilt in the
17th century: the part framed
by towers dates from this phase.
The interior contains Breton
Renaissance furniture and a

The fishing port of Erquy, base of many
deep-sea trawlers

monumental stairway. There
is also a formal garden.

🏰 **Château de Bienassis**
Sur la D786. **Tel** (02) 96 72 22 03.
🕐 Mid-Jun–mid-Sep: Mon–Sat,
Sun pm; mid-Sep–mid-Jun: by
arrangement. 🚫

❷❾ Sables-d'Or-les-Pins

Road map: E1. 8 km (5 miles)
southwest of Cap Fréhel via the
D34a. 🏔 2,100. ➔ 🚉 Lamballe.
ℹ️ Plurien; (02) 96 72 18 52 all year.
🛒 Tue.

This coastal resort with smart villas
in the neo-Norman style was
created in the early 1920s as a rival
to Deauville. With a 3-km (2-mile)
long sandy beach and pine trees, it
is very popular with holidaymakers.

Environs

Erquy, on the D786 west of
Sables-d'Or, is renowned for its
clams and scallops. It is also the
base for a large fleet of deep-
sea trawlers. Of all the beaches
nearby, the Plage de Caroual is
the best. In summer, the tourist
office organizes boat trips to the
Île de Bréhat (see p104) and
the Baie de St-Brieuc (see p109).

Cap d'Erquy is less well
known than Cap Fréhel, yet it
is one of the most beautiful
headlands in Brittany. Many
marked footpaths cross the
flower-covered heath here and
run along the indented cliffs,
beneath which are shingle
beaches. The views from the
headland are stunning; to
the west, there is a panorama
across the Baie de St-Brieuc and
to Pointe de Pléneuf beyond.

One of the paths on the
promontory passes an *oppidum*
popularly known as Caesar's
Camp; it was, in fact, a fortified
Gaulish settlement and its Iron
Age earthworks are still visible.
Classified in 1978, the site was
bought by the local authority
in 1982 so as to protect it from
erosion caused by motorcyclists
using it as a rough circuit. In
summer, daily walks on Cap
d'Erquy are organized by the
Syndicat des Caps (02 96 41
50 83).

Fort La Latte, built in the 13th century, with a commanding view of the sea

❸⓪ Cap Fréhel

Road map: E1. 🛈 Fréhel; (02) 96 41 57 23. 🚶 Mid-Jun–mid-Sep & school holidays of season: daily. 🚢 Compagnie Corsaire Dinard/St Malo; 08 25 13 81 00.
ⓦ **compagniecorsaire.com**

The spectacular headland of Cap Fréhel is one of the most beautiful landscapes in Brittany. Heathland covered with heather and gorse stretches to infinity, and sheer pink limestone cliffs rise vertically from the sea to heights of 70 m (230 ft).

The view from here stretches from Pointe du Grouin in the east to the Île de Bréhat in the west. In clear weather, it is even possible to see the Channel Islands. Sea birds, such as fulmars, kittiwakes, cormorants, guillemots and pied oystercatchers, nest in nooks in the cliffs and on the neighbouring small islands.

There are two lighthouses on the promontory: one built by Vauban in the 17th century and the other dating from 1950. The latter is open to visitors; the effort of climbing to the top is rewarded by the view. In summer, the Syndicat des Caps organizes walks on the promontory every day. Trips by motorboat from Dinard and St-Malo allow visitors to admire the cliffs from the sea.

🏰 Lighthouse
Tel (02) 96 41 40 03. 🗓 Apr–Oct; free.

❸① Fort La Latte

Road map: E1. 4 km (3 miles) southwest of Cap Fréhel via the D16. **Tel** (02) 96 41 57 71. 🗓 Apr–Sep: daily; Oct–Mar: Sat & Sun pm; winter school holidays: daily pm. 🚢 Compagnie Corsaire Dinard/St Cast, St Malo; 08 25 13 81 00.

This impressive fortress overlooking the sea was built in the 13th century by the powerful Goyon-Matignon family. It was captured by Bertrand du Guesclin *(see p47)* in 1379 and was besieged by the English in 1490, then by the Holy League in 1597. On Vauban's orders, Garangeau *(see p86)* restored it in the 17th century. The keep and the cannon-ball foundry are of particular interest to visitors.

From the rampart walk, there is a sublime view of the Côte d'Émeraude. Abandoned in the 19th century, the fort passed into private ownership in 1892, and was classified as a historic monument in 1931.

The spectacular headland at Cap Fréhel, with sheer limestone cliffs

❸② St-Cast-Le Guildo

Road map: E1. 🚌 🚉 Lamballe. 🏠 3,290. 🛈 Place Charles-de-Gaulle; (02) 96 41 81 52. 🛒 Mon & Fri. 🎵 Concerts (Jul–Aug).

Now a popular coastal resort, St-Cast-Le Guildo has no less than seven beaches, and in summer its population increases ten-fold. Its expansion began at the end of the 19th century, when the painter Marinier purchased the headland and set about developing it.

The ruins of the **Château du Guildo**, in the parish of Créhen, recall the fratricidal conflict between Giles of Brittany, son of Jean V, Duke of Brittany, whose allegiance was to the English crown, and his brother François I of Brittany, a supporter of the king of France. François murdered Giles, but the latter had prayed to God that his brother might outlive him by just 40 days; François indeed died exactly 40 days later. It was not until 1758 that the English, who suffered defeat at St-Cast, finally relinquished their intentions of invading the coast of Brittany.

From here, visitors may enjoy two walks along part of the GR34 long-distance footpath. One goes south to Pointe de la Garde, which offers a beautiful panorama of the Ebihens archipelago and Presqu'île St-Jacut; the other goes north, to the Pointe de St-Cast, which commands a fine view of Fort La Latte and Cap Fréhel.

The fort and Cap Fréhel can also be admired from the sea by taking a trip in the **Dragous**, an old sailing boat, which leaves from St-Cast-Le-Guildo.

The town's **church** contains a 12th-century Romanesque stoup decorated with grotesques and a statue of St Cast, the monk who established a hermitage here in the 6th century.

🚢 Dragous
Port de St-Cast. Tel (02) 96 41 71 71. **Open** Jul–Aug: daily; Easter–Nov: by arrangement. 🚢

⊕ Street-by-Street: Dinan

In the words of Victor Hugo, Dinan perches "on an overhanging precipice…like a swallow's nest". From the 14th to the 18th centuries, a flourishing trade in linen cloth, leather, wood and cereals – cargoes that left Dinan from its harbour on the Rance – led to the creation of an exceptionally rich architectural heritage: the old town has some extremely fine half-timbered houses. The town is enclosed by 3 km (2 miles) of walls that are both the most massive and the oldest in Brittany. The 14th-century machicolated keep, as well as the Basilique St-Sauveur, with a magnificent Romanesque porch, are some of the other attractions of this medieval town.

★ **Basilique St-Sauveur**
This is built in a style combining Gothic and Romanesque influences.

Tour Ste-Catherine
One of the oldest towers in the town's 13th-century walls commands a splendid panorama of the harbour and the Rance valley.

★ **Rue de Jerzual**
Until 1852, when the viaduct was built, travellers entering Dinan would follow this street, which was once a steep track.

Tour du Gouverneur

Porte de St-Malo

Franciscan Monastery
Built in the 13th century, this former Franciscan monastery now houses a private school.

RUE DU

RUE

RUE NÉEL DE LA VIGNE

RUE DU REMPART

RUE HAUT

RUE MICHEL

RUE DU

RUE DU PETIT FORT

RUE DE

PROMENADE DES

★ **Castle and Town Walls**
The castle consists of a keep, the Tour de Coëtquen and the Porte du Guichet. The 14th-century keep houses a museum of local history.

0 metres   100
0 yards   100

Key

— Suggested route

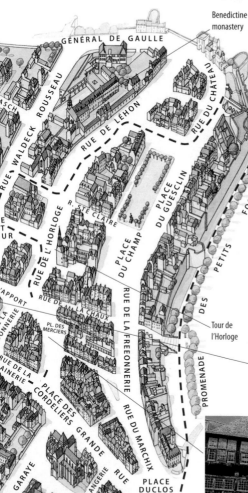

Benedictine monastery

GÉNÉRAL DE GAULLE

RUE WALDECK ROUSSEAU

BASCH

CE NT EUR

RUE DE LÉHON

RUE DU CHÂTEAU

R. STE CLAIRE

RUE DE L'HORLOGE

PLACE DU CHAMP

PLACE GUESCLIN

DU GUESCLIN

DES PETITS FOSSÉS

FOSSÉS

Tour de l'Horloge

L'APPORT

SONNERIE

RUE DE LA CHAUX

RUE DE LA FREECONNERIE

PROMENADE

PL. DES MERCIERS

RUE DE LA LAINERIE

PLACE DES CORDELIERS

GRANDE RUE

RUE DU MARCHIX

DE LA GARAYE

RUE DE LA BOULANGERIE

RUE DE LA CROIX

PLACE DUCLOS

SÉS

Porch of the Hôtel Beaumanoir
The street entrance of this residence is framed by a stone archway decorated with carved dolphins.

★ **Place des Merciers**
In the heart of the old town, the Place des Merciers (Haberdashers' Square) is lined with medieval timber-framed houses. Among these is Restaurant de la Mère Pourcel, a 15th-century timber-framed building with overhanging upper storey.

Exploring Dinan

The history of Dinan is closely linked to events in Breton political history. In about 1000, noblemen from a family called Dinan took possession of the town and, in 1283, it came under the control of the duchy of Brittany. Dinan enjoyed an initial period of prosperity thanks to its maritime trading links with Flanders and England, and to the trade in linen sheets and cloth. In the 14th century, the Wars of the Breton Succession, during which Dinan supported the king of France, curtailed the town's development. However, from the 16th century, Dinan was again prosperous and it enjoyed a second golden age in the 17th and 18th centuries. This can be seen from the fine timber-framed houses that line the town's streets. At this time, religious orders also established several large convents and founded new churches in Dinan.

The old town of Dinan, on the banks of the Rance

🏛 Old Town and Harbour

In the harbour, the commercial activity that once brought Dinan such riches has been replaced by a flotilla of pleasure boats. The leafy banks of the Rance offer the opportunity for scenic walks.

Rue du Quai leads to **Rue du Petit-Fort**. At No. 24 is the **Maison du Gouverneur**, a fine 15th-century residence. Before the viaduct was built in 1852, travellers would enter Dinan via **Porte du Jerzual**, a 14th-century gate with Gothic arcades. They would then follow **Rue du Jerzual**, which is lined with timber-framed houses dating from the 15th and 16th centuries. Once filled with traders, the street has been taken over by cabinet-makers and gilders.

Rue de l'Apport has several well-restored houses. This street leads to **Place des Merciers**, which also contains attractive houses with wooden porches and overhanging upper storeys.

The **Hôtel de Keratry**, a 16th-century mansion with granite columns, is housed at No 6 **Rue de l'Horloge**.

🏛 Town Walls

These were built in the 13th century and strengthened in the 15th century by François I, Duke of Brittany. They were renovated in the 17th century by Garangeau (*see p86*) on the orders of Vauban. The walls are set with 10 towers, the most impressive of which is the Tour Beaumanoir.

Two walks along the walls, the Promenade de la Duchesse Anne and the Promenade des Grands Fossés, offer views of the town and of the Rance.

🏛 Franciscan Monastery

Place des Cordeliers. **Open** Mon–Fri. This former monastery was established in the 13th century by a Crusader who became a Franciscan friar.

Several 15th-century buildings survive. Among them are the Gothic cloisters, the main courtyard and the chapter-house, which is used as a refectory by the school that now occupies the monastery.

🏛 Église St-Malo

Grande-Rue. **Open** daily, 9am–4pm. **Closed** to visitors during services.

The church, with a slate-covered bell-turret, was begun in the 15th century and completed 400 years later. The exterior has a remarkable Renaissance doorway. Pillaged during the Revolution, the interior is somewhat bare, apart from more recent additions such as the high altar (1955) in granite carved by Gallé and a series of stained-glass windows (1927) by Merklen, depicting various quarters of Dinan, such as the Jerzual and Place des Cordeliers.

🏛 Basilique St-Sauveur

Place St-Sauveur. **Open** daily, 9am–4pm. **Closed** to visitors during services.

Built in a combination of Romanesque and Gothic styles, the basilica is unique in Brittany. It was founded by a knight who had safely returned from a crusade against the Saracens. Begun in the 12th century, it was not completed until the 16th century.

The façade has a remarkable Romanesque doorway carved

Rue du Petit-Fort, lined with fine 15th-century houses

Birth of a Legend

In 850, some monks dressed in rags met King Nominoë (see p43) and asked him to help them. The king agreed on condition that he be given some relics in return. To fulfil this obligation, the monks set sail for Sark, in the Channel Islands, where they found the body of St Magloire (525–605), Bishop of Dol. On their return, the king fell to his knees before the relic and founded the Prieuré de St-Magloire-de-Lehon.

Relic of St Magloire

VISITORS' CHECKLIST

Practical Information
Road map: E2. 🚶 15,000. 🛈 9 Rue du Château; (02) 96 87 69 76. 📅 Apr–Jun & Sep: Sat; Jul–Aug: daily. 🚌 Thu. 🎵 Festival de Harpe Celtique (second week in Jul); Fête des Remparts (every 2 years from 2016; third weekend in Jul); Fête de la Pomme (first weekend in Nov).
🌐 dinan-tourisme.com

Transport
🚉 🚌 Place du 11-Novembre-1918.

with depictions of the vices and with such monstrosities as sirens, human-headed serpents and a toad at a woman's breast. The interior combines the Romanesque and Flamboyant Gothic styles. The heart of Bertrand du Guesclin (see p47) is entombed in the north transept. There are also some fine stained-glass windows, both ancient and modern.

The former cemetery is now a terraced garden with a view of the Rance valley. In the garden are busts of the explorer Auguste Pavie and of Néel de la Vigne, mayor of Dinan during the Revolution.

Statue from the castle

🕐 Tour de l'Horloge
Rue de l'Horloge. **Tel** (02) 96 87 02 26. **Open** Easter–May: daily pm; Jun–Sep: daily. 🏛
The top of the tower offers impressive views of Dinan. The bell was a gift from Anne of Brittany in 1507.

🕐 Benedictine Monastery
Rue de Léhon. **Open** Mon–Fri.
Built in the 17th and 18th centuries, the monastery now houses a private school where Chateaubriand (see p75) was once a pupil.

🏰 Castle & Museum
Rue du Château. **Tel** (02) 96 39 45 20. **Open** Jun–Sep: daily; Easter–May; Oct–mid-Nov: daily pm. **Closed** mid-Nov–Easter. 🏛
The castle consists of a 14th-century keep, the 13th-century Porte du Guichet and the Tour de Coëtquen. Strengthened by Mercœur,

leader of the Holy League (see p50), the castle withstood attack by Protestant soldiers but, with the help of the people of Dinan, Henri IV managed to break through the Porte de St-Malo. The keep, built in 1380, must have served both as a fortress and as living quarters, as it features spy-holes and lookouts as well as mullioned windows and monumental chimneys. A platform at the top of the keep offers a magnificent view of Dinan and its environs.

Tour Coëtquen, with tomb effigies, was built in the 15th century, nearly a hundred years after its keep was built.

The **museum** of local history, which is located in the keep, displays interesting archaeological artifacts, paintings and sculpture.

🏛 Maison d'Artiste de la Grande-Vigne
103 Rue du Quai. **Tel** (02) 96 87 90 80. **Open** mid–May–Sep: daily pm. 🏛
This house was the home of Yvonne Jean-Haffen

The Tour de l'Horloge, offering a wide view over Dinan

(1895–1993), an artist who was a pupil and friend of Mathurin Méheut (see p111). Among the 4,000 works that Jean-Haffen bequeathed to the town are engravings, ceramics and watercolours depicting scenes of Brittany.

Exhibited in rotation, these works illustrate a variety of themes.

Tour de Coëtquen, built by the architect Estienne Le Fur

NORTHERN FINISTÈRE

Two very distinct geographical and historical entities make up northern Finistère. West of the Morlaix river lies the territory of the former diocese of the Léon, whose religious and economical capital was St-Pol. East of Morlaix is a small section of the Trégor, the neighbouring diocese that became part of Finistère after the Revolution.

The Trégor Finistérien, that part of the Trégor annexed to Finistère, is a charming part of Brittany, a patchwork of valleys and sunken lanes. The Léon, by contrast, is a large plateau that in the 1960s was stripped of its trees to maximize intensive agriculture. This is especially true of the Haut-Léon, a prime producer of artichokes and cauliflowers. Its commercial dynamism even led to the creation of Brittany Ferries, founded to export the Léon's prized local produce.

Commercially successful, the Haut-Léon is also deeply religious. Not for nothing is it known as "the land of priests", and it boasts some of Brittany's architectural jewels: the parish closes, built with funds provided by local rural inhabitants who, from the 13th century, had grown rich through the thriving linen cloth trade.

The Bas-Léon, surrounded on three sides by the sea (the Abers, the Mer d'Iroise and the Rade de Brest), has quite a different landscape. Here are wide deserted beaches and narrow secret creeks, wooded estuaries and cliffs topped by lighthouses, banks of dunes and wind-swept promontories. In the extreme west, battered by the Atlantic Ocean, lies Ouessant, the end of the known world in ancient times, and the low-lying islands of the Molène archipelago, which, like the Monts d'Arrée and the magical forest of Huelgoat, form part of the Parc Régional d'Armorique.

Halyards and stays coiled and hung to dry on belaying pins after fishing

◀ Cavalry dating from 1581 to 1588, Passion of Christ in Guimiliau parish in Finistère

Exploring Northern Finistère

The northern part of Finistère, meaning "Land's End", consists of several protected environments. Among these are the Baie de Morlaix, the heathland of the Monts d'Arrée *(see pp146–7)*, the dunes of Keremma, the deeply indented Côte des Abers and the Ouessant archipelago, battered by wind and spray. As the distances between these areas are small, it is easy to explore them while also stopping off to visit the chateaux, manor houses and parish closes that make up the rich architectural heritage of the area, once the diocese of Léon. Alternating between coastal and inland areas, particularly around Landerneau and Landivisiau, visitors will appreciate the many facets of this rugged region, which is bathed in a pearly light.

The church at Lannédern, north of Pleyben

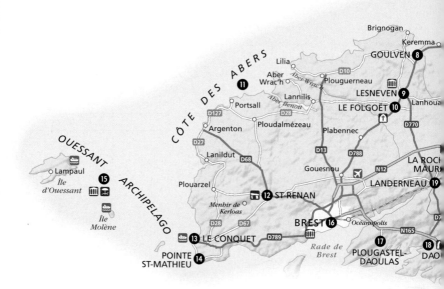

Sights at a Glance

0 kilometres 20

0 miles 10

The small town on the Île de Batz

Getting Around

Morlaix and Brest, the two major towns in northern Finistère, are linked by a motorway, the N12, and by the TGV (high-speed train) service. The TGV journey time between these two towns is 45 minutes. The port of Roscoff, a ferry terminal for services to and from Britain and Ireland, is served by buses and TER trains run by the French state railway company, SNCF. Several coach companies (such as Bihan, CAT, Cars de l'Élorn, Kreisker and Le Roux) provide regular links between the towns of the Léon. Particularly scenic routes are the coast roads D73 (Morlaix to Carantec), D76 (Plouézoc'h to Térénez) and D127 (Portsall to Argenton), as well as those that follow the estuaries of the Côte des Abers and along the banks of the Élorn (D712 and D30) and Queffleuth rivers (D769).

Key

— Major road

— Secondary road

= Minor road

--- Main railway

---- Minor railway

— Regional border

Wooded countryside around St-Rivoal, southeast of Sizun

For keys to symbols see back flap

❶ Street-by-Street: Morlaix

On the border of the Léon to the west and the Trégor to the east, and with the sea to the north and the Monts d'Arrée to the south, Morlaix (*Montroulez* in Breton) was once one of the largest ports on the English Channel. From early times, shipowners, privateers and merchants exploited to the full the town's favourable geographical location. Its focal point were the docks, from which ships bound for Spain were laden with delicate linen cloth woven inland, and those bound for Holland with salt from Guérande, lead from the mines of Huelgoat, leather and wine from the vineyards of Bordeaux. In the 19th century, ships could still sail up the estuary to a point level with Morlaix's town hall. Lined with arcades and warehouses, the quays were as busy as any modern stock exchange.

The Morlaix viaduct, with a pedestrian bridge on the lower of its two levels

★ Place des Otages
The square is lined with 17th-century mansions, such as that at No. 15, built for a member of the Breton parliament, and with charming timber-framed houses, like that at No. 32, shown here. It contains the bookshop *La Nuit Bleu Marine*.

0 metres   100
0 yards   100

Église St-Melaine and Viaduct
The impressive viaduct that bestrides Morlaix's old town was built by the engineer Victor Fenoux in 1861 to carry a stretch of the Paris–Brest railway. The church is dedicated to Melaine (462–530), a priest who was chancellor to Hoel II, a Breton king, and counsellor to Clovis, king of France.

PLACE ÉMILE SOUVESTRE

The town hall was built in 1841.

The old town walls are vestiges of medieval Morlaix.

Rue Ange-de-Guernisac is lined by houses with slate-clad façades.

★ No. 9 Grand'Rue
This was the street where the linen cloth market was once held. The house at No. 9 has a *pondalez*, a staircase that is typical of residences in Morlaix. The building also features windows with sliding shutters and 17th-century painted beams.

Maison de la Duchesse Anne
This is one of the fine town houses built in the 15th and 16th centuries for the nobility of Morlaix and for rich merchants in the linen cloth trade.

Musée de Morlaix
Together with the nearby Maison à Pondalez, this Jacobin convent houses part of the museum's collection. Art exhibitions are held in the gallery space.

Église St-Mathieu
The tower (1548) was once crowned by a dome. Inside the church is a rare "*vierge ouvrante*", a statue of the Virgin and Child that opens to reveal the Holy Trinity.

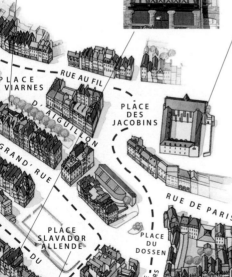

Place Allende was once the market square.

Key

— Suggested route

Exploring Morlaix

Morlaix sadly lost much of its character when, in 1897, its docks were filled in and covered by two squares, the Place des Otages and Place Cornic. Efforts are now being made to make the town more vibrant and to renovate the historic quayside buildings – mansions with dormer windows and houses with *pondalez* (spiral staircases) – that merchants built in a more prosperous age. Pleasure boats are the only vessels that now tie up in the harbour, as, with the closure of the tobacco-processing plant, it is now devoid of the ships that once serviced that industry. The resulting loss of 2,000 jobs has forced Morlaix, the third-largest town in the Finistère, to seek prosperity in other industries.

Stained-glass window in the Église St-Mathieu

Timber-framed and slate-clad houses in Morlaix

Église St-Melaine
Rue Ange-de-Guernisac. **Tel** (02) 98 88 05 65.
Built in the Flamboyant Gothic style by the Beaumanoirs and completed in 1489, St-Melaine is the oldest church in Morlaix. As well as an organ built by Thomas Dallam in 1682, it contains painted wooden statues of saints and has fine 16th-century beams carved with plant motifs, angels, animals, including ermines (emblem of Anne of Brittany) and, amusingly, caricatures of prominent people of the time.

Les Jacobins
Place des Jacobins. **Tel** (02) 98 88 68 88. **Open** Oct–Jun: Tue–Sat; Jul–Sep: daily.
The main collection of the Musée de Morlaix is housed at La Maison à Pondalez, but here, in a former convent founded in the 13th century, is a small collection with several themes: local history, painting inspired

Furniture detail, Musée de Morlaix

by Brittany, and contemporary art. Not all of the collection can be displayed at the same time, so exhibits are regularly changed. Pieces from the permanent collection are also alternated with temporary exhibits.

Église St-Mathieu
East of the Rue de Paris. **Tel** (02) 98 88 05 65.
This church, rebuilt in 1824, is notable for its tower, one of the earliest examples of the Renaissance style in Brittany, and for the curious statue that it contains. Made in about 1390 in a workshop in Westphalia, it depicts the Virgin and Child but opens to reveal the Holy Trinity. It is especially precious since most such statues were destroyed after the Council of Trent (1563): theologians feared that they might give rise to the idea that the Virgin could have engendered the Holy Trinity.

Maison de la Duchesse Anne
33 Rue du Mur. **Tel** (02) 98 88 23 26. **Open** May–Sep: Mon–Sat, Sun pm. **Closed** public holidays.
This house, one of several in the region where Anne of Brittany is reputed to have stayed, consists of three sections, the central part with a monumental chimney piece rising the full height of the building.
The house also has a staircase known as a *pondalez*. This is a spiral staircase that, by means of a walkway, allows access to the rooms in the different parts of the house.

Windows of the Maison de la Duchesse Anne

La Maison à Pondalez
9 Grand'Rue. **Tel** (02) 98 88 68 88. **Open** Oct–Jun: Tue–Sat; Jul–Sep: daily.
The house at No.9 Grand'Rue is another 16th-century residence with a *pondalez* staircase, profusely carved, and a monumental granite fireplace. The windows were designed to allow merchants to display their wares.
The main collection of the Musée de Morlaix is found here (the other is at Les Jacobins). On four levels, the collection details the history and architecture of the town.

Caplan & Co

This café and bookshop, which opened in 1933, is one of the most atmospheric places in Finistère Nord. It is housed in a former grocer's shop overlooking the beach at Poul-Rodou, on the coast road between Locquirec and Guimaëc. Outside, there is a terrace with tables. Inside, where the décor replicates a school classroom, is an excellent selection of books by an international range of authors.

Caplan & Co, one of the region's most famous cafés

Environs

The **Trégor Finistérien**, the small region of heath and woodland between Morlaix and Locquirec, is worth exploring, not least for its archaeological sites and beautiful coastal landscapes. From Morlaix, take the D76 that runs along the estuary to Dourduff-en-Mer.

🗼 Cairn de Barnenez

Presqu'île de Barnenez, Plouézoc'h. **Tel** (02) 98 67 24 73. **Open** Sep–Apr: Tue–Sun; May–Aug: daily. 🗷

This megalithic monument crowns the Presqu'île de Barnenez. Built in about 4,500 BC, it is the largest and oldest cairn in Europe. It contains 11 dolmens, and excavations have uncovered pottery, bones and engraved motifs. From the tip of the peninsula, there is a superb view of the Château du Taureau *(see p126)*, the Île Stérec and the small fishing harbour of Térénez.

🏖 Plages de Plougasnou

The beaches tucked away along the coast between Térénez and St-Jean-du-Doigt are the most beautiful in the Trégor Finistérien. They are at Samson, Guerzit and Port-Blanc (reached via the D46A2) and Primel-Trégastel (via the D46).

Walkers will enjoy the coast path that runs round the Pointe du Diben. The headland bristles with rocks in strange zoomorphic shapes, such as those of a dromedary and a sphinx. The Pointe de Trégastel offers a wide panorama of the English Channel, the Île de Batz and the Île Grande.

St-Jean-du-Doigt

6 km (4 miles) northeast of Morlaix via the D46. 🚌 from Morlaix.

In the late 19th century, the pardon held in this small town (*Sant Yann ar Biz* in Breton) would attract up to 12,000 faithful. It is named after a famous relic, the finger of St John the Baptist, that is kept in the church here.

The relic reputedly has the power to restore sight, and, in the 16th century, Anne of Brittany came to seek a cure for a troublesome left eye. Duly healed, she funded the building of the church, whose spire and three bell-turrets were struck by lightning in 1925. The town also has an elegant fountain decorated with lead statues.

🏛 Musée Rural du Trégor

Le Prajou, Guimaec, 13 km (8 miles) northeast of Morlaix. **Tel** (02) 98 67 64 77. **Open** Jul-Aug: daily; Sep–Jun: (timings vary, phone ahead). 🗷

The museum is housed in a barn on the road running between the small town of Guimaec and the wild coast around Beg an Fry. It contains almost 2,500 traditional tools and implements of the Trégor, including flails, gorse-crushing hammers, combs for carding linen and cream separators.

Fountain in St-Jean-du-Doigt, decorated with lead statues

Locquirec

Road map C1. 19 km (12 miles) northwest of Morlaix on the D786 then the D64. 🚹 1,200. 🚌 🚌 from Morlaix. 🚩 Place du Port; (02) 98 67 40 83. 🛒 Wed am.

It was in this small fishing village on the border between the Trégor and the Côtes d'Armor that the thick, heavy Locquirec slate – with which almost all local buildings are roofed – was once mined. Locquirec (*Lokireg* in Breton) is now a coastal resort, with nine beaches, a large hotel and a coast path that offers a fine view of the bay. The church, with a belfry built by Beaumanoirs in 1634, is as dainty and intimate as the village itself. It has a painted wooden ceiling and a charming statue of Our Lady of Succour. The **Chapelle Notre-Dame-des-Joies**, 5 km (3 miles) further south, has a 16th-century oak chancel decorated with fruits, flowers and chimeras, and a *Virgin and Child*.

Cairn de Barnenez, one of the most remarkable burial mounds in Europe

The beach at the elegant coastal resort of Carantec

❷ Carantec

Road map B1. 🏔 2,800. 🚌 from Morlaix. 🛈 4 Rue Pasteur; (02) 98 67 00 43. 🔄 Thu am. 🏛 Pardon de Notre-Dame-de-Callot (Sun after 15 Aug). 🌐 **tourisme-morlaix.fr**

With the arrival of the first foreign visitors, between the 1870s and the 1900s, the history of Carantec (*Karanteg* in Breton) took a decisive turn. One of these visitors found the location enchanting and, largely thanks to him, a fashionable coastal resort was created. Its smart hotels and elegant villas no longer exist, however.

The magical views here can be enjoyed by following a marked footpath running from Grève Blanche to the pine wood at Penn al Lann. The two-hour walk takes in Porspol beach, a rocky platform known as the Chaise du Curé (Parson's Chair) and another beach, Le Cosmeur. There are also views of the **Île Callot**, with sandy inlets, and the Île Louët, a small island with a lighthouse and a keeper's cottage, as well as the **Château du Taureau**. The castle was built by the inhabitants of Morlaix as a defence against the incursions of English pirates. Strengthened by Vauban, it later became a prison. Guided tours of the château include not just the garrison but also a boat trip.

In Carantec itself, the small **Musée Maritime** contains some vintage sailing boats, including a boat in which 193 British pilots and members of the Résistance crossed the Channel during World War II.

🏠 Château du Taureau
Open Guided tours, which include a boat trip, available from Apr–Sep. **Tel** (02) 98 62 29 73. 🚗 🌐 **chateaudutaureau.com.**

🏝 Île Callot
Accessible from Grève Blanche at low tide. Check with the tourist office.

🏛 Musée Maritime
8 Rue Albert-Louppe. **Tel** (02) 98 67 00 43. **Open** mid-Jun–mid-Sep: Fri–Wed pm. 🚗

❸ St-Pol-de-Léon

Road map B1. 🏔 7,400. 🚉 🛈 Place de l'Évêché; (02) 98 69 05 69. 🔄 Tue. 🌐 free in summer. 🌐 **saintpoldeleon.fr**

This city is the capital of Brittany's artichoke- and cauliflower-growing region. St-Pol (*Kastell Paol* in Breton) is named after Pol-Aurélien, a Welsh evangelist who founded a monastery here in the 6th century. Soon after, it became the see of the diocese of Léon. The clergy's powerful influence here is evident both from the number of religious institutions – monastic

communities and seminaries – and from its religious buildings. The 12th-century **cathedral**, which towers over the market square, is one of the very few churches in Brittany still to have its original ciborium (canopy). This one takes the form of a palm tree, its spreading branches covered in putti, vine leaves and ears of corn. According to an ancient tradition, the ciborium is suspended over the altar. Other notable features are a 16-petal rose window (1431), trompe-l'œil decoration on the organ, built by Robert Dallam, 16th-century choir stalls with carvings of fabulous animals, and reliquaries containing skulls.

The most remarkable building in St-Pol is, however, the **Chapelle Notre-Dame-du-Kreisker**, whose belfry is the tallest in Brittany; the climb up its 170-step spiral staircase is rewarded by a breathtaking view of the bay, the fields forming the Ceinture Dorée (the "golden belt" that is a prime producer of early vegetables), and, below, the old town of St-Pol. From this vantage point there is a bird's-eye view of other jewels of St-Pol's Renaissance architecture, such as the Maison Prébendale (canons' house) on Place du 4-Août-1944, the Hôtel de Keroulas in Rue du Collège, and the Manoir de Kersaliou, on the road to Roscoff, a charming 16th-century manor house.

🏠 Chapelle Notre-Dame-du-Kreisker
Town centre. **Tel** (02) 98 69 05 69. **Open** daily. 🌐 Belfry (summer). 🚗

View of St-Pol-de-Léon from the belfry of Notre-Dame-du-Kreisker

The Story of the Johnnies

When Henri Olivier, an inhabitant of Roscoff, sailed for Plymouth in a ship loaded with onions, he was unwittingly establishing a tradition. Hundreds of agricultural workers, many of whom were very young, followed Olivier's example, going from port to port in Wales, Scotland and England selling strings of onions to housewives, who nicknamed them Johnnies. Until the 1930s, this seasonal migration was an essential opportunity for trade, and many families who lived on the coast of Brittany began to adopt such British habits as drinking tea and playing darts. They also began to speak Breton interspersed with various English words and expressions.

Johnnies with their strings of onions

❹ Roscoff

Road map B1. ⛰️ 3,700. 🚉 🚌 from Morlaix. 🚢 **i** Quai d'Auxerre; (02) 98 61 12 13. 🗓️ Wed am. 🎭 Pardon de Ste-Barbe (mid-Jul); Fête de l'Oignon (mid-Aug). 🌐 roscoff-tourisme.com

From the fish farms at Ste-Barbe to the seaweed boats in the old harbour, most of Roscoff is focused on the sea. The **Église Notre-Dame-de-Kroaz-Baz**, built with funds from merchants and privateers (in 1515), has caravels carved on its exterior walls.

Roscoff (*Rosk o Gozen* in Breton), whose port handles ferry links with Plymouth, has a long, if stormy history with Britain. Not only did Roscovites fight naval battles with the British and suffer their raids, they were also accomplices in smuggling. In the 18th century, contraband tea, brandy and other liquor left Roscoff to be landed in Britain. Shipowners grew prosperous, as the fine houses that they built in Rue Armand-Rousseau, Rue Amiral-Réveillère and Place Lacaze-Duthiers clearly show.

A small museum presents the history of the Johnnies, which was the name given to the Roscoff producers who went to Great Britain to sell their distinctive pink onions.

🏛️ **Maison des Johnnies et de l'Oignon Rose**
48 Rue Brizeau. **Tel** (02) 98 61 25 48. **Open** mid-Jun–mid-Sep: Mon–Fri; mid-Sep–mid-Jun: Mon, Tue, Thu & Fri pm. **Closed** Jan. 🎦 🎥 obligatory.

❺ Île de Batz

Road map B1. ⛰️ 740. 🚢 4 motorboats run by CFTM (02 98 61 78 87), Armein (02 98 61 74 04) and Armor Excursions (02 98 61 79 66) from Roscoff. **i** (02) 98 61 75 70. 🎭 Pardon de Ste-Anne (late Jul).

Separated from Roscoff by a narrow channel, the Îsle de Batz (*Enez Vaz* in Breton) is a small island just 4 km (3 miles) long and 2 km (1 mile) wide. It has about 20 sandy beaches and creeks.

The crossing from Roscoff's old harbour, or from the groyne, takes only 20 minutes, and the island attracts up to 4,000 visitors a day over certain summer weekends. Outside the high season, Batz is a haven of tranquillity, with far fewer visitors than continue to flock to the Île de Bréhat (*see p104*).

Most of the islanders are market gardeners. The seaweed that they spread on their small plots of land helps produce the best fruit and vegetables in the region.

From the landing stage, an alley to the right leads to the

Jardin Exotique Georges-Delaselle, the colonial garden on the Île de Batz

ruined Romanesque Chapelle de Ste-Anne and the **Jardin Exotique George-Delaselle**, in the southeast of the island, created in 1897. Some 1,500 plants from southern Africa, California and New Zealand thrive in the island's gentle microclimate.

🌿 **Jardin Exotique Georges-Delaselle**
Porzan lliz. **Tel** (02) 98 61 75 65. **Open** Apr–Oct: daily. 🎦 🎥

Île de Batz, a small treeless island with sandy beaches, off Roscoff

The 16th-century covered market in Plouescat, a rare sight in Brittany

❻ Plouescat

Road map B1. 14 km (9 miles) west of St-Pol-de-Léon via the D10. 🚗 3,780. 🚍 Brest then change at Lesneven. 🛈 5 Rue des Halles; (02) 98 69 62 18. 🐎 Sat am. 🏇 Horse racing in the Baie du Kernic (Aug). 🌐 **tourisme-plouescat.com**

The two most memorable features of Plouescat (*Ploueskad* in Breton), a major coastal resort and centre of vegetable production, are its beach, the Plage du Pors Meur, and the 16th-century covered market, one of the few remaining in Brittany.

Environs
Further inland are several interesting chateaux. Among them is the **Château de Traonjoly**, an attractive Renaissance manor 4 km (3 miles) northeast of Plouescat. The main building is flanked by wings set at right angles to it. A balustraded terrace closes the

Château de Kerouzéré near Plouescat

fourth side, thus forming the main courtyard. The more austere **Château de Kerouzéré**, 9 km (5 miles) east of Plouescat, is a fortified castle with a machicolated rampart walk and thick granite walls. Built between 1425 and 1458 by Jehan de Kerouzéré, it was twice besieged during the Wars of the Holy League (*see p50*).

The **Château de Maillé**, 3 km (2 miles) south of Plouescat, is different again. Remodelled in about 1560 in the late Renaissance style by the Carman-Goulaine family, it has an elegant pavilion.

The most romantic of all the castles here is the **Château de Kergournadeac'h**, 6 km (4 miles) south of Plouescat, although it is gutted. Built in the 17th century by the Kerc'hoënt and Rosmadec-Molac families, it was destroyed a century later on the orders of its owner, the Marchioness of Granville; it is said that she feared that so beautiful a residence would keep her son away from the royal court.

🏰 **Château de Traonjoly**
Cléder. **Tel** (02) 98 69 43 01 (tourist office).

🏰 **Château de Kerouzéré**
Sibiril. **Tel** (02) 98 29 96 05. 🗓 Jul–Aug: timings vary, phone ahead.

🏰 **Château de Maillé**
Plounévez-Lochrist. **Tel** (02) 98 61 44 68. 🗓 🗓

🏰 **Château de Kergounadeac'h**
5 km (3 miles) south of Plouescat on the D30. 🗓 Jul–Aug: by arrangement with the tourist office in Cléder (see above).

In the countryside around Plouescat are two jewels of religious architecture: the parish close of Notre-Dame de Berven, 5 km (3 miles) northeast of Plouescat, and the Chapelle Notre-Dame-de-Lambader, 9 km (5 miles) to the east of the town.

In the **Église Notre-Dame-de-Berven**, the Virgin is traditionally invoked to help young children learn to walk at an early age. The church has a stone chancel and a wooden rood screen with reliefs showing the four scenes from the Passion of Christ. A superb late 16th-century *Virgin of Jesse* of Flemish or Rhenish inspiration stands in a shuttered niche.

Notre-Dame-de-Lambader has a balustraded belfry with four corner-towers like that of Notre-Dame-du-Kreisker in St-Pol-de-Léon (*see p126*). The Flamboyant Gothic rood screen (1481) is flanked by a spiral staircase and a 16th-century statue of the Virgin that is carried in procession at the Whitsun pardon.

❼ Château de Kerjean

See pp130–31.

❽ Goulven

Road map B1. 23 km (14 miles) west of St-Pol-de-Léon via the D10. 🚗 460. 🛈 Plounéour-Trez; (02) 98 83 45 03.

The 16th-century church in Goulven has an interesting interior. It contains a small altar with reliefs of the six miracles performed by St Goulven, and painted wooden panels depicting the saint with Count Even de Charruel, who fought at the Battle of Thirty (*see p46*). The belfry, built on the model of that of Notre-Dame-du Kreisker in St-Pol-de-Léon (*see p126*), overlooks a wide bay. At low tide the sea retreats 5 km (3 miles), making the bay a favourite spot for sand yachting. It also attracts many different species of birds, including curlew, teal and sandpiper.

The Pontusval lighthouse, near Brignogan

Environs

Keremma, 3 km (2 miles) east of Goulven, is one of the most scenic places on the coast of the Léon. It has a long string of dunes created in 1823 by one Louis Rousseau (1787–1856). With his wife Emma, Rousseau purchased the marshy Plaine de Tréflez. Having installed a dyke and drained the land, he built over 80 farms and villas. This newly created polder (see p77) increased the agricultural land of the parish by a quarter.

Louis Rousseau's descendants, who still come to spend the summer here, have entrusted the dunes to the Conservatoire du Littoral, a conservation body.

The coastal resort of **Brignogan**, 5 km (3 miles) further north, has a beautiful white sandy beach (below the Pontusval lighthouse) and a men marz, 8.5 m (28 ft) high, one of a small number of Christianized menhirs.

❾ Lesneven

Road map B2. 22 km (13.5 miles) north of Brest on the D788. 🚊 6,920. 🚌 Brest or Landerneau. 🅸 Place des 3 Piliers; (02) 98 83 01 47. 🚍 Mon. 🆆 **tourisme-lesneven-cotedeslegendes.fr**

Apart from some old houses – at No. 21 Place du Général-Le-Flô and No. 1 Rue du Comte-Even – the main focus of interest in Lesneven is the **Musée du Léon**, housed in a former Ursuline convent.

The collection traces local history from prehistoric times to the present day. Until the Revolution, the parish was the seat of the seneschalsy (stewardship) of Léon. One exhibit documents the frightful scenes of terror that occurred in the town in 1793, when many local peasants resisted conscription to the revolutionary cause and were massacred by Republican soldiers.

The museum also has a number of costumes of the 1830s on display, including a red silk skirt, an embroidered apron and a gold-embroidered bodice (see pp32–3), a feast-day outfit that would be worn, with a square coiffe, by the women of Kerlouan.

🏛 **Musée du Léon**
Place des 3 Piliers. **Tel** (02) 98 83 01 47. **Open** Apr–Jun & Sep: Mon–Fri; mid-Jul–mid-Aug: daily; Oct–Mar: Mon–Sat. 🖼

❿ Le Folgoët

Road map B2. 20 km (13 miles) north of Brest via the D788. 🚊 3,094. 🚌 Brest. 🎿 Grand Pardon (first weekend in Sep).

The name of this small town – "Fool's Wood" – has its origins in a strange story. There was once a simpleton named Salaün. He lived near a spring on the edge of the wood near Lesneven, and would tirelessly repeat the words "Ave Maria". The villagers nicknamed him fol goad (madman of the woods). One day, in 1358, Salaün was found dead near the spring. Some time later, a lily sprouted on his neglected grave; it bore two words in golden letters: Ave Maria.

The story of this miracle was broadcast throughout the duchy. Jean V, Duke of Brittany, and the duchy's noble families then financed the building of a chapel in Le Folgoët. This is the imposing **Basilique Notre-Dame** (1422–60). One of the most illustrious places of pilgrimage in Brittany, it has a delicate kersanton (granite) rood screen and a small museum.

🏰 **Basilique Notre-Dame**
Tel (02) 98 83 01 47 (tourist office, Lesneven). 🖼 Jul–Aug.

Basilique Notre-Dame, in Folgoët

❼ Château de Kerjean

In 1618, Louis XIII described this stately residence as "one of the most beautiful in the kingdom". It was built between 1566 and 1595 by Louis Barbier, with the fortune that his uncle Hamon, a rich canon of St-Pol-de-Léon, had amassed. It has the characteristics both of a traditional Breton manor and of a French chateau. The architect in charge of the project was clearly familiar with the architectural treatises of the period and also with Renaissance decorative motifs. He remains anonymous, but his style was to influence future buildings in the Léon, including the churches at Berven and Bodilis and the parish close at St-Thégonnec. Ransacked in 1793, Kerjean was sold to the state in 1911. It now contains a fine collection of 17th- and 18th-century furniture of the Léon.

Dormer Windows
The richly decorated dormer windows relieve the plainness of the façades.

Kitchen
This large, 6-m (20-ft) high room has two hearths and a bread oven.

Pediment over the Central Doorways
The doorways of the stable wing are topped by pediments set with urns.

Main entrance

KEY

① **A museum of stonework** is housed in one of the guardrooms.

② **The wooden beams** of the chapel ceiling are decorated with representations of the Four Evangelists and Mary Magdalen.

③ **Surviving walls** of the part of the chateau destroyed by fire in 1755. It contained the armoury.

④ **In the projection room**, a film traces the history of the chateau.

★ **Main Entrance**
Elaborate ornamentation, with caryatids and volutes, crowns the main entrance.

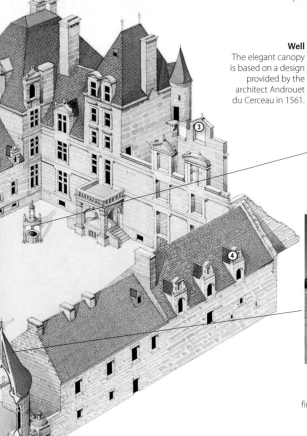

General view of the chateau from the grounds

VISITORS' CHECKLIST

Practical Information
Road map B1. St-Vougay. 32 km (20 miles) west of Morlaix via the N12 then the D30. **Tel** (02) 98 69 93 69. **Open** Mar–Jun & Sep–Oct: Wed–Mon pm; Jul–Aug: daily; Christmas hols & Feb (phone for timings). Theatre and live music: phone for details.

Well
The elegant canopy is based on a design provided by the architect Androuet du Cerceau in 1561.

★ **Chapel**
The chapel has interesting vaulting and contains some fine carved reclining figures. It is located above a room that was used as a guardroom.

Breton Furniture at Kerjean

As well as grain bins and chests that double as seats, Kerjean contains a few pieces of furniture that are typical of the Léon. These are *gwele kloz* (box beds), some of which are decorated with the monograms of Christ and of the Virgin, and *pres lin* (linen presses), in which cloth was kept before it was taken for sale. These presses are valuable items associated with the weaving industry that brought prosperity to the region.

Linen press

Box bed

⓫ Côte des Abers

Three long, fjord-like indentations scar the coastline between Brignogan and Le Conquet. These are known as *abers* – a Celtic word meaning "estuary". They were formed as glaciers began to melt at the end of the Ice Age, 10,000 years ago. As the sea level rose, sea water flowed up the valleys far inland, where it met the fresh water of the streams. These estuaries are very characteristic of this part of Brittany, and they are strikingly different from the coastline itself. There are no gleaming mud flats along the *abers* but piles of rocks and white, sandy dunes where the local inhabitants once spread seaweed out to dry.

Aber Wrac'h, a popular sailing and diving centre

Key

- Suggested route
- Other roads

0 kilometres 5
0 miles 3

⑤ Portsall

It was on the rocks of Portsall that the Liberian oil tanker *Amoco Cadiz* foundered in 1978. The whole area has still not forgotten this ecological disaster. Tragic for wildlife, the oil spill was doubly unfortunate as the stretch of coastline between St-Pabu and Argenton is one of the most beautiful and least developed in the Léon.

St-
⑤
Lampaul-
Ploudalmézeau
Trémazan
D 168
D 127
D 27
Ploudalmézeau
Argenton
Plou
D 27
D 28
D 168
Porspoder
D 68
D 27
D 268
Lanrivoaré
⑥
Aber Ildut
D 28
D 27
St-Renan
Lampaul-
Plouarzel
D 5
Le Conquet
Plouarzel
St-Renan

⑥ Lanildut

The village (*Lannildud* in Breton) is the largest seaweed-processing port in France, handling almost 50 per cent of the national harvest. The coastline is riddled with the ovens in which laminaria, a green seaweed, was once burned to produce soda, from which iodine was in turn extracted.

Mission Pictures

In 1613, Mikael Le Nobletz, a native of Plouguerneau and a zealous missionary, developed an ingenious method of teaching Christian doctrine and backing up the teachings of the Church. On his evangelizing missions, he showed the inhabitants of local coastal parishes pictures of biblical scenes and parables annotated in Breton. These moralizing paintings *(taolennou)* were highly successful. Used until 1950 by missionaries in other countries, they have been translated into 256 languages.

Le Miroir du Monde, by Mikael Le Nobletz

Tips for Drivers

Tour length: 56 km (35 miles).
Stopping-off places: The coast has many crêperies where you can enjoy a pancake and local cider. There is also the Auberge de Vieux Puits in Lampaul-Plouarzel. Alternatively, the oyster farms and bakeries in Lannilis will provide all you need for a picnic on one of the small islands along the abers (but take care not to become marooned by rising tides). For a night stop, there is the Hôtel de la Baie des Anges, 350 Route des Anges, Aber Wrac'h village.

① Lilia

At 82.5 m (270 ft) high, the Île Vierge lighthouse, opposite Lilia, is the tallest lighthouse in Europe. It was built in 1902 to protect shipping from treacherous rocks along a stretch of the coast known as Bro Bagan, "pagan country".

② Plouguerneau

The Écomusée des Goémoniers de Plouguerneau is an open-air museum devoted to the local seaweed-gathering industry. Also of interest is Iliz Koz, where ruins of a church engulfed by sand in the 18th century have been uncovered.

④ Aber Benoît

A footpath runs along the south bank of the *aber*. The walk from the coast to the end of the *aber* takes three to four hours, and reveals every aspect of the estuary.

③ Aber Wrac'h Harbour

This small fishing harbour is now a very popular stopping-place for pleasure boats, and has a diving centre. It is also an ideal base for exploring Aber Wrac'h, the longest and least developed of the three *abers* that indent this stretch of the coast of Brittany.

⓬ St-Renan

Road map: A1. 9 km (6 miles) northwest of Brest via the D5. 🏛 7,900. 🚌 from Brest or Landerneau. 𝒊 Place du Vieux Marché; (02) 98 84 23 78. ⛺ Sat.

Until the early 17th century, St-Renan (*Lokournan* in Breton) was an important town with a court of justice that served 37 parishes, including Brest. The town's few surviving granite or timber-framed houses, the finest of which are around the Église Notre-Dame-de-Liesse and on Place de la Mairie, date from this period. The weekly market held on this square is widely renowned for the local produce sold there.

The history of these markets and of the horse fairs for which St-Renan was also famous is illustrated in a small museum, the **Musée du Patrimoine**. Breton headdresses, furniture, domestic objects and exhibits relating to the rich tin mines of the parish are also displayed.

The **Menhir de Kerloas** stands 4 km (2.5 miles) west of St-Renan. Erected on a crest, it is one of the tallest megaliths in Brittany. Newly married couples who wanted children would come to rub their abdomens against the stone.

🏛 Musée du Patrimoine

16 Rue St-Mathieu. **Tel** (02) 98 32 44 94. **Open** Sep–Jun: Sat am; Jul–Aug: Mon–Fri pm, Sat am. 🅿

Timber-framed houses on Place du Marché in St-Renan

The fishing harbour at Le Conquet, seen from Pointe de Kermorvan

⓭ Le Conquet

Road map: A2. 20 km (12 miles) southwest of Brest via the D789. 🏛 2,400. 🚌 from Brest or Plougonvelin. ⛴ Île Molène & Île d'Ouessant. 𝒊 Parc de Beauséjour; (02) 98 89 11 31. ⛺ Tue am. 🎉 Blessing the sea (mid-Jul).

For many Bretons, the name of this small, busy fishing port is associated with the radio station on Pointe des Renards that, from 1948 to 2000, broadcast shipping forecasts.

Le Conquet (*Konk Leon* in Breton) has few old buildings besides those known as the *maisons anglaises* (English houses), which the English spared when they attacked the port in 1558, and the Chapelle Notre-Dame-de-Bon-Secours, which contains mission pictures invented by Mikeal an Nobletz (*see p133*).

By contrast, the coast between Le Conquet and Lampaul-Plouarzel has some splendid and varied landscapes for walkers. Beyond the Presqu'île de Kermorvan, a peninsula that offers a fine view of the Île Molène and Île d'Ouessant, the long-distance footpath GR34 runs along the dunes of Blancs-Sablons, the beach at Porsmoguer and the cliffs of Le Corsen, 12 km (7.5 miles) to the north. On this rocky headland, the most westerly point in France, stands CROSS, the centre that coordinates rescue operations and monitors maritime traffic in the approaches to Ouessant.

The **Trézien lighthouse**, 2 km (1 mile) northeast, is open to visitors. It is part of the navigation aids (17 lighthouses on land and 13 at sea, 85 lightships and 204 buoys) installed in the 19th century to alert seamen to the hidden dangers of the Mer d'Iroise.

🗼 Phare de Trézien

Trézien en Plouarzel. **Tel** (02) 98 89 69 46. 🕐 Jul–Aug: Mon–Sat pm, Sun am; Jun & Sep: Tue am. 🅿

Lobster pots stacked on the quay at Le Conquet

⓮ Pointe St-Mathieu

Road map: A2. 22 km (14 miles) southwest of Brest via the D789 then the D85. 🚌 from Brest, changing at Plougonvelin. 𝒊 Trez Hir in Plougonvelin, Boulevard de la Mer. **Tel** (02) 98 48 30 18.

The lighthouse on Pointe St-Mathieu, built in 1835, is open to visitors. Its beams project 60 km (37 miles) across the Mer d'Iroise and its many reefs, including those known as Les Vieux-Moines and La Chaussée des Pierres-Noires.

At the foot of the lighthouse are the ruins of a monastery that was probably founded in the 6th century. At nightfall, the Benedictine monks who settled in this windswept abbey in 1656 would light a fire at the top of the church tower in order to guide ships.

⑮ Ouessant Archipelago

Road map: A1. 🗻 1,207.
🚤 Motorboats run by Penn Ar Bed (02 98 80 80 80). Flights from Finist'Air, (02) 98 84 64 87. ℹ️ Place de L'Eglise, Ouessant (02) 98 48 85 83.
W ot-ouessant.fr

Pointe St-Mathieu, where Benedictine monks once settled

Battered by strong westerly winds and lashed by the sea, the seven islands and dozen islets that make up the Ouessant archipelago lie some 20 km (13 miles) off the mainland. Only two of the islands – Ouessant (*Eussa* in Breton*)* and Molène (*Molenez*) are inhabited. Each of these islands preserves its identity and rich natural environment and wildlife.

With heathland lapped by the waves, piles of lichen-covered rocks and an exceptionally varied plant life that thrives in the moist salt air, the fascinating Ouessant archipelago is a world like no other. In 1989 Unesco declared it a World Biosphere Reserve.

Shelduck on the Ile d'Ouessant

Just 1.2 km (0.75 mile) long and 800 m (875 yds) wide, the **Île Molène** can be walked around in half an hour. At first sight, the tiny bare, low-lying island's only interesting feature is a small town of 277 inhabitants huddled behind a breakwater. But Molène deserves a closer look: it is a welcoming place in which to linger. Quirkily, it keeps English time. It offers one great advantage – no cars – and three specialities: lobster, seaweed-smoked sausage and sea rescue.

From the top of the former signal station there is a view of the islands of the archipelago: Beniget, with a population of wild rabbits, and Banneg, Balaneg and Trielen, which were inhabited until the 1950s and which are today classified nature reserves. They are home to a small colony of otters, shelducks and gulls, and 120 species of plants, including the curiously named Sabot du Petit Jésus (Baby Jesus's Slipper) and Cierge de Marie (Mary's Candle). The island's **Semaphore de Molène** houses a museum with interactive displays on the daily life of a watchman.

The largest and highest island in the archipelago, the **Île d'Ouessant** is a wild granite plateau. With its rugged landscapes, the island has been the subject of the most fanciful legends. In ancient times, the Celts considered it to be the final gateway to the Otherworld.

A striking feature of Ouessant is that it is divided into extremely small parcels of land, of which there are about 55,000. The population is widely spread over 92 hamlets and a small main town, Lampaul.

The parish church of St-Pol-Aurélien, in Lampaul, has a spire that was built with funds provided by the British crown. Queen Victoria wished to thank the islanders for their valiant actions after the *Drummond Castle* was shipwrecked off the coast of Ouessant in 1896.

Walkers who do not have time to explore the whole island should make for the northwestern part, starting with a visit to the open-air museum in Le Niou Huella and the Musée des Phares et Balises (*see pp136–7*).

🏛 Sémaphore de Molène
Île Molène. **Tel** (02) 98 07 39 47.
Open Jun & Sep: 9am–6pm daily; Jul & Aug: 10am–7pm daily; call ahead for rest of year.

The Ile d'Ouessant, the largest and highest island in the Ouessant archipelago, seen from Corz

Exploring Ouessant

With its 45km (28 miles) of coastal paths and its breathtakingly beautiful landscape, Ouessant attracts some 120,000 visitors – walkers and city-dwellers in search of fresh air – every year. The island's wildness is accentuated by its location. At the point where the Atlantic Ocean and English Channel meet, Ouessant is ceaselessly washed by waves and salt spray.

The Phare du Stiff, and to the right, a radar station, on Ouessant

Lampaul, 4km (2.5 miles) from the landing stage, is Ouessant's main town. A good place to start out from on an exploration of the island is the hamlet of Niou Huella, where the **Écomusée d'Ouessant** opened in 1968.

This open-air museum has two traditional houses which themselves make a perfect introduction to the island's history and traditions. One of the houses contains pieces of furniture made with *pense an aod* (wood from wrecks washed up on the shore) and painted in blue, white and other bright colours, the remains of the paint used to decorate the hulls of ships. The other house contains a display of tools, costumes, souvenirs of shipwrecks and objects relating to the ritual of the *proëlla*, a small wax candle symbolizing the body of a sailor lost at sea. The **Phare de Créac'h**, which towers over the surrounding heathland, is one of the most powerful lighthouses in the world, with a beam that carries for 80 nautical miles (150 km/93 miles). Since it was inaugurated in 1863, its xenon lamps (which emit two white flashes every 10 seconds) have guided more than 100,000 vessels through one of the busiest and most hazardous shipping lanes – the infamous Ouessant strait linking the Atlantic Ocean and the English Channel.

The **Musée des Phares et Balises**, on the subject of lighthouses and buoys, has

Exhibits in the Musée des Phares et Balises, in the Phare de Créac'h

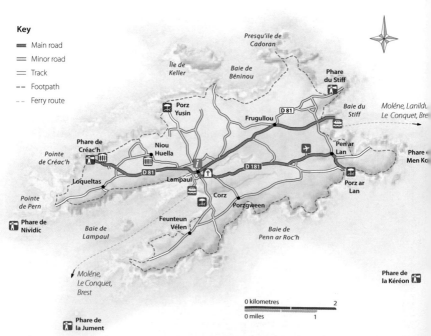

Key

▬ Main road

═ Minor road

═ Track

−− Footpath

-- Ferry route

Presqu'île de Cadoran

Île de Keller

Baie de Béninou

Phare du Stiff

Porz Yusin

Frugullou

Baie du Stiff

Moléne, Lanildu Le Conquet, Bre

Phare de Créac'h

Niou Huella

Pointe de Créac'h

D 81

Pen ar Lan

Phare Men Ko

Lampaul

D 181

Loqueltas

Corz

Porz ar Lan

Pointe de Pern

Porzgween

Phare de Nividic

Baie de Lampaul

Feunteun Vélen

Baie de Penn ar Roc'h

Moléne, Le Conquet, Brest

Phare de la Kéréon

0 kilometres — 2

0 miles — 1

Phare de la Jument

For keys to symbols *see back flap*

Ouessant's Sheep

One of Ouessant's black sheep

Out of the high season, Ouessant's sheep graze freely on the island's salty pastures. Then, on the first Wednesday in February, the day of Porzgwenn's traditional fair, they are collected by their owners. Although sheep-rearing has always been an important activity on Ouessant, the local breed, which is related to the ancient wild sheep of Asia Minor, has almost disappeared from the island. This small, hardy black sheep is being rivalled by the white-fleeced merino.

The Phare du Stiff, built by Vauban in 1695

opened in the lighthouse's former generator room. From the Musée des Phares et Balises, a coast path runs between pebble ridges and low dry-stone walls, leading to the **Pointe de Pern**, the island's most westerly point. Beyond the tip of this spectacular promontory, with rocks eroded into strange and fantastic shapes, rises the Phare de Nividic, bathed in spray.

The island's northern coast has been colonized by sea birds, including herring gulls, common gulls, puffins, pied oystercatchers and kittiwakes. Further east, grey seals can be seen in the narrow inlets of the Presqu'île de Cadoran. They can also sometimes be seen basking in the sun on rocks at Toull Auroz and Beninou.

The path continues towards the **Phare du Stiff**, which

stands on the island's highest point (65 m/213 ft). Built by Vauban in 1695, it is one of the oldest lighthouses in France. From here, in clear conditions, it is possible to see the whole archipelago, the west coast of the Léon and the Île de Sein. Below nestles Stiff harbour, where the *Enez Eussa*, the *Fromveur* and other vessels from the mainland tie up each day.

The **Presqu'île de Pen ar Lan**, southeast of Stiff, is worth a visit primarily for its small sandy inlet, which attracts fewer visitors than Corz, the beach at Lampaul, and for its cromlech, dating from 2,000 BC. This is an elliptical arrangement of menhirs that probably served astronomical purposes.

These are not the only signs of prehistoric habitation on Ouessant. At the foot of the

Colline St-Michel, in Mez Notariou, archaeologists have discovered fragments of pottery and pieces of amphora that show that Ouessant was an early and important centre of trade.

Out at sea opposite Porz ar Lan is the Phare de Kéréon, built in 1907 in extremely difficult conditions. Another lighthouse, the Phare de la Jument, dating from 1904, protects shipping from the dangerous rocks that extend the **Presqu'île de Feunteun Velen**, to the southwest.

Écomusée d'Ouessant
Niou Huella. **Tel** (02) 98 48 86 37.
Open daily (by arrangement only).

Musée des Phares et Balises
Créac'h. **Tel** (02) 98 48 80 70. **Open** Apr–Sep: daily; Oct–Mar: Tue–Sun pm only.

The rocky Pointe du Créac'h, on the southwest side of Ouessant

For hotels and restaurants see pp226–7 and pp238–9

⑯ Brest

The second-largest town in Brittany after Rennes, Brest has always played a leading military role. From the early days of the Roman Empire, legionnaires had seen the advantage of establishing a secure base on the rocky spur here, overlooking a river, the Penfeld, and perfectly protected by a peninsula, the Presqu'île de Crozon. At the instigation of Richelieu, Colbert and Vauban, who throughout the 17th century worked to transform this natural harbour into the kingdom's foremost naval base, life in the city revolved around the naval dockyard. Brest remained a major shipyard until World War II. After 165 bombing raids and 43 days of siege, the conflict reduced Brest to rubble.

French Navy training ships at the start of the "Challenge of Schooners" in Brest

Exploring Brest

A city of rigidly straight streets, regimented residential blocks and lifeless districts, Brest, which was entirely rebuilt after World War II, cannot be described as a prime tourist destination. Yet, visitors who take the trouble to explore it will be rewarded.

Although there are few old buildings here, the town has a pervading and stimulating naval atmosphere. There are dry docks, warships in the naval dockyard, vessels in the roadstead (sheltered anchorage), where there is a viewing platform, and

Rue de Siam, Brest's lively commercial thoroughfare

everywhere the cry of seagulls. Of special interest are the opportunity to experience the undersea world at Océanopolis (see p141) and, every four years, the great international gathering of tall ships in the harbour.

🚇 Rue de Siam

The name of this lively commercial thoroughfare commemorates the arrival in Brest of ambassadors sent by the king of Siam to the court of Louis XIV in 1686.

More prosaically, Rue de Siam is a perfect example of 1950s town planning. It has a very uniform appearance. Here, as in the entire district between the Pont de Recouvrance and the town hall, large four-storey residential buildings are arranged symmetrically on a strictly rectilinear axis. However, the installation, in 1988, of seven black fountains by the Hungarian sculptor Marta Pan has given the Rue de Siam a noticeable lift.

🏛 Église St-Louis

Place St-Louis, Rue de Lyon.
Open daily. ♿

Built between 1953 and 1958 on the site of the original church of St-Louis, which was destroyed in 1944, this place of worship is the largest of all those built in France in the post-war period.

The materials used – yellow stone from Logonna-Daoulas and reinforced concrete – are a clear departure from Breton architectural traditions, and they produce an admirable effect. The bold lines and restrained decoration of the interior are no less impressive.

The church has two notable features: stained-glass windows on the west front, by Paul Bony, and a lectern in the shape of an eagle, one of the very few pieces that were salvaged from the original church.

🚇 Quartier St-Martin

The former outlying district of St-Martin, which became part of Brest in 1861, is one of the few surviving quarters of the old town. It is also one of the most convivial, judging by the cafés and Irish pubs here, which attract many students from the Université de Bretagne Occidentale.

Retired people and idle onlookers also gather here, to stroll in the market or play boules on Place Guérin, between the school and the Église St-Martin (1875), two buildings that survived the wartime bombings.

The Neo-Romanesque-Gothic church in the Quartier St-Martin

La Mer Jaune, by Georges Lacombe, Musée des Beaux-Arts

VISITORS' CHECKLIST

Practical Information
Road map: B2. 156,200.
Place de la Liberté; (02) 98 44 24 96. Mon–Sat in Halles St-Martin. Fête Internationale de la Mer et des Marins (mid-Jul; every four years; next in 2016); Jeudis du Port (Jul–Aug); Festival International du Film Court (Nov); Astropolis electro music festival (late Jul/Aug).
W brestetvous.fr

Transport
Brest-Bretagne, 9 km (5.5 miles) from the town centre.
Place du 19e-R-I.
Place du 19e-R-I.

Musée des Beaux-Arts

24 Rue Traverse. **Tel** (02) 98 00 87 96. **Open** Tue–Sat, Sun pm. **Closed** Public holidays.

The original collection held by this museum was quite literally annihilated by bombing in 1941. However, thanks to the efforts of the curator, the collection has been rebuilt, now consisting of around 300 works of art.

There is a fine collection of Baroque paintings on the first floor, where Guerchin's *Judith and Holophernes* is the centrepiece, and an interesting assemblage of paintings by members of the Pont-Aven School *(see p175)* on the ground floor. Among the most notable works in the collection are *Vue du Port de Brest* by Louis-Nicolas Van Blarenberghe,

a Dutch artist who painted siege and battle scenes for Louis XV. Although the artist took liberties with his depiction of the course of the Penfeld river, this painting is of great documentary value as it shows in minute detail the work carried out by convicts and carpenters in the naval dockyards of Brest in 1774.

Brest City Centre

1. Rue de Siam
2. Église St-Louis
3. Musée des Beaux-Arts
4. Cours Dajot
5. Quartier St-Martin
6. Musée National de la Marine
7. Naval Dockyard
8. Quartier de Recouvrance
9. Musée du Vieux Brest

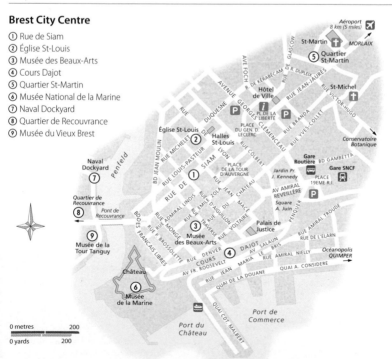

🏛 Cours Dajot

This promenade on the southern part of the town walls was built by convicts in 1769, to a plan by Dajot, a pupil of Vauban. It offers a panoramic view of the commercial port, built in 1860, and of Brest's famous roadstead, which has long given it a strategic and military advantage. Like a huge marine amphitheatre, the roadstead covers 150 sq km (60 sq miles) between the Elorn estuary and the Pointe des Espagnols, with the Île Longue, where there is a nuclear submarine base, in the background.

Of passing interest is the 1900s-style Maison Crosnier, on the corner of Rue Traverse. This is the only house on Cours Dajot that was not destroyed during the war.

Château de Brest, built in the 15th and 16th centuries

🏛 Musée National de la Marine

Château de Brest. **Tel** (02) 98 22 12 39. **Open** Apr–Sep: daily; Oct–Mar: Wed–Mon pm. **Closed** Jan. 🗓 Jul–Aug. 🎫

Built in the 15th and 16th centuries, this great fortress on the Penfeld estuary was a lynchpin in the duchy of Brittany's defences; for many years the English had designs on it. It withstood assaults by the Holy League, the Bonnets Rouges, and many more. Later it was used as barracks and as a prison. The castle now houses the naval prefecture as well as a small naval museum. The keep,

built by Vauban in 1683, contains the oldest exhibits, which include ship models, lanterns, pieces salvaged from wrecks and wooden figure-heads carved in the workshops of the naval dockyard. The modern collections, with navigational instruments, a German mini-submarine, and other exhibits, are displayed in the gatehouse towers.

From the top of the keep there is a fine view of the Quartier de Recouvrance and the Penfeld river.

🏛 Quartier de Recouvrance

The Penfeld river, like a fjord, separates the town centre from the Quartier de Recouvrance. The river is spanned by the Pont de Recouvrance, a vertical-lift bridge built in 1954. Its 525-tonne roadway can be raised 26 m (85 ft) in less than three minutes.

The Quartier de Recouvrance used to be a run-down district, as can be seen from the derelict houses in Rue de St-Malo. Before World War II, it was populated by the families of fishermen and of naval dockyard workers. Though slightly insalubrious, with illegal bars and inebriated sailors, the quarter inspired the writers Mac Orlan and Jean Genet (in *Querelle de Brest*).

The 18th-century Maison de la Fontaine, at No. 18 Rue de l'Église, is one of the oldest houses in Brest. It has a fountain dating from 1761 and a 15th-century medieval granite cross.

Crew hoisting sails in the rigging of a tallship

🏛 Musée du Vieux Brest

Tour Tanguy. **Tel** (02) 98 00 87 93. **Open** Jun–Sep: daily; Oct–May: Wed–Thu & Sat–Sun pm. 🗓 Groups only, by arrangement.

A fuller picture of the Quartier de Recouvrance as it was in the past, with its dives and its shady streets, can be gained through a visit to the Musée du Vieux Brest, in the Tour Tanguy.

Built in the 14th century, the Tour de la Motte-Tanguy was once owned by the powerful Chastel family. In 1964, the tower was converted into a museum devoted to historic Brest.

By means of dioramas, documents and other exhibits, the museum illustrates such major events in the town's history as the naval battle fought by Hervé de Portzmoguer in 1512, the arrival of ambassadors from Siam in 1686, and a visit by Napoleon III in 1858.

The Pont de Recouvrance, a vertical-lift bridge across the Penfeld river

Le Tour du Monde

The regular haunt of the famous yachtsman Olivier de Kersauson, this bar is located above the port authority building. Le Tour du Monde (Round the World) was opened in 1997, the year that Kersauson won the Jules Verne round-the-world yachting trophy in his trimaran *Port-Elec*. The yacht

The bar Le Tour du Monde

is moored near the bar. When he is not at sea, the Admiral, as Kersauson is affectionately known, can often be seen in this wood-panelled bar, which is filled with all manner of souvenirs of his yachting exploits.

Part of the tropical pavilion at Océanopolis

Rope-works on the banks of the Penfeld

🏛 Naval Dockyard

Porte de la Grande-Rivière, Route de la Corniche. **Tel** (02) 98 22 11 78. **Open** Easter, mid-Jun–mid-Sep: daily pm. 🎫 Admission restricted to nationals of countries that are members of EU. Identification compulsory. 🎥 obligatory.

Brest's naval dockyard (Arsenal) was established at the instigation of Cardinal Richelieu. Work began in 1631, and workshops, dry docks and rope-works appeared on the banks of the Penfeld. It was here also that workmen and convicts fitted out ocean-going vessels and provided the labour for further installations. Between 1749 and 1858, 70,000 convicts worked here. Replaced by the penal settlement in Cayenne, French Guiana, the convict centre in Brest closed in 1858.

The guided tour of the naval dockyard takes in the installations that were built at the mouth of the estuary after 1889. They include the naval college, the former submarine base and the quays, where the most

advanced vessels of the French navy are tied up. The reorganization of the French navy and of its dockyards threatens the future of Brest, which is focused on naval defence.

🌿 Conservatoire Botanique

52 Allée du Bot. **Tel** (02) 98 41 88 95. Park: **Open** daily. Greenhouses: **Open** Apr–Oct: Wed, Sat & Sun pm. 🎫 greenhouses. 🎥 for groups, by arrangement.

This, one of eight similar institutes established in France, is the first to have seriously addressed the issue of saving endangered species of plants from extinction.

Specializing in the plants of the Armorican massif and of the former French colonies (including Madagascar, Martinique and Mauritius), the institute has four greenhouses, in each of which different climatactic zones have been re-created.

A Noah's Ark of the plant kingdom, the institute has been able to successfully reintroduce certain species into their original environment. One such is loose-strife, which became extinct in Spain's Balearic Islands in about 1925.

The park, covering 22 ha (54 acres), is laid out in the little valley of the Stangalar, just north of the greenhouses. It is a paradise for both nature-lovers and joggers.

🐟 Océanopolis

Moulin-Blanc Marina. **Tel** (02) 98 34 40 40. **Open** daily. **Closed** Jan–Apr & mid-Sep–Dec: Mon. 🎫 🍴 🎥

A day is hardly long enough to explore Océanopolis. Three pavilions re-create polar, temperate and tropical marine conditions. With a spectacular presentation and state-of-the-art technology, the centre is simultaneously educational, fascinating and entertaining.

Visitors can ride in a glass-sided lift that descends through a pod of sharks, or step into a bathyscaph (submersible vessel) to float through leathery fronds of seaweed. In environments ranging from from ice floes to coral reefs, 1,000 species of sea creatures can be observed in elaborate aquariums with viewing tunnels running through them. There is also a colony of penguins.

The Tour Tanguy, home to the Musée du Vieux Brest

⑰ Plougastel-Daoulas

Road map B2. 🏠 12,000. 🚌 from Brest. 🚏 Place du Calvaire; (02) 98 40 34 98. 🕐 Thu am. 🎭 Fête des Fraises (second Sun in Jun); Pardon de la Fontaine-Blanche (15 Aug).

Lying between the Elorn and Daoulas rivers, the Plougastel peninsula is a world apart. Plougastel-Daoulas (*Plougastell-Daoulaz* in Breton) itself only came under the administration of Brest in 1930.

The character of the area is well illustrated in the **Musée de la Fraise et du Patrimoine**, which focuses on local culture (furniture, ceremonial dress and the tradition of *pain des âmes*, special loaves eaten on All Soul's Day) and on the history of local strawberry-growing, from the time that the first plants were brought back from Chile by Amédée-François Frézier in 1712, to the conquest of the British market in the early years of the 20th century.

In 1602, the inhabitants built an elaborate calvary to thank God for the passing of an epidemic of plague. Similar to that at Guimiliau (*see p144*), it has 180 figures depicting scenes from the life of Christ.

Poster, Musée de la Fraise

🏛 Musée de la Fraise et du Patrimoine

Rue Louis-Nicolle. **Tel** (02) 98 40 21 18. **Open** Feb–May: Wed–Fri, Sun pm; Jun & Sep: Tue–Fri, Sat–Sun pm; Jul–Aug: Mon–Fri, Sat–Sun pm; Oct–Dec: Tue–Fri, Sun pm. 🎥 by arrangement. 🚻 ♿

Abbaye de Daoulas, founded in 1167 by Augustinians

⑱ Daoulas

Road map B2. 🏠 1,866. 🚌 From Brest. 🚏 Landerneau; (02) 98 85 13 09. 🕐 Sun am.

The town of Daoulas (Breton: *Daoulaz*) developed thanks to the linen-weaving and kaolin-extraction industries.

Augustinian canons founded the **abbey** here in 1167. When they left in 1984, the *département* of Finistère bought the buildings and con-verted them into a cultural centre devoted to the world's great civilizations.

Of particular interest are the remains of the cloisters, with 32 arcades and a monolithic fountain, decorated with masks and geometric motifs such as stars, guilloche patterns, wheels and crosses. The monastic tradition of growing medicinal herbs continues in a garden near the cloisters that contains 300 species native to Brittany, Asia, Africa and Oceania. At the far end of the abbey grounds is Notre-Dame-des-Fontaines, a charming oratory of 1550.

🏠 Abbaye de Daoulas

21 Rue de l'Église. **Tel** (02) 98 25 84 39. Abbey **Open** times vary, phone ahead. Gardens **Open** Apr–Jun & Sep–mid-Nov: Tue–Sun pm; Jul–Aug: daily. 🚻 🎥

⑲ Landerneau

Road map B2. 🏠 15,035. 🚏 9 Place Gén. de Gaulle; (02) 98 85 13 09. 🚉 Place François-Mitterrand. 🚌 Quai Barthélemy-Kerros. 🕐 Tue & Fri, am, Sat. 🎭 Festival Kann al Loar (Jul); Festival du Bruit (mid-Aug).

One of the most striking features of Landerneau (*Landerne* in Breton) is the **Pont de Rohan**, built in 1510 and one of the few surviving habitable bridges in Europe. The houses

The historic Pont de Rohan in Landerneau, a bridge all but hidden by the buildings on it

and shops of metalworkers, millers and cloth merchants were built on piles or, like the superb house of the magistrate Gillart (1639), built directly on the riverbed.

Although the Elorn, which flows through the town, now carries hardly any river traffic, Landerneau was for centuries a busy port. All kinds of goods bound for the naval dockyard in Brest, as well as linen cloth, passed through Landerneau.

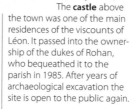

Rood screen figure, La Roche-Maurice

Most of the old houses beside the river date from this age of prosperity (1660–1720). Built in yellow stone from Logonna, they have dormer windows, pepperpot roofs and ornate cornices.

Throughout the summer, the tourist office here organizes an architectural walk through the town.

Of particular interest on the south bank are the old Auberge de Notre-Dame-de-Rumengol, at No. 5 Rue St-Thomas, and the houses at Nos. 11, 13 and 15 Rue Rolland. On the north bank is the Maison de la Sénéchaussée at No. 9 Place du Général-de-Gaulle, with one façade of dressed stone and another clad in slates; the residence of the shipowner Mazurié de Keroualin at No. 26 Quai de Léon; the Ostaleri an Dihuner (Inn of the Alarm Clock) at No. 18 Rue du Chanoine-Kerbrat; and the house of the merchant Arnaud Duthoya, at Nos. 3–5 Rue du Commerce.

⑳ La Roche-Maurice

Road map B2. 4 km (3 miles) northeast of Landerneau via the D712. 🚂 1,740. 🚌 Landerneau. *i* Mairie; (02) 98 20 43 57. 🎭 Pardon de Pont-Christ (15 Aug).

As in many other small towns and villages in the Léon, the **church** here is an architectural gem. The belfry, which has two superimposed bell chambers, is decorated with Gothic spires, gargoyles and Renaissance

lanterns. Inside, the wooden ceiling features angels on a blue background, while the rood screen is striking for its skilled craftsmanship and decoration of fauns and gorgons, apostles and saints. Other notable features are the stained-glass window of the Passion of Christ (1539) by Laurent Sodec, of Quimper, and, above the stoup at the ossuary (1639), an *Ankou* (skeletal figure) with his spear and his motto "Je vous tue tous" ("I kill you all").

The **castle** above the town was one of the main residences of the viscounts of Léon. It passed into the ownership of the dukes of Rohan, who bequeathed it to the parish in 1985. After years of archaeological excavation the site is open to the public again.

㉑ La Martyre

Road map B2. 7 km (4 miles) east of Landerneau via the D35. 🚂 610. *i* Town Hall; (02) 98 25 13 19; tourist office: (02) 98 25 12 94 (Jul–Aug). 🚌 Landerneau.

This fortified close was begun in the 9th century. The house on the left of the entrance was once the look-out post from which the borders of the medieval kingdom, then duchy, of Cornouaille were watched.

The annual fair that was held here would draw crowds of merchants from England, Holland and Touraine, who

came to deal in linen cloth, livestock and horses. As it levied taxes on every transaction that took place, the parish grew rich and could thus afford to commission the best workshops to decorate the close and the church.

Everything about the church, dedicated to St Salomon, is, indeed, remarkable: from the 16th-century door and rampart walk, to the tympanum over the south porch, the beams over the north aisle and the stained-glass window of the Crucifixion. Over the ossuary, two angels hold banners that are inscribed in Breton with words that, loosely translated, read: "Death, judgment, freezing hell. Think on that and fear it. Foolish is he who does not know that he must die."

㉒ Bodilis

Road map B2. 21 km (13 miles) northeast of Landerneau via the D770, the N12 and the D30. 🚂 1,400. *i* Town Hall; (02) 98 68 07 01.

The 16th-century church in Bodilis is another jewel of religious architecture in Haut-Léon. It has a superb Renaissance porch (1585–1601), which the stoneworkers of Kerjean decorated with statues of the 12 apostles. The interior has a painted wooden ceiling, a Baroque high altar and beams richly decorated with scenes of labour and, somewhat unexpectedly, of drunkenness: a man is shown drinking from a barrel while worms infest a skull.

The fortified close of La Martyre, built by Hervé VII of Léon

The church in St-Thégonnec, once one of the richest in Léon

or pathetic attitudes make up an earthy and unusual depiction of the life of Christ.

Inside the church is an organ built by Thomas Dallam, and an altarpiece of St Joseph in the Laval style. The baptismal fonts, dating from 1675, are graced by elegant spiral columns.

㉓ Lampaul-Guimiliau

Road map B2. 3 km (2 miles) west of Guimiliau. ⌖ 2,037. ⌖ Landivisiau. *i* Kerven, Landivisiau; (02) 98 68 33 33.

The parish close at Lampaul (*Lambaol* in Breton) was built in stages, starting with the porch in 1533 and ending with the sacristy in 1679. Masterpieces here are six stunning altarpieces and an *Entombment of Christ* by Antoine Chavagnac, a sculptor to the French Navy in Brest.

㉔ Guimiliau

Road map B2. ⌖ 850. ⌖ Landivisiau. *i* Kerven, Landivisiau; (02) 98 68 33 33.

The calvary in the parish close at Guimiliau (*Gwimilio* in Breton) dates from 1588. Almost 200 figures in amusing

㉕ St-Thégonnec

Road map B2. 13 km (8 miles) south of Morlaix via the D769. ⌖ 2,310. ⌖ Morlaix. *i* Town Hall; (02) 98 79 61 06.

The porch of the **parish close** here is in a triumphal and ostentatious style that perfectly reflects the opulence that St-Thégonnec (*Sant Tegoneg* in Breton) enjoyed during the Renaissance, when it was one of the richest parishes in the Léon.

Although the church was severely damaged by fire in 1988, some 16th- and 17th-century masterpieces survive. Among them is a priest's chair decorated with medallions and putti, and with armrests in the shape of dolphins' heads. There is also a Rosary altarpiece; a shuttered niche with the Tree of Jesse; a pulpit, which was originally gilded; and an organ built by Thomas Dallam.

The ossuary contains a beautiful painted wood *Emtombment of Christ* dating from 1702. Like the triumphal porch, the architecture of the ossuary is exuberant, with bell-turrets, windows and slender columns.

The altarpiece, set at the back of the altar, provides a focal point for prayer. This one depicts St Joseph.

Guimiliau Parish Close

This is a typical parish close, with three essential features: an entrance framed by an arch or a monumental gateway, a calvary with figures depicting biblical scenes, and an ossuary attached to the church.

The cemetery, where members of the small parish community were buried.

Calvaries were built for the elevation of the souls of believers towards God, but they also provide an insight into daily life in the past.

The Entombment of Christ, part of the calvary at Lampaul-Guimiliau

Parish Closes

The phenomenon of Brittany's parish closes *(enclos paroissiaux)*, of which there are almost 70 in Lower Brittany, is closely connected to the rise of the linen industry in the 16th and 17th centuries. The most numerous and elaborate parish closes are those in the Élorn valley. Here, encouraged by evangelizing missions, the religious fervour of the faithful and the generosity of the rich *juloded* (local linen merchants), parishes would virtually rival one another in their efforts to build the finest close. Centred around cemeteries, these remarkable religious complexes consist of a church, an ossuary, a calvary and a triumphal entrance, with Baroque altarpieces and sculptures carved in lacelike detail.

In the ossuary, the bones of the deceased exhumed from the cemetery would be stored. The ossuary was considered a bridge between the living and the dead.

The triumphal entrance was the gateway through which the faithful entered the close. It was intended to prefigure the entry of the righteous into the kingdom of heaven.

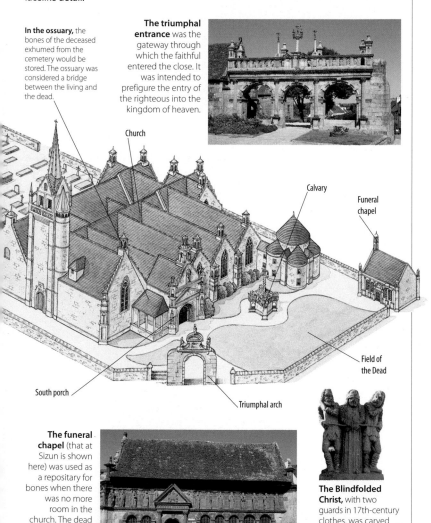

Church

Calvary

Funeral chapel

South porch

Triumphal arch

Field of the Dead

The funeral chapel (that at Sizun is shown here) was used as a repository for bones when there was no more room in the church. The dead were originally buried beneath the floor of the church.

The Blindfolded Christ, with two guards in 17th-century clothes, was carved by Roland Doré. The sculpture is from the calvary at St-Thégonnec.

The Moulin du Chaos, at the start of Huelgoat's impressive rocks

❷ Huelgoat

Road map C2. 🚉 Morlaix. 🏠 1,748.
ℹ️ 18 Place Aristide Briand; (02) 98 99 72 32. 🏪 Thu.

A shining river, a mass of strangely shaped fallen rocks, great moss-covered trees and menhirs make Huelgoat (High Wood) a mysterious and atmospheric place around which popular imagination has woven many legends.

From the Moulin du Chaos, marked footpaths link various places of interest in the area around Huelgoat, which is now part of the Parc Naturel Régional d'Armorique *(see right)*. The river, which from 1750 to 1867 worked the wheels of a lead mine, winds between the Grotte du Diable (Devil's Cave), the first stop on the Chemin de l'Enfer (Path to Hell) of legend, and the famous Roche Tremblante (Shaking Rock), a 100-tonne stone that can be made to rock back and forth simply by applying pressure to it in the right place.

Keen walkers will want to continue to the Mare aux Sangliers (Wild Boars' Pond) and the Camp d'Artus, a Gaulish *oppidum* (fortified settlement), where the fabulous treasure of King Arthur *(see p69)*, is said to lie.

The botanical gardens **Les Arbres du Monde** contain plants and trees from five continents, with over 4,000 different varieties, including 145 species of magnolia and orchards with ancient varieties of fruit trees.

🌳 **Les Arbres du Monde**
55 Rue des Cieux. **Tel** (02) 98 32 43 93. **Open** Apr–Jun & Sep–Oct: Thu–Sun pm; Jul–Aug: Tue–Sun. 🅿️

❷ Tour of the Monts d'Arrée

The hilly area between Léon and Cornouaille can hardly be described as mountainous, as nowhere does it exceed an altitude of 384 m (1,260 ft). Nevertheless, the Monts d'Arrée, covering 60,000 ha (148,000 acres), are the spine of Finistère. With fewer than 40 inhabitants per square kilometre (103 per square mile), it is sparsely populated. It contains spectacular landscapes, with huge areas of heath, hilly crests and peat bogs, level expanses of granite, ubiquitous lichens and rare species of ferns. Rich in legends and tales of sorcery, this arid region becomes even more extraordinary when the marshy Yeun Elez depression is shrouded in mist. Threatened by forest fires, encroaching wasteland and desertification, it is a fragile environment. The Parc Naturel Régional d'Armorique is working to protect its plant life and to ensure that the local economy remains viable.

Key

 Suggested route
 Other roads

④ Sizun
Renowned for its salmon-rich rivers, Sizun is also worth a visit for its church, with a fine organ case by Thomas Dallam and a 17th-century high altar with dramatic décor. The triumphal entrance leads to the ossuary, which is decorated with apostles and contains a small museum of religious art.

③ Maison Cornec
This historic farm just outside the small town of St-Rivoal is a prime example of rural architecture. It also offers an excellent insight into country life in Brittany in the 18th century.

⑤ Les Moulins de Kerhouat
This hamlet, with buildings dating from 1610, has been converted into an open-air museum of the daily life and work of local millers.

⑥ Commana
The parish church here contains two painted wooden altarpieces, one depicting St Anne and the other, of 1682, Christ displaying his wounds.

⑦ Brennilis
A village strongly associated with legends, Brennilis is located near a strange peat bog – the Yeun Elez – which reputedly marks the entrance to Hell. The church has two 16th-century altars.

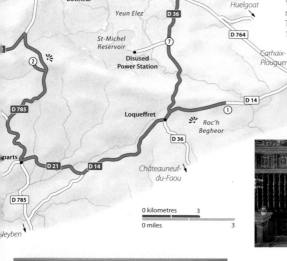

① St-Herbot
The chapel, dedicated to St Herbot, patron saint of livestock, has a chancel and two stone tables on which people placed offerings when requesting his aid.

② Montagne St-Michel
A stony track leads to the summit of this bare mountain, 380 m (1,247 ft) high, from which there is a panoramic view of one of the wildest areas of Brittany.

LES MACARONS
DE PHILOMENE

SOUTHERN FINISTÈRE

This part of Brittany has a wild and rugged coastline but also some very sheltered beaches, and is swept by strong winds while also enjoying a temperate climate. The outstanding cultural heritage of southern Finistère is amply evident in Quimper, the capital city, and during the Festival de Cornouaille that is held here.

Corresponding to the historic kingdom of Cornouaille, southern Finistère is bordered to the north by the Monts d'Arrée and the Presqu'île de Crozon, and to the east by the Montagnes Noires. Like northern Finistère, to the north, and the Morbihan, to the southeast, the region has an indented coastline with impressive promontories, wide bays and sheltered coves.

The Pointe du Van and Pointe du Raz, two promontories at the western extremity of southern Finistère, are among the region's wildest and most beautiful places. It is here, on the edge of the Atlantic, that the four of the largest inshore and deep-sea fishing ports in Brittany – Concarneau, Douarnenez, Le Guilvinec and Camaret – have developed. Inland, southern Finistère is an area of unspoiled countryside, with lush woods and narrow rivers running through deep valleys where unexpectedly splendid chapels, many with splendid altarpieces and calvaries, can be discovered.

It is also in southern Finistère, together with the Morbihan, that the spirit of ancient, mythical, pre-Christian Brittany most tangibly lives on. The Breton spirit is suffused with the otherworldy, with ancient pagan ideas and rituals that have given birth to legends surrounding countless saints. Armorica is also the land of the Knights of the Round Table and the companions of King Arthur, whose legends enliven a part of this region's enthralling and romantic history.

Spectacular beach view at Pointe du Raz with Phare de la Vieille, the lighthouse, at a distance

◀ Old timber-framed buidling in Quimper

Exploring Southern Finistère

The northwestern part of this region is made up of the Parc Naturel Régional d'Armorique, which consists of a small section of the Montagnes Noires and the whole Presqu'île de Crozon, with its long sandy beaches, forests and moors. The Châteaulin basin, in the centre of Finistère Sud, is drained by the Aulne river. Further south, at the confluence of the Steir and the Odet, is the historic city of Quimper, Cornouaille's administrative and cultural capital. The region has two major towns: Douarnenez, in the west, a seafaring town built around an extensive bay, and the fortified town of Concarneau in the south. With a mainly southern orientation, southern Finistère encourages a relaxed way of life. Sheltered coastal resorts, like Morgat, contrast strongly with the rugged Ménez-Hom and the dramatic Pointe du Raz. Never far away are nature reserves that are of particular interest to bird-watchers. The Glénan archipelago, the Île Tristan and Île de Sein each offer superb ports of call for yachtsmen and much that will appeal to divers.

0 kilometres 10

0 miles 10

The wide Plage de Veryach at Camaret

For hotels and restaurants see p227 and pp239–41

Getting Around

From Paris, Quimper can be reached in four hours by TGV (high-speed train). The principal roads linking Quimper and Nantes and Quimper and Rennes are, respectively, the N165 motorway in the south and the N24 going east to Rennes. The N165 heading north leads to Châteaulin and goes onto Brest, and the Presqu'île de Crozon via the D791. Quimper-Cornouaille, the regional airport, is located at Pluguffan, 10 km (6 miles) from Quimper via the D785.

Sights at a Glance

1. Landévennec
2. Crozon
3. Pointe des Espagnols
4. Camaret
5. Pointe de Pen-Hir
6. Morgat
7. Ménez-Hom
8. Châteaulin
9. Pleyben
10. Locronan
11. Douarnenez
12. Réserve du Cap Sizun
13. Pointe du Van
14. Pointe du Raz
15. Île de Sein
16. Audierne
17. Notre-Dame-de-Tronoën
18. Penmarc'h
19. Le Guilvinec
20. Loctudy
21. Manoir de Kérazan
22. Pont-l'Abbé
23. Îles de Glénan
24. *Quimper pp64–71*
25. Bénodet
26. Fouesnant
27. *Concarneau pp172–4*
28. Rosporden
29. Pont-Aven
30. Quimperlé

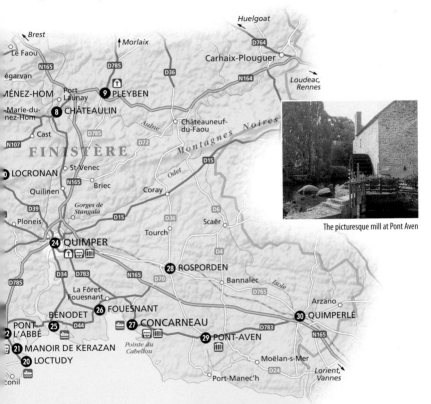

The picturesque mill at Pont Aven

ÎLES DE GLÉNAN
23

The Pointe du Van, where the cliffs are 65 m (210 ft) high

Key

— Major road
— Secondary road
═ Minor road
⋯ Main railway
— Regional border
— Minor railway

For keys to symbols *see back flap*

Ruins of the Abbaye de Landévennec, founded in the 5th century

❶ Landévennec

Road map B2. 18 km (11 miles) south of Crozon via the D791 and the D60. 🏠 370. 🚌 Brest or Quimper, then taxi or bus. 🚕 ⓘ (02) 98 27 78 46 (summer); (02) 98 27 72 65 (winter).

In the fifth century, where Landévennec (*Landevenneg* in Breton) now stands, St Guénolé founded an abbey. Destroyed by the Normans in 913, rebuilt in the 13th century, pillaged by the English in the 16th and dissolved during the Revolution, the abbey remained an important centre of Christianity despite these vicissitudes.

Among the ruins of this fine example of Romanesque architecture are a 16th-century statue of St Guénolé and a tomb that is said to be that of Gradlon, legendary king of Cornouaille. The capitals and the bases of the abbey's columns are well preserved, and they bear Celtic patterns and animal motifs.

The **Musée de l'Ancienne Abbaye** presents the history of this religious centre in the context of Christianity in Brittany. Artifacts, such as manuscripts and statues, that were discovered during archaeological excavations here, are also on display.

The **Corniche de Térénez**, leading towards Le Faou, follows the Aulne estuary and leads to a viewpoint offering a splendid panorama of the meandering river and a view of the French navy's scrapyard.

🏛 **Musée de l'Ancienne Abbaye**
Tel (02) 98 27 35 90. **Open** May & Oct: Sun–Fri pm; Jun–Sep: daily. 🎫 📷

❷ Crozon

Road map B2. 🏠 7,800. 🚌 Brest or Quimper. 🚍 🚏 to Brest (summer only). ⓘ Boulevard de Pralognan-la-Vanoise; (02) 98 27 07 92. 🗓 Tue–Sun.

With its beautiful turquoise lagoons and white sandy creeks, the coast here is a paradise, specially in summers.

According to the Cartulaire de Landévennec, King Gradlon gave a third of the land around Crauthon (the old name of Crozon) and its church to St Guénolé. Because of its strategic location, Crozon (*Kraozon* in Breton) was invaded by Normans in the 10th century, by English allies of the Montforts in the 14th century, by the English again in the 15th and 16th centuries and later by the Spanish. It also suffered bombing during World War II.

Although the **Église St-Pierre** has been damaged by vandals and the ravages of time, it still has its 16th-century porch and a magnificent painted wooden altarpiece of the Ten Thousand Martyrs (*see pp154–5*), also dating from the 16th century.

❸ Pointe des Espagnols

This promontory on the north side of the Presqu'île de Crozon encloses Brest's roadstead (*see p140*) and also offers a view of Île Longue, where there is a nuclear submarine base.

The promontory (Spaniards' Point) is named after a fort that the Spaniards, allies of the Holy League, built in 1594 during their war with Henry IV. It was, however, captured and destroyed by the king's soldiers.

❹ Camaret

Road map A2. 9 km (6 miles) west of Crozon via the D8. 🏠 2,735. 🚌 🚍 ✈ Brest-Guipavas or Quimper-Cornouaille. ⓘ Quai Kléber; (02) 98 27 93 60. 🎉 Pardon de Notre-Dame de Rocamadour (first Sun in Sep). 🗓 third Tue in the month (every Tue eve from Jun–Sep).

Once a sardine port, Camaret (*Kameled* in Breton) turned to the crayfish industry at the beginning of the 20th century. Ships take on cargoes of crayfish from the farms located all along the coast of Brittany. Foreign competition has, however, somewhat curtailed this industry.

The **Tour Vauban**, begun in 1689 and rendered in orange, is the focal point of the

Pointe du Tourlinguet, between Pointe de Pen-Hir and Camaret

One of the beaches at the small coastal resort of Morgat

fortifications that Vauban *(see p173)* built around Camaret. It was these fortifications that made possible the destruction of the Anglo-Dutch fleet when it made an attempted landing here in 1694.

The **Chapelle de Notre-Dame-de-Rocamadour** was built on a shingly spit, the Sillon de Camaret, in the 16th century. It is named for the pilgrims who stopped there on their way to the Église de Notre-Dame in Rocamadour, southwestern France. The top of the belfry was destroyed by a cannon ball fired by the English in 1694. In stormy weather, the church bells are rung to guide seamen.

Environs

Just off the road from Camaret to Pointe du Tourlinguet are the **Alignements de Lagatjar**, 142 menhirs that stand facing the sea. Opposite are the ruins of the Manoir de Coecilian, where St-Pol Roux, a poet and pioneer of Surrealism, lived from 1905.

🏛 **Tour Vauban**
Closed for restoration; check with tourist office. 📷 Jul–Aug: Tue 🅿
🚩 Alignements de Lagatjar D8, towards the Pointe du Tourlinguet.

❺ Pointe de Pen-Hir

Road map A2. 5 km (3 miles) west of Crozon via the D8, or 6 km (4 miles) via the D355.

Rising to a height of 63 m (207 ft), Pointe de Pen-Hir offers one of the most breathtaking panoramas in Brittany. Breaking the waves just below the point is a cluster of rocks, the Tas de Pois (Pile of Peas). On the left is Pointe de Dinan (from which there is a fine view of a rock known as the Château) and on the right Pointe du Tourlinguet and Pointe de St-Mathieu.

The **Musée Memorial de la Bataille de l'Atlantique**, on the road running round Pointe de Pen-Hir, describes the German occupation here, and is a memorial to the Bretons who died in World War II.

Cormorant on Pen-Hir

🏛 **Musée Memorial de la Bataille de l'Atlantique**
Kerbonn, commune of Camaret.
Tel (02) 98 27 92 58. **Open** school hols: daily pm, phone to check times. 🅿

❻ Morgat

Road map A2. 4 km (3 miles) south of Crozon via the D887. 🚂 7,880. 🚌
ℹ Place d'Ys; (02) 98 27 29 49 (Jul–Aug). 🛥 Jul–Aug: first & third Wed in the month. 🎣 Fête du Thon (14 Jul).

The small coastal resort of Morgat (*Morgad* in Breton) developed at the beginning of the 20th century, thanks to the publicity that it gained from its association with the Peugeot family, who built hotels here. The villas in the resort date from this era. Morgat is now administratively part of Crozon, and this has contributed to the latter's development.

Although Morgat has pleasant beaches, today it is the large nature reserves nearby, such as the Marais de l'Aber, that draw visitors. With its population of birds and otters, the Étang de Kerloc'h, covering 110 ha (270 acres) between Camaret and Crozon, is of particular interest to lovers of wildlife. A fascinating feature here are the sea caves carved out of the schist cliffs by the waves.

Environs
The **Maison des Minéraux** in St-Hernot, on the road to Cap de la Chèvre, contains a splendid collection of local minerals and a rare display of fluorescent rocks.

🏛 **Maison des Minéraux**
St-Hernot, Crozon. **Tel** (02) 98 27 19 73. **Open** Jul–Aug: daily; Sep–Jun: Mon–Fri, Sun pm. 🅿 ♿

Cartulaire de Landèvennec

This ninth-century book of gospels demonstrates Landévennec's importance in the production of religious texts. Written in Latin, in Carolingian minuscule – the clear calligraphic style introduced by Charlemagne – it contains more than 300 parchment pages. The Four Evangelists are symbolized by animals. St Mark is associated with the horse (*marc'h* means "horse" in Breton), an animal that, in Armorican tradition, replaces the lion. The two feast days honouring St Guénolé, held on 3 March and 28 April, are mentioned. This rare manuscript was presented to the New York Public Library by an American collector in 1929.

Cartulaire de Landévennec, the oldest manuscript created in Finistère

Crozon: Altarpiece of the Ten Thousand Martyrs

The Église St-Pierre in Crozon *(see p152)* contains an altarpiece that gives a magnificent visual account of the story of the Ten Thousand Martyrs. It tells the story of the 10,000 soldiers of the Theban Legion who, as punishment for their Christian faith, were put to death on Mount Ararat by Emperor Hadrian during his Armenian campaign in the second century. The soldiers' crucifixion and their composure in the face of death were intended to reflect the Passion of Christ. The altarpiece, made in 1602, is certainly the work of several artists, and it is one of many depictions of the theme that were created during the Renaissance. The story also appears in Anne of Brittany's *Book of Hours*.

Acace Garcère and His Troops
The legionnaires, under the command of the orator Acace Garcère, choose death rather than denial of their Christian faith. The Roman soldiers, meanwhile, show their determination as they prepare for war and execute an ostentatious military parade.

10,000 Legionnaires
During the reign of Emperor Hadrian, an army was raised to put down a revolt by the inhabitants of Armenia.

Angel
On the eve of battle, the angel invites the martyrs to embrace their faith.

Confusion of Battle
The future martyrs throw themselves into battle. Despite their entreaties to the gods, fear spreads among the pagan ranks.

KEY

① **Hadrian's soldiers** gather stones to throw at those who profess their faith in Christ, but the stones fly back to hit them.

② **The upper triptych** depicts the martyrs receiving communion.

③ **The Crown of Thorns**, which was suffered by Christ, is inflicted on the martyrs.

④ **The condemned** reassert their faith after they have been led by the angel to the place of their execution.

Pagan Soldiers
Hadrian's pagan troops are depicted kneeling before an idol, while the newly converted Christians are shown turning their backs on it.

Grotesque Figure
Kneeling in front of the martyrs, this figure acts out a parody of the Scourging of Christ.

Way to Mount Ararat
The blood that flows from the martyrs' chests is used for their baptism into the Christian faith. They then make their way up to Mount Ararat.

The Martyrs' Death
The martyrs die on Mount Ararat, at the same hour as Christ died on the Cross.

View from the summit of Ménez-Hom, with the Aulne river below

❼ Ménez-Hom

Road map B2. West of Châteaulin via the D887.

A peak on the western edge of the Montagnes Noires, Ménez-Hom (*Menez-C'hom* in Breton) rises to a height of 330 m (1,083 ft). It overlooks the Baie de Douarnenez and, in clear weather, Pointe du Van and Cap de la Chèvre can be seen from the summit.

Sacred in Celtic lore, the mountain is also the land of the *korrigans* (evil spirits) and of the elves of Armorican popular belief and literature. Wildlife here includes Montagu's harrier and warblers. The marshes of the Aulne estuary at the foot of the mountain are home to herons and ducks, and many species of plants. On 15 August each year, during the Festival du Ménez-Hom, the sound of bombards and Breton bagpipes *(see pp28–9)* fills the air.

The chapel in the hamlet of Ste-Marie-du-Ménez-Hom contains a beautiful altarpiece. There is also a parish close and a 16th-century calvary here. In Trégarvan, about 12 km (8 miles) away, an early 20th-century school has been converted into the **Musée de l'École Rurale en Bretagne**.

🏛 **Musée de l'École Rurale en Bretagne**
Trégarvan. **Tel** (02) 98 26 04 72.
Open phone for timings. 🛇

❽ Châteaulin

Road map B2. 🏘 5,700. 🚉 🚍 Quimper-Cornouaille. **ℹ** Quai Amiral Cosmao; (02) 98 86 02 11 (Apr–Sep). 🍽 Thu. 🎪 Boucles de l'Aulne (late May/early Jun).

The Grand Prix des Boucles de l'Aulne that is held here has made this town the Breton capital of cycle racing. The Aulne is the most salmon-rich river in France, so Châteaulin (*Castellin* in Breton) also attracts large numbers of anglers. Trips along the Aulne on a restored riverboat, the **Notre-Dame-de-Rumengol**, leave from here (Jul–Aug).

A short walk upriver leads to the Chapelle Notre-Dame, on a wooded hill on the left bank of the Aulne. The church has a 15th-century calvary with a depiction of the Last Judgment.

Port-Launay, where the salmon-rich river attracts many anglers

Port-Launay, on a bend in the Aulne 2 km (1 mile) north-east of Châteaulin, was once the town's port. With low houses lining the riverbank, it offers a timeless picture of Brittany.

In the 16th century, when the plague was taking a heavy toll, a chapel dedicated to St Sebastian, patron saint of healing, was built in St-Ségal, 3 km (2 miles) northwest of Port-Launay. The calvary, monumental entrance and altarpiece are among the finest in southern Finistère.

🚤 **Notre-Dame-de-Rumengol**
Châteaulin. **Tel** (02) 98 20 06 58.

❾ Pleyben

Road map B2. 🏘 3,800. **ℹ** Place Charles-de-Gaulle; (02) 98 26 71 05. 🎪 Pardon (1st Sun Aug). 🍽 Sat.

The parish of Pleyben (*Pleiben* in Breton) is mentioned in the 12th-century Cartulaire de Landévennec *(see p153)*. Pleyben – a conflation of "Iben", the name of a Breton saint, and the prefix "ple" *(see pp43)* – was one of the parishes established when immigrants from Britain arrived in the fifth to seventh centuries.

The **parish close** consists of a calvary – one of the finest in Brittany – an ossuary, a monumental entrance and a church. The latter, dedicated to St Germain of Auxerre, has two belfries. The one on the right is a Renaissance tower, and the one on the left a Gothic spire. Between them is a stair turret with pinnacles and an ornate spire. The nave has a 16th-century painted ceiling with beams carved and painted with sacred and secular scenes. The high altar, dating from 1667, is lit by 16th- and 17th-century stained-glass windows.

The 16th-century ossuary has been converted into a museum of the history of Pleyben. The triumphal entrance, or *porz ar maro* (gate of the dead), through which every deceased member of the parish used to be carried, was built in 1725.

The Pleyben Calvary

This gospel in stone, designed for the edification of illiterate worshippers, was constructed in 1555 and completed in 1650 with the addition of sculptures by Julien Ozanne, of Brest. These, carved in *kersanton*, the dark Breton granite, are on the first tier of the east side of the calvary. They depict The Last Supper, The Entry into Jerusalem, and Christ Washing the Feet of his Disciples. In 1738, the calvary was given the monumental appearance that it has today. There are two curious depictions. One, on the northeastern spur, shows the Devil disguised as a monk who tempts Christ. The other, on the western side, is of Peter weeping for his denial of Christ before a cockerel, of which only the feet survive. The scenes are arranged in sequence, starting with The Visitation, in which the angel appears to Mary. The next scene is The Nativity.

The Passion of Christ

The focal point of the parish close, the visual account of the Passion of Christ expresses the fundamental Christian belief in the Death and Resurrection of Christ.

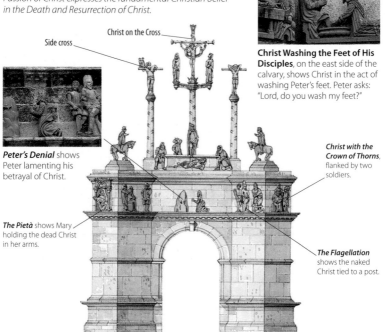

Christ on the Cross

Side cross

Christ Washing the Feet of His Disciples, on the east side of the calvary, shows Christ in the act of washing Peter's feet. Peter asks: "Lord, do you wash my feet?"

Peter's Denial shows Peter lamenting his betrayal of Christ.

Christ with the Crown of Thorns, flanked by two soldiers.

The Pietà shows Mary holding the dead Christ in her arms.

The Flagellation shows the naked Christ tied to a post.

The Last Supper, on the east side of the calvary.

Cardinal Points

The scenes on the four sides of the calvary were intended to be read by the faithful as they processed round it. The scenes of the life of Christ are arranged in sequence from west to east, east representing Golgotha and the Resurrection.

North

West   East

South

The plinth of the Pleyben Calvary, in the shape of a cross.

Granite-built house, typical of buildings in Locronan

⑩ Locronan

Road map B2. 🚹 800. 🚗 Quimper.
🛈 Place de la Mairie; (02) 98 91 70 14.
🏛 Tue. 🎭 Pardon La Petite Troménie
(2nd Sun July). 🎪 Jul–Aug: Tue & Thu
3pm 🔳 **locronan-tourisme.com**

A legend tells that Ronan, an Irish monk, came to Cornouaille. He worked tirelessly to evangelize the area, and it became an important place of pilgrimage. In the 15th century, Locronan (*Lokorn* in Breton) developed thanks to the linen and hemp-weaving industry that provided Europe with sailcloth. Old looms and local costumes are displayed in the **Musée d'Art et d'Histoire**.

The **Église St-Ronan**, built in the 15th century, is connected to the 16th-century **Chapelle du Pénity**. The apse of the church is lit by a large 15th-century stained-glass window of the Passion of Christ, and the pulpit (1707) is carved with medallions with scenes from the life of St Ronan. There is also a rosary altarpiece, dating from the 17th century. The chapel contains a recumbent figure of St Ronan and a magnificent *Descent from the Cross* in painted stone.

The square, in which there is a well, is lined with houses with granite façades. Built in the 17th and 18th centuries, they were the residences of Locronan's wealthy citizens.

The **Chapelle Bonne-Nouvelle**, in Rue Moal, has a small calvary and an attractive fountain.

🏛 **Musée d'Art et d'Histoire**
Tel (02) 98 91 70 14. **Open** Apr–Sep:
daily. 🅿

⬆ **Église St-Ronan and Chapelle du Pénity**
Place de l'Église. **Open** daily.

⬆ **Chapelle Bonne-Nouvelle**
Rue Moal. **Open** Easter–Sep. For other times, phone Mairie (02) 98 51 80 80.

⑪ Douarnenez

Road map B2. 🚹 15,820.
🚗 Quimper. ✈ Quimper-
Cornouaille. 🛈 2 Rue du Dr-Mével;
(02) 98 92 13 35. 🏛 Halles de la
Grande-Place de Tréboul (Mon–Sat,
am); Tréboul harbour (Wed & Sat am).
🎭 Rosmeur harbour, organized by
the tourist office (Apr–Oct).
🔳 **douarnenez-tourisme.com**

Douarnenez was once the largest sardine port in France, and its was here that the first canning factories opened, in 1853. Fishing, in which about 1,000 people are engaged, can no longer support the population of Douarnenez, although the fresh fish auction held here is still one of the largest in Brittany.

Remains of a *garum* factory discovered at Les Plomarc'h, a small fishing village next to Douarnenez, indicate that the site was settled in the Gallo-Roman period. *Garum* was a fish sauce highly prized throughout the Roman world.

Today, it is the cove at Tréboul and the **Le Port Musée**, at Port Rhu, a centre for the preservation of the local seafaring heritage, that together draw visitors to Douarnenez.

Between the quays and the town centre is the 17th-century **Chapelle St-Michel**, which contains a collection of 52 mission pictures created by Michel Le Nobletz (*see p133*). During the summer months, exhibitions are held here.

🏛 **Le Port Musée**
Place de l'Enfer. **Tel** (02) 98 92 65 20.
Open Jul–Aug: daily; Apr–Jun & Sep–
Oct: Tue–Sun. 🅿 🎫

⬆ **Chapelle St-Michel**
Rue du Port-Rhu. **Tel** (02) 98 92 13 35.
Open by arrangement. For exhibitions, phone to check times.

⑫ Réserve du Cap Sizun

Road map A2. 20 km (13 miles) west of Douarnenez via the D7, Chemin de Kérisit. 🛈 64 Rue de Bruyères, Beuzec Capsizun (02) 98 70 55 51. Bretagne Vivante SEPNB: **Tel** (02) 98 70 13 53.

This nature reserve, created in 1959 by Michel-Hervé Julien and Bretagne Vivante SEPNB (Société d'Étude et de Protection de la Nature en Bretagne), covers 25 ha (62 acres) on the north coast of Cap Sizun. It attracts many ornithologists, as, from April to the end of August, sea birds come here to breed in their thousands. Migrating birds are also seen here. There are marked footpaths to help visitors explore, and guided walks are available.

At Pont-Croix, on the right bank of the Goyen river, which runs along the southern part of Cap Sizun, stands **Notre-Dame-de-Roscudon**, founded in the

Port Rhu and the maritime museum in Douarnenez, with vessels tied up at the quayside

Pointe du Van, with Cap Sizun visible in the far distance

13th century. The church's Romanesque vaulting is supported by clustered columns typical of an English-influenced style that became known as the school of Pont-Croix. Le Marquisat, a 16th-century residence, houses the **Musée du Patrimoine**.

The Goyen estuary, with salmon-rich waters and large numbers of birds, offers a walk in an unspoiled environment running for 12 km (8 miles) from Pont-Croix to Audierne.

🏛 Musée du Patrimoine
Tel (02) 98 70 51 86. **Open** Jul–Aug: Tue–Fri & Sat–Mon pm; other times, phone to check. 🐾

⓭ Pointe du Van
Road map A2. 27 km (17 miles) west of Douarnenez via the D7.

With high cliffs and the 17th-century Chapelle St-They perching on rocks, the Pointe du Van is a magnificent sight, and the views of Pointe de Brézellec, Cap de la Chèvre, Pointe St-Mathieu and the rocks known as the Tas de Pois

(Pile of Peas) are superb. To the left is Pointe du Raz, the Phare de la Vieille and, behind it, Île de Sein. A walk along the GR34 long-distance path will reveal several small fishing villages tucked away along the coast here.

⓮ Pointe du Raz
Road map A2. 16 km (10 miles) west of Audierne via the D784. 🚌 Douarnenez, Audierne, Quimper. 🛈 Maison de la Pointe du Raz, Plogoff; (02) 98 70 67 18. 🅿 compulsory; pay and display. 🆆 la-pointe-du-raz.com

Wild and majestic, this spur shaped by the action of waves

rises to height of more than 70 m (230 ft). Pointe du Raz (*Beg ar Raz* in Breton) is extended by a spine of submerged rocks, on the most distant of which stands a lighthouse, the Phare de la Vieille.

In fine weather, the Île de Sein and the Ar Men lighthouse are visible from here. On the north side, the sea has carved potholes known as the Enfer de Plogoff, where the legendary Princesse Dahud would cast her unfortunate lovers. The Raz de Sein, a notorious tide race, is much feared by sailors.

Pointe du Raz is now a conservation area with a network of footpaths. There is also a visitor centre, the Maison de la Pointe du Raz, which has car parks nearby.

Environs
The Baie des Trépassés (Bay of the Dead) has a beautiful beach with caves in the cliffs that can be explored at low tide. According to local legend, the bodies of those who had died at sea would be washed up on this beach by strong currents.

The lighthouse, Phare de la Vieille, seen from Pointe du Raz

Christians processing during the Troménie in Locronan

The Troménie, Tour of Monastery Land

Some 2,500 years ago, Locronan was a centre of Celtic religion unlike any other in Europe. Here, Celtic astronomical points of reference were used to create a *nemeton*, a quadrilateral circuit 12 km (7.5 miles) long punctuated by 12 markers corresponding to the 12 cycles of the lunar calendar. Although Benedictine monks took over this Celtic site to build a priory, the outline of the sacred itinerary survived the imposition of Christianity. The Celtic astronomical markers became the 12 stations of the Christian procession. The word *troménie* is derived from the Breton words *tro* (tour) and *minihy* (monastery land). The oldest-established *troménie* goes back to 1299. The *grande troménie* secures pilgrims' entry into heaven and equals three *petites troménies*.

⓯ Île de Sein

Road map A2 🗺 250. ℹ Mairie; (02)
98 70 90 35. ⛴ Audierne (daily), Brest,
Camaret (summer only). No cars
allowed on the island. 🎭 Pardon de
St-Guénolé (Trinity Sunday, Jun), Pardon
de St-Corentin (first Sun in Aug).

This island, an extension of
Pointe du Raz, is no more than
about 2 km (1 mile) long and
800 m (875 yds) wide, and its
highest point is just 6 m (20 ft)
above sea level. The landscape
here is bare and the small town
consists of a maze of narrow
streets that give welcome
shelter from the wind.

The Île de Sein (*Enez-Sun* in
Breton) has a few megalithic
monuments, including two
menhirs known as Les Causeurs
(The Talkers) and the Nifran
tumulus. The island may have
been a burial place for druids.

The islanders' greatest
moment in history came at
the outbreak of World War II,
when they answered the call
of General de Gaulle.

A track leads to the lighthouse and the Chapelle
St-Corentin. The **Musée Jardin
de l'Espérance** documents
daily life on the island.

Environs
The **Phare d'Ar Men**, 12 km
(7.5 miles) west of the island, was
built on a reef that is permanently
battered by the waves. It took
the islanders 14 years to build.
The unmanned lighthouse
protects shipping negotiating
these dangerous waters.

🏛 **Musée Jardin de l'Espérance**
Quai des Paintolais.
Open Jun–Sep: daily. 📷

Les Causeurs, a pair of menhirs on
the Île de Sein

The lighthouse, Phare Île de Sein, off the western tip of the Île de Sein

⓰ Audierne

Road map A2. 🗺 2,500.
🚗 Quimper-Cornouaille.
🚌 Quimper then by bus. ℹ 8 Rue
Victor-Hugo; (02) 98 70 12 20.
🎭 Pardon (last Sun in Aug). 🛒 Sat.
🌐 **audierne-tourisme.com**

The seafaring town of
Audierne (*Gwaien* in Breton)
still has a busy harbour, with
an inshore fishing industry
specializing in such highly
prized fish as sea bream and
monkfish caught with seine
nets, and sea bass caught on
the line, as well as crayfish. The
boat scrapyard in the Anse de
Locquéran, with old lobster
boats, is a protected historic
site. Also of historic interest
are exhibits in the **Musée
Maritime**. They include
a reconstruction of a fisherman's cottage.

The 17th-century **Église
St-Raymond-Nonnat**, which
overlooks the town, is
decorated with carvings
of ships and has a striking
Baroque belfry.

The **L'Aquashow** on the
outskirts of the town, offers
the opportunity to view
marine life.

Environs
At Primelin, 3 km (2 miles)
west of Audierne on the
D784, is the beautiful **Chapelle
de St-Tugen**, built in 1535.
While the nave and square
tower are both in the
Flamboyant Gothic style, the
transept and apse date from
the Renaissance.

🏛 **Musée Maritime**
Rue Lesné. **Tel** (02) 98 70 27 49.
Open mid-Jun–Sep: daily. 📷

🐟 **L'Aquashow**
Rue du Goyen. **Tel** (02) 98 70 03 03.
Open Apr–Sep: daily; Oct & school
hols Nov–Mar: daily pm. 📷 by
arrangement. ♿ 📷

🏠 **Chapelle de St-Tugen**
Open daily (summer only).

Audierne harbour, with the Église
St-Raymond-Nonnat on the right

⓱ Notre-Dame-de-Tronoën

Road map B3. 9 km (5.5 miles) west
of Pont-l'Abbé, commune of St-Jean-
Trolimon. **Tel** (02) 98 82 00 34.
Open daily. 📷 summer only.

A landscape of bare dunes
surrounds the chapel and
calvary of Tronoën (*Tornoan*
in Breton). The vaulted chapel
has a rose window, and two
doorways frame an open belfry
set with turrets.

The calvary (c. 1450–70) is
the oldest in Brittany, and the
detail of its carvings has been
obliterated by the passage of
time. On the platform are Christ
on the Cross, flanked by the two
thieves. The rectangular base is
decorated by a double frieze
illustrating The Childhood of
Christ and The Passion of Christ.

The sequence of scenes
begins on the east side with
The Annunciation, continuing on
the north side with The Visitation
and The Nativity. The scenes are

carved in granite from Scaër. This stone is prone to becoming covered in lichen, as can be seen in The Last Judgment and The Last Supper (on the south side). The Visitation, The Nativity and The Three Kings bringing their gifts (north side) are carved in tougher *kersanton* (black granite).

The elegant belfry on the church of Notre-Dame-de-Tronoën

General de Gaulle's Call to Arms

The harsh existence that generations of Sénans (inhabitants of the Île de Sein) had endured gave them a fighting spirit. When, on 18 June 1940, General de Gaulle made his appeal by radio from London, calling on all Frenchmen to fight the German invasion, the men of Sein readily left the island to join other volunteers in England. When the Germans reached Sein, the only people left were women and children. In July 1940, the leader of Free France reviewed the first 600 volunteers, 150 of whom were Sénans. "The Île de Sein therefore represents a quarter of France," exclaimed the

General de Gaulle with seamen on the Île de Sein

general. Of the Sénan seamen who answered the call, only 114 returned. In 1946, de Gaulle came to the island to award it the Croix de la Libération.

⑱ Penmarc'h

Road map B3. 12 km (7.5 miles) southwest of Pont-l'Abbé via the D785. ✈ Quimper-Cornouaille. 🚌 🚐 🏛 6,030. 🛈 Place du Maréchal-Davout; (02) 98 58 81 44. 🎪 Pardon de Notre-Dame-de-la-Joie (15 Aug). ⛵ Jun–Sep: Fri am (St-Guénolé harbour) & Wed (Kérity harbour). 🌐 penmarch.fr

The story goes that the cruel Princess Dahud cast a spell on Marc'h, legendary king of Poulmarc'h, as the result of which his head was turned into that of a horse *(penmarc'h)*.

Penmarc'h consists of three parishes: that of Penmarc'h itself, and those of St-Guénolé and Kérity. St-Guénolé is the second-largest port in the Bigouden and the sixth-largest in France. The computerized fish auction that is held there is the most advanced in Europe.

The **Phare d'Eckmühl** is the pride of the town. Built in 1897 with funds provided by the daughter of Général Davout, Prince of Eckmühl, the lighthouse is made of Breton granite known as *kersanton*. Its beams carry for 50 km

(30 miles). The **Musée de la Préhistoire**, near the Plage de Pors-Carn, documents the region's prehistory.

🗼 **Phare d'Eckmühl**
Tel (06) 07 21 37 34. **Open** Apr–Sep *(phone to check, depends on weather conditions).* 🚹

🏛 **Musée de la Préhistoire**
Rue du Musée-Préhistorique.
Tel (02) 98 58 60 35. **Open** Jun–Sep: Mon–Fri & Sun pm. 🎫 🚹

⑲ Le Guilvinec

Road map B3. 10 km (6 miles) south of Pont-l'Abbé via the D785 and D57. 🏛 3,040. ✈ Quimper-Cornouaille. 🚌 🚐 🛈 62 Rue de la Marine; (02) 98 58 29 29. 🎪 Les Estivales Jul–Aug: Fri. ⛵ Tue & Sun (summer). 🌐 leguilvinec.com

This fishing village began to develop in the 19th century when it became Quimper's main supplier of fresh fish. Today, Le Guilvinec is still a large, traditional fishing village. The quayside comes to life in the late afternoon when the boats return. **Haliotika**, a sea-fishing discovery centre, can also be found here, with exciting interactive exhibits.

A seaweed oven at Pointe du Men-Meur bears witness to the importance of seaweed-harvesting in the past. Further on is the **Manoir de Kergoz**, an attractive manor built in the 15th century and now restored. It has a 16th-century dovecote. Footpaths lead to Lesconil, a charming fishing village with white houses.

The harbour at Le Guilvinec, where visitors come for sea fishing

The pleasant little fishing port of Île-Tudy

⑳ Loctudy

Road map B3. 6 km (4 miles) southeast of Pont-l'Abbé via the D2. 🏔 3,700. ✈ Quimper-Cornouaille. 🚐 🚌 **ℹ** Place des Anciens-Combattants; (02) 98 87 53 78. 🎪 Pardon de St-Tudy (Sun after 11 May). 🛒 Tue am.

The well-known coastal resort of Loctudy (*Loktudi* in Breton) is pleasantly located on the Pont-l'Abbé river, with a fine view of Île Garo and Île Chevalier and of Île-Tudy, a peninsula. Loctudy's fishing port is the foremost provider of live crayfish, the famous "demoiselles de Loctudy". When the trawlers return to the harbour, there is a fish auction on the quay, which is always a high point in daily life everywhere in Armorica. Trips out to sea with rods and bait are organized by the tourist office, and visitors can also learn how to fish with nets and lay lobster pots.

The 12th-century Romanesque Église St-Tudy is very well preserved. The capitals are carved with flowers, masks, human figures and animals; the apse has an ambulatory and chapels. Beside the church is the small chapel of Pors-Bihan, and just outside the town, on the road to Pont-l'Abbé, is the pretty Chapelle de Croaziou, with a Celtic cross.

Environs

When, having sailed from Britain, St Tudy reached Brittany, he founded a monastery on what was, in the early 5th century, an island. After the saint's death, the monastery was transferred to Loctudy. **Île-Tudy**, now a peninsula, is a small, pleasant fishing village accessible by boat from Loctudy.

㉑ Manoir de Kérazan

Road map B2. 4 km (2.5 miles) south of Pont-l'Abbé via the D2. **Tel** (02) 98 87 50 10. **Open** Apr–mid-Jun & mid-end Sep: Tue–Sun pm; mid-Jun–mid-Sep: daily. 🎫 groups by arrangement. 🅿 ♿ 🎪 mini-festivals, exhibitions in summer. **W kerazan.fr**

This magnificent country residence, built in the 16th century and restored in the 18th, was bequeathed by Joseph Astor to the Institut de France in 1928. The manor, sturdily built in granite, is set in 5 ha (12 acres) of parkland and was obviously designed for a luxurious and sophisticated lifestyle.

The Astor family devoted themselves to the development of Bigouden culture and to local politics. In 1930, a school of embroidery was opened in the house. Later, at the instigation of his father, a patron of the arts,

Joseph Astor assembled a collection of 16th- to 20th-century paintings and drawings, and a large collection of faience from the former faience factory at Porquier. These now form part of a museum collection which also includes costumes and traditional Breton furniture.

㉒ Pont-l'Abbé

Road map B3. 🏔 8,425. ✈ Quimper-Cornouaille. 🚐 Quimper. 🚌 **ℹ** 11 Place Gambetta; (02) 98 82 37 99. 🎪 Fête des Brodeuses (second Sun in Jul). 🛒 Thu.

The town is named after the monks (*abbés*) of Loctudy who built the first bridge (*pont*) across the river at this spot. The site had already drawn the attention of the Romans, who built a fortified camp here.

Pont-l'Abbé (*Pont-N'-Abad* in Breton) later became the capital of the Bigouden. During the Middle Ages, the lord of Pont-l'Abbé built a castle surmounted by a huge oval tower. During the Wars of the Holy League (*see p50*), the town's barons converted to Protestantism, and the castle was damaged by attacks, especially during the revolt of the Bonnets Rouges (Red Caps). In 1675, this revolt let to the uprising of hundreds of protestors in Lower Brittany. All wore red hats and all demanded the abolition of the *corvée* (unpaid labour for the feudal lord), of taxation on harvest and of the tithe paid to the clergy, and the universal right to hunt. The repression with which the governor of Brittany responded quelled further attempts at protest. While the main part of the castle contains

Granite buildings of the Manoir de Kérazan, built in the 16th century

Église Notre-Dame-des-Carmes, built in 1383, Pont-l'Abbé

the town hall, the keep houses the **Musée Bigouden**. This contains an interesting collection of traditional costumes and headdresses, as well as furniture and other objects.

The **Église Notre-Dame-des-Carmes**, built in 1383 and formerly the chapel of the Carmelite convent, has an outstanding 15th-century stained-glass window. It also contains a beautiful representation of the Virgin, embroidered in coloured silks on a banner made by the Le Minor workshop.

Not far from the quays are the ruins of the church of Lambour, which was destroyed by the Duke of Chaulnes during the Bonnets Rouges uprising. The arches and columns of the church are in the style of the Pont-Croix School *(see pp159)*.

The towpath along the Pont-l'Abbé river makes for a pleasant walk. The river flows into an estuary dotted with small islands, Les Rats, Queffen and Garo, which are inhabited by flocks of birds, including common spoonbill and heron. At Pointe Bodillo is the largest colony of herons in Finistère.

Traditional costume, displayed in the Musée Bigouden

Ⅲ Musée Bigouden
Tel (02) 98 66 00 40. **Open** Jun–Aug: daily; Sep: Tue–Fri, Sat & Sun pm; Oct: Sat & Sun pm; May: Tue–Sun pm.

⬆ Église Notre-Dame-des-Carmes
Place des Carmes. **Open** varies.
🕊 6:30pm Sat; 11am Sun.

㉓ Îles de Glénan

Road map B3. 🛈 Fouesnant; (02) 98 51 18 88. 🚢 from Port-La-Forêt, Beg-Meil, Concarneau and Benodet. Also from Concarneau, Le Corentin (02 98 57 00 58, Jul–Aug) arrange cruises on a replica of a 19th-century lugger.

This archipelago, 12 nautical miles (14 miles) off the mainland and opposite the Baie de La Forêt, consists of eight large islands and a dozen islets. Its white sandy beaches, clear water and plant and animal life make it an exceptionally suitable place for the sailing and deep-sea diving courses that are organized here.

On Penfret, the largest island, is the **Centre Nautique des Glénan**. Established in 1947, the school is world-famous for its training in dinghy and catamaran sailing. Students are housed in an 18th-century fort.

The Île St-Nicolas is the base from which the **Centre International de Plongée** holds its diving courses.

The Île Guiautec is a bird sanctuary. A rare flower – the Glénan narcissus, which was brought by the Phoenicians and which flowers in April – also grows on the island.

⚓ Centre Nautique des Glénan
Office on Place Pierre-Viannay, Concarneau. **Tel** (02) 98 97 14 84.

⚓ Centre International de Plongée Île St Nicolas, Fouesnant. **Tel** (02) 98 50 57 02.

The lighthouse at Penfret, the largest island in Îles de Glénan

Street-by-Street: Quimper

Founded by Gauls on the site of the present Locmaria district, downstream from the present city centre, the town was later named *Aquilonia* (Town of Eagles) by the Romans. For centuries, it was then known as Quimper-Corentin, after Corentine, its first bishop. The city stands at the confluence *(kemper)* of the Steir and the Odet rivers. Rampart walks, projecting towers and walls survive in the old town, although old timber-framed houses now alternate with later mansions and modern architecture. Recent building work has revealed substantial remains of the medieval city.

Musée Departemental Breton
Founded in 1846, the museum is housed in the bishops' palace.

BOULEVARD AMIRAL DE KERGUÉNLEN

ODET

RUE DU FROUT

RUE DU ROI GRADLON

★ **Cathédrale St-Corentin**
Built in the 13th and 14th centuries, on the site of a Roman temple, the cathedral was later sumptuously renovated *(see pp168–9)*.

RUE DE LA MAIRIE

PLACE SAINT-CORENTIN

RUE KÉRÉON

RUE ÉLIE FRÉRON

RUE DU GUÉODET

RUE DES BOUCHERIES

PL. AU BEURRE

RUE DU SALLÉ

René Laënnec
This statue honours the inventor of the stethoscope, who died in 1826.

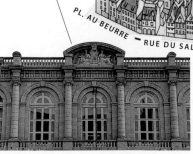

RUE

★ **Musée des Beaux-Arts**
Built in 1872 by the Quimper architect Joseph Bigot, it contains collections of Flemis and Italian paintings.

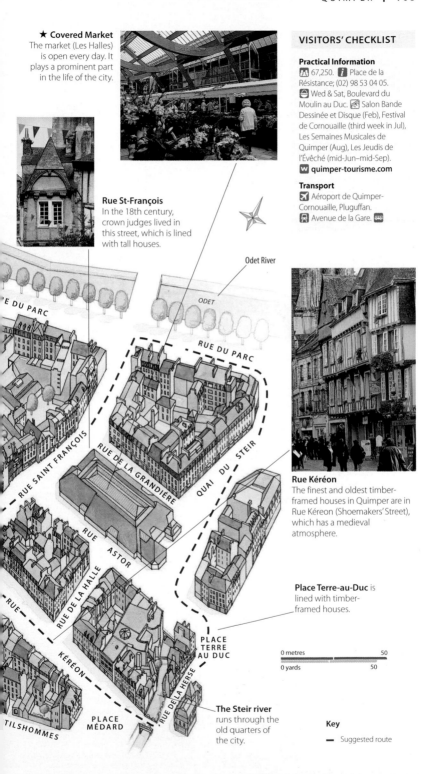

★ **Covered Market**
The market (Les Halles) is open every day. It plays a prominent part in the life of the city.

Rue St-François
In the 18th century, crown judges lived in this street, which is lined with tall houses.

Odet River

E DU PARC

ODET

RUE DU PARC

RUE SAINT FRANÇOIS

RUE DE LA GRANDIERE

QUAI DU STEIR

RUE ASTOR

RUE DE LA HALLE

RUE

KÉRÉON

TILSHOMMES

PLACE MÉDARD

RUE DE LA HERSE

PLACE TERRE AU DUC

Rue Kéréon
The finest and oldest timber-framed houses in Quimper are in Rue Kéréon (Shoemakers' Street), which has a medieval atmosphere.

Place Terre-au-Duc is lined with timber-framed houses.

The Steir river runs through the old quarters of the city.

| 0 metres | | 50 |
| 0 yards | | 50 |

Key

— Suggested route

Exploring Quimper

Listed as a historic town, Quimper (*Kemper* in Breton) has an unusually rich heritage, and great care is being taken to show it to best advantage. The cathedral has been restored and three squares – Place Laënnec, Place St-Corentin and Place Terre-au-Duc – have been totally remodelled. A 12th-century cemetery and 14th-century esplanades have been discovered, and there's a thriving contemporary cultural centre, Le Quartier. Quimper has an illustrious past: it is the birthplace of Fréron (1719–76), Voltaire's famous adversary, of the adventurer René Madec (1736–84), of the poet Max Jacob (1876–1944) and of René Laënnec (1781–1826), inventor of the stethoscope. Yves de Kerguelen, the explorer, is also a native of the Quimper area. The city naturally has a strong Celtic identity, and Celtic culture is celebrated at the Festival de Cornouaille every July. It is also famous for its faience, which has been made here since 1690.

Banner carried in procession during the Grand Pardon

▦ Old Town

The city's finest medieval streets are those opposite the cathedral, and they are faced with decorative ceramic tiles. Half-timbered houses, slate roofs and cobbled streets also fill this old part of the city.

Faces on the Maison des Cariatides

Rue Kéréon (Shoemakers' Street) is lined with corbelled houses. Other street names, such as Place au Beurre (Butter Square) and Rue des Boucheries (Butchers' Street), also echo the trades that were once practised here.

At No.10 **Rue du Sallé** is the Minuellou, a former residence of the Mahaut family. Rue des Boucheries is intersected by Rue du Guéodet, which contains the famous 16th-century **Maison des Cariatides**. The faces carved into the stonework of the house are those of Quimpérois who distinguished themselves in the Wars of the Holy League. Further on, the **Rue des Gentilshommes**, which is lined with mansions, leads down to the banks of the Steir, ending at **Rue de la Herse**, which has a projecting turret.

The right bank of the Steir, on the other side of the Pont Médard, was once the territory of the dukes of Brittany. Half-timbered houses line **Place Terre-au-Duc**. Not far from here is the **Église St-Mathieu**, a church with a particularly fine 16th-century stained-glass window.

The quays along the Odet lead to **Rue St-François** and, further on, there is a business centre and shopping mall. In **Rue du Parc**, which follows the Odet, is the Café de l'Épée, once patronized by writers and artists from Gustave Flaubert to Max Jacob and now a Quimper institution.

On the opposite side of the Odet, footpaths lead to **Mont Frugy** (70 m/230 ft high), which offers a good view over the city centre.

The Du Plessis distillery, in the Quartier d'Ergué-Armel, contains an interesting collection of antique stills.

▥ Musée Départemental Breton d'Art et de Traditions Populaires

1 Rue du Roi-Gradlon. **Tel** (02) 98 95 21 60. **Open** mid-Jun–mid-Sep: daily; mid-Sep–mid-Jun: Tue–Sat, Sun pm. 🖼

The museum is housed in the former bishops' palace on the south side of the cathedral. The palace consists of two wings flanking a Renaissance tower known at the Logis de Rohan, built in the Flamboyant Gothic style in 1507 by Bishop Claude de Rohan and restored in the 19th century. Inside the tower is a spiral staircase, which gives access to all the rooms. The staircase is finished with decorative wood carvings.

The museum, which documents 3,000 years of Breton history, was established by the

Timber-framed houses on Place Terre-au-Duc

For hotels and restaurants see p227 and pp239–41

Société d'Archéologie du Finistère in 1846. Devoted to cultural anthropology, it contains an important collection of folk art.

The ground floor contains prehistoric artifacts (spear points, hand axes, Gaulish stele and weapons), a fine collection of painted wooden religious statues and two recumbent figures of knights.

The first and second floors of the museum contain magnificent displays of traditional costumes, 17th- to 19th-century furniture, including chests, box beds and wardrobes, and everyday objects, including an unusual folding spoon.

On the third floor is a collection of 300 pieces of Quimper faience (see p170) and stoneware dating from the 17th to the 20th centuries. Medieval and modern religious art is also exhibited. The tour of the museum ends in a room devoted to temporary exhibitions.

Le Génie à la Guirlande, by Charles Filiger, Musée des Beaux-Arts

🏛 Musée des Beaux-Arts
40 Place St-Corentin. **Tel** (02) 98 95 45 20. **Open** Jul–Aug: daily; Sep–Oct & Apr–Jun: Wed–Mon; Nov–Mar: Wed–Sat, Sun pm–Mon. **Closed** public holidays. 🖼

The gallery was built by the architect Joseph Bigot to house the collection that Jean-Marie Silguy bequeathed to the city. The gallery contains Flemish, Italian and French painting, including works by Sérusier, Denis and Lacombe, members of the Pont-Aven School (see p175).

One room is devoted to the life and work of the poet and painter Max Jacob, a native of Quimper, and that of his friend Jean Moulin. Watercolours and drawings, as well as portraits of Jacob's artist friends, including Cocteau and Picasso, are displayed. Also shown are major works by Rubens, Fragonard and Corot, and 20th-century paintings (by Delaunay and Tal Coat), as well as the work of Breton painters, such as Guillou, Boudin and Noël. There are also some splendid prints and drawings, especially by Charles Filiger.

Quimper City Centre

① Cathédrale St-Corentin
② Hôtel de Ville
③ Musée Départemental Breton d'Art et de Traditions Populaires
④ Faïencerie HB-Henriot
⑤ Musée de la Faïence
⑥ Église St-Mathieu
⑦ Musée des Beaux-Arts

Key

🔲 See pp164–5

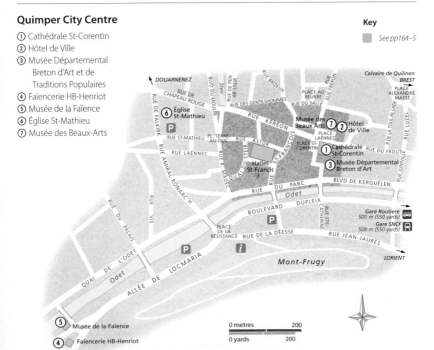

🏛 Musée de la Faïence
14 Rue Jean-Baptiste-Bousquet.
Tel (02) 98 90 12 72. **Open** Apr–Sep:
Mon–Sat. 🖼

The museum is laid out in the Maison Porquier, a former faience factory in the heart of the Locmaria district, where the 18th-century kilns are also located. Recent building work in this district is in keeping with the character of the area.

The museum highlights the elements necessary for making pottery, namely water, clay and fire. The natural occurrence of clay and water in the vicinity is the reason why Quimper became a prime centre of pottery manufacture.

Odetta vase with hydrangea motif

There is also a display of Quimper pottery, with work by Alfred Beau, and pieces by major throwers and painters. The creation of the mark Odetta HB Quimper in 1922 and the beginnings of studio pottery are also documented.

Faïencerie HB-Henriot
16 Rue Haute. **Tel** (02) 98 53 04 05.
Open Jul–Aug: Mon–Sat; Apr–Jun &
Sep: Tue, Thu, Fri pm. 🎥 obligatory. 🖼

In 1984, two Americans, Paul and Sarah Janssens, acquired the HB-Henriot faience factory. Continuing Quimper's faience-making tradition, the factory is the only one still to produce pieces with freehand decoration.

Environs
The 16th-century **Calvaire de Quilinen**, in open countryside between Quimper and Châteaulin, is worth a visit. About 1 km (0.5 mile) further on is the Gothic **Chapelle de St-Venec**, dedicated to the brother of St Guénolé, which has a fountain framed by slender twisted columns. The church at **Cast**, 8 km (5 miles) south of Châteaulin, is known for a 16th-century sculpture called *St Hubert's Hunt*. The belvedere at **Griffonez**, on a bend of the Odet 7 km (4 miles) north of Quimper, offers a view of the **Gorges de Stangala**.

Cathédrale St-Corentin

Impressed by the religious faith of Corentine, whom he met on Ménez-Hom, so the legend goes, King Gradlon invited the hermit to become Bishop of Quimper and gave him land on which to build a cathedral. History records that in 1239 Bishop Rainaud decided to start building the choir of his projected cathedral. The light and airy building that resulted was achieved by means of new construction techniques: ribbed vaulting supported by flying buttresses. The choir was built out of line with the nave to accommodate an older chapel containing the tomb of Alain Canhiart, who repelled Norman invasions in 913.

★ **Stained-Glass Windows**
The great vertical spaces of the nave, the choir and the transept are lit by superb stained-glass windows made in a local workshop in the 15th century.

KEY

① **Small chapel**

② **The old high altar** beneath a canopy decorated with seraphim, was shown at the Exposition Universelle in Paris in 1867.

③ **Spires**, in the Pont-Croix style, were added in 1854.

④ **Twin towers**, 76 m (250 ft) high, are pierced by double openings.

⑤ **Bell turret on the tower**

⑥ **St-Guénolé and St-Ronan Window**, dating from the 19th century, depicts the two saints, one the founder of the Abbaye de Landévennec and the other the hermit of Locronan.

⑦ **West door**

★ Romanesque Nave
Rebuilt in the 15th century, the Romanesque nave and transept are lit by ten windows in the Flamboyant Gothic style. The tombs of bishops of Quimper laid out here and in the transept are covered by recumbent figures of the deceased.

Portal
Seven carved archivolts frame a rose window above which runs a balustrade. Between the two square galleried towers is a statue of King Gradlon.

Pulpit
Of painted and gilded wood, the Baroque pulpit was made in 1679 by Olivier Daniel, of Quimper. It is decorated with medallions showing scenes from the life of St Corentine.

The apse of the cathedral and the gardens of the former bishop's residence

Quimper Faience

The history of Quimper faience began in 1690, when Jean-Baptiste Bousquet settled in the Locmaria district of the town. He came from Moustiers, in Provence, but competition and the lack of wood to fire the kilns had forced him to seek his fortune elsewhere. In Cornouaille, forests were more plentiful and royal permission to cut firewood easier to obtain. Clay in the area was also abundant, and the Odet river provided a convenient means of transport. Bousquet's Manufacture de Pipes et Fayences soon prospered, and, thanks to his granddaughter's marriage, he benefited from Italian influence brought by a potter from Nevers, a leading centre of faience manufacture. He was then joined by a manufacturer from Rouen, another prestigious centre of faience production. In the 19th century, Alfred Beau, a photographer and amateur painter from Morlaix, created a new style, based on colourful scenes of daily life.

History of Faience

Faience was first made in southern France and in Italy. Faience made in Nevers, in central France, features scenes of daily life and shows a predominant use of yellow. Faience made in Rouen, a major and distinctive centre of production, is remarkably colourful and displays a variety of elaborate motifs, including flowers, trees, birds and cornucopiae. In the 19th century, faience production was dominated by the influence of Alfred Beau and by the distinctive Quimper style, with scenes of daily life depicted in bright colours by the "single stroke" technique, by which shape was defined and colour applied by a single touch of the brush.

View of the Odet at Quimper, overglaze decoration by Alfred Beau, late 19th century

Plate in the Nevers and Moustiers style (1773).

"Single stroke" decoration (early 19th century).

New style Porquier-Beau (late 19th century).

Vase with Odetta design (20th century).

Decoration

After being removed from the mould and dried, the piece of faience was fired in the kiln and glazed. It was then passed to the decorators. Each design was reproduced on paper, its outline pierced with holes. The paper was applied to the glaze and the outlines transferred with charcoal. The design was then filled in with a fine brush and the piece re-fired.

Piece by Berthe Savigny, a mid-20th century modeller.

Statue of Quillivic (mid-20th century)

Potting

There are several ways of modelling clay. While circular pieces are shaped on the wheel, more complex pieces are press-moulded. To make highly complex pieces, liquid clay is poured into moulds.

The potter throws a piece on the wheel.

The decorator adds the finishing touches.

Vase by Louis Garin (mid-20th century).

Dish with contemporary decoration.

㉕ Bénodet

Road map B3 ㊂ 2,750. ㊐
㊑ Quimper-Cornouaille. ℹ 29 Avenue de la Mer; (02) 98 57 00 14. ㊗ Place du Meneyer, Mon am.

On the border between the Bigouden and the Fouesnant area, Bénodet (*Benoded* in Breton) is a well-known coastal resort on the Odet estuary. Comfortable residences, manor houses and chateaux line the river. The chapel in Le Perguet, just east of Bénodet, was once the parish church. It was rebuilt in the 12th century and has a Romanesque interior and a 15th-century porch.

Housed in the tourist office is the **Musée du Bord de Mer**, a small museum devoted to yachting in the Odet Estuary.

Penfoul harbour, where boat races and regattas are held, is very lively. Cruises and trips out to sea are offered here. At Le Letty, just south of Bénodet and opposite the Îles de Glénan, is a lagoon known as the **Mer Blanche**, which attracts numerous birds.

🏛 Musée de Bord de Mer
Maison du tourisme, Avenue de la Mer. **Tel** (02) 98 57 00 14. **Open** Jul–Aug: daily; Sep–Jun: Thu–Mon. ㊟

🚤 Vedettes de l'Odet
Motorboats. **Tel** (02) 98 57 00 58.

The Mer Blanche at Bénodet, a lagoon attracting many birds

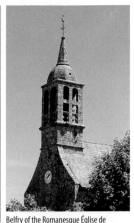

Belfry of the Romanesque Église de St-Pierre, in Fouesnant

㉖ Fouesnant

Road map B3 ㊂ 8,460. ㊐
㊑ Quimper-Cornouaille. ℹ 4 Espace Kernévéleck; (02) 98 51 18 88. ㊗ Wed am in Beg-Meil (summer only); Fri am in Fouesnant, Sun am & Tue eve in La Forêt-Fouesnant (summer only).
🌐 tourisme-fouesnant.fr

At an altitude of 60 m (300 ft) above sea level, Fouesnant (*Fouenant* in Breton) looks across the Baie de La Forêt to the Îles de Glénan. The town is in the centre of an area of lush and fertile valleys. Butter biscuits and the best cider in Brittany have largely made the reputation of the area.

At the Fête des Pommiers (Cider Festival), which takes place during the third week of July, the women wear traditional costumes and headdresses with large back-folded wings, waffle collar and lace wimple.

The Romanesque **Église de St-Pierre**, which was restored in the 18th century, has a pitched roof. Inside, tall semicircular arches rest on capitals carved with acanthus leaves, stars and human figures. The calvary dates from the 18th century, and the war memorial is by the sculptor René Quillivic.

Cap-Coz, on the eastern side of the Anse de Penfoulic at Fouesnant, is a pleasant place for a walk along the coast. From there it is posible to reach the resort of Beg-Meil.

For hotels and restaurants see p227 and pp239–41

㉗ Street-by-Street: Concarneau

The walled town *(ville close)*, Concarneau's ancient centre, is set on an islet in the Moros estuary that is just 350 m (380 yds) wide and 100 m (110 yds) long. With narrow paved streets and picturesque houses, the islet is very popular with visitors. It is accessible via two bridges leading to a postern bearing the royal coat of arms. The outer defences here, consisting of a triangular courtyard surrounded by high walls and flanked by two towers, made the town impregnable. Visitors enter this town of medieval streets by crossing an inner moat. At the western end of Rue Vauban, with old, crooked houses, is the Maison du Gouverneur, one of the oldest houses in the *ville close*.

The walled town, Concarneau's historic nucleus, seen from the fishing harbour

★ Logis du Major
Beyond the triangular courtyard, which is defended by the Tour du Major and Tour du Gouverneur at two of its corners, is the Logis du Major, built in 1730.

Musée de la Pêche

RUE MILITAIRE

RUE VAUBAN

RUE VAUBAN

RUE VAUBAN

RUE THÉOPHILE LOUARN

Maison du Gouverneur

Postern

Causeway

★ Belfry
Fronting the towers, and set at the third corner of the triangle, the belfry was once a watchtower.

Tour de la Fortune
The tower commands a magnificent view of the yachting harbour.

★ **Ramparts**
Beyond the two small bridges at the entrance, a stairway on the left leads to the ramparts. The wall walk gives an impressive view of the *ville close*.

PORTE AU VIN

QUAI DE LA

RUE SAINT GUÉNOLÉ

PLACE
NT-GUÉNOLÉ

RUE

DE L'ÉGLISE

QUAI DU PASSAGE

PLACE
DU PETIT
CHÂTEAU

Powder
magazine

The Amphitheatre,
facing into the ramparts, is a venue for summer shows.

0 metres	50
0 yards	50

Key

— Suggested route

Porte du Passage
This gateway leads to the embarkation point for the ferry across the Moros.

Façade of the former hospital
Not far from the amphi-theatre, is a fine building that was once a church, then later a hospital. The façade is in the late Gothic style.

Vauban

Sébastien Le Prestre de Vauban (1633–1707), Marshal of France and superintendent of fortifications, is France's most famous military builder. Fascinated by military techniques, he also wrote on the art of warfare and on politics. Brittany's strategic location and new methods of warfare that were developing at the time led Vauban to remodel military defences on Belle-Île and at Concarneau, Port-Louis, Brest and St-Malo, and to build fortifications at Hoëdic and Houat and the Tour Dorée in Camaret.

Sébastien Le Prestre
de Vauban

Exploring Concarneau

The "Blue Town", as it is known, after the blue fishing nets that were used in the early 20th century, has an important historic heritage. The islet of Le Conq was inhabited from the 10th century by monks from Landévennec, and the earliest fortifications date from the 13th century. By the 14th century, the island settlement had become the fourth-largest fortified town in Brittany. Briefly occupied by the English, the town returned to the duchy of Brittany in 1373, then, with the marriage of Anne of Brittany and Charles VIII, king of France, in 1491, it became a royal town. Vauban reinforced its defences in the 18th century. The first fish cannery opened in 1851, and 50 years later there were about 30 canning factories in Concarneau. The disappearance of sardine stocks led to hardship from 1905, but the Fête des Filets Bleus helped to raise funds for families in difficulties. Today, the sixth-largest fishing port in France, Concarneau produces 10,000 tonnes of fresh fish a year.

Château de Kériolet, in a recreated Flamboyant Gothic style

Concarneau's attractive walled town, with the Îles de Glénan beyond

🏛 Musée de la Pêche

4 Rue Vauban. **Tel** (02) 98 97 10 20. **Open** Feb–mid-Nov & Christmas hols: daily. 🅿

With dioramas and models complementing the displays of artifacts, the Museum of Fishing traces the development of Concarneau and its seafaring activities from its beginnings to the present day. Fishing methods and the town's maritime heritage are the main focus here. There is also an aquarium containing species of fish caught in the Atlantic, and, against the ramparts, an open-air maritime museum with docks where a trawler, the *Hémérica*, and a tuna boat are open to visitors.

Old-style tin of Breton sardines

⚓ Fishing Harbour

Guided tours to auctions, trawlers and canning factories **Tel** (02) 98 50 55 18.

Trawlers, tuna boats and sardine boats are tied up along the **Quai d'Aiguillon**. Refrigerator ships that fish in tropical waters berth along the **Quai Est**.

🐟 Marinarium

Place de la Croix. **Tel** (02) 98 50 81 64. **Open** Feb–Mar & Oct–Dec: daily pm; Apr–Sep: daily. **Closed** Jan. 🅿

The Marinarium du Collège de France, created in 1859, was one of the first maritime research stations in Europe. The flora and fauna of Brittany's coasts can be seen in ten aquariums and seawater tanks. The use of audiovisual facilities, the opportunity to view certain species under the microscope, and guided tours along the coastline make for a comprehensive understanding of marine and coastal life.

🏯 Château de Kériolet

Beuzec-Conq, 2 km (1.5 miles) north of Concarneau. **Tel** (02) 98 97 36 50. **Open** Jun–Sep: Sun–Fri, Sat am. 🅿 groups by arrangement. 🅿

Built in the 13th century by the architect Joseph Bigot, of Quimper, the chateau was much remodelled in the 19th century in the Flamboyant Gothic style. Among its guests was Princess Youssoupova, aunt of the last Russian tzar, Nicolas Romanov.

The chateau, surrounded by a lovely garden, is now used as a venue for artistic events.

🌊 Pointe du Cabellou

Road map B3. 3 km (2 miles) south of Concarneau via the D783.

Fine views of Concarneau and the bay can be seen from this charming promontory just a short car ride from the town. A chic residential quarter of villas and gardens, shaded by pine trees, it has a coastal footpath leading to sheltered sandy coves with quiet beaches. A 17th-century fort with a stone roof stands at the tip of the promontory. The path continues to the Minaouët river, where there is a 16th-century tidal mill.

㉘ Rosporden

Road map B3. 10 km (6 miles) north of Concarneau via the D70. ⚏ 6,430. ✈ Quimper. 🚌 Quimperlé. 🛈 8 Rue Earnest Prévost; (02) 98 59 27 26.

In the midst of lush country-side dotted with picturesque chapels, Rosporden stands on the edge of a pond formed by the Aven river. The **Église Notre-Dame**, built in the 14th century and restored in the 17th, has a fine belfry. Inside are a notable altarpiece and several interesting statues.

The many footpaths here, and the disused Rosporden-Scaër railway line allows walkers and cyclists to explore.

㉙ Pont-Aven

Road map B3. ⚏ 3,000. ✈ Quimper. 🚌 Quimperlé. 🛈 5 Place de l'Hôtel-de-Ville; (02) 98 06 04 70. 🎉 La Fête des Fleurs d'Ajonc (first weekend in Aug); Pardon de Trémalo (last Sun in Jul). 🅦 pontaven.com

Pont-Aven was originally a small fishing harbour set at the end of a *ria* (ancient flooded valley) and surrounded by mills. Luggers trading eastwards towards Nantes and southwards towards Bordeaux gradually transformed this small town into a busy port. The 17th- and 18th-century granite houses and paved streets that rise in tiers between Rue des Meunières and Place Royale date from this prosperous period in the port's history.

From the 1860s, Pont-Aven owed its fame to the painters

who settled here. Paul Gauguin's *Christ Jaune* takes as its subject the Christ on the Cross that still hangs in the **Chapelle de Trémalo** at the top of the town, just on the edge of Bois d'Amour woods. The **Musée de Pont-Aven** documents the town's history and has paintings of the Pont-Aven School, where a style called

Pont-Aven's
Christ on
the Cross

The quay at Quimperlé, founded in the 11th century

Syntheticism was created. This style used bold dashes of colour and strong symbolism.

🏛 Musée de Pont-Aven
Place de l'Hôtel-de-Ville. **Tel** (02) 98 06 14 43. **Closed** until mid-2015. 🎨 🎫

⛪ Chapelle de Trémalo
Place de l'Hôtel-de-Ville. **Tel** (02) 98 06 01 68. **Open** daily.

㉚ Quimperlé

Road map C3. ⚏ 11,500. 🚌 Quimperlé. 🛈 3 Place Charles de Gaulle; (02) 98 96 04 32. 🛒 Fri in Place St-Michel; Sun am, in the covered market. 🎉 Fest Noz (Aug). 🅦 quimperle-terreoceane.com

This town, at the confluence of the Isole and Ellé rivers, was founded by Benedictine monks in the 11th century, although it began to develop only in the 17th century.

Capuchins and Ursulines also settled here, and nobles built fine residences in **Rue Dom-Morice** and **Rue Brémond-d'Ars**, in the lower town. Other notable buildings are the **Hôtel du Cosquer** and the houses in **Rue Savary**.

Quimperlé (*Kemperle* in Breton) later expanded beyond its old boundaries, developing around the **Église Ste-Croix**, in the lower town, and Place St-Michel, in the higher town. Because of the strongly influential presence of the monks and nuns here, the principal monuments in Quimperlé are religious. They include the Baroque **Chapelle des Ursulines**, which holds temporary art exhibitions, and the **Église Notre Dame d'Assomption** built in a Flamboyant Gothic style.

The Pont-Aven School

In 1866, a colony of American painters settled in Pont-Aven. Fascinated by the picturesque character of the surroundings, they painted scenes of the daily life that they observed around them. Paul Gauguin arrived in Pont-Aven in 1886, and there he met Charles Laval, Émile Bernard, Ferdinand du Puigaudeau and Paul Sérusier, artists who were later to form part of the Nabis group. Soon after, seeking refuge from the bustle of this coastal town, the group moved to the quieter surroundings of Le Pouldu, east of Pont-Aven. Influenced by primitive art, these painters used colour expressively and evocatively, and imbued images with a symbolic meaning. Their paintings were not intended to reflect reality but to embody reality itself, with line and colour producing a flat image devoid of shading and perspective. Their use of tonal contrasts, their novel approach to composition and their asceticism were at odds with Impressionism.

La Belle Angèle, by Paul Gauguin, a leading member of the Pont-Aven School

MORBIHAN

Occupying the central southern part of Brittany, the Morbihan, which means "little sea" in Breton, takes its name from the .Golfe du Morbihan on the *département*'s southeasterly side. With gentle landscapes bathed in sunshine, a deeply indented coastline washed by the Atlantic Ocean, historic towns and cities and harbours thronged with boats, the Morbihan holds many attractions.

The history of the Morbihan goes back to the remote past. Neolithic people raised an impressive number of large and mysterious standing stones here: the alignments at Carnac and Locmariaquer between them constitute the largest concentration of megalithic monuments in the world.

The Golfe du Morbihan, which is extended inland by the Auray and Vannes rivers, is almost like an inland sea. Marshland and mud flats are home to flocks of birds of various species. The gentle climate, in which a Mediterranean vegetation flourishes, the beauty of a landscape of ever-changing colours, and the soft sand beaches here combine to make the Morbihan a popular tourist destination.

The gulf is dotted with a host of small islands, whose number is said to equal that of the days in the year. The islands include the Île d'Arz, the aptly named Belle-Île, the Île de Groix and the Île d'Houat, which are a delight for nature lovers. The Presqu'île de Quiberon, a narrow spit of land protruding out to sea, is almost like a separate region. The peninsula's indented Côte Sauvage (Wild Coast) to the west contrasts with its more sheltered eastern side, where there are many beaches.

Great vitality characterizes towns and cities in the Morbihan, from Vannes, which was established in Gallo-Roman times, to Lorient, which was rebuilt after World War II. In the interior are such monuments to past glories as the Château de Josselin and Château de Pontivy, picturesque houses in Rochefort-en-Terre, and the fine historic covered markets in Questembert and Le Faoüet.

The Neolithic alignment of 540 menhirs at Kerlescan, outside Carnac

◀ The beautiful village of Rochefort-en-Terre in Morbihan

Exploring the Morbihan

The south of the Morbihan is crossed by the Vilaine, which flows into the Atlantic just west of La Roche-Bernard. Vannes, on the far northern side of the gulf, is the capital of the Morbihan, and a lively city with an ever-expanding student population. The Morbihan's two other major conurbations – Lorient, a port with five harbours, and Auray, a charming medieval town – are located further northwest. Water is ubiquitous in this region; countless rivers have carved deep canyons, and *rias* (ancient valleys flooded by the sea) go far inland. The Golfe du Morbihan is almost closed and is thus sheltered from the rigours of the open sea. Although the Morbihan's inland region attracts fewer visitors, it has beautiful countryside and pretty villages.

Basilica at Ste-Anne-d'Auray

The citadel at Port-Louis

Getting Around

From Paris, Vannes can be reached in 3 hours and 10 minutes by TGV (high-speed train), and Lorient in 3 hours 45 minutes. The N24 and its continuation, the N166, link Rennes and Vannes. The fast N165, almost all of it a dual carriageway, links Nantes with Vannes, Auray and Lorient. Several minor roads, including the D780, D781, D199 and D101, run around the edge of the Golfe du Morbihan. The best way of exploring the gulf is, however, by boat, which provides a comprehensive view of the islands and their beautiful coastlines.

Key

━━ Major road

━ Secondary road

═ Minor road

┅ Main railway

╌ Minor railway

━ Regional border

For keys to symbols *see back flap*

Bagpipe-player at the Festival Interceltique held in Lorient

❶ Lorient

Road map C3. 🏔 121,820. 🚆 Rue Beauvais. 🚌 Cour de Chazelles. 🚢 Rue Gahinet; (08) 20 05 61 56. Sailings to the Île de Groix (all year). 🛈 Maison de la Mer, Quai de Rohan; (02) 97 84 78 00. 🛒 Wed & Sat. 🎭 Carnaval (Apr); Festival des Sept Chapelles (classical music, mid-Jul–mid-Aug); Festival Interceltique (Aug). 🌐 lorientbretagnesudtourisme.fr

It was in the 17th century, when the French East India Company, based in Port-Louis, needed to expand, that Lorient was created. The new port became the base for trade with the East (l'Orient), hence its name, and in 1770 was chosen as the site of the royal dockyard. Almost totally destroyed in World War II, Lorient has been rebuilt.

Today, Lorient is France's second-largest port. Not only a fishing port, it handles cargo and passenger ships and is a yachting centre.

Keroman harbour, which has a large covered fish market, caters to the fishing industry.

The **Quayside Buildings** in the naval dockyard stand on the site of the East India Company, while in the location of the World War II German submarine base is **La Cité de la Voile Éric Tabarly**, a museum exploring the world of ocean racing. Interactive simulators bring the experience to life, or you can design your own boat. Outside, moored to the quay, is a sailing ship that offers trips around the bay. Also on the quay is the submarine La Flore, which houses a museum explaining the strategic military importance of Lorient. Discover life aboard by visiting the engine room, living quarters and operations room.

On Place Alsace-Lorraine is an **Air-Raid Shelter** (abri) for 400 people which now gives a flavour of life during the war years (1939–45). In the Quartier de Merville are houses in the Art Nouveau and Art Deco styles that survived the bombing raids.

The tourist office here organizes trips to the roadstead (Rade de Lorient) and along the Blavet river, including a visit to the market at Hennebont (see p201).

Painted altarpiece in the choir of the church at Larmor-Plage

Teapot, 18th-century, Musée de la Compagnie des Indes

🏛 La Cité de la Voile Éric Tabarly
Base des sous-marins, 56200 Lorient. **Tel** (02) 97 65 56 56. **Open** mid-Feb–Dec; times vary, call ahead. ♿

🏛 Quayside Buildings
Porte Gabriel. 📷 obligatory; Jul–early Sep & school holidays: daily. **Tel** (02) 97 02 23 29. **Open** Jul–Aug: daily; May–Jun & Sep–Oct: Mon–Fri, Sat–Sun pm. ♿

🏛 Air-Raid Shelter
Place Alsace-Lorraine. **Tel** (02) 97 02 23 29. 📷 ♿

Environs
Larmor-Plage, to the south-west, has beaches and a fortified Gothic church. To the east, at the mouth of the river, lies the Barre d'Étel, a notorious sandbar. Further north, Belz leads to St-Cado, a small island that is popular with painters.

❷ Port-Louis

Road map C3. 12 km (7.5 miles) southeast of Lorient via the D194 then the D781. 🏔 3,000. 🚆 Lorient. 🛈 1 Ave Marcel-Charrier (02) 97 84 78 00. 🛒 Sat. 🎭 Regattas (Jun).

The 17th-century citadel in Port-Louis, at the entrance to Lorient's roadstead, guards the mouth of the Blavet and Scorff rivers. Begun by the Spaniards, it was completed during the reign of Louis XIII, after whom it is named. Elegant residences dating from this period can be seen in the town, although they suffered damage during World War II.

With maps, models and examples of the highly prized goods that they brought back from the East, the **Musée de la Compagnie des Indes et de la Marine**, within the citadel, describes the illustrious history of the French East India Company.

🏛 Musée de la Compagnie des Indes et de la Marine
Citadelle de Port-Louis. **Tel** (02) 97 82 56 72. **Open** May–Aug: daily; Feb–Apr & Sep–mid-Dec: Wed–Mon pm. ♿

Port-Tudy, on the Île de Groix, built in the 19th century

❸ Île de Groix

Road map C3. 🏠 2,320.
🚢 Compagnie Océane; 0820 05
61 56. 🛈 Quai de Port-Tudy; (02)
97 84 78 00. 🛒 Tue & Sat, in Le Bourg.
🎭 Fête de la Mer (late Jul).
🌐 lorientbretagnesudtourisme.fr

This picturesque island, with an area of 24 sq km (9 sq miles), is best explored on foot, by bicycle or on horseback. Between 1870 and 1940, tuna fishing provided employment for up to 2,000 of the island's seamen. The harbour at **Port-Tudy** would then be filled with tuna boats rather than the pleasure boats that are moored here today.

The **Écomusée** in Port-Tudy describes daily life on Groix as well as its natural environment. The island's interesting geology is the subject of the displays in the **Maison de la Réserve**.

At the end of the road running south from Créhal, a coast path leads to the Trou de l'Enfer, an impressively deep recess in the cliff face on the southern side of the island.

On the west coast is the beautiful Plage des Grands-Sables, the only convex beach in Europe, and there is a bird sanctuary on the northwesterly Pointe de Groix.

🏛 Écomusée
Port-Tudy. **Tel** (02) 97 86 84 60.
Open May–Sep: daily; Oct–Apr: Tue–Sun. **Closed** public hols 🖼

🖼 Maison de la Réserve
Île de Groix. **Tel** (02) 97 86 55 97.
Open Jul–Aug & school holidays: Tue–Sat am; rest of year: Thu am.

❹ Presqu'île de Quiberon

Road map C4. 🚉 Auray or Quiberon (route served by the Tire-Bouchon train in Jul–Aug). 🚌 Auray. 🛈 14 Rue de Verdun, Quiberon; (02) 97 50 07 84. 🛒 Thu in St-Pierre, Sat in Quiberon & Wed in Port-Haliguen (mid-Jun–mid-Sep). 🎭 Regatta (Jun), Fête de la Mer et du Nautisme (Jun), Fête de la Sardine, Port-Maria (Jul). 🌐 quiberon.com

Of all the areas of Brittany that attract visitors, the beautiful Presqu'île de Quiberon justifiably draws the greatest number. It is also an exceptional environment for sailing and watersports. The peninsula, 14 km (9 miles) long, is linked to the mainland by a sandbank, the Isthme de Penthièvre.

At Plouharnel, just above the peninsula, is **La Belle Iloise,** a sardine cannery with a museum dedicated to the history of this important local industry. The **Musée de la Chouannerie**, in an old blockhouse nearby at Plouharmel, tells the story of the Chouans (see p52).

The Fort de Penthièvre, rebuilt in the 19th century and now owned by the French Army, controls access to the peninsula. To the west, Portivy, a fishing harbour, leads to Pointe de Percho, from where there is a splendid view of Belle-Île (see pp182–3) and the Île de Groix.

Exposed to the rigours of the sea, the cliffs of the **Côte Sauvage** (Wild Coast) are indented with caves and chasms, and on stormy days the windswept sea at Ber-er-Goalennec is an impressive sight. **Quiberon**, once a busy sardine port, is a resort now known mainly for its institute of thalassotherapy. The town was launched as a coastal resort in the early 20th century, when silk manufacturers from Lyon built villas on the seafront here. From Port-Maria, once a sardine port, boats sail for Belle-Île, the Île de Houat and Île de Hoëdic (see pp182–3). Pointe du Conguel, with the Phare de la Teignouse, is the peninsula's most southerly point. During the summer, regattas are regularly held at Port-Haliguen.

St-Pierre-de-Quiberon, a family holiday resort on the eastern side, has good beaches and interesting prehistoric standing stones. There are also many sailing schools here.

🏛 La Belle Iloise
Zone Activité Plein Ouest. **Tel** (02) 97 50 08 77. **Open** Mon–Fri, Sat am. ♿

🏛 Musée de la Chouannerie
Plouharnel. On the D 768. **Tel** (02) 97 52 31 31. **Open** Apr–mid-Jun: daily pm; mid-Jun–Sep: daily. 🖼

Alignment of menhirs at St-Pierre-de-Quiberon

❺ Belle-Île-en-Mer

The largest island in Brittany, Belle-Île (Beautiful Island) well deserves its name. Its unspoiled environment, of heathland carpeted in gorse alternating with lush valleys, its beaches and well-kept villages attract numerous holiday-makers. Continually fought over on account of its strategic position south of Quiberon, the island was held by the English in 1761. It was finally exchanged for Minorca in 1763.

Pointe des Poulains
The lighthouse and its setting held great appeal for Sarah Bernhardt.

Pinte des Poulains

Stêr-Vraz

Grotte de l'Apothicairerie

↗ *Quiberon*

D 25

Sauzon

D 30

D 30

D 25

Sauzon
The town's colourfully painted houses and the steep-banked inlet here captivated painters and poets, including Victor Vasarely and Jacques Prévert in the 1950s and '60s.

Port-Donnant is framed by sheer cliffs. The beach here is spectacular.

Grand Phare
commands a view stretching from Lorient to Le Croisic.

Bangor

D 190a

D 190

Port-Goulphar
The cove at Port-Goulphar and the jagged rocks at Port-Coton, where breakers foam furiously, were portrayed by the painter Claude Monet in 1886.

Île de Bangor

Bangor is a small town near some of the wildest stretches of coast.

❻ Île de Houat

Road map D4. 🏠 345. 🚢 from Quiberon, Compagnie Océane; 0820 056 156; In summer, also from Port-Narvalo, Vannes, Locqmariaquer; 0825 132 100. **ℹ** Mairie; (02) 97 30 68 04. 🎉 Fête de la Mer (15 Aug).
w iles-du-ponant.com

Like the neighbouring Île de Hoëdic, the Île de Houat (Duck Island in Breton) forms part of the Ponant archipelago. Just 5 km (3 miles) long and 1 km (0.5 mile) wide, Houat can be explored easily on foot. A coast path encircles the island, taking in Pointe Beg-er-Vachif, where, at sunset,

Cyclists riding through the quiet village of Houat

the grey granite rocks are flecked with red.

Four fifths of the island are covered with heathland. **Houat**, the island's only village, has neat whitewashed houses. The Église St-Gildas, built in 1766, is dedicated to the 6th-century saint who came to live here as a

hermit. In **Port-St-Gildas**, the harbour below Houat, fishing boats come and go.

Vestiges of Houat's former importance as a military base include the Beniguet battery, the En-Tal redoubt and a ruined fort.

The **Éclosarium**, just outside the village, is a plankton research and breeding centre where visitors can see microscopic marine life. The Plage de Treac'h-er-Goured, on the southeastern side, is one of Houat's more sheltered beaches.

🏛 Éclosarium
1 km (0.5 mile) from Houat. **Tel** (02) 97 52 38 38. **Open** Easter–Sep: daily. 🅿

Sarah Bernhardt

Born Rosine Bernard in Paris, the actress known as Sarah Bernhardt (1844–1923) made her debut at the Comédie Française. From 1870 to 1900, she dominated Parisian theatre and made successful tours abroad. In 1893, she discovered Belle-Île and fell in love with the island. She purchased the Bastion de Basse-Hiot, bought land at Pointe des Poulains, and in 1909 became the owner of the Domaine de Penhoët. There is a museum at the Pointe des Poulains dedicated to her life.

Sarah Bernhardt on Belle-Île

VISITORS' CHECKLIST

Practical Information
Road map C4. 🔼 5,000.
i Quai Bonnelle, Le Palais; (02) 97 31 81 93. 🚢 daily in Le Palais & Locmaria (Jul–Aug) & Sun in Sauzon. 🚩 Regattas (May/Jun); Festival Lyrique (Jul–Aug); Fête de la Mer (15 Aug). **W** belle-ile.com

Transport
🚢 all year from Quiberon (Compagnie Océane: 0820 056 156); Apr–Oct also from Port-Navalo, Vannes, Locmariaquer (Navix: 0825 132 100). Jul–Aug from La Turbie, Le Croisic (Navix).

Pointe de Taillefer

Quiberon

Le Palais

Port Navalo, Vannes

Le Palais
The harbour of this town, the capital of Belle-Île, is dominated by a citadel. The museum here documents the island's history.

Pointe de Kerdonis

D 25

Locmaria

Key
▬▬ Main road
═══ Minor road
---- Ferry route

| 0 kilometres | 4 |
| 0 miles | 2 |

Locmaria has several beaches that are ideal for watersports. The town also contains the island's oldest church, built in 1714.

Plage des Grands-Sables is the island's largest beach.

Pointe du Skuel

❼ Île de Hoëdic

Road map D4. 🔼 140. 🚢 from Quiberon, Compagnie Océane; 0820 056 156. *i* Mairie; (02) 97 52 48 88. 🚩 Fête de la Mer (15 Aug).

As its Breton name suggests, the Île de Hoëdic (Little Duck Island) is smaller than its big sister, the neighbouring Île de Houat, just 5 km (3 miles) to the northwest. Hoëdic is 2.5 km (1.5 miles) long and 1 km (0.5 mile) wide, and like Houat, it is easy to explore on foot.

The island's ubiquitous heathland is scattered with sea pinks and sea bindweed. Along the coast, superb beaches alternate with jagged, rocky creeks.

Le Bourg, in the centre of Hoëdic, is a traditional village with long, low houses, white-washed and south-facing. The Église St-Goustan is worth a visit for its attractive blue and gold ceiling and its thanksgiving plaques. Northeast of Bourg, the 19th-century **Fort d'Hoëdic** contains a short-stay gîte and exhibitions devoted to the island's plants, animals and local history.

🏛 Fort d'Hoëdic
Tel (02) 97 52 48 82. **Open** Jun–Aug: daily. **Closed** Mon am.

Sailing off the Île de Hoëdic, an island with a beautiful coastline

For keys to symbols *see back flap*

❽ Carnac

Brittany's best-known prehistoric site is, without doubt, Carnac. The alignments of 3,000 standing stones – which may originally have numbered over 6,000 – are the most extraordinary group of menhirs in the world. The oldest date from the Neolithic period and the most recent from the Bronze Age. Although their significance remains unknown, they were probably connected to religion. Apart from its famous megaliths, Carnac also has wide sandy beaches and a lively commercial centre, making it a popular coastal resort for summer visitors.

The Alignements de Kerlescan, with 240 standing stones

Exploring Carnac

Carnac consists of the town itself and of Carnac-Plage, the beach that was created from scratch out of a lagoon in 1903.

The Renaissance **Église St-Cornély**, in the centre of the town, was built in the 17th century and is dedicated to the local patron saint of horned animals. This honour highlights the importance of agriculture, and of oxen in particular, to the local community. The figure of St Cornély, framed by oxen, can be seen above the pediment of the west door. The wooden ceiling inside the church is decorated with 18th-century frescoes, those over the nave showing scenes from the life of St Cornély.

Southwest of Carnac, overlooking the Anse du Pô, is **St-Colomban**, a picturesque fishing village where oysters are farmed. A few old houses cluster around the Flamboyant Gothic chapel, built in 1575. There is also a 16th-century fountain with two troughs, one for washerwomen and the other for animals to drink from.

🏛 Musée de Préhistoire

10 Place de la Chapelle, Carnac-Ville. **Tel** (02) 97 52 22 04. **Open** mid-Mar–Jun & Sep–Nov: Wed–Mon; mid-Feb–mid-Mar & Jul–Aug: daily. **Closed** Jan–mid-Feb. 🅰 🅲

This important museum contains a collection of some 500,000 artifacts, although only 6,000 pieces are shown at a time. They are presented in chronological order.

The ground floor is devoted to the Palaeolithic (450,000–12000 BC), Mesolithic (12,000–5000 BC), and Neolithic (4500–2000 BC) periods. The Neolithic period, when the megaliths were built (see p41), is particularly well illustrated. Menhirs (standing stones), cromlechs (menhirs in a semicircle), dolmens (tombs consisting of two upright stones roofed by a third), cairns (galleried graves), tumuli (burial mounds), and allées couvertes (graves in the form of covered alleys) are each explained. Axes made of polished jadeite (a green stone), pottery, jewellery, bone and horn tools, and flint arrowheads, blades and handaxes provide a picture of daily life in Neolithic times. There are also models and reconstructions.

The first floor is devoted to subsequent periods: the Chalcolithic and the appearance of the earliest bronze tools, the Bronze Age (1800–750 BC), the Iron Age, and the Gallo-Roman period, which is fittingly illustrated by objects found at the Villa des Bosséno, near Carnac.

🏠 Alignements de Kerzérho

Along the D781 heading north from Carnac to Lorient, just before arriving at Erdeven. **Tel** (02) 97 55 64 60. **Open** daily. 🅲 arranged at tourist office, 7 Rue Abbé Le Barh, Erdeven.

These alignments are made up of 1,130 menhirs arranged east to west in 11 rows. A line consisting of 29 menhirs, perpendicular to the west, has two stones over 4 m (13 ft) high. These standing stones are known locally as the "Soldiers of St Cornely", and the location "Caesar's Camp", recalling Erdeven's history, from Roman occupation to Christian times.

The fountain with two troughs in St-Colomban

🏠 Alignements de Carnac

Northeast Of Carnac-Ville. 🛈 Visitor centre at la Maison des Megaliths, Ménec. **Tel** (02) 97 52 29 81. **Open** all year. 🅰 (free Oct–Apr) 🅲 May–Sep: obligatory, check times with visitor centre.

Carnac's standing stones, just outside the town, consist of three groups, the alignments at **Ménec**, **Kermario** and **Kerlescan**, which are framed at their eastern and western limits by cromlechs. To protect the site from large numbers of visitors, wire fencing has been erected around the alignments.

The precise purpose of the alignments remains unknown. The most likely explanation is that they were great religious centres where regular gatherings took place, perhaps where rituals connected to a sun god were performed.

The Alignements de Kerlescan, in the direction of La Trinité, consist of 555 menhirs arranged in 13 lines. The southwest end is marked by a cromlech of 39 stones. On the heath is the Géant du Manio, a menhir 6 m (20 ft) high.

The Alignements de Kermario consists of 1,029 menhirs laid out in ten rows. This alignment has some of the most beautiful standing stones in Carnac.

The Alignements du Ménec, further west, contain the most representative stones. The 1,099 menhirs here are arranged in

Fresco in the Église
St-Cornély, Carnac

11 rows and the tallest stones are 4 m (13 ft) high. Other megaliths here include the Tumulus de Kercado (east of Kermario), a dolmen dating from 4670 BC with a gallery leading to a burial chamber with engraved walls, and the dolmens at Mané-Kerioned.

The best time to see Carnac's menhirs is at sunrise, when the stones cast extraordinary shadows, and it is best to walk the alignment from east to west.

Carnac's tourist office supplies an itinerary and map for a 5-km (3-mile) tour of the most important sites. From April to September there is also a tourist train that makes

VISITORS' CHECKLIST

Practical Information
Road map C3-4. 🏘 4,320. 🅸 74 Avenue des Druides; (02) 97 52 13 52. Place de l'Église, Carnac-Ville (Apr–Sep). 🏛 Wed & Sun. 🏛 Pardon de la St-Colomban (Aug); Marché Nocturne (Thu, summer); Breton tales legends, at the menhir known as the Géant du Manio (Wed, late Jul–early Aug); Pardon de la St-Cornély (Sep). 🆆 ot-carnac.fr

Transport
🚍 Auray. 🚌

daily 50-minute tours of the alignments and beaches. A running commentary is given in several languages, including English. Further information is available at www.petittrain-carnac.com.

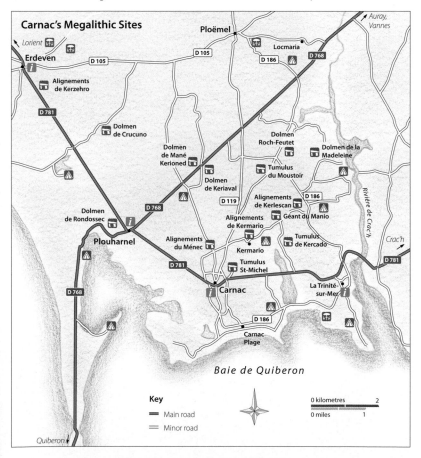

Carnac's Megalithic Sites

Auray, Vannes

Lorient
Erdeven
Ploëmel
Locmaria
D 105
D 105
D 186
D 768

Alignements de Kerzehro

D 781

Dolmen de Crucuno

Dolmen de Mané Kerioned

Dolmen Roch-Feutet

Dolmen de la Madeleine

Tumulus du Moustoir

Dolmen de Keriaval

D 119

Alignements de Kerlescan

D 186

Dolmen de Rondossec

D 768

Géant du Manio

Rivière de Crac'h

Alignements de Kermario

Plouharnel

Alignements du Ménec

Kermario

Crac'h

Tumulus de Kercado

D 781

D 781

D 768

Tumulus St-Michel

Carnac

La Trinité-sur-Mer

D 186

Carnac Plage

Baie de Quiberon

Key

▬ Main road
═ Minor road

0 kilometres   2
0 miles   1

Quiberon

The Grand Menhir Brisé (Great Broken Menhir) at Locmariaquer, 5 m (16 ft) wide and originally 20–30 m (65–98 ft) high

❾ La Trinité-sur-Mer

Road map C4. ⛰ 1,530. 🚉 Auray.
🚌 🚌 Navix; 0825 132 100. Sailings to Ile d'Arz & Ile Aux Moines & cruises in the Golfe du Morbihan. ℹ 30 Cours des Quais; (02 97 55 72 21).
🍴 Tue & Fri. 🎿 Spi Ouest France (regattas; Easter); Ar-Men Race (Ascension). 🌐 ot-trinite-sur-mer.fr

Nestling in a sheltered *ria*, La Trinité-sur-Mer is the time-honoured meeting place of sailing enthusiasts. The town's sailing club, founded in 1879, is one of the oldest in France, and it was here that Éric Tabarly, Peyron and other yachtsmen began their careers. From April to September, regattas take place in the harbour, which is large enough to accommodate 1,250 yachts. La Trinité also has a fishing industry, which supplies the town's lively fish market.

A coast path leads from the harbour to the beaches, taking in Pointe de Kerbihan. The Pont de Kérisper, in the direction of Carnac and spanning the Crac'h river, offers a breathtaking view of the river, which incorporates both the oyster farms further upstream and the marina further downstream. Trips out

The Table des Marchands, a Neolithic galleried grave near Locmariaquer

to sea in an old sailing boat and boat rides on the Crac'h are available in summer.

❿ Locmariaquer

Road map D4. 10 km (6 miles) east of La Trinité-sur-Mer via the D 781.
⛰ 1,400. 🚉 Auray. 🚌 Navix; 0825 132 100. Trips to Belle-Île & cruises in the Golfe de Morbihan (Jul–Aug).
ℹ Rue de la Victoire; (02) 97 57 33 05.
🍴 Tue & Sat (Jul–Aug). 🎿 Pardon (Jul); Troc et Puces (Jul); Fête de l'Huître (Aug). 🌐 morbihan-way.fr

This charming coastal resort also has some of the most impressive megalithic monuments in Brittany. Just outside the town is the **Table des Marchands**, a Neolithic galleried grave dating from 3700 BC. Its stones are engraved with scrolls, an axe shape and depictions of cattle. Behind the Table des Marchands, a path leads to the Mané-Lud tumulus, consisting of 22 engraved stones forming a corridor. The Er-Grah Tumulus, 140 m (460 ft) long, is a burial mound.

These monuments date from a time when people were using polished stone axes, had learned to make pottery, and had begun to keep animals and plant crops. Having adopted a settled way of life, they turned to raising impressive monuments.

The **Grand Menhir Brisé**, dating from 4500 BC, is 20 m (65 ft) long and weighs 350 tonnes. It lies broken into four pieces, but is the largest known menhir in the western world.

🏛 **Megaliths (Grand Menhir Brisé, Table des Marchands & Er-Grah Tumulus)**
At the entrance to the town, near the cemetery. **Tel** (02) 97 57 37 59.
Open daily. **Closed** 1 Jan, 1 May, 25 Dec. ♿🎫

Environs

The Pointe de Kerpenhir, opposite Port-Navalo (*see p188*), southeast of Locmariaquer, offers a panoramic view of the Golfe du Morbihan. The granite statue of Notre-Dame de Kerdro protects sailors and yachtsmen. Behind Plage de Kerpenhir is the Allé Couverte des Pierres-Plates, a corridor grave with two burial chambers engraved with motifs, and connected by a long passage.

⓫ Auray

Road map D3. ⛰ 10,590. 🚉 2 km (1 mile) from the town centre.
ℹ Chapelle de la Congrégation, 20 Rue du Lait; (02) 97 24 09 75. 🍴 Jul–Aug: Thu. 🍴 Mon & Fri on Place Notre-Dame; Thu–Sat (Jul-Aug) at St-Goustan farm. 🎿 St-Goustan Book & Postcard Fair (Fri, May–Sep).
🌐 auray-tourisme.com

Tucked away at the end of a *ria*, Auray (*An alre* in Breton) stands on a promontory overlooking the Loch river. With its old houses and attractive harbour, this is a delightful town. It also has its place in the history of Brittany. It was the Battle of

Detail of the 17th-century altarpiece in the Église St-Gildas in Auray

The Imp of the High Seas

Éric Tabarly (1931–98), once a captain in the French Navy, was the ultimate yachtsman of the second half of the 20th century. Such eulogy would have embarrassed this shy man, who would face cameras with a modest smile. He had a long list of victories to his name. His first came in 1964, sailing in the *Pen Duick II*, when he won the second Solo Transatlantic Race, beating the British. Tabarly became a French yachting legend in the process and, as the newly popular art of sailing gripped the nation, others were inspired to emulate him.

Éric Tabarly aboard the *Côte d'Or*

Timber-framed houses in the Quartier St-Goustan, Auray

Auray, in 1364, that brought an end to the War of the Breton Succession *(see p46)* .

The **Église St-Gildas** has a Renaissance doorway (1636) and contains a remarkable Baroque altarpiece *(see p70)* made by a sculptor from Lavalle in 1657. Place de la République is surrounded by elegant houses, including the Maison Martin and the Hôtel de Trévegat, both dating from the 17th century, and the town hall, built in 1776.

From the belvedere and the promenade above the Loch, where terraced gardens are laid out in tiers below the castle, there is a beautiful view of the river and the harbour.

A 17th-century stone bridge at the bottom of the town leads to **St-Goustan**, which was once Auray's port. Here, medieval timber-framed houses line the quay, whose peaceful

atmosphere has captivated many painters. The steep, narrow streets behind the harbour are also worth exploring.

Environs

Just north of Auray is the magnificent **Abbaye de Chartreuse**. Inside is a black-and-white marble mausoleum with sculpted reliefs by David d'Angers. At St Dégan, near Brech, is the **Ecomusée St Dégan**. Housed in a group of renovated farm buildings, its exhibits recount early-19th-century peasant life. The picturesque fishing village of Le Bono lies 6 km (4 miles) southeast of Auray. The view from the suspension bridge (1840) is spectacular.

🏛 Ecomusée St-Dégan

Venelle de l'Ecomusée. **Tel** (02) 97 57 66 00. **Open** Feb–Jun & Sep: Mon–Fri pm; Jul–Aug: daily. 🖉

The 17th-century cloisters at Ste-Anne-d'Auray

Waxwork of John Paul II in the Musée de Cire, Ste-Anne-d'Auray

⑫ Ste-Anne-d'Auray

Road map D3. 7 km (4 miles) north of Auray via the D17. 👥 1,950. 🚉 Auray. 🛈 9 Rue de Vannes; (02) 97 24 34 94. 🗓 Wed. 🎭 Grand Pardon (late Jul).

The second-greatest shrine in France after Lourdes, and honoured by a visit from Pope John Paul II in 1999, Ste-Anne-d'Auray became a major place of pilgrimage in the 17th century.

St Anne, mother of the Virgin Mary, appeared numerous times to a humble ploughman, Yves Nicolazic, whom she instructed to build a chapel. When a statue was discovered at the spot that she had indicated, a church was built there. It was replaced by the present basilica in 1872. The church contains stained-glass windows depicting scenes from the life of St Anne and of the ploughman. The **Trésor** (Treasury) in the cloisters contains votive plaques, seascapes and model ships, and statues dating from the 15th to the 19th centuries.

The **Musée de Cire de l'Historial**, opposite the basilica, traces the origins of the town as a place of pilgrimage and describes the life of Nicolazic. The town is also the site of the Monument aux Morts, a memorial to the 250,000 Bretons who died in World War I.

⛪ Trésor de la Basilique
Tel (02) 97 57 68 80. **Open** daily pm. **Closed** Jan–Feb. 🖉

🏛 Musée de Cire de l'Historial
6 Rue de Vannes. **Tel** (02) 97 57 64 05. **Open** Mar–Oct: daily. 🖉

⓭ Golfe du Morbihan

This large bay was created 9,000 years ago, when global warming caused the sea level to rise. About 15,000 years earlier, the sea level was 100 m (330 ft) lower than it is today, and Belle-Île was attached to the mainland. The rising sea gradually created hundreds of islands, the largest of which are the Île d'Arz and the Île aux Moines. The Golfe du Morbihan consists of two parts: an eastern basin, which is flatter, rather like a lagoon; and a western basin, which is defined by a rocky coastline and where there are strong currents. Here, the sea bed is uneven, particularly around Port-Navalo, where depressions can be as much as 30 m (100 ft) deep. The constant ebb and flow of the tide circulates volumes of water from the Atlantic, encouraging thousands of species of marine plant and animal life to thrive. These in turn provide food for indigenous and migratory birds.

Île Berder
At low tide, it is possible to walk across the sand to the island.

★ Port-Navalo
This small port is also a holiday resort. The coast path offers beautiful views in all directions.

0 kilometres — 5

0 miles — 3

Église St-Gildas-de-Rhuys
Founded in the 11th century, the church still has its original transept and choir.

★ **Pointe d'Arradon**
This promontory commands spectacular views of the Île aux Moines and the Île d'Arz.

VISITORS' CHECKLIST

Practical Information
Road map: D 4. ℹ Auray (02) 97 24 09 75; Locmariaquer (02) 97 57 33 05; Sarzeau (02) 97 41 82 37; Vannes (02) 97 01 63 00.

Transport
🚉 Auray & Vannes. 🛥 Arradon, Arzon, Baden, Île aux Moines, Île d'Arz, Locmariaquer, Sarzeau. 🚶

Île d'Arz
A walk around the island takes in this old restored tidal mill.

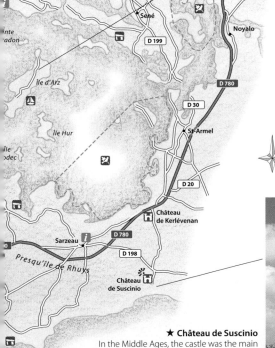

Key

━━ Main road
══ Minor road
-- Ferry route

★ **Château de Suscinio**
In the Middle Ages, the castle was the main residence of the dukes of Brittany. It was abandoned after the Revolution but, at the suggestion of the writer Prosper Mérimée, it was classified as a historic monument in 1835. Now under municipal ownership, it contains a museum of Breton history.

For keys to symbols *see back flap*

Exploring the Golfe du Morbihan

Focal point of the Morbihan region, the Golfe du Morbihan is 20 km (12 miles) wide and covers 12,000 ha (30,000 acres). The gulf, with its deeply indented coastline and many islands, can be explored by boat from Vannes, Port-Navalo, Auray, La Trinité or Locmariaquer. Tourism, together with shellfish and oyster farming, are major industries here, and, although fishing, sailing and other activities have also developed, the gulf is a haven for bird life. The land around it is dotted with menhirs, dolmens and tumuli.

Detail of the stoup in the Église St-Gildas-de-Rhuys

🦜 Pointe d'Arradon

Road map D3. 9 km (6 miles) south-west of Vannes via the D101 then the D101a. 🛈 2 Bouruet Aubertot, Arradon; (02) 97 44 77 44. 🚤 Tue & Fri.

The Pointe d'Arradon is sometimes referred to as the "Riviera of the Gulf". There are some stunning houses here and the view takes in the Îles Logoden, Île Holavre and Île aux Moines.

🦜 Île d'Arz

Road map D4. 🚤 15 mins from Vannes-Conleau, (02) 97 01 22 80; Navix, 0825 132 100. 🛈 Mairie, Île d'Arz; (02) 97 44 31 14. 🎏 Pardon, on Île d'Hur (late Jul); regattas (Aug).

The Île d'Arz (Bear Island), which attracts fewer visitors than the Île aux Moines, can be explored on foot as it is only 3 km (2 miles) long and 1 km (0.5 mile) wide. The low, whitewashed, slate-roofed houses and lush vegetation here create a typical image of Brittany.

The island is dotted with menhirs and dolmens, with a particular concentration on Pointe de Liouse. The Église Notre-Dame, in the town, has Romanesque capitals decorated with grotesque figures. Boating enthusiasts will find two sailing schools on the island.

🏛 Cairn de Gavrinis

Road map D4. Île Gavrinis. **Tel** (02) 97 57 19 38 🚤 Larmor-Baden. **Open** Apr, Jun–Sep: daily; May: Mon–Fri pm, Sat & Sun (make reservations 24 hrs in advance). 🚫 🎥

Discovered in 1832, this single-chambered passage grave is considered to be unusual both on account of its construction – of a type that makes it one of the oldest in the region – and because of its engravings. When the writer Prosper Mérimée visited it in 1835, he was struck by "stones covered in peculiar drawings… curved, straight, broken and wavy lines combined in a hundred different ways".

Cairn de Gavrinis

Measuring 16 m (52 ft), the Cairn de Gavrinis is the longest dolmen in France. The gallery leading to the burial chamber consists of 29 stones, some of which are engraved with symbolic motifs including shields, scrolls, axes, horn shapes and other signs. Inferences about the significance of these signs gives an insight into the meaning of such inscriptions.

Carved Stone No. 8 has engravings in which the central motif is a shield. This is usually a schematic depiction of an anthropomorphic deity.

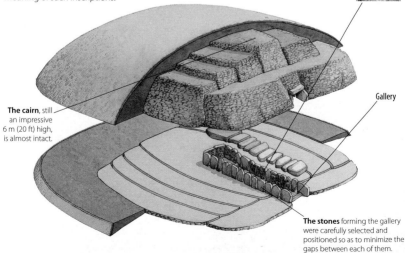

The cairn, still an impressive 6 m (20 ft) high, is almost intact.

Gallery

The stones forming the gallery were carefully selected and positioned so as to minimize the gaps between each of them.

⛴ Île aux Moines

Road map D4. 🚢 from Port-Blanc, with Izenah Crosières (02) 97 26 31 45. 🛈 The harbour; (02) 97 26 32 45. 🏛 summer: daily; winter: Wed & Fri. 🎭 Semaine du Golfe (gathering of old sailing ships, May/Jun, every 2 years from 2015); Festival de la Voile (Aug).

This cruciform island, 6 km (4 miles) long and 3 km (2 miles) wide, once belonged to the Abbaye de St-Sauveur in Redon *(see p70)*. The largest island in the Golfe du Morbihan, it has been inhabited since Neolithic times, and it has several megalithic sites. The most notable are the cromlech at Kergonan, the largest in France, and, further south, the dolmen of Pen-Hap.

Like the neighbouring Île d'Arz, the Île aux Moines has fine 17th- and 18th-century houses. Its mild microclimate supports a vegetation associated with more southerly climes. Eucalyptus, mimosa, camellia and fig all thrive here. As for the island's forests – Bois d'Amour (Wood of Love), Bois des Soupirs (Wood of Sighs) and Bois des Regrets (Wood of Regrets) – their names alone are conducive to gentle reverie.

Each of the promontories on the island's indented coastline offers spectacular views of the gulf.

⛴ Presqu'île de Rhuys

Road map D4. South of the Golfe du Morbihan, via the D780 from Vannes. 🛈 Sarzeau, (02) 97 41 82 37; St-Gildas-de-Rhuys, (02) 97 45 31 45; Port du Crouesty, (02) 97 53 69 69. 🏛 Sun in St-Gildas-de-Rhuys; Tue in Port du Crouesty; Mon in Port du Crouesty (Jul–Aug). 🎭 Semaine du Golfe (gathering of old sailing boats; Ascension, 40 days after Easter, every 2 years, next 2015); Spectacles Historiques, (summer); Fête de la Mer (Aug).

Like Quiberon *(see p181)*, this peninsula has two different aspects: a sheltered north-facing side, and a southern side that is exposed to the rigours of the Atlantic.

The Italianate **Château de Kerlévenan** dates from the 18th century. The building is closed to the public, but its huge walled gardens, planted

An attractive 18th-century building on the Île aux Moines

with shrubs and trees, are open to visitors. A small Chinese bandstand lends a touch of exoticism. The **Château de Suscinio**, on the south coast, is surrounded by marshland. Built as a hunting lodge in the 13th century, it was converted into a fortress in the 14th century. It has a draw-bridge flanked by towers, walls set with watchtowers, and a moat fed by the sea. In the 15th century, François II and his daughter, Anne of Brittany, chose Nantes rather than Suscinio as their place of residence, and the castle fell into neglect. It houses a permanent exhibition on the restoration of the Château, as well as temporary exhibitions. **St-Gildas-de-Rhuys**, further west, is named after an English monk who established a monastery here in the 6th century.

The **Musée des Arts et des Métiers**, at the Le Net roundabout, contains reconstructions of workshops and shops dating from the 1600s to the 1950s. Between here and Arzon stands the Tumulus de Tumiac, also known as Caesar's Mound because the future Roman emperor is reputed to have used it as a lookout.

At the western tip of the peninsula, Port-Navalo and Port du Crouesty are modern coastal resorts. The coast path here commands impressive views of the gulf. It is also worth calling at the pretty little port of Le Logeo, opposite the Îles Branec.

Sarzeau, in the centre of the peninsula, has fine 17th- and 18th-century residences. The chapel at Penvins, nearby, dates from 1897.

Migratory birds can be observed from footpaths on the peninsula's north coast.

🏰 Château de Kerlévenan

On the D780. **Tel** (02) 97 26 46 79. Park: **Open** Jul–mid-Sep: Sat–Thu pm; mid-Sep–Jun: by arrangement. 🅿 🏰

🏰 Château de Suscinio

From Sarzeau, take the D198. **Tel** (02) 97 41 91 91. **Open** Apr–Sep: daily; Oct–Mar: daily pm. 🅿 🏰

🏛 Musée des Arts et Métiers

RD780. **Tel** (02) 97 53 68 25. **Open** Jul–Aug: Mon–Sat & Sun pm; Sep–Jun: Tue–Sun pm (only groups). **Closed** mid-Nov–mid-Mar. 🅿

The chapel at Penvins, near Sarzeau, in the form of a Greek cross

⑭ Street-by-Street: Vannes

The medieval centre of Vannes is a honeycomb of narrow streets which, like those around the Cathédrale St-Pierre, are lined with well-restored timber-framed houses. The main entrance into the walled town, a busy commercial district, is Porte St-Vincent, near Place Gambetta. The walls on the eastern side offer a fine view of the town, with formal gardens laid out below, and also pass the city's old wash houses. The harbour, to the south, is a lively centre of activity.

★ City Walls and Gardens
Part of the Gallo-Roman walls around the old town survives.

Place Gambetta
This square, opposite the marina, is always busy. It is a central meeting place for the inhabitants of Vannes, who fill the café terraces here.

The fish market takes place twice a week, on Wednesdays and Saturdays.

RUE DE LA POISSONNERIE

RUE LE HELLEC

RUE NO

PLACE GAMBETTA

PLACE DU POIDS PUBLIC

RUE SAINT VINCENT

PLACE DES LIC

PORTE POTERNE

RUE DE LA

RUE

Château de l'Hermine
The chateau was built in the 18th century on the site of the residence of the dukes of Brittany. It is fronted by extensive formal gardens, where it is pleasant to walk.

The new market sells fresh produce year-round.

Porte Poterne leads to the gardens beneath the city walls.

Wash Houses
Located beside the Marle river, the city's wash houses date from 1820. They were still in use after World War II.

| 0 meters | 100 |
| 0 yards | 100 |

For hotels and restaurants see pp228–9 and pp241–3

Place Henri-IV
The square is lined with timber-framed houses dating from the 15th and 16th centuries, the oldest in Vannes. In the Middle Ages, a popular bird market was held here.

Musée d'Histoire et d'Archéologie

Musée de la Cohue is the main art gallery of Vannes, set in a building of great historic interest.

VISITORS' CHECKLIST

Practical Information
Road map D3. 🗺 54,000.
ℹ Office du Tourisme du Pays de Vannes, Quai Tabarly, (02) 97 47 24 34. 🚍 Tue–Sun.
🎭 Fêtes Historiques (Jul); Festival de Jazz (Jul); Nuits Musicales du Golfe (Jul–Aug); Fêtes d'Arvor (traditional dancing and music, Aug).
W tourisme-vannes.com

★ **Doorway of the Cathédrale St-Pierre**
Built in the 16th century in the Flamboyant Gothic style, the doorway is lined with niches that, in keeping with Breton tradition, contain statues of the Apostles.

Porte St-Jean was the home of executioners, whose profession passed from father to son.

★ **Place des Lices**
The square is surrounded by well-kept timber-framed houses, the most recent dating from the 17th century.

Porte Prison, dating from the 13th and 15th centuries, was the main gateway into Vannes. Criminals were imprisoned there.

Tour du Connétable
The tower, the highest in Vannes, was built in the 16th century and is now owned by the city authorities, who have restored it. It has a pointed roof and mullioned windows.

Key

— Suggested route

RUE SAINT SALOMON
RUE BURGAULT
RUE DES HALLES
PLACE HENRI IV
RUE BILLAUT
ACE DE ENCIA
RUE DES ORFÈVRES
PLACE SAINT-PIERRE
RUE SAINT CHANOINES
RUE BRIZEUX
RUE DE LA MONNAIE
RUE SAINT GUENAËL
PLACE LAROCHE
PLACE BRÛLÉE
PARTS
RUE DES VIERGES
RUE PORTE PRISON

Exploring Vannes

The history of Vannes goes back to Roman times, when it was known as Darioritum. In the 5th century, it was a diocese and, in the Middle Ages, a city of major importance. Vannes expanded during the 14th century, when it became the capital of Brittany. As a university town, an administrative centre and the capital of the Morbihan, it is again expanding rapidly today. The city also attracts large numbers of sightseers and holiday-makers.

Porte Poterne, the city's postern gate, built in the 17th century

🔲 Town Walls

Vannes was once completely surrounded by defensive walls. Two thirds of these remain, and some have been incorporated into more recent buildings. Part of the Gallo-Roman walls survive on the north side of the city.

Vannes' finest gateway is on its southern side, opposite the harbour. This is Porte St-Vincent, built in 1624. It was restored in 1747, when the gate's existing arrow slits and machicolation were replaced by niches with shell motifs and columns with capitals.

From here to Porte Prison, on the north side of the town, the wall walk overlooks formal gardens laid out in the former moat. It also passes Porte Poterne (1678), and the historic wash houses nearby. Other towers in the town walls include Tour de la Trompette, Tour de la Poudrière, Tour de la Joliette, and Tour du Bourreau. The highest is Tour du Connétable.

⛪ Cathédrale St-Pierre

Open 8:30am–6:30pm daily. 🖼
From a vantage point on the Colline du Mené, the Cathédrale St-Pierre dominates the old town. It was built in the Flamboyant Gothic style, but has neo-Gothic additions dating from the 19th century.

A rotunda chapel dedicated to the Holy Sacrament is built into the north aisle. A jewel of Renaissance architecture, it has a double tier of niches with pediments and high windows framed by semicircular arches. It contains the tomb of St Vincent-Ferrier, a Spanish monk renowned for his preaching. A Gobelins tapestry decorates the wall and there is an outstanding 16th-century Flemish altarpiece.

The cathedral treasury contains some fine metalwork.

Statue of the Virgin in the Cathédrale St-Pierre

🔲 Old Town

Place Henri-IV, at the heart of the old town, is lined with 15th- and 16th-century half-timbered houses, the oldest in Vannes. Many of the houses in the area around the square have unusual decoration. The house at No. 13 Rue Salomon has animal carvings and, on the corner of Rue Noé, is the famous inn sign in the form of "Vannes et sa Femme", the couple who ran the tavern.

In the 17th century, when the Breton parliament was exiled in Vannes, many fine granite or stone town houses (hôtels) were built here. The Hôtel de Lannion, in Impasse de la Psalette, flanked by a projecting turret, was once the residence of the governors of Vannes and Auray. The Hôtel de Limur, in Rue Thiers, with a Neo-Classical façade, is a three-storey residence with a courtyard and a garden.

🏛 Musée de la Cohue

9 & 15 Place St-Pierre. **Tel** (02) 97 01 63 00. **Open** mid-Jun–Sep: daily; Jan–mid-Jun: Tue–Sun pm. **Closed** Oct–Dec. 🖼

The museum is laid out in a restored covered market (cohue) whose origins go back to the 13th century. While market stalls occupied the ground floor, the first floor housed the ducal courts of the Breton parliament, when the latter was exiled to Vannes in 1675 on the orders of Louis XIV. The building was then used as a theatre until the 1950s.

The Musée de la Cohue is an art gallery whose most highly prized exhibit is Delacroix's Crucifixion. Millet, Corot and Goya are also represented. The work of Breton painters, including Maufra, Henri Moret, Paul Helleu, and of engravers native to Vannes, such as Frélaut and Dubreuil, are also displayed, as is that of contemporary artists, including Tal Coat, Soulages and Geneviève Asse. Two other rooms in the museum are devoted to pieces relating to seafaring.

🏛 Musée d'Histoire et d'Archelogie

Château Gaillard, 2 Rue Noé. **Tel** (02) 97 01 63 00. **Open** mid-Jun–mid-Sep: daily. 🖼

Housed in the 15th-century Château Gaillard, which once accommodated the Breton parliament, this archaeological museum contains prehistoric artifacts from sites in the Morbihan. These include axes of polished jadeite and jewellery made of variscite (a kind of turquoise). Coins struck by the Veneti, a local Gaulish tribe, pieces from Roman Gaul, and medieval and Renaissance artifacts are also displayed.

🏛 Place Gambetta

This semicircular square, lined with the white façades of residential blocks, was laid out in the 19th century and is today one of the liveliest parts of Vannes. The harbour lies immediately to the south, so that pleasure boats can sail right up into the heart of the city.

The marina in Vannes, just south of Place Gambetta

From the square, Promenade de la Rabine, a wide walkway which is continued by a coast road, leads to the Presqu'île de Conleau, 4 km (3 miles) downstream.

Environs

The **Forteresse de Largoët d'Elven**, 14 km (9 miles) northeast of Vannes, is an example of medieval Breton architecture. The fortress has two towers and a curtain wall dating from the 13th century, a 14th-century keep, a gatehouse and a 15th-century circular tower. The surrounding **Landes de Lanvaux**, heathland with lakes and woods, is traversed by footpaths and cycle tracks.

🏰 Forteresse de Largoët d'Elven

From Vannes, take the N166 then the D135 at St-Nolff. The fortress is about 3 km (2 miles) further north. **Tel** (02) 97 53 35 96. **Open** mid-Mar–May: Sat & Sun pm; Jun & Sep: Wed–Mon; Jul–Aug: daily. **Closed** Oct–mid-Mar. 🖼

Vannes City Centre

① Cathédrale St-Pierre
② Old Town
③ Musée de la Cohue
④ Musée d'Histoire et d'Archéologie
⑤ Place Gambetta

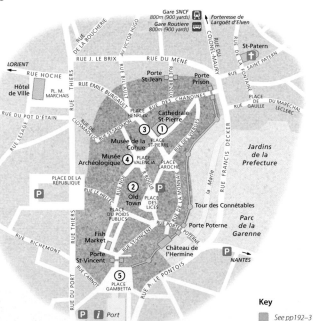

0 metres   300
0 yards   300

Key

■ See pp192–3

The 16th-century town hall in
La Roche-Bernard

⓯ La Roche-Bernard

Road map E4. 34 km (21 miles)
southeast of Vannes on the N165.
🚌 Ponchâteau. 🛈 14 Rue du
Docteur-Cornudet; (02) 99 90 67 98.
🚍 Thu.

Perched on a rocky spur, La
Roche-Bernard stands at an
important intersection on
the estuary of the Vilaine. In the
11th century, a village grew
up around the fortress and,
six centuries later, Richelieu
ordered naval dockyards to
be installed. It was here that
the three-decker *La Couronne*,
pride of the French navy, was
built in 1634.

The port consists of a
marina, along the Vilaine, and
of the old harbour that was later
abandoned in favour of the
Quai de la Douane. Salt, corn,
wine, quicklime and chestnut
wood once passed through
the docks here. In the old
town, which rises in tiers, is the
16th-century Maison du Canon,
which houses the town hall, and
the Auberge des Deux Magots,
on Place du Bouffay. There
are former salt warehouses in
Rue de la Saulnerie.

The **Musée de la Vilaine
Maritime** is laid out in the
16th-century Maison des
Basses-Fosses, where the
ground floor is carved out of
the living rock. The museum

traces the history of navigation
on the Vilaine and documents
the rural life of the region.

Environs
The **Parc Zoologique de
Branféré**, 20 km (12 miles)
northwest of La Roche-Bernard,
has over 100 species of animals
that roam in relative freedom.

🏛 **Musée de la Vilaine Maritime**
6 Rue Ruicard. **Tel** (02) 99 90 83 47.
Open mid-Jun–mid-Sep: daily. 🐾

🐾 **Parc Zoologique de Branféré**
Le Guerno, via the N165. **Tel** (02) 97 42
94 66. **Open** mid-Feb–mid-Apr: daily
pm; mid-Apr–early Nov: daily. 🐾

⓰ Questembert

Road map D3. 28 km (17 miles) east
of Vannes, via the N165, the D775 and
the D5. 🚌 Bel Air. 🛈 15 Rue des
Halles; (02) 97 26 56 00. 🚍 Mon am,
Wed pm. 🎉 Pardon in Bréhardec
(15 Aug); Soirées Estivales (Sat in Jul–
Aug). 🆆 rochefortenterre-
tourisme.com

This small town – "chestnut-
tree land" in Breton – owes its
former prosperity to the fairs
that took place here, in the
covered market (1675). Nearby
is the former Hostellerie Jehan
le Guenego, built in 1450 and
the oldest house in the town.
The 16th-century Hôtel Belmont
next door, now the tourist
office, is enlivened by some
remarkable wooden caryatids.
There are many producers of
duck foie gras in the area.

⓱ Rochefort-en-Terre

Road map E3. 33 km (20 miles) east of
Vannes via the N166, the D775 and
the D774. 🚌 Bel Air. 🛈 Place du
Puits; (02) 97 43 33 57. 🎉 Pardon
(mid-Aug); Festival de Musique (late
Aug). 🆆 rochefortenterre-
tourisme.com

Built on a promontory above
the Gueuzon river, this village
has a medieval atmosphere.
Because of its strategic position,
the site has been fortified
since Roman times. A keep
overlooking Rochefort was built
in the 12th century, and in the
15th the town was enclosed
by walls. Demolished on three
previous occasions, the castle
was again destroyed during
the Revolution. In 1907, Alfred
Klots, an American painter,
restored it and moved into
the castle's 17th-century
outbuildings. The **castle
museum** (closed until the
end of 2015 or longer) contains
antique furniture, paintings by
Alfred Klots and various items
illustrating life in the area. The
moat walk offers a good view
of the surroundings. The finest
houses in Rochefort, with
granite or schist façades carved
with decorative motifs, are in
Grande-Rue and Place du Puits.
The Église Notre-Dame-de-la-
Tronchaye, built on the hillside
and dating from the 15th and
16th centuries, has a façade in
the Flamboyant Gothic style.

Wooden roof of the 17th-century covered market in Questembert

Place du Puits, in the flower-filled village of Rochefort-en-Terre

Features of interest within include beams decorated with monsters, woodcarvings on the theme of death (left of the pulpit) and a Renaissance altarpiece. A 16th-century calvary stands on the church square.

🏰 Castle and Museum
Tel (02) 97 43 31 56. **Closed** for renovation until late 2015. 🅿

⑱ Ploërmel

Road map D3. 🚉 Vannes. 🚹 8,000.
ℹ 5 Rue du Val; (02) 97 74 02 70.
🕑 Jul–Aug: Mon & Thu. 🍴 Fri.
🎉 Fest Noz (Oct); Free concerts (Jul–Aug). 🌐 tourisme-ploermel.com

This town was one of the places of residence of the dukes of Brittany. The tombs of Jean II and Jean III lie in the 16th-century Église St-Armel, near the tomb of Philippe de Montauban. The fine stained-glass window with the Tree of Jesse is the work of Jehan le Flamand. The north entrance is decorated with some strikingly expressive reliefs depicting the vices and the Last Judgment. The **Maison des Marmousets** (1586), opposite the tourist office in Rue Beau-manoir, has some unusual reliefs. Next door is the Hôtel des Ducs de Bretagne, which, built in 1150, is

Figure, Maison des Marmousets

the town's oldest building. The astronomical clock (1855), near the Lycée Lamennais, was made by a member of the Ploërmel brotherhood, which was founded by the older brother of the writer Félicité de Lamennais (see pp31 & 53).

Environs
The Circuit de l'Hortensia is a walk around the Lac au Duc, 1 km (0.5 mile) northwest of Ploërmel. The lake is bordered by 2,000 hydrangeas representing 12 different types of these colourful flowering shrubs.

⑲ Josselin

Road map D3. 🚉 Vannes. 🚹 2,500.
ℹ 4 Rue des Remparts; (02) 97 22 36 43.
🍴 Sat. 🎉 Festival Médiéval (14 Jul), free concerts (Jul–Aug); Pardon St-Eloi (8 Sep). 🌐 josselin-communaute.fr

Linen weaving and the linen trade created Josselin's wealth. The town has at least two important buildings: the **Château de Josselin** (see pp198–9) and the **Basilique Notre-Dame-du-Roncier**, with legendary origins. A miraculous statue of the Virgin was found under brambles (ronces) and a church was built on the holy spot. The basilica that now stands on this legendary site is in the Flamboyant Gothic style, with typically Gothic gargoyles,

but Romanesque columns survive in the choir. Recumbent statues of Olivier de Clisson (see p198) and of his wife, Marguerite de Rohan, lie near the miraculous statue.

Rues des Vierges, Olivier-de-Clisson and Trente are lined with fine 16th- and 17th-century houses. The **Musée des Poupées**, at No. 3 Rue Trente, contains some 600 wax, wooden and porcelain dolls dating from the 17th and 18th centuries. Chapelle Ste-Croix (1050), on the banks of the Oust, is the oldest chapel in the Morbihan.

🏛 Musée des Poupées
3 Rue Trente. **Tel** (02) 97 22 36 45.
Open Apr–mid-Jul & Sep: daily pm; mid-Jul–Aug: daily; Oct: Sat & Sun.
Closed Nov–Mar. 🅿

Environs
From the Middle Ages, the Forêt de Lanouée, 10 km (6 miles) north of Josselin, provided firewood for the ironworks where cannon balls were made. They were at their most productive in the 18th century.

The parish close at Guéhenno, 11 km (7 miles) southwest of Josselin, is the only complete example in the Morbihan. Two statues of soldiers guard the entrance to the ossuary, where there is a figure of the resurrected Christ. The calvary is the most spectacular part of the close. It dates from 1550 but was badly damaged in the Revolution. Eventually a parish priest undertook its restoration. A column with the symbols of the Passion of Christ stands in front of it.

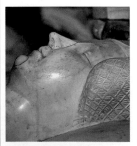

Marguerite de Rohan, Basilique Notre-Dame-du-Roncier, Josselin

Château de Josselin

Perched on rocks opposite the Oust river, the Château de Josselin, once the stronghold of the Rohan dynasty, is an impressive sight. It is defended by four towers built by Olivier de Clisson in the 14th century. The castle's military severity is softened by the more delicate inner façade, dating from the early 16th century and looking onto gardens. A fine Flamboyant Gothic building, the castle has delicately carved granite galleries, pinnacles, balustrades and chimney pieces, and is decorated with a range of motifs, including fleurs-de-lis, stoats and lozenges.

Detail of the chimney piece, with the Rohans' motto, "A Plus"

★ Library
Containing 3,000 volumes, the library was remodelled in the Neo-Gothic style in the 19th century.

★ Interior North Façade
This side of the castle has dormer windows with ornamental pediments. Each window is different, and together they embody the decorative repertoire of the time.

Olivier de Clisson

One of the most illustrious owners of the Château de Josselin was Olivier de Clisson (1336–1407). He married Marguerite de Rohan and in 1370 acquired the castle. De Clisson harboured a long hatred of the king of France, who had ordered his father's execution because of his support of the English. During the War of the Breton Succession, de Clisson sided with the English. However, he later transferred his allegiance to the French, befriending Bertrand du Guesclin and succeeding him as constable of France. De Clisson finally gave his daughter in marriage to the son of Charles of Blois, his erstwhile enemy.

Equestrian statue of Olivier de Clisson

KEY

① **Prison tower**

② **Ten dormer windows** rising through two storeys cover almost half the façade.

③ **The main courtyard** is an ideal place from which to take in this fine Gothic building.

★ Grand Salon
The room has a chimney piece decorated with garlands and hunting scenes, as well as 18th-century furniture and a portrait of Louis XIV painted by Rigaud.

VISITORS' CHECKLIST

Practical Information
Place de la Congrégation.
Tel (02) 97 22 36 45. Ground floor: **Open** Apr–mid-Jul: 2–6pm daily; mid-Jul–Aug: 11am–6pm daily; Sep: 2–5:30pm daily; Oct: Sat–Sun pm; school hols: pm daily. **Closed** Nov–Mar.

Façade over the Oust
The fortress stands on an outcrop of schist at the foot of which runs the Oust river. Only four of the nine towers raised by Olivier de Clisson survive.

③

Entrance gate

Entrance Gate
Beyond the entrance gate is an inner façade with a wealth of intricate carving.

Dining Room
The Neo-Gothic furniture in the dining room is the work of a local cabinetmaker and the design of the chimney piece echoes that in the Grand Salon.

Machicolated defences at the Château des Rohan in Pontivy

⓴ Baud

Road map D3. 24 km (15 miles) north of Auray via the D768. 🚉 Auray. 🚌 4,930. 🛈 Place de L'Eglise, Plumeliau (Apr–Oct). **Tel** (02) 97 08 04 07. 🚍 Sat.
🌐 **tourisme-baud-communaute.fr**

The small town of Baud overlooks the Evel valley. In the upper town is the Chapelle Notre-Dame, with an interesting 16th-century apse. In the lower town is the 16th-century **Fontaine Notre-Dame-de-la-Clarté**, which provides water for the old wash houses here.

Also of interest is the **Cartopole Conservatoire de la Carte Postale**, with a collection of 20,000 postcards depicting local history.

Environs
About 2 km (1 mile) southwest of Baud, near a ruined castle, is a statue known as the Vénus de Quinipily. Standing about 2 m (7 ft) high, the almost naked figure is inscribed with the mysterious letters "LIT". Either Egyptian or Roman, it may represent Isis, a fertility goddess revered by Roman legionaries.

Public footpaths traverse the woods around Baud. The Blavet valley also contains a large number of interesting calvaries, fountains and chapels. In summer, exhibitions of contemporary art are held in many of the villages.

🏛 **Cartopole Conservatoire de la Carte Postale**
3 Avenue Jean Moulin, Baud.
Tel (02) 97 51 15 14. **Open** mid-Jun–mid-Sep: Tue pm, Wed–Sat, Sun pm; mid-Sep–mid-Jun: Tue pm, Wed, Thu–Fri pm, Sat. **Closed** Nov–Easter. 🎨

㉑ Pontivy

Road map D3. 🚌 14,500. 🚉 🚌 Rue d'Iéna. 🛈 Duchesse Anne (barge), Quai Niémen; (02) 97 25 04 10. 🚍 Mon. 🎉 Kan ar Bol (Breton tales and songs, late Apr).
🌐 **tourisme-pontivycommunaute.com**

Fontaine Notre-Dame-de-la-Clarté in Baud

This town, the capital of the Rohan dynasty, consists of two distinct parts: the medieval town, with timber-framed houses and a great castle; and an imperial town, with straight avenues arranged around Place Aristide-Briand. This latter district was laid out on the orders of Napoleon, who aimed to make Pontivy a base from which to fight back against the Chouans (see p52).

The **Château des Rohan**, which was begun in 1479 by Jean II de Rohan, is a fine example of military architecture. The seignorial living quarters overlooking the courtyard were remodelled in the 18th century. Exhibitions and shows take place at the castle in summer.

The old town spreads out around the castle. Of the old town walls, only la Porte de Carhaix survives. The finest houses here, built in the 16th and 17th centuries, are those on Place du Martray and along Rue du Fil and Rue du Pont.

A canal runs alongside Pontivy, making the town an important intersection for river traffic. The towpath also offers the chance of walks through beautiful countryside.

🏰 **Château des Rohan**
Tel (02) 97 25 12 93. **Open** Feb–mid-Jun & mid-Sep–Nov: Wed– Sun pm; mid-Jun–mid-Sep: daily (phone first). 🎨

Napoleon-ville

In 1790, Pontivy sided with the Republicans and the town became the focus of the Chouan royalists' war (see p52). In March 1793, 10,000 recalcitrant peasants attacked the town. Napoleon chose Pontivy as a base from which to lead a counter-attack. He also decided to canalize the Blavet river between Brest and Nantes and built a new town. When the Napoleonic Empire collapsed, the project was still unfinished. An imperial district was, however, built during the reign of Napoleon III.

Mairie de Pontivy, built during the Napoleonic period

㉒ Guéméné-sur-Scorff

Road map C2. 19 km (12 miles) west of Pontivy via the D782. 🚉 1,500 🚇 Lorient. 🛈 1 Rue Haha; (02) 97 39 33 47. 🕒 Thu. 🎪 Fête de l'Andouille (late Aug). 🖥 **tourismepaysroimorvan.com**

Once the seat of the Dukes of Rohan, Guéméné-sur-Scorff was the object of bitter dispute during the War of the Breton Succession *(see p46)*. The town is now a centre of *andouille* (sausage) production. The buildings on Place Bisson reflect its former prosperity.

Frescoes in the choir of the church in Kernascléden

㉓ Kernascléden

Road map C3. 30 km (19 miles) southwest of Pontivy via the D782. 🛈 🖥 **tourismepaysroimorvan.com**.

It is worth stopping at this little village to visit the 15th-century church, which contains frescoes that are among the finest of their period. The choir is decorated with scenes of the life of the Virgin and of Christ's childhood. In the crossing is a chillingly realistic depiction of the Dance of Death, similar to that in the Chapelle Kermaria-an-Iskuit *(see p107)*, in the Côtes d'Armor.

The Oratoire St-Michel, attached to the Chapelle Ste-Barbe, near Le Faouët

㉔ Le Faouët

Road map C3. 35 km (22 miles) north of Lorient via the D769. 🚉 3,000. 🚇 Quimperlé. 🛈 3 Rue de Cendres; (02) 97 23 23 23. 🕒 first and third Wed in the month. 🎪 Pardons (last Sun in Jun, third Sun in Aug). 🖥 **tourismepaysroimorvan.com**

Isolated in undulating wooded landscape, the village of Le Faouët has a fine 16th-century covered market.

Set in a former convent, the **Musée des Peintres du Faouët** contains paintings of Breton country life. In the **Musée de l'Abeille Vivante et La Cité des Fourmis**, visitors can observe bees and ants.

Environs

The chapels in the vicinity of Le Faouët – St-Nicolas, Ste-Barbe and St-Fiacre – are each worth a visit. The most interesting is the Chapelle St-Fiacre, 3 km (2 miles) southeast of Le Faouët, in the Flamboyant Gothic style and with a gabled belfry. It also contains a beautiful rood screen.

The **Parc Aquanature Le Stérou**, 6 km (4 miles) southeast of Le Faouët, is a 70-ha (170-acre) nature park with a population of deer.

🏛 **Musée des Peintres du Faouët**
1 Rue de Quimper. **Tel** (02) 97 23 15 27. **Open** Apr–Jun & Sep–mid-Nov: Tue–Sat, Sun pm; Jul–Aug: daily. 🖼

🏛 **Musée de l'Abeille Vivante**
Kercadoret, Le Faouët. **Tel** (02) 97 23 08 05. **Open** Apr–Jun: daily pm; Jul–Aug: daily; Sep–mid-Nov: Tue–Sun pm. 🖼

🐾 **Parc Aquanature Le Stérou**
Route de Priziac. **Tel** (02) 97 34 63 84. **Open** Apr–Oct: daily. 🖼

The stud at Hennebont, housed in a former Cistercian abbey

㉕ Hennebont

Road map C3. 13 km (8 miles) northeast of Lorient, via the D769 then the D769 bis. 🚉 14,000. 🚇 🛈 9 Place du Maréchal-Foch; (02) 97 84 78 14. 🕒 Thu. 🎪 Medieval festivals (late Jul); Pardon (late Sep). 🖥 **lorientbretagnesudtourisme.fr**

Overlooking the steep banks of the Blavet river, Hennebont was once one of the largest fortified towns in the area. On Place Foch, with a central well (1623), is the Basilique Notre-Dame-du-Paradis, built in the 16th century. The walled town, damaged during World War II, is defended by the Porte du Broërec'h. This 13th-century gatehouse contains a **museum** of local history. A view of the gardens and the river can be enjoyed from the rampart walk.

The **Haras National** (National Stud), where 75 thoroughbreds (including Breton post-horses, Arabs and Selle Français) are kept, is housed in a former Cistercian abbey. Visitors can see the farrier's forge, the tack room, the stables, the school and a collection of carriages.

At Inzinzac, the former Forges d'Hennebont ironworks operated from 1860 to 1966 and played a role in the local economy. Now a museum, the **Écomusée Industriel**, exhibits metalworking techniques, and workers' living and working conditions at the time.

🏛 **Musée des Tours Broërec'h**
Rue de la Prison. **Tel** (02) 97 36 29 18. **Open** Jun–Sep: daily.🖼

♘ **Haras National**
Rue Victor-Hugo. **Tel** (02) 97 89 40 30. **Open** mid-Apr–mid-May & Sep: Mon–Fri, Sat–Sun pm; Jul–Aug: daily. 🖼

🏛 **Écomusée Industriel**
Inzinzac, Zone Industrielle des Forges. **Tel** (02) 97 36 98 21. **Open** Jun & Sep: Mon–Fri, Sun pm; Jul–Aug: Mon–Fri, Sat & Sun pm. 🖼

LOIRE-ATLANTIQUE

Between Ancenis in the east and St-Nazaire in the west, the great Loire river winds lazily, cutting through verdant lands and flowing through Nantes, the region's capital, before broadening into an estuary as it empties into the Atlantic. While the north of the Loire-Atlantique is a region of lakes and woodland, the south is characterized by mud flats, especially on the Guérande peninsula to the west.

Both in historical and in geographical terms, the Loire-Atlantique is assuredly Breton. Yet, incorporated into the Pays de la Loire in 1969, the region is also oriented towards the south and the Vendée, to the southwest.

The central axis of the Loire-Atlantique is the Loire estuary, which provides a link with the Atlantic. On it stands Nantes, the former capital of the dukes of Brittany, and today not only the capital of the Pays de la Loire but also the largest city in western France. Until the mid-19th century, the Loire was a major artery for the transport of commercial goods: salt from Guérande and fish from the Atlantic were transported inland by boat.

The Loire-Atlantique is made up of a mosaic of distinct areas. While the Presqu'île de Guérande and the coastal town of Le Croisic grew rich long ago from salt-panning, La Baule and the surrounding coastal resorts came into their own in the late 19th century. The industrial city of St-Nazaire enjoyed a golden age in the first half of the 20th century.

While the Pays de Retz, to the west, is a land of pasture, beaches and mud flats fringed by the sea, the Pays d'Ancenis, to the east, is a major wine-producing area, where hillsides are dotted with terracotta-roofed houses. The Forêt de Gâvre and the countryside around Châteaubriant, to the north, offer yet more lush landscapes.

View over the bridge near the port of Le Croisic

◀ Boats moored on the banks at Port St Martin

Exploring the Loire-Atlantique

Named after the river that traverses it from east to west, flowing into the Atlantic Ocean at St-Nazaire, the Loire-Atlantique is Brittany's most southerly region. The northwest of this *département*, consisting of the Presqu'île de Guérande and the great nature reserve of La Grande Brière, is dominated by heathland with outcrops of granite, by marshland and by a rocky coastline. Slate-roofed or thatched houses are ubiquitous here. The area around Châteaubriant, in the north, contains a central expanse of woodland with outcrops of blue-grey schist. This is good walking country. South of the Loire, vineyards where Muscadet and Gros Plant are grown stretch as far as the eye can see. In the Pays de Retz, which borders the Atlantic in the west, wide sandy beaches alternate with marshes where salt has been gathered since ancient times.

La Guérandière in Guérande

Sights at a Glance

1 Guérande
2 Le Croisic
3 La Baule
4 Pornichet
5 St-Nazaire
7 *Nantes pp210–15*
8 Pornic
9 Pays de Retz
10 Clisson
11 Pays d'Ancenis
12 Châteaubriant
13 Forêt du Gâvre

Tour

6 Parc Naturel Régional de la Grande Brière

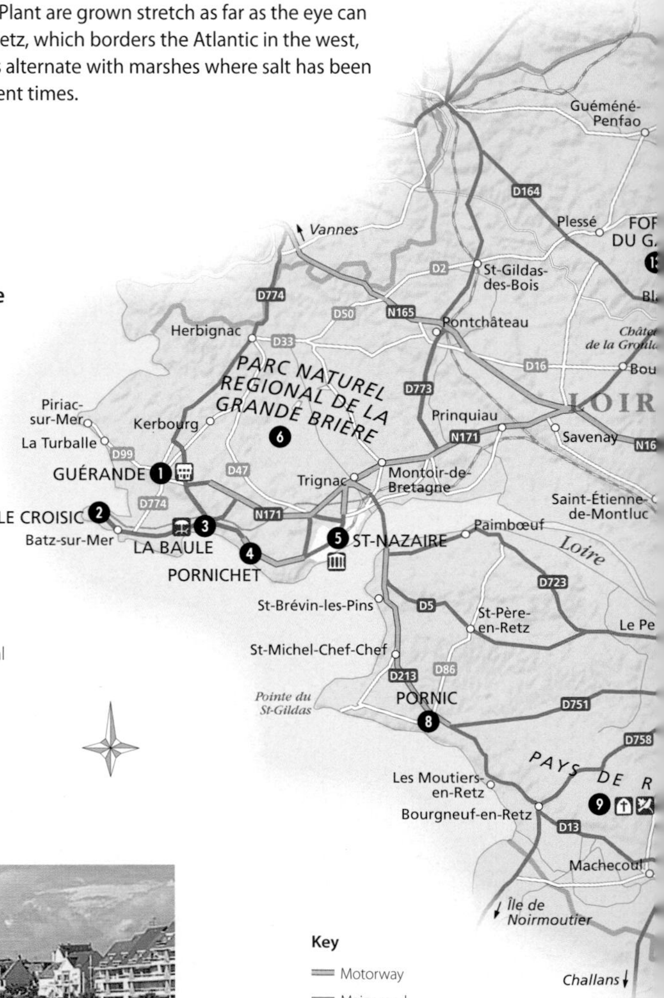

Key

═══ Motorway
═══ Major road
─── Secondary road
∙∙∙∙ Minor road
╌╌╌ Main railway
──── Minor railway
═══ Regional border

The harbour at Le Croisic

For hotels and restaurants see p229 and p243

0 kilometres 20
0 miles 10

↑ Vitré

CHÂTEAUBRIANT 🏠 **12**

→ Laval

← Rennes

D178

Derval

D775

D163

D771

St-Julien-
de-Vouvantes

Moisdon-
la-Rivière

N137

Treffieux

Don

D178

Nozay

La Meilleraye-
de-Bretagne

St-Mars-
la-Jaille

→ Angers

Saffiré

D33

Riaillé

Joué-s-Erdre

anal de Nantes

Nort-sur-
Érdre

→ Angers

éric

D16

D164

Mésanger

Ligné

PAYS D'ANCENIS

A11

D723

ATLANTIQUE

N137

Treillières

D178

Oudon

Ancenis ⓫

Varades

Carquefou

D723

Loire

Orvault

A11

A811

D751

Le Loroux-
Bottereau

NANTES 🏛 **7**

Château de Goulaine

D37

Rezé

Vertou

Vallet

N249

ouaye

✈

D763

→ Cholet

c de
ndé-
ieu

Passay

Aigrefeuille-
sur-Maine

D59

10 🏠 **CLISSON**

D937

D137

Gétigné

St-Philbert-
de-Grand-Lieu

A83

↓ Niort

Touvois

Legé

↓ La Roche-
sur-Yon

Allée Turenne, in Île Feydau, Nantes

The ruins of Château de Clisson

Getting Around

Nantes has an international airport and is also only 2 hours 15 minutes from Paris by TGV (high-speed train). The most direct road route from Paris to Nantes is the A11 motorway. From there, the N165, which becomes the N171, leads to St-Nazaire. The Pays de Retz, in the west, can be explored by taking the D213 from St-Nazaire or the D751 from Nantes. The N137 leads to the Pays de Gâvre, in the north, while the D178 runs north to Châteaubriant. The D723, along the Loire, leads to Ancenis, to the east. To the south, the N249 then the D763 run to Clisson.

For keys to symbols *see back flap*

Porte St-Michel, the main entrance into the walled town of Guérande

❶ Guérande

Road map D4. 🗾 12,000.
🚆 La Baule. ✈ Nantes-Atlantique.
🛈 1 Place du Marché-au-Bois; 0820 150 044. 🕘 Wed & Sat. 🎭 Remontée du Sel de Guérande (Apr–May), Fête Medievale (May), La Salicorne (Jun).
🅦 ot-guerande.fr

Overlooking extensive salt marshes on the Presqu'île de Guérande, this town has long depended on the salt-panning industry. Although this industry began in Roman times, it became important only in the 15th century.

The old town is enclosed within 14th- and 15th-century ramparts. The Porte St-Michel, the gatehouse and main entrance on the eastern side, contains the **Musée Château du Pays de Guérande** in which local furniture, costumes, faience and religious art are displayed. The Collégiale St-Aubin, the collegiate church in the centre of the old town,

was built in the 13th century and later remodelled. The interior has 14th- and 15th-century stained glass, and Romanesque capitals carved with scenes of martyrdom and fantastic animals. The **Musée de la Poupée et du Jouet Ancien** contains dolls and toys dating from 1830 to the present day.

Environs
The D99 running northwest out of Guérande leads to La Turballe, the largest sardine port on the Atlantic coast. The market where the fish auction takes place has an exhibiton on fishing. Past Pointe du Castelli, the road reaches the resort of Piriac-sur-Mer, where a granite church stands amid narrow streets.

The D774 south from Guérande winds through salt marshes, leading to Saillé, a typical salt-panning village. The **Maison des Paludiers** documents the history of salt-panning on the peninsula.

🏰 Musée Château du Pays de Guérande
Porte St-Michel. **Tel** (02) 28 55 05 05. **Open** Apr–Oct: Tue–Sun, Mon pm. 🖼

🏛 Musée de la Poupée
23 Rue de Saillé. **Tel** (02) 40 15 69 13. **Open** Apr–Oct: daily; other times, phone to check. **Closed** Jan. 🖼

🏛 Maison des Paludiers
18 Rue des Prés. Garnier, Saillé.
Tel (02) 40 62 21 96. **Open** Apr–Jun & Sep: daily pm; Jul–Aug: daily. 🖼

❷ Le Croisic

Road map D4. 🗾 4,450. 🚆 🚌 La Baule. ✈ Nantes-Atlantique. 🛈 6 Rue du Pilory; (02) 40 23 00 70.
🕘 Thu & Sat. 🎭 Fête de la Mer (Jun), Les Vieux Métiers de la Mer (Jul–Aug).

Set on a peninsula reaching 5 km (3 km) into the Atlantic, Le Croisic is both an active fishing port and a popular resort. The old town has some fine houses dating from the time when salt was shipped from Le Croisic to destinations as distant as the Baltic. In the **Océarium du Croisic**, one of the largest private aquariums in France, the marine life of the Atlantic coast can be observed.

The Flamboyant Gothic Église St-Guénolé has a high tower from which Batz-sur-Mer can be seen. The granite Chapelle Notre-Dame-du-Mûrier, built in the 15th century, is now in ruins.

Environs
The **Musée des Marais Salants** in Batz-sur-Mer, 5 km (3 miles) southeast of Le Croisic, documents the history of the salt marshes and the lives of salt panners in the 19th century.

🏛 Océarium du Croisic
Avenue de St-Goustan, Le Croisic.
Tel (02) 40 23 02 44. **Open** daily.
Closed Three weeks in Jan. 🖼 ♿
🅦 ocearium-croisic.fr

🏛 Musée des Marais Salants
29 bis, Rue Pasteur, Batz-sur-Mer.
Tel (02) 40 23 82 79. **Open** Jul–Aug: daily; Sep–Jun: Tue–Sun **Closed** two weeks in Jan. 🖼

The harbour at Le Croisic, with active fishing and shellfish-farming industries

The beautiful crescent-shaped beach at La Baule

❸ La Baule

Road map D4. 🗺 16,400. 🚍 🚌
🛈 8 Place de la Victoire; (02) 40 24 34 44. 🏛 Apr–Sep & school holidays: daily am (Jul & Aug all day); Oct–Mar: Tue–Sun, am. 🎭 Pardon d'Escoublac (Aug). La Baule Jazz Festival (Jul-Aug). 🌐 **labaule.fr**

Famous for its exceptionally long beach, which stretches for some 8 km (5 miles), La Baule became a holiday resort when the rail link with the interior opened in 1879. Residential districts were then created, and a multitude of villas and luxury hotels sprang up. The seafront promenade was opened in 1929. Later, however, apartment blocks replaced the seaside villas, although a few fine examples survive, particularly in the resort's eastern extension, La Baule-les-Pins. About 10 km (7 miles) inland is the large Forêt d'Escoublac, which is traversed by footpaths.

Detail from an elegant villa in Pornichet

❹ Pornichet

Road map D4. 🗺 8,160. 🚍 🚌 La Baule. 🛈 3 Boulevard de la République; (02) 40 61 33 33. 🏛 Wed & Sat; covered market daily Jun–Sep. 🌐 **pornichet.fr**

Occupying the eastern third of a wide bay, Pornichet is extended on its eastern side by several beaches and smaller bays. "Port Niché" (Nestling Harbour) began to grow into a fashionable resort in 1860, when publishers and other literary people came to enjoy the coast here. The Plage des Libraires (Booksellers' Beach) recalls those days.

This smart resort also boasts a number of elegant villas built between 1880 and 1930.

❺ St-Nazaire

Road map E4. 🗺 66,000. 🚍 🚌
🛩 Nantes-Atlantique. 🛈 Boulevard Légion d'Honneur; (02) 40 22 40 65. 🏛 Tue, Fri & Sun. 🎭 Les Escales (world-music festival, late July); Consonances (chamber music, Sep). 🌐 **saint-nazaire-tourisme.com**

The great shipyards of St-Nazaire began to develop in the 19th century, when ships too large to sail up the Loire to Nantes would dock here. The port is still a major industrial and shipbuilding centre today.

The **Écomusée**, in the harbour, illustrates the wildlife and history of the Loire estuary. It also gives access to *L'Espadon*, a French submarine built in 1957, in which the life of submariners is re-created. A monument commemorating the abolition of slavery stands near the ecomuseum.

The **STX Chantiers de l'Atlantique**, shipyards from which such legendary liners as *Normandie* (1932) and *France* (1960) were launched, and where impressive cruise liners are still built today, are open to visitors.

Escal-Atlantic, an exhibition tracing the history of ocean liners, is laid out in a huge Nazi blockhouse in the submarine base here.

🏛 **STX Chantiers de l'Atlantique, Ecomusée, Escal'Atlantic, L'Espadon submarine**
Port de St-Nazaire. **Tel** (02) 28 54 06 40. **Open** Each site has different opening hours, call for more detailed information. 🎫

Pont de St-Nazaire over the Loire estuary, the longest bridge in France

❻ Tour of the Parc Naturel Régional de la Grande Brière

Consisting of a landscape of reed beds crossed by canals, the Parc Naturel Régional de la Grande Brière occupies the centre of the Presqu'île de Guérande. This natural environment of 49,000 ha (121,000 acres) was made a protected area in 1970. It has an abundant population of birds, and also contains about 3,000 traditional stone-built, thatched houses, the highest concentration in France. One way of exploring the park is by boat, accompanied by local guide. Alternative ways to enjoy it are on foot, by bicycle, on horseback or by horse-drawn carriage.

① **Château de Ranrouet**
The origins of this imposing fortress, now in ruins, go back to the 13th century.

② **Les Jardins du Marais**
Over a hectare of land in size (2.5 acres), this private organic garden includes a vegetable plot, a flower garden, an experimental garden and a small wood. The grounds are cultivated without the use of pesticides.

③ **St-Lyphard**
From the belfry of the church in the village of St-Lyphard, there is a stunning view of Grande Brière.

④ **Kerhinet**
This village came to life again when Grande Brière was declared a protected area. It consists of a cluster of 18 thatched houses, including the park's Visitor Centre (Maison du Parc). About 1 km (0.5 mile) further west is a well-preserved Neolithic galleried grave.

⑤ **Bréca**
This barge port is located at the western extremity of the Bréca Canal, which opened in 1937–8 and which crosses Grande Brière from east to west, starting at Rozé.

⑩ La Barbière
The Dolmen de la Barbière at Crossac testifies to human habitation of this area 5,000 years ago. There are also megaliths at Herbignac and St-Lyphard.

⑪ Chapelle-des-Marais
The church contains a statue of St Cornély, protector of horned animals. Until 1966, each September the statue of carved wood was paraded through the town in a chariot drawn by 20 pairs of oxen crowned with roses.

⑨ Île de Fédrun
The centre of the island, inhabited since ancient times, was reserved for growing staple crops. A road running around the edge links the island's houses. The Maison de la Mariée (Bride's House) is at No. 182.

⑧ Rozé
This port, with a lock on its west side, is one of the points from which the water level is controlled. It was through Rozé that peat, Grande Brière's "black gold", was transported. The Reserve Pierre Constant is an ornithological reserve with look-out posts, information panels and hides.

⑦ Pont de Paille at Trignac
With its locks and pounds (holding areas for barges), Trignac is the largest barge port in Grande Brière. The bridge spans the Canal de Rozé, one of the major canals across the reserve.

⑥ La Chaussée-Neuve
This barge port, which once handled consignments of peat, now attracts people who come to the park to for bird-watching. At the beginning of each year, reed-cutters land their harvest here. The reeds are used to roof the houses in Grande Brière.

Key
▬ Suggested route
═ Other routes

❼ Nantes

Historic capital of the dukes of Brittany, Nantes is today capital of the Pays de la Loire. Such dual importance enhances the cultural diversity of this vibrant city. Connected to the Atlantic via the wide lower reaches of the Loire, Nantes is a port city, and historically the slave trade ensured its prosperity. But, in the heart of vegetable-growing country, Nantes is now focused on a land-based economy. A stately city but also a modern metropolis, an industrial and cultural centre with a well-respected university, Nantes is one of the most dynamic towns in France, with a steadily growing population and pleasant, well-kept districts.

Doorway and balcony in Rue Kervégan

🏛 Place du Bouffay

This is the heart of Nantes, where the founders of the future city settled, near the confluence of the Loire and the Erdre. In the Middle Ages, a fortress (destroyed in the 18th century) was built to serve as a prison and law tribunal, and executions took place on the square.

The street names in the vicinity echo the past: Rue de la Bâclerie (Bolt Street), with 15th-century timber-framed houses, Rue de la Juiverie (Jewry Street), Rue des Halles (Market Street), Place du Pilori (Stocks Square). The Église Ste-Croix, on Place Ste-Croix, was begun in the 17th century and completed 200 years later. The clock and bell were transferred from the destroyed Tour du Bouffay in 1860. This pedestrianized area is a part of Nantes that has been least affected by the city's rapid development.

🏛 Quartier Graslin

Place Royale links the medieval quarter of Nantes with the Neo-Classical Quartier Graslin. Laid out by the architect Mathurin Crucy in 1790, the square is lined with tall residential buildings of elegant restrained design. The blue granite fountain, dating from 1865, is decorated with personifications of the Loire and its tributaries.

Place Graslin, nearby, is named after Jean Graslin, a Parisian barrister who came to seek his fortune in Nantes in 1750. A shrewd speculator, he purchased land and commissioned Crucy to develop the district. Part of this development was the Neo-Classical **theatre**, centrepiece of the square. The building, fronted by eight Corinthian columns crowned with eight muses, is a focal point of cultural life in Nantes. Opposite

Statue in Passage Pommeraye

stands **La Cigale**, a famous brasserie that opened in 1895. The decoration of the interior, by Émile Libaudière, is in the Art Nouveau style: large areas of dark wood carvings are surrounded by motifs in ceramic, wrought iron, mosaic and plaster, featuring stylized cicadas *(cigales)*. This is somewhere to go as much to feast the eyes as to enjoy good food.

🏛 Île Feydeau

This district, a former island, was created when branches of the Loire were filled in in the 1930s and 1940s, and it is here that the wealth generated by a profitable trade in slaves and sugar is most evident. The luxurious private residences here were built in the 18th century by traders who bought slaves with cheap jewellery, sold them and then returned from Africa with vessels loaded with sugar.

Allée Turenne, Allée Duguay-Trouin, Allée Brancas, Rue Kervégan and Place de la Petite-Hollande are lined with houses decorated with masks, shells, the faces of bearded spirits and ears of corn, and faced with wrought-iron balconies – all outward signs of wealth.

🏛 Passage Pommeraye

Opened in 1843, this unusual arcade is named after the man who built it. Pommeraye, a lawyer, joined forces with Guilloux, a restaurateur, to create the arcade, designed on the model of those that were built in Paris at the time. The shops, cafés

The Neo-Classical theatre on Place Graslin

and restaurants that opened here soon attracted Nantes' wealthy inhabitants. The film-maker Jacques Demy, who was born in Nantes, chose the arcade as the location for two of his films, *Lola* and *Une Chambre en Ville*. An elegant wooden staircase, decorated with lamps and statues, gives access to the arcade's three galleries, on different levels. Between those on the upper floor is a Neo-Classical porch decorated with medallions.

🏛 Musée Thomas Dobrée

18 Rue Voltaire. **Tel** (02) 40 71 03 50. **Closed** temporary exhibitions as it is closed for renovation; due to reopen in 2015. 🛗

At the age of 28, Thomas Dobrée (1810–95), heir to a family business going back 300 years, turned down a career as a shipowner to concentrate on collecting art. In time, his collection came to encompass painting, sculpture and drawings, tapestries, furniture and porcelain, arms and armour,

Painting of Louis XII and Anne of Brittany, Musée Thomas Dobrée

and religious art. From 1862 until his death, Dobrée devoted himself to creating a suitable building in which to house the 10,000 pieces that his collection by then comprised. For this he commissioned the architect Viollet-le-Duc, who built the Neo-Gothic chateau that is now the Musée Thomas Dobrée.

Among the finest pieces on display here are a gold reliquary with a crown containing the heart of Anne of Brittany (1514), enamels, such as the 12th-century Reliquary of the True Cross, and the 13th-century Reliquary of St Calminius.

Engravings by Dürer, Schongauer, Rembrandt, Ruysdael and Jacques Callot are among the museum's masterpieces.

Two other buildings stand in the palace precinct. One is the Musée Archéologique, which is devoted to prehistory, ancient Egyptian and Greek artifacts and local Gaulish and Gallo-Roman history. The other is the Manoir de la Touche, which documents local history during the Revolution, especially the Vendée Wars.

Nantes City Centre

① Place du Bouffay
② Quartier Graslin
③ Île Feydeau
④ Passage Pommeraye
⑤ Musée Thomas Dobrée
⑥ Château des Ducs de Bretagne
⑦ Cathédrale St-Pierre-et-St-Paul
⑧ Musée des Beaux-Arts
⑨ Usine LU
⑩ Musée Jules-Verne
⑪ Jardin des Plantes

0 metres 400
0 yards 400

Around the Chateau and Beyond

The Château des Ducs de Bretagne *(see pp214–15)*, with Place du Bouffay and the Cathédrale St-Pierre-et-St-Paul, once formed the hub of Nantes. This nucleus is on the eastern side of the present city. The Jardin des Plantes, the Musée des Beaux-Arts and the picturesque Lieu Unique are other landmarks. The Musée Jules-Verne, devoted to this famous native of Nantes, is on the western side of the city, well beyond the port.

The Musée des Beaux-Arts, late 19th-century façade

Statue of Marguerite de Foix, Cathédrale St-Pierre-et-St-Paul

⛪ Cathédrale St-Pierre-et-St-Paul

Place St-Pierre. **Open** daily. 🅿

Standing on the site of a Roman building, vestiges of which remain in the crypt, the Flamboyant Gothic cathedral was begun in 1434. Its construction continued until the 19th century, when the apse was completed.

The cathedral has richly decorated doorways and an impressively lofty nave, 37 m (120 ft) high. The choir and ambulatory are lit by contemporary stained-glass windows. A fine example of the Renaissance style, the black and white marble tomb of François II and his wife Marguerite de Foix was carved by Michel Colombe in 1507. It is surrounded by allegorical statues; that of Justice is thought to portray their daughter, Anne of Brittany.

Porte St-Pierre, next to the cathedral and once part of the walls that surrounded Nantes, leads to Cours St-Pierre, a walkway where there are remains of the 13th-century ramparts. Impasse St-Laurent, on the left of the cathedral, leads to La Psalette, a charming 15th-century Gothic house.

🏛 Musée des Beaux-Arts

10 Rue Georges-Clémenceau. **Tel** (02) 51 17 45 00. **Closed** for renovations until 2016. 🅿

Built by the architect Josso, a native of Nantes, in the late 19th century, this is one of the best-designed museums of its period.

The ground floor, of simple design and lit by natural light, is devoted to modern and contemporary art, from Impressionism to the present day, and including abstract art of the 1950s. Besides paintings by the Fauves and the Nabis, there are two Monets *(Water-lilies* and *Gondolas in Venice)*, *Lighthouse at Antibes* by Signac, and works by Dufy, Émile Bernard, Mauffra and the Pont-Aven School *(see p175)*, as well as 11 paintings by Kandinsky.

The first floor is devoted to major periods in the history of art from the 13th century to the first half of the 19th. The collection of early Italian painting includes a *Virgin in Majesty* by the Master of Bigallo. A typically full-blooded Rubens, *Judas Maccabaeus Praying for the Dead* (1635), provides a dramatic and strong contrast to peaceful Dutch and Flemish landscapes and still-life paintings.

French painting of the 17th century is represented by three works by Georges de la Tour, a master of the depiction of light: *The Hurdy-Gurdy Player, St Peter's*

The Revolution in Nantes

During the civil war fought between royalists and republicans during the French Revolution, one man in particular stood out in the political climate that prevailed in Nantes. Jean-Baptiste Carrier, a member of the Convention (revolutionary assembly), was sent to Brittany on a mission to pacify the region. After the royalist Chouans were defeated at Savenay, he inflicted on the citizens of Nantes a cruel repression. He designed boats with a hull that could be opened when the vessel reached the middle of the Loire, drowning as many as 100 people at a time. "Republican weddings" consisted of tying a man and a woman together and tossing them into the river. Some 5,000 people lost their lives under this regime. Executions of royalists also took place on Place Viarme, in Nantes.

Mass drownings organized by Jean-Baptiste Carrier in Nantes in June 1793

Le Gaulage des Pommes, by Émile Bernard, Musée des Beaux-Arts

Denial and *Apparition of the Angel before St Joseph*.

Highlights of the 19th-century collections include works by Ingres, particularly his beautiful portrait of *Madame de Senonnes* (1814), by Delacroix *(Caïd, Moroccan Chief)*, and by Corot *(Democrites and the Abderitans)*, as well as paintings by the Barbizon School. In the room devoted to Courbet, the subject matter and composition of *The Gleaners* demonstrates his skill as a realist.

🏛 Les Machines de l'Îles des Nantes

l'Îles de Nantes.
This former scrap of wasteland on the banks of the Loire is an ongoing urban redevelopment project. The Nefs, the ancient naval workshops, are home to Les Machines de l'Îles des Nantes. Visitors can ride the Grand Elephant, an articulated wooden elephant, and visit bars and restaurants.

🏛 Usine LU, Lieu Unique

Rue de la Biscuiterie, Quai Ferdinand-Favre. **Tel** (02) 40 12 14 34. **Open** Tue–Sun pm, Jul–Aug: daily pm. 📷

The history of Nantes is inseparable from that of the almost legendary biscuit, the Petit-Beurre LU, which people have enjoyed for over a century.

In 1846, the Lefèvre-Utile, a couple from Lorraine who settled in Nantes, opened their first pâtisserie. To challenge competition from British imports, they began making biscuits on an industrial scale and in 1885 built a factory. The Petit-Beurre was launched, followed by the Paille d'Or. From 1913, the factory turned out 20 tonnes of biscuits per day. When it became too small to meet the growing demand, the site was abandoned.

Threatened with demolition in 1995, the factory was rescued and, since 1999, what became known as the Lieu Unique (Unique Place) has become a cultural centre where festivals, shows and exhibitions take place. It is very popular with the people of Nantes.

🌿 Jardin des Plantes

Boulevard Stalingrad & Place Sophie-Trébuchet. **Open** daily.

Opened in the early 19th century, the botanical garden – the second-largest in France after the Jardin des Plantes in Paris – covers 7 ha (17 acres) and contains 12,000 species of plants. It was originally a garden of mostly medicinal plants, but sea captains brought back exotic specimens that rapidly broadened its scope. Today, the garden contains over 200 varieties of camellia, which grow beneath the oldest magnolias in Europe. In the tropical greenhouses flourish a great many species of orchid.

🏛 Musée Jules-Verne

3 Rue de l'Hermitage. **Tel** (02) 40 69 72 52. **Open** Jul–Aug: daily; Sep–Jun: Mon, Wed–Sat, Sun pm. 📷 🎫 Jul–Aug.

This small house at the top of a steep street is the birthplace of the writer Jules Verne. The museum that it now contains gives a detailed account of his life and work, and of the peculiar world that he created in his novels. Books, souvenirs, quotations, humorous drawings, cards, magic lanterns and models draw the visitor into the imaginary world created by the writer. There is also furniture from his house in Amiens, where Verne spent most of his life.

Jules Verne, born in Nantes in 1828

Environs

The 11th-century **Château de Goulaine**, 13 km (8 miles) southeast of Nantes, contains a collection of tropical butterflies, and an exhibition documenting the history of the LU biscuit factory. The reception rooms are sumptuously decorated.

🏰 Château de Goulaine

Haute-Goulaine. **Tel** (02) 40 54 91 42. **Open** mid-Jul–mid-Sep: daily; rest of year: call ahead. 📷 🎫 for groups, all year round by arrangement. ♿

Musée Jules-Verne in Nantes, the birthplace of writer Jules Verne

Château des Ducs de Bretagne

On the banks of the Loire, the Château des Ducs de Bretagne was founded in the 13th century, and served both as a residential palace and military fortress. Anne of Brittany was born here in 1477, and it is here that Henri IV is supposed to have signed the Edict of Nantes in 1598. Over the centuries, the castle was continually remodelled. The sturdy towers and drawbridge are counterbalanced by delicate Renaissance buildings facing on to the courtyard. Converted into barracks in the 18th century, the castle passed into state ownership after World War I. A restoration programme to return the buildings to their original appearance was carried out between 1993 and 2006. The castle now contains a major museum of the history of Nantes, with more than 850 historical objects arranged across 32 rooms.

★ **Grand Logis**
The façade bears the coat of arms of Louis XII and Anne of Brittany.

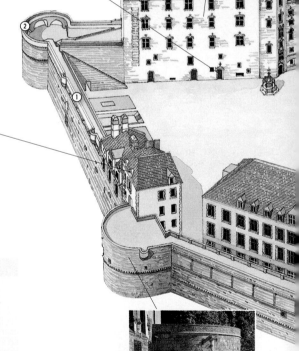

Entrance to museum

Petit Gouvernement
Built in the 16th century, during the reign of François I, the king's apartments are now known as the Petit Gouvernement (Governor's Small Palace). The dormer windows are typical of the Renaissance.

KEY

① **Courtine de la Loire**, the wall linking Tour de la Rivière and Tour du Port, was built in the 15th and 16th centuries.

② **Tour du Port** was hidden by a bastion for 200 years. The bastion was demolished in 1853.

③ **The castle museum** is devoted to regional folk art of the 16th to 20th centuries.

④ **Bastion St-Pierre**, built in the 16th century, was levelled off in 1904.

⑤ **The Harness Room** was built by the army in the 17th and 18th centuries.

Tour de la Rivière
Forming part of the castle's system of defences, the Tour de la Rivière consists of two floors with a terrace above.

Grand Gouvernement
The ducal palace, known since the 17th century as the Grand Gouvernement (Governor's Great Palace), has been restored to its original splendour. The double staircase leads up to a single row of steps beneath a porch.

VISITORS' CHECKLIST

Practical Information
4 Place Marc-Elder. **Tel** 08 11 46 46 44. Ramparts and courtyard: **Open** daily. Musée d'Histoire: **Open** Sep–Jun: Tue–Sun; Jul–Aug: daily. ♿ ⬛ ⬛ (museum only; moat ditches, courtyard and sentry walk free). 🅦 **chateau-nantes.fr**

★ Vieux Donjon
The polygonal keep, built in the 14th century on the orders of Jean IV de Montfort, is the oldest part of the castle. It is attached to the 18th-century caretaker's lodge.

★ Tour du Fer-à-Cheval
This shield decorates the keystone of the vaulting inside the Tour du Fer-à-Cheval (Horseshoe Tower). Guarding the northwest corner of the castle, it is a fine example of 15th-century military architecture.

Illustrious Guests

Henri IV
(1553–1610)

Many famous people have passed through the gates of the Château des Ducs de Bretagne. The wedding of François II of Brittany and Marguerite de Foix took place here in 1471, and it was also here that their daughter, Anne, Duchess of Brittany, was married to Louis XII in 1499. In 1532, François I of France came here to mark the "permanent union of the duchy and country of Brittany with the kingdom of France", as an inscription in the courtyard recalls. Henri II, then Charles IX, also stayed in the castle. In 1598, Henri IV thrashed out the terms of the Edict de Nantes, which legalized Protestantism. He may even have signed the edict at the castle. Louis XIV also stayed here when he came to Nantes in 1661, during a gathering of the States of Brittany.

The thalassotherapy centre on Plage de l'Alliance, in Pornic

8 Pornic

Road map E5. 14,000. 🚃 🚌 ⛴. ℹ️ Place de la Gare; (02) 40 82 04 40. ⛴ Thu & Sun. 🎪 Fête de St-Gilles (traditional music and dance festival, Aug). 🌐 ot-pornic.fr

This small fishing port is also a coastal resort with yachting harbours and a thalassotherapy centre. The lower town, with brightly painted fishermen's houses, is dominated by the outline of the castle, which was owned by Gilles de Rais *(see p47)* in the 15th century. It was remodelled by Viollet-le-Duc in the 19th century. The coast road beyond Pornic is lined with 19th-century villas where the writers Michelet and Flaubert and the painter Renoir once stayed.

St-Michel-Chef-Chef, 9 km (5 miles) further north, is renowned for its biscuits made with salted butter, and for its wide beach.

9 Pays de Retz

Road map E5. Machecoul. Between the D751 and the D13. 🚃 🚌 Nantes. ℹ️ 3 Chausée du Pays de Retz Bernerie; (02) 40 82 70 99. 🌐 paysderetzatlantatlantique.fr

Machecoul, once the capital of the Pays de Retz, was the fiefdom of Gilles de Rais, the local Bluebeard *(see p47)*. The ruins of one of his castles still stand here.

The **Musée du Pays de Retz** at Bourgneuf-en-Retz, 12 km (9 miles) further west on the D13, describes the local salt-panning and fishing industries, as well as the crafts of the past. Les Moutiers-en-Retz, on the coast, owes its name to two 11th-century monasteries. Vestiges of these buildings can be seen in the Église St-Pierre, which was built in the 16th century in the Gothic style. Close to this church is an 11th-century lantern whose flame was intended to cast light into the darkness for the benefit of the dead.

The Lac de Grand-Lieu, to the east, is an unusually rich bird sanctuary. The **Maison du Lac** here documents the local wildlife, including 225 species of birds, among which are heron and teal. Built in the 9th century, the Carolingian abbey church of **Abbaye de St-Philbert**, at St Philbert-de-Grand-Lieu, is one of the oldest churches in France. In the crypt lies the tomb of St Philbert, the abbey's founder.

🏛 Musée du Pays de Retz
Rue des Moines, Bourgneuf-en-Retz. **Tel** (02) 40 21 40 83. **Open** Mar–Jun: Tue–Sun pm; Jul–Aug: daily. **Closed** Oct–Feb. 🔲 🦽

⚜ Maison Guerlain
St-Philbert-de-Grand-Lieu. **Tel** (02) 40 78 73 88. **Open** Apr–Sep: daily; Oct–Mar: Tue–Sat, Sun pm.

🏛 Abbaye de St-Philbert
ℹ️ St-Philbert de Grand-Lieu; (02) 40 78 73 88. **Open** daily.

🔟 Clisson

Road map F5. 20 km (12 miles) south of Nantes via the D59. 5,900. 🚃 Place du Minage; (02) 40 54 02 95. ⛴ Tue. 🎪 Les Italiennes de Clisson (theatre, music & film, Jul); Les Médiévales (Aug, every two years). 🌐 levignobledenantestourisme. com

A romantic dream led to the development of Clisson. In the 19th century, the Cacault brothers, natives of Nantes who loved Italy, built themselves a Tuscan-style villa here. This set a trend, and ochre-walled, red-roofed houses, in contrast to those roofed in the customary slate, began to spring up.

Although it is in ruins, the **Château de Clisson** here, built in stages between the 13th and the 16th centuries, well illustrates the evolution of military architecture. **La Garenne Lemot**, an estate near the town's eastern exit, has two further examples of the Italianate style: the estate office, by the architect Crucy (1815), and the Villa Lemot, designed by the sculptor Lemot (1824). The surrounding parkland is decorated with antique columns, obelisks, follies and other ornaments. Muscadet and Gros Plant vines are grown in the vineyards between Clisson and the Loire.

🏰 Château de Clisson
Place du Minage. **Tel** (02) 40 54 02 22. **Open** Oct–Apr: Wed–Sun pm; May–Sep: Wed–Mon. 🔲 🦽

🏰 La Garenne Lemot
Gétigné. **Tel** (02) 40 54 75 85. Park: **Open** daily. Estate office: **Open** May–Sep: daily; Oct–Apr: Tue–Sun pm. Villa Lemot: **Open** temporary exhibitions.

Château de Clisson at Place du Minage

⑪ Pays d'Ancenis

Road map F4. Ancenis. 30 km (19 miles) east of Nantes via the A11 or the N23. 🚶 7,000. 🚌 ✈ Nantes-Atlantique. 🛈 27 Rue du Château; (02) 40 83 07 44. 🎭 Fête de la Loire et des Vins (every two years in May, next festival 2016). 🛍 Thu & Sat.

This area of countryside, whose focal point is the town of Ancenis, flanks a stretch of the Loire that in places runs between high cliffs.

Ancenis, set in the midst of vineyards, has some elegant wine merchants' houses and the 16th-century **Château d'Ancenis**.

Further downstream is the **Donjon d'Oudon**, a 14th-century keep. Overlooking Ancenis, the keep is also ideally situated to survey the Loire, once the main traffic artery in western France. Further upstream is Varades. The elegant 19th-century Italian-style **château**, Palais Briau, here was built by an engineer who had made his fortune during the reign of Napoleon III.

🏰 Château d'Ancenis
Rue du Pont. **Tel** (02) 40 83 07 44.
Closed for renovations until 2016.

🏰 Château de Varades
Palais Briau. **Tel** (02) 40 83 45 00. Park:
Open Apr–Sep: Wed–Mon pm. Palais:
Open Apr–Sep: Sat, Sun & public holidays pm; Aug: Wed–Mon pm.
🎟 obligatory. 🅿

🏰 Donjon d'Oudon
Rue du Pont-Levis. **Tel** (02) 40 83 60 00. **Open** Mar: Sun & public hols pm; Apr–Sep: daily; Oct: Sat & Sun. 🅿

The Nantes–Brest Canal at Blain, just south of the Forêt du Gâvre

⑫ Châteaubriant

Road map F3. 🚶 13,380. 🚌 🛒 🛈 29 Place Charles de Gaulle (02) 40 28 20 90. 🛍 Wed am. 🎭 Foire de Béré (Sep). 🌐 **tourisme-chateaubriant.fr**

The few surviving schist-built medieval houses here give the walled town of Châteaubriant a historic atmosphere. Two **chateaux** stand in close proximity on a hill overlooking the Chère river: a medieval fortress, with a keep, and an

South gallery of the Renaissance chateau in Châteaubriant

elegant Renaissance chateau with a main building flanked by wings.

The Romanesque Église St-Jean-de-Béré, built in contrasting blue schist and red granite, contains a 17th-century Baroque altarpiece.

🏰 Châteaux
Access via Place Charles-de-Gaulle.
Tel (02) 40 28 20 20. **Open** May–Sep: Wed–Mon; Oct–Apr: Sat–Sun pm.
🎟 interiors of the castles. 🅿 (entry to the park is free).

⑬ Forêt du Gâvre

Road map E4. Blain.35 km (22 miles) north of Nantes via the N137 then the D164. 🚶 7,450. 🛈 2 Place Jean-Guilhard, Blain; (02) 40 87 15 11. 🛍 Tue & Sat am. 🎭 St-Laurent (Aug).

Covering a large massif enclosed by the Don, Isac and Brivet rivers, the forest is good walking country. There is also an interesting museum and a chateau to explore here.

The **Musée de Blain**, in Blain, on the D164, is devoted to popular art and tradition from prehistoric and Gallo-Roman times to the early 20th century. The **Château de la Groulais**, in the direction of St-Nazaire, was the residence of the Clisson and Rohan families during the Middle Ages. There is a restaurant in the cellars.

🏛 Musée de Blain
2 Place Jean-Guilhard, Blain. **Tel** (02) 40 79 98 51. **Open** Tue–Sat, pm. 🅿

🏰 Château de la Groulais
South exit from Blain. **Tel** (02) 40 79 07 81. **Open** Jul–Aug: Tue–Fri pm.
Closed Nov–Mar: groups only, by arrangement.

Vendée Wars

In 1793, the persecution of the clergy, the execution of Louis XVI and a rise in taxation provoked an anti-republican uprising in the Vendée. Royalists soon followed up with acts of barbarism, and the execution of republicans in Machecoul began on 11 March. Catelineau, a carter, and Stofflet, a gamekeeper, joined by various aristocrats, stirred up revolt among the peasantry. In June, the Armée Catholique et Royale Vendée seized control of the Vendée, as well as the towns of Saumur and Angers, but it was defeated by the republicans at Cholet on 17 October. On the orders of General Turreau, the latter led punitive expeditions in the Vendée in 1794–5.

Republican prisoners being given their freedom

TRAVELLERS' NEEDS

WHERE TO STAY

For many decades, Brittany has been among the most popular tourist destinations in France. As a result, the region is well equipped to cater for the needs of visitors. From grand chateaux to basic camping sites, and including a number of familiar hotel chains, there is accommodation to suit every taste and budget. Even at individual locations the choice is wide. Accommodation along Brittany's coasts is, of course, more varied and plentiful, even though there is much to interest visitors in areas further inland. While the resorts are oriented towards beaches, watersports and sailing, a warm welcome at a countryside guesthouse brings visitors closer to the soul of Brittany.

Reservations

In the summer season, Brittany, like any other holiday destination that attracts large numbers of visitors, becomes very crowded. This is particularly true during school holidays and over long holiday weekends, and also when local festivals and other events take place.

It is, therefore, essential to book accommodation well in advance. Nearly all hotels, *chambres d'hôtes* (bed and breakfast) and gîtes have websites that allow visitors to reserve online, although some still prefer phone reservations. Whether you would like to stay in a characterful hotel or B&B, or if you have in mind a particular area of Brittany or simply need a suggestion for a weekend break, the regional tourism office **Tourisme Bretagne** can provide all the information.

Hotel Categories

The **French Ministry of Tourism** grades hotels into five categories, with a rating of one to five stars. However, the system was reformed and now rates all accommodation (except for B&Bs) according to three criteria: comfort of facilities, quality of services, and good practice with regard to respecting the environment and welcoming disabled customers.

Prices

In Brittany, as in the rest of France, advertised prices include tax and service. Charges are per room rather than per person, except when board or half-board is offered. In rural areas, half-board may occasionally be compulsory, or even the sole option when the hotel is the only place in the area where visitors can have a meal.

Most establishments add a small charge for a third person or a child sharing a double room. Some hotels close during the winter, and those that stay open often offer advantageous rates

La Ferme Saint-Vennec in Combrit (*see p227*)

during the low season. Check websites for information on off-season rates and deals.

Chain Hotels

Hotel chains are well represented in Brittany, including **Louvre Hotels**, which includes the Campanile, Kyriad and Première Classe subchains and **Accor Hotels**, with the **Ibis**, **Novotel**, **Sofitel** and **Mercure** subchains. Strict quality controls ensure that these establishments offer a high standard of comfort and cleanliness as well as an excellent range of amenities. For travellers on a tighter budget, **Formule 1**, **B+B Hotels** and **Balladins** are some of the hotel chains designed to provide basic facilities at a low price.

Traditional Family-run Hotels

Establishments affiliated to **Logis de France**, the leading independent association of hotels in Europe, will suit visitors who prefer smaller

Castel Beau Site in Perros-Guirec (*see p225*)

◀ Cafés under half-timbered houses lining the street at Place de Ste-Anne, Rennes

hotels with local character. Hotels in this chain offer a more personal welcome and an authentic flavour of their particular locality. The hotels themselves are usually characterful buildings that are very much in keeping with their surroundings.

Relais du Silence is an affiliation of distinguished hotels with a friendly atmosphere and where peace and relaxation are a prime consideration. They have a two- to five-star rating.

Luxury Hotels

Those who like a little luxury and a memorable gastronomic experience will not be disappointed by the finest hotels in Brittany. A large number of chateaux and listed buildings have been converted into upmarket accommodation, some of which employ the services of prestigious chefs. Such hotels are ideal for visitors seeking the very best in French hospitality and cuisine.

These luxury establishments often belong to either of the two main associations. One is **Relais et Châteaux**, with 13 hotel-restaurants in Brittany, including the **Château de Locguénolé in Hennebont** (see p228). The other is **Châteaux et Hôtels de France**, with 18 establishments in Brittany, including the **Hôtel Reine Hortense** in Dinard

The Grand Hôtel des Thermes in St-Malo *(see p225)*

The Hôtel Reine Hortense in Dinard *(see p224)*

(see p224) and the **Auberge Bretonne** in La Roche-Bernard (see p228).

Thalassotherapy

This therapeutic treatment uses the curative powers of sea water, which is rich in iodine and trace elements, and whose curative effects and revitalizing properties are widely known. Between St-Malo in the north and La Baule in the south, Brittany has 13 thalassotherapy centres. Among the best known are the Thermes Marins in St-Malo, where there are six sea-water swimming pools.

Thalassotherapy centres offer several options that also include accommodation. There are, for instance, antistress treatments, cures to combat the effects of smoking, and post-natal courses. Full details on thalassotherapy in Brittany are available from Tourisme Bretagne.

Chambres d'Hôtes

Private houses or chateaux with rooms to let are a popular option. Staying in a B&B provides the opportunity to meet local people and to experience Breton culture at a more authentic level than is possible when staying in a hotel. Like hotels, they vary from the basic to extremely luxurious. Many also offer cottages and apartments for families.

Some B&B offer *table d'hôte* (meals) for guests. These offer an opportunity to enjoy local specialities in informal surroundings, often for less than the price of a meal at a restaurant.

Local tourist offices can provide lists of private houses offering B&B accommodation in their areas. The **Gîtes de France** publish the *Chambres d'Hôtes en Bretagne*, a full listing giving all details to their members; the details can also be found on their website, www.gites-de-france-bretagne.com.

The Hôtel Ker Moor in St-Quay-Portrieux *(see p226)*

Country Gîtes

Gîtes ruraux (country gîtes) are fully furnished houses or apartments built in the local rural style. All are privately owned, and a good many are affiliated to the national **Gîtes de France** association. Each *département* in Brittany has its own office and website listing gîtes and B&Bs with booking information.

Gîtes de France also issues lists of specific types of accommodation: *gîtes de caractère* (picturesque houses), *gîtes de charme* (usually more luxurious houses), *ecogîtes* (environment-friendly), *gîtes de pêche* (for fishing), *gîtes d'étape* (dormitory accommodation for groups), *gîtes Panda* (in the Parc Naturel Régional d'Armorique; (*see pp146–7*), *gîtes au jardin* (houses with access to private gardens), *gîtes bébé* (safe for young children) and *gîtes de grande capacité* (sleeping 9 or more).

The Gîtes de France association also issues a free guide, *Bienvenue à la Ferme en Bretagne*, sponsored by the Chambres d'agriculture. It lists places to stay on working farms, either in *gîtes ruraux*, B&B rooms or campsites. There are over 120 listings on its website, and often prices are very reasonable.

Self-Catering Accommodation

Self-catering accommodation is often also available in seaside apartments or cottages. Rental is by the week, usually starting on Saturdays. Weekend bookings may also be possible, except in the high season. Check local tourist office websites for lists of self-catering accommodation. The **Federation Nationale des Locations de France Clévances** lists over 2,000 holiday rentals in Brittany; other good sources are **Owners Direct** and **Homeaway**.

Youth Hostels

Some of the least expensive accommodation may be found in *auberges de jeunesse* (youth hostels). They are available to everyone, regardless of age, as long as they have a **Youth Hostel Association** or a **Hostelling International** card. If you are not a member of the YHA in your home country, you will have to pay a surcharge each time you stay in a French youth hostel. A full list of youth hostels is available on YHA's website.

Campsites

Many campsites in Brittany are set in fine locations, perhaps beside the sea or, inland, deep in a forest. The **Fédération Française de Camping et de Caravaning** publishes an official guide of approved campsites, which can be downloaded online. Gîtes de France also provides a guide to campsites on its website. In all cases, it is advisable to book in advance, especially in July and August.

Campsites are subject to an official classification system, which runs from a one- to a four-star rating according to toilet, washing and other facilities such as swimming pools and television. Three- and four-star sites are usually very spacious with plenty of amenities and electricity connections for tents and caravans. One- and two-star sites, often in more remote areas, always have toilets and running water. It is sometimes possible to hire tents and camper vans, or rent bungalows.

Camping rough, or camping nature, at one of the unofficial campsites along the coast also has its attractions. Such sites often have stunning locations and charge very little.

Disabled Travellers

Various organizations provide information on holidays and establishments with facilities for disabled people. The **Association des Paralysés de France** (APF) and **Handitourisme Bretagne** provide all information on their special holiday website. Gîtes de France publishes a list of *gîtes tourisme et Handicap* for people with disabilities. These gîtes

Camper vans at a site on Pointe de l'Arcouest, on the Côtes d'Armor *(see p105)*

come with wheelchair access and special equipment adapted for those with hearing, visual and mental disabilities.

Other useful sources of information are **Tourism for All** (UK) and **Mobility International** (US) who list specialized tour operators for disabled visitors.

Due to the age of many Breton hotels, few are able to offer unrestricted wheelchair access to the entire hotel. Larger hotels have lifts, and hotel staff will go out of their way to aid disabled guests. Most resort hotels, and many B&Bs have at least one accessible room.

Recommended Hotels

The hotels and B&Bs featured in this guide have been chosen for the quality of accommodation, location, historical character

A pretty youth hostel close to the old town district of Quimper

and, in some cases, for good value. They are listed by department and town, and categorized by a theme that best denotes their character. Besides **Luxury** hotels and **B&Bs**, there are **Historic** hotels located in châteaux, manor houses, long houses, turn-of-the-century seaside villas or even thatched cottages. **Classic** hotels are the ones that are especially built as

hotels – this encompasses both chain and independent hotels. **Family** hotels are particularly welcoming to people travelling with children.

Look out for establishments designated as "DK Choice" in recognition of one or more outstanding features – excellent facilities, a stunning location and superb views, evocative history, boutique design or charm.

DIRECTORY

Reservations

French Government Tourist Offices
UK: Lincoln House, 300 High Holborn, London WC1V 7JH.
Tel 020 7061 6600 (within UK only).
US (east coast): 825 Third Ave, New York NY 10022.
Tel 212 838 7800.
North America (Canada): 1800 Avenue McGill College Bereau 1010, Montreal, Quebec.
Tel 00 1 514 288 20 26.
w int.rendezvous-enfrance.com

Tourisme Bretagne
8 Rue de l'Arrivée, 75015 Paris. **Tel** (01) 53 63 11 50.
w bretagne.fr

Chain Hotels

Accor Hotels
Tel 08 25 88 00 00.
w accorhotels.com

B+B Hotels
Tel 08 92 78 29 29.
w hotel-bb.com

Balladins
Tel 08 25 08 84 53.
w balladins.com

Formule 1
Tel 0892 685 685.
w hotelf1.com

Ibis, Novotel, Sofitel, Mercure
Tel 0871 663 0624 (UK).
w accor.com

Louvre Hotels
w louvrehotels.com

Traditional Family-run Hotels

Logis de France
Tel (01) 45 84 70 00.
w logishotels.com

Relais du Silence
Tel (01) 70 23 81 63.
w relaisdusilence.com

Luxury Hotels

Châteaux et Hôtels de France
Tel 08 92 23 00 75.
w chateaux hotels.com

Relais et Châteaux
Tel (01) 76 49 39 39.
w relaischateaux.com

Chambres d'Hôtes

Gîtes de France
56 Rue St-Lazare, 75439 Paris.
Tel 0826 10 44 44.
w gites-de-france.com

Self-Catering Accommodation

Federation Nationale des Locations de France Clévacances
54 Blvd de l'Embouchure CS 22361 31022 Toulouse Cedex 2.
Tel 05 32 10 82 30.

Homeaway
w homeaway.co.uk

Owners Direct
w ownersdirect.co.uk

Youth Hostels

Hostelling International-American Youth Hostels (HI-AYH)
8401 Colesville Rd, Suite 600, Silver Spring MD 2091D.
Tel 240 650 2100.
w hiusa.org

Youth Hostel Association (YHA)
Trevelyan House, Dimple Rd, Matlock, Derbyshire DE4 3YH.
Tel 01629 592 700.
w yha.org.uk

Campsites

Fédération Française de Camping et de Caravaning
78 Rue de Rivoli, 75004 Paris.
Tel 01 42 72 84 08.
w ffcc.fr

Disabled Travellers

Association des Paralysés de France (APF)
w vacances-accessibles.apf.asso.fr

Handitourisme Bretagne
w handi.tourisme bretagne.com

Mobility International
w miusa.org

Tourism for All
w tourismforall.org.uk

Where to Stay

Ille-et-Vilaine

DK Choice

BAZOUGES-LA-PÉROUSE:
Château de la Ballue €€€
B&B **Map** F2
Bazouges-la-Pérouse, 35560
Tel *(02) 99 97 47 86*
🔲 la-ballue.com
This 17th-century chateau is
among the most elegant places
to stay near Mont-St-Michel. It is
surrounded by remarkable landscaped gardens planted in the
1970s with topiary twists, sculptures, and a labyrinth of 1500
yews inspired by a La Corbusier
design. Period furnishings adorn
the luxurious bedrooms and
salons. Exceptional breakfasts.

CANCALE: Le Grand Large €
Classic **Map** E1
4 Quai Jacques Cartier, 35260
Tel *(02) 99 89 82 90*
🔲 hotellegrandlarge.com
Traditionally furnished rooms
sleeping up to six, some with
views of Baie du Mont-St-Michel.

COMBOURG: Hôtel du Château €
Classic **Map** E2
1 Pl Chateaubriand, 35270
Tel *(02) 99 73 00 38*
🔲 hotelduchateau.com
Granite hotel set in a park offers
pretty rooms in cream and pastel
hues. Excellent restaurant.

DINARD: Hôtel Printania €
Family **Map** E1
5 Ave Georges V, 35801
Tel *(02) 99 46 13 07*
🔲 printaniahotel.com
The Breton-style rooms here come
with box beds, Quimper faience
and carved wooden furniture.

The elegant Château de la Ballue in Bazouges-la-Pérouse

DK Choice

DINARD: Hôtel Reine
Hortense €€€
Historic **Map** F1
19 Rue Malouine, 35800
Tel *(02) 99 46 54 31*
🔲 villa-reine-hortense.com
Charming, intimate 19th-century
villa built by a mysterious
Russian prince, and named
after Queen Hortense, the
daughter of Napoleon's wife
Josephine. The public rooms
retain the Louix XV character
and lovely *trompe loeil* ceiling
frescoes. Run by delightful
owners, it is located right on
the beach, and has stunning
views of St-Malo.

DOL-DE-BRETAGNE: Domaine
des Ormes €
Family **Map** E2
Epiniac, 35120
Tel *(02) 99 73 53 00*
🔲 lesormes.com
This campsite offers the option
of staying in a treehouse. Golf
course and water park on site.

HÉDÉ: Hostellerie du
Vieux Moulin €
Family **Map** E2
La Vallée du Moulin 35360
Tel *(02) 99 45 45 70*
🔲 levieuxmoulin-hede.com
A 17th-century miller's residence,
with bright, simple rooms and a
garden with ruins of a watermill.

IFFENDIC: Château du Pin €€
B&B **Map** E2
D125, near Montfort, 35750
Tel *(02) 99 09 34 05*
🔲 chateau-pin.fr
Pretty, colourful rooms in an
18th-century mansion surrounded
by parkland, in the heart of
the Brocéliande.

MONT-ST-MICHEL:
Croix Blanche €€€
Classic **Map** F1
16 Grand Rue, 50116
Tel *(02) 33 60 14 04*
🔲 hotel-la-croix-blanche.com
Quaint hotel sheltered by
ramparts. Cosy rooms on the top
floor offer spectacular views.

MONT-ST-MICHEL:
Terrasses Poulard €€€
Classic **Map** F1
Grand Rue, 50116
Tel *(02) 33 89 02 02*
🔲 terrasses-poulard.fr
Old-world charm fills this popular
hotel. All rooms are comfortable;
some afford scenic views.

PAIMPONT: Le Relais de
Brocéliande €€
Classic **Map** E3
Rue des Forges, 35380
Tel *(02) 99 07 84 94*
🔲 le-relais-de-broceliande.fr
Situated in Paimpont forest,
this hotel has smart rooms and
an excellent spa, with special
algae and fruit treatments.

PLOUËR-SUR-RANCE: Hôtel
Manoir de Rigourdaine €€
Historic **Map** E2
Route de Langrolay, 22490
Tel *(02) 96 86 89 96*
🔲 hotel-rigourdaine.fr
Spacious rooms in a stone-built
manor, with a terrace for
breakfast or aperitifs.

REDON: Hôtel Chandouineau €
Classic **Map** E3
1 Rue Thiers, 35600
Tel *(02) 99 71 02 04*
🔲 hotel-restaurant-
chandouineau.com
Choose from stylish attic rooms
in soft hues, located above a
well-known restaurant of the
same name. Free garage and
Wi-Fi for guests.

RENNES: Hôtel des Lices €
Family **Map** E3
7 Pl des Lices, 35000
Tel *(02) 99 79 14 81*
🔲 hotel-des-lices.com
Contemporary rooms with
good soundproofing and chic
furnishings. Nearly all rooms
come with balconies.

The reception at Castel Beau Site in Ploumanach, Côtes d'Armor

RENNES: Le Coq-Gadby €€
Classic   Map E3
156 Rue d'Antrain, 35700
Tel *(02) 99 38 05 55*
W lecoq-gadby.com
Evocative period rooms in a 17th-century building and others in a new one. Good spa next door.

DK Choice

ST-MALO: Le Beaufort €
Classic   Map E1
25 Chaussée du Sillon, 35400
Tel *(02) 99 40 99 99*
W hotel-beaufort.com
Retaining the warmth and charm of a mid-19th-century residence that makes it especially welcoming for families, Beaufort was one of the town's first hotels. It occupies a prime location with direct access to the beach and the walled town is a half-hour walk along the promenade.

ST-MALO: Le Grand Hôtel des Thermes €€€
Luxury   Map E1
100 Boulevard Hébert, 35400
Tel *(02) 99 40 75 75*
W le-grand-hotel-des-thermes.com
Classic 19th-century seaside palace hotel, with direct access to the thalassotherapy centre. Excellent children's facilities.

ST-MÉLOIR-DES-ONDES: Tirel Guérin €€
Classic   Map E1
1 Le Limonay, 35350
Tel *(02) 99 89 10 46*
W tirelguerin.com
A haven of peace near St-Malo, with landscaped gardens, spacious rooms and a superb restaurant.

ST-RÉMY-DU-PLAIN: Château la Haye d'Irée €€
B&B   Map F2
35560
Tel *(02) 99 73 62 07*
W chateaubreton.com
Luxurious Louis XVI-style rooms in an 18th-century chateau with magnificent views.

Côtes d'Armor

BRÉLIDY: Château de Brélidy €€
Historic   Map C1
22140
Tel *(02) 96 95 69 38*
W chateau-brelidy.com
Imposing 16th-century manor house in a park with elegant rooms and a spa. Bicycles are available for hire.

CAP FRÉHEL: Le Relais de Fréhel €
B&B   Map E1
Rue du Cap, Plévenon, 22240
Tel *(02) 96 41 43 02*
W relaiscapfrehel.fr
Renovated Breton longhouse, surrounded by woodland and a garden with tennis courts.

DINAN: Hôtel Arvor €€€
Family   Map E2
5 Rue Augustus-Pavie, 22120
Tel *(02) 96 39 21 22*
W hotelarvordinan.com
An 18th-century building with a cosy lounge and comfortable modern rooms that sleep up to six.

GUINGAMP: La Demeure de Ville Blanche €
Historic   Map C2
5 Rue du Général-de-Gaulle, 22200
Tel *(02) 96 44 28 53*
W demeure-vb.com
Outstanding 17th-century guesthouse with elegant period furnishings in the rooms, and an attractive little garden.

DK Choice

HILLION: Château de Bonabry €€
B&B   Map D2
Hillion, 22120
Tel *(02) 96 32 21 06*
W chambre-au-chateau.com
Set amid flower gardens and woodlands, this 15th- and 16th-century chateau features rooms full of old-fashioned charm. The B&B is run by the delightful Vicomte and Vicomtesse Louis du Fou de Kerdaniel. Breakfast features fruits from the home orchard. There's a path that leads down to the beach.

PAIMPOL: K'Loys €
Historic   Map D1
21 Quai Morand, 22500
Tel *(02) 96 20 40 01*
W hotel-kloys.com
A former sea merchant's house by the marina, with chintzy English style and a warm ambience.

PERROS-GUIREC: Le Manoir du Sphinx €€
Historic   Map C1
67 Chemin de la Messe, 22700
Tel *(02) 96 23 25 42*
W lemanoirdusphinx.com
Spectacular cliff-edge location. Nearly all the rooms overlook the sea and seven islands.

PERROS-GUIREC: Castel Beau Site €€€
Luxury   Map C1
Plage de Saint-Guirec, Ploumanach, 22700
Tel *(02) 96 91 40 87*
W castelbeausite.com
Luminous boutique rooms, all equipped with the latest amenities. Many have sunset sea views.

PLANCOËT: Manoir de la Hazaie €€€
Historic   Map E2
Planguenoual 22400
Tel *(02) 96 32 73 71*
W manoir-hazaie.com
Beautifully restored 16-century manor house. Period rooms equipped with spa tubs.

PLELO: La Maison des Lamour €
B&B   Map D2
La Ville Guerfault, 22170
Tel *(02) 96 79 51 25*
W lamaisondeslamour.com
Exceptionally attractive, beamed rooms located in an old mill, surrounded by a charming flower garden and woodland. There are also four delightful self-catering cottages.

PLÉVEN: Manoir du Vaumadeuc €€
Historic   Map E2
Le Vaumadeuc, 22130
Tel *(02) 96 84 46 17*
W vaumadeuc.com
Peaceful 15th-century manor house with comfortably furnished rooms under old oak beams. Beautiful French garden and lake.

PLOUBAZLANEC: Les Agapanthes €
Family   Map D1
1 Rue Adrien Rebours, 22620
Tel *(02) 96 55 89 06*
W hotel-les-agapanthes.com
An 18th-century hotel with a modern interior. Some rooms afford views of Paimpol Bay.

For more information on types of hotels *see page 223*

**QUEMPER GUÉZENNEC: Le
Manoir de Kermodest** €€
Historic Map D1
22260
Tel (02) 96 95 38 46
W kermodest.com
Old granite manor in a park,
with a relaxed country house
atmosphere and warm lounge.

ST-BRIEUC: Hôtel de Clisson €
Classic Map D2
36 Rue Gouët, 22000
Tel (02) 96 62 19 29
W hoteldeclisson.com
Set in a charming garden, with
a pond and fountain. Splurge
on the VIP room with the colour-
therapy Jacuzzi.

**ST-QUAY-PORTRIEUX:
Ker Moor** €€
Historic Map D1
13 Rue-du-Président-le-Sénéchal,
22410
Tel (02) 96 70 52 22
W ker-moor.com
Delightful, smart rooms in a
flamboyant Moorish-style cliff-
top villa with lovely views.

**TRÉBEURDEN: Manoir de
Lan-Kerellec** €€
Luxury Map C1
Allée Centrale de Lan-Kerellec, 22560
Tel (02) 96 15 00 00
W lankerellec.com
A Relais & Châteaux hotel in a
19th-century Breton manor
house with seafront gardens and
gorgeous views.

**TRÉGASTEL: Park Hôtel
Bellevue** €€
Historic Map C1
20 Rue des Calculots, 22730
Tel (02) 96 23 88 18
W hotelbellevuetregastel.com
The gracious 1930s Bellevue is
set in a flower-filled garden and
looks out over the sea.

La Manoir de Lan-Kerellec, a 19th-century
manor house in Trébeurden

TRÉGUIER: Aigue Marine €
Family Map C1
5 Rue M-Berthelot, 22220
Tel (02) 96 92 97 00
W aiguemarine-hotel.com
Bright hotel with a wide choice
of family rooms, good facilities
and excellent buffet breakfasts.

Northern Finistère

BREST: Hôtel de la Corniche €
Family Map B2
1 Rue Amiral-Nicol, 29200
Tel (02) 98 45 12 42
W hotel-la-corniche.com
Set in a peaceful area near the
scenic coastline, this hotel offers
pretty pastel-hued rooms.

**CARANTEC: Hôtel de
Carantec** €€€
Classic Map B1
20 Rue de Kelenn, 29660
Tel (02) 98 67 00 47
W hoteldecarantec.com
Elegant clifftop hotel from the
1930s, with splendid sea views
and Michelin-starred chef Patrick
Jeffroy's excellent restaurant.

**HANVEC: Les Chaumières de
Kerguan** €
B&B Map B2
Kerguan, 29460
Tel (02) 98 21 97 75
Authentic thatched longère
(farmhouse) and other farm
buildings housing simply
furnished rooms and a gîte.

HUELGOAT: Hôtel du Lac €
Family Map C2
12 Rue de Général-du-Gaulle, 29690
Tel (02) 98 99 71 14
W hoteldulac-huelgoat.com
Lovely well-refurbished rooms
beside a wooded lake in the
Monts d'Arrée. There is a
restaurant-pizzeria on site.

**ÎLE D'OUESSANT: Le Ti Jan
Ar C'Hafe** €
Classic Map A2
Kernigou, 29242
Tel (02) 98 48 82 64
W tijan.fr
Beautifully renovated house run
by a delightful owner. Rooms are
in warm tones, and there is a
neat garden and wooden terrace.

LANDÉDA: La Baie des Anges €€
Luxury Map A1
350 Rue des Anges, 29870
Tel (02) 98 04 90 04
W baie-des-anges.com
Seaside resort hotel overlooking
the splendid coastline. Contemporary and smartly decorated
rooms. Hearty breakfasts.

LANILDUT: Le Nid d'Iroise €
B&B Map A1
4 Hent Kergaradoc, 29840
Tel (02) 98 04 38 41
W hebergement-nature-
bretagne.com
Three rooms in an 18th-century
longère surrounded by exotic
gardens with cockatiels. Also
offers two rooms in rustic cabins.

**LOGONNA-DAOULAS: Domaine
de Moulin Mer** €
B&B Map B2
34 Rue de Moulin Mer, 29460
Tel (02) 98 07 24 45
W domaine-moulin-mer.com
A 19th-century mansion on
a sheltered coast with stylish
rooms and a wellness spa,
located amid palms and mimosa.

MORLAIX: Hôtel de l'Europe €
Family Map C1
1 Rue d'Aiguillon, 29600
Tel (02) 98 62 11 99
W hoteleurope-morlaix.com
A Second Empire hotel with
elegant woodwork in the lobby.
Rooms are modern, comfortable
and soundproofed.

DK Choice

**PLOUGONVELIN: Hostellerie
de la Pointe St-Mathieu** €€
Classic Map A2
Pointe de St-Mathieu, 29217
Tel (02) 98 89 00 19
W pointe-saint-mathieu.com
Splendidly situated over a
rocky shore on the extreme
western point of France, this hotel affords
beautiful views of the lighthouse
and ruins of St-Mathieu Abbey.
The contemporary designed
rooms are comfortable and
well-equipped. There is a
spa, an indoor pool and a
restaurant serving delicious
cuisine by the fireplace.

**PLOUGONVEN: La Grange
de Coatélan** €
B&B Map C2
D109, Coatélan, 29640
Tel (02) 98 72 60 16
W les-gites-en-bretagne.fr
A converted 16th-century
farm set amid gardens, with
a terrace facing a meadow.

ROSCOFF: Hôtel aux Tamaris €
Classic Map B1
49 Rue Edouard Corbière, 29680
Tel (02) 98 61 22 99
W hotel-aux-tamaris.com
Built in 1935, this is a modernized
seafront hotel close to the thalassotherapy centre. The dining
room offers panoramic views.

ROSCOFF: Le Brittany €€€
Luxury   Map B1
Blvd Ste-Barbe, 29681
Tel *(02) 98 69 70 78*
🆆 hotel-brittany.com
A beautiful Breton manor house,
with period pieces, luxurious
amenities and a superb restaurant.

**ST-POL-DE-LÉON: Hôtel de
France** €
Classic   Map B1
29 Rue Minimes, 29250
Tel *(02) 98 29 14 14*
🆆 hotel-saint-pol.com
Relaxed, tranquil and friendly
spot set in extensive gardens
that are great for breakfast
outdoors in fine weather.

Southern Finistère

AUDIERNE: Au Roi Gradlon €
Family   Map A2
3 Ave Manu-Brusq, 29770
Tel *(02) 98 70 04 51*
🆆 auroigradlon.com
Modern hotel on the beach,
with blue-and-white rooms, most
offering splendid ocean views.

**BÉNODET: Domaine de
Kereven** €
Historic   Map B3
Kereven, 29950
Tel *(02) 98 57 02 46*
🆆 kereven.fr
The natural charm of this 1742
farmhouse is enhanced by its
lush garden setting. Just a mile
away from the sea.

DK Choice

**COMBRIT: La Ferme Saint-
Vennec** €€€
Luxury   Map B3
Rue de la Clarté, 29120
Tel *(02) 98 56 74 53*
🆆 lafermesaintvennec.com
An idyllic collection of 18th-
century farms, completely
secluded in the countryside,
and stunningly restored with
top-notch five-star furnishings.
Offers both rooms as well as
self-catering cottages that sleep
up to six, and a heated pool.
Baby-sitting is available on
request. It is also popular for
weddings and seminars.

CONCARNEAU: Ker-Moor €€
Classic   Map B3
Plage des Sables-Blancs, 29900
Tel *(02) 98 97 02 96*
🆆 hotel-kermor.com
An early 20th-century former villa
charmingly furnished with items
recovered from old cargo ships.

The luxurious La Ferme Saint-Vennec in Combrit

**CONCARNEAU:
Les Sables Blancs** €€
Luxury   Map B3
45 Rue des Sables Blancs
Tel *02 98 50 10 12*
🆆 hotel-les-sables-blancs.com
Modern, white-and-wood hotel
on a soft sandy beach, with a
gorgeous seaside terrace.

**DOUARNENEZ: Hostellerie Le
Clos de Vallombreuse** €€
Historic   Map B2
7 Rue d'Estienne-d'Orves, 29100
Tel *02 98 92 63 64*
🆆 closvallombreuse.com
Elegant hotel in an early 20th-
century villa, in a quiet park with
views across the bay.

**FORÊT FOUESNANT: Le Manoir
du Stang** €€
Historic   Map B3
Le Stang, 29940
Tel *(02) 98 56 96 38*
🆆 manoirdustang.com
Stunning manor house on a lake
with carved fireplaces, antiques
and gardens.

**FOUESNANT: Mona Lisa à
Cap Coz** €
Family   Map B3
Plage de Cap Coz, 29170
Tel *(02) 98 51 18 10*
🆆 bestwestern-capcoz.monalisa.fr
Big, white hotel with direct
access to the beach. Most rooms
have sea views.

ÎLE DE SEIN: Hôtel d'Ar Men €
Classic   Map A2
32 Rue Ferdinand Crouton, 29170
Tel *(02) 98 70 90 77*
🆆 hotel-armen.net
Friendly, peaceful hotel and
restaurant near the lighthouse,
on the western tip of the island.

**LANDUDEC: Château de
Guilguiffin** €€
Historic   Map B3
29710
Tel *(02) 98 91 52 11*
🆆 chateau-guilguiffin.com
Magnificent 18th-century chateau,
surrounded by an enormous park

of woodland. Rooms are
decorated with stunning
period pieces. There are also
gîtes on the estate, sleeping
up to five.

**MOËLAN-SUR-MER: Manoir
de Kertalg** €€
Luxury   Map C3
Rue de Riec-sur-Belon, 29350
Tel *(02) 98 39 77 77*
🆆 manoirdekertalg.com
Elegantly furnished
rooms in the stone-built
stables of a delightful chateau.

PONT-AVEN: Roz Aven €
Historic   Map B3
11 Quai Theodore-Botrel, 29930
Tel *(02) 98 06 13 06*
🆆 hotelpontaven.com
Stay in a room overlooking the
harbour in this picture-perfect
16th-century thatched cottage
and adjacent modern extension.

**PONT-L'ABBÉ:
Hôtel de Bretagne** €
Family   Map B3
24 Pl de la République, 29120
Tel *(02) 98 87 17 22*
🆆 hoteldebretagne29.com
Centrally located, family-run
hotel-restaurant with stylish
rooms, a walled garden and
a pretty terrace.

QUIMPER: Hôtel Gradlon €€
Classic   Map B3
30 Rue de Brest, 29000
Tel *(02) 98 95 04 39*
🆆 hotel-gradlon.fr
Charming rooms located near
the historic centre, with a few
looking across the garden
and fountain.

**TRÉGUNC: Les Grandes
Roches** €€
Historic   Map B3
Rue des Grandes Roches, 29910
Tel *(02) 98 97 62 97*
🆆 hotel-lesgrandesroches.com
Peaceful place, with two
charming suites in thatched
cottages. Lovely gardens
and breakfast terrace.

For more information on types of hotels *see page 223*

Morbihan

AURAY: Hôtel du Golf Saint-Laurent €
Classic **Map** D3
Golf de Saint-Laurent, 56400
Tel *(02) 97 56 88 88*
🔲 hotel-golf-saint-laurent.com
Modern hotel with its own golf course. Rooms have private terraces overlooking the gardens.

**BELLE-ÎLE-EN-MER:
La Désirade** €€€
Family **Map** C4
Petit Cosquet, Bangor, 56360
Tel *(02) 97 31 70 70*
🔲 hotel-la-desirade.com
Rooms in this hotel come in soothing pastel tones and are spread over several traditional houses. A good base for exploring the island.

DK Choice

BELLE-ÎLE-EN-MER: Castel Clara €€€
Luxury **Map** C4
Port-Goulphar, 56360
Tel *(02) 97 31 84 21*
🔲 castel-clara.com
Relais & Château hotel in an idyllic location looking out over the Goulphar cove. The almost luminous, contemporary rooms and suites are done up in soft tones and fitted with all amenities. Many have terraces with sea views. There is also an excellent spa and thalassotherapy centre as well as a superb restaurant.

BILLIERS: Domaine de Rochevilaine €€€
Luxury **Map** D4
16 Rue du Phare, 56190
Tel *(02) 97 41 61 61*
🔲 domainerochevilaine.com
Stunning rooms in a beautiful 16th- and 17th-century estate overlooking the ocean.

CARNAC: Hôtel An Ti Gwenn €
Family **Map** C4
2 Rue Poulperson, 56340
Tel *(02) 97 52 00 73*
🔲 hotel-antigwenn.com
Situated near the Grande Plage, the "white house" offers modern rooms. Bicycles available for hire.

CARNAC: Hôtel Celtique €€
Classic **Map** C4
17 Ave Kermario/82 Ave des Druides, 56190
Tel *(02) 97 52 14 15*
🔲 hotel-celtique.com
Near one of the bay's most lovely beaches. Rooms look across a garden with ancient pines.

HENNEBONT: Château de Locguénolé €€€
Luxury **Map** C3
1 km (half a mile) south of Hennebont, 56700
Tel *(02) 97 76 76 76*
🔲 chateau-de-locguenole.com
Elegant period rooms in a romantic 18th-century chateau and manor house, surrounded by a wooded park.

**ÎLE DE GROIX:
Hôtel de la Marine** €€
Classic **Map** C3
7 Rue de Général de Gaulle, 56590
Tel *(02) 97 86 80 05*
🔲 hoteldelamarine.com
Expect a warm welcome at this relaxing hideaway, with rooms overlooking the sea or garden.

**LA ROCHE-BERNARD:
L'Auberge Bretonne** €
Historic **Map** E4
2 Pl du Guesclin, 56130
Tel *(02) 99 90 60 28*
🔲 auberge-bretonne.com
This early 20th-century Breton town house offers a choice of lovely airy, period rooms.

**LA TRINITÉ-SUR-MER:
Le Lodge Kerisper** €€€
Luxury **Map** C3
4 Rue de Latz, 56470
Tel *(02) 97 52 88 56*
🔲 lodge-kerisper.com
Charming boutique hotel set in a former farm building, with a conservatory, parquet floors and terrace gardens.

LOCMARIAQUER: Les Trois Fontaines €
Classic **Map** D4
Rosnarho, Golfe de Morbihan, 56470
Tel *(02) 97 57 42 70*
🔲 hotel-troisfontaines.com
Elegant rooms facing colourful flowerbeds at the edge of an oyster-farming village.

LORIENT: Hôtel Escale Oceania €€
Classic **Map** C3
30 Rue du Couedic, 56100
Tel *(02) 97 64 13 27*
🔲 oceaniahotels.com
Friendly city centre hotel with comfortable, soundproofed rooms.

LORIENT: Les Pecheurs €
Classic **Map** C3
7 Rue Jean La Garde, 56100
Tel *(02) 97 21 19 24*
🔲 hotel-lespecheurs.com
Refurbished one-star hotel near the marina. Tidy rooms and a lively bar popular with locals.

DK Choice

PLOËRMEL: Dihan €€€
Family **Map** D3
Kerganiet, 56400
Tel *(02) 97 56 88 27*
🔲 dihan-evasion.org
This former working farm is a delight for nature lovers, offering rooms in a barn; suspended in a treehouse; a Mongolian yurt; a Nordic chalet; a gypsy caravan; and a bubble tent. There is a spa as well as various activities, including paddle boards, kite surfing, hiking and bicycle hire.

PLOËRMEL: Hôtel Le Cobh €
Family **Map** D3
10 Rue des Forges, 56800
Tel *(02) 97 74 00 49*
🔲 hotel-lecobh.com
Inspired by Brocéliande legends, Le Cobh offers three types of themed rooms: sacred rites and literature, forest, and opalescence.

PONTIVY: Hôtel de l'Europe €
Historic **Map** D3
12 Rue François-Mitterand, 56300
Tel *(02) 97 25 11 14*
🔲 hotellerieurope.com
A 19th-century mansion set in a walled garden. Well-kept rooms, some with canopy beds.

Gypsy caravan, one of the rooms available at Hotel Dihan in Ploërmel

**PRESQU'ÎLE DE QUIBERON:
Hôtel Bellevue** €
Family **Map** C4
Rue de Tiviec, 56173
Tel *(02) 97 50 16 28*
w hotel-bellevuequiberon.com
Located near the thalassotherapy
centre, this modern seaside hotel
is built around a heated pool.

QUESTEMBERT: Le Bretagne €€
Classic **Map** D3
13 Rue St-Michel, 56230
Tel *(02) 97 26 11 12*
w residence-le-bretagne.com
Set in lush gardens, an ivy-
covered country house with
smart rooms. Superb breakfasts.
Gift shop on site.

SARZEAU: Le Mur du Roy €
Classic **Map** D4
43 Chemin du Mur du Roy, 56370
Tel *(02) 97 67 34 08*
w lemurduroy.com
Informal, friendly place with
direct access to the beach and
a fine restaurant with panoramic
sea views.

**VANNES: Hôtel La
Marébaudière** €€
Family **Map** D3
4 Rue Aristide Briand, 56000
Tel *(02) 97 47 34 29*
w marebaudiere.com
Peaceful hotel located near
the old walled town. Modern,
stylish rooms overlook a garden
courtyard. Free car parking and
Wi-Fi available.

DK Choice

VANNES: Villa Kerasy €€€
Classic **Map** D3
20 Ave Favrel & Lincy, 56000
Tel *(02) 97 68 36 83*
w villakerasy.com
Villa Kerasy is a unique boutique
hotel near Vannes' medieval
centre. The decor of each room
evokes one of the 15 spice
ports of the 17th-century East
India Company. There is a lovely
terrace, a Japanese garden,
Ayurvedic Indian cuisine, and
relaxing massages to be enjoyed
in a private spa.

Loire-Atlantique

**BERNERIE-EN-RETZ: Château
de la Gressière** €
Historic **Map** E5
Rue Noue-Fleurie, 44500
Tel *(02) 51 74 60 06*
w lagressiere.com
Lavish, regency-style furnishings
in a 19th-century manor house

The classic Villa Kerasy hotel
in Vannes

overlooking the sea and Île de
Noirmoitier. Rooms have views of
the beach or garden.

GUÉRANDE: La Guérandière €
B&B **Map** D4
5 Rue Vannetaise, 44350
Tel *(02) 40 62 17 15*
w guerandiere.com
A former *hôtel particulier* (town
house) with a walled garden,
stained glass, wood-carved
panels and parquet floors.

DK Choice

**LA BAULE:
Saint-Christophe** €€€
Family **Map** D4
1 Ave Alcyons, 44500
Tel *(02) 40 62 40 00*
w st-christophe.com
Housed in four ivy-covered
villas dating from the 1910s,
in a quiet corner of La Baule,
this hotel offers a comfortable
country-house atmosphere.
There is a pretty garden and
terrace, as well as exceptional
family facilities: eight family
rooms, toys, DVDs, baby
equipment and special dinners
for kids in the summer.

LE CROISIC: Hôtel de France €€€
Classic **Map** D4
24 Rue Crebillon, 44000
Tel *(02) 40 23 00 63*
w oceaniahotels.com
This boutique, 18-century *hôtel
particulier* in the city centre has
quirky rooms.

LE CROISIC: Fort de l'Océan €€€
Luxury **Map** D4
Pointe de Croisic, 44490
Tel *(02) 40 15 77 77*
w hotelfortocean.com
Ramparts from the 17th century
enclose this sumptuous hotel
that was formerly a seafront fort.

NANTES: Hôtel La Pérouse €
Classic **Map** F4
3 Allée Duquesne, 44000
Tel *(02) 40 89 75 00*
w hotel-laperouse.fr
A peaceful hotel, with glossy
wooden flooring and designer
furniture. Good buffet breakfast.

PORNIC: Hôtel Beau Soleil €
Family **Map** E5
70 Quai Leray, 44210
Tel *(02) 40 82 34 58*
w hotel-beausoleil-pornic.com
Small, soundproofed rooms
on the harbour, nearly all offering
sea views.

PORNICHET: Le Régent €€
Classic **Map** D4
150 Blvd des Océanides, 44210
Tel *(02) 40 61 04 04*
w le-regent.fr
Smart hotel with themed
rooms: choose from pop, design,
romantic, retro or Baroque.

**SORINIÈRES: Abbaye de
Villeneuve** €€
Historic **Map** F5
Rue de La Roche-sur-Yon, 44840
Tel *(02) 40 04 40 25*
w abbayedevilleneuve.com
Beautiful abbey restored in 1977,
with lovely furnished rooms and
a gourmet restaurant.

DK Choice

**ST-JOACHIM: La Mare Aux
Oiseaux** €€€
Classic **Map** E4
223 Rue du Chef de l'Île, 44720
Tel *(02) 40 88 53 01*
w mareauxoiseaux.com
In the bird-filled Grande Brière
marshlands, this Relais du
Silence hotel offers chic boutique bedrooms plus three
rooms in wooden cabins. There
is a spa and a superb contemporary restaurant, specializing
in locally sourced ingredients.

ST-NAZAIRE: Au Bon Acceuil €
Family **Map** E4
39 Rue Marceau, 44600
Tel *(02) 40 22 07 05*
w au-bon-accueil44.com
This friendly hotel is in one of
the few buildings that escaped
destruction during World War II.

**ST-SAVEUR DE LANDEMONT:
Château de la Colaissière** €€
Historic **Map** F4
37 Rue du Calvaire, 49270
Tel *(02) 40 98 75 04*
w colaissiere.com
Renaissance chateau encircled
by a moat, with beautiful period
rooms and lounges with fireplaces.

For more information on types of hotels *see page 223*

WHERE TO EAT AND DRINK

The foremost agricultural region of France, Brittany abounds in produce that is the basis of the region's cuisine. Brittany is best known for its fish and shellfish, but locally produced cooked meats and free-range poultry find place on the menu as well. The region also grows excellent fruit and vegetables, including strawberries and artichokes. Other specialities include Breton cider and the prized Muscadet from the vineyards around Nantes. From the finest meals served in some of the most highly reputed establishments in France to a delicious plate of pancakes enjoyed in a simple crêperie, Brittany's restaurants cater for all tastes and all pockets.

L'Auberge Bretonne in La Roche-Bernard *(see p242)*

Types of Restaurants

Bretons are fond of good food, and locally grown produce provides plenty of opportunities for creating excellent dishes. Away from the coasts, especially, there are restaurants that offer authentic Breton cuisine at reasonable prices. The *fermes-auberges* (farmhouse inns) and *tables d'hôtes* are good options for enjoying simple, inexpensive dishes made with local produce. On the coasts, the choice is wider, but the quality may not be the best. There are fast-food outlets, pizzerias, snack bars and *crêperies* (pancake houses) as well as upmarket restaurants to choose from.

Tables et Saveurs de Bretagne is an association of 44 restaurants in Brittany that offer original Breton cuisine based on local produce. Information on these restaurants is available from the **Comité Régional du Tourisme**.

Local Produce

Breton cuisine is renowned chiefly for its fish and seafood dishes. The grilled mackerel and sardines served in the region are particularly delicious because of the freshness of local catches. Monkfish, sea bass, yellow pollack, turbot, red mullet, sole or sea bream, gently baked or served with *beurre blanc* (a butter, vinegar and shallot sauce) are succulent dishes. In the Loire-Atlantique, shad, elvers and lamprey also appear on the menu. Seafood, such as oysters from Cancale, Paimpol, Aven-Belon, Quiberon and Croisic; mussels from Vivier and Pénestin; as well as whelks, winkles, shrimps, spider crabs and lobsters, can be found piled high in almost every market near the coast. While lovers of seafood never tire of Brittany's scallops, top chefs are now beginning to use edible seaweed and samphire in their dishes as well.

Depending on the season, Brittany's inland areas also offer a range of culinary delights. Potatoes, a basic ingredient in all Breton cuisine, artichokes, cauliflowers, beans (such as those known as *coco de Paimpol*), lamb's lettuce from the Nantes area, asparagus, onions from Roscoff, turnips and leeks are all popular ingredients. Locally grown fruit includes apples, pears and kiwi fruit, as well as juicy melons from the Rennes area.

Breton Specialities

Brittany is famous for its traditional butter biscuits and delectable pancakes, as well as for the tempting *plateau de fruits mer* (seafood platter) and *homard à l'armoricaine* (lobster served in a spicy garlic and tomato sauce). Another great classic, albeit in a different league, is a dish of mussels known as *moules marinière* (mussels cooked in wine).

The region is also a prime producer of pork and offers a range of products made from pig meat. Two of the most prominent are *andouilles* (chitterling sausages made with lard) from Guéméné-sur-Scorff, and sausages and pâté (including the famous Hénaff brand) from Baye.

Les Filets Bleus in Lannion *(see p236)*

Les Forges, a restaurant near the Forêt de Brocéliande *(see p235)*

As for meat dishes, there is the mouth-watering *agneau de pré-salé* (salt-pasture lamb) from Mont-St-Michel, roast duckling and cold duck galantine.

Breton salted butter (French butter is otherwise unsalted) is also highly prized. In the days before refrigerators existed, salt was added to butter as a preservative, and to this day salted butter is an essential ingredient in Breton cuisine. Salt from Guérande, meanwhile, is famous across France.

Breton cakes include the *kouign amann* (cake made with wheat flour, butter and sugar), which is eaten warm. *Far* (Breton prune flan) and *quatre-quarts* (a rich sponge cake) are other deservedly famous specialities, along with Traou-Mad de Pont-Aven (cookies), Pleyben or St-Michel *galettes* (butter biscuits) and the wafer-thin *crêpes-dentelles* from Quimper.

Cider is the most popular drink in Brittany. Although many people like *cidre doux* (sweet cider), connoisseurs prefer *cidre brut* (dry cider). The best cider-producing regions of Brittany are the areas around Dol-de-Bretagne and the Arguenon, Rance, Messac, Fouesnant and Domagné valleys. *Chouchen*, a kind of mead (or hydromel) is also worth sampling, as is the locally brewed beer. Among the best brands are

Coreff, of Morlaix, and Telenn Du, a wheat beer. Muscadet from the Loire-Atlantique is a delicate, crisp, dry wine.

Practicalities

Irrespective of the season, it is advisable to book a restaurant table in advance. While informal dress is perfectly acceptable in most restaurants, such casual wear as shorts is likely to attract disapproval in high-end establishments. Swimming costumes are unacceptable, except in beach-side restaurants.

Most restaurants in Brittany offer set price menus that are far cheaper than ordering à la carte. Most places across the region accept the main credit cards. However, in country areas, be sure to carry cash in case any other form of payment is not accepted.

Children

Children are welcomed in Brittany, and many restaurants, such as *crêperies*, are suitable for families. Most establishments offer special menus for children, and some provide highchairs for toddlers.

Recommended Restaurants

The restaurants in this guide have been selected for their excellent food, outstanding

Le Jardin Gourmand in Lorient *(see p242)*

Tables outside a *crêperie* on the Rue St-Georges in Rennes

location and good value. The restaurants run across a wide price range and cuisine types. Fine Dining refers to formal, elegant restaurants that offer some of the best dining experiences in France. Visitors can try new exciting dishes that make imaginative use of Brittany's splendid meats, seafood and produce at the creative restaurants. Seafood restaurants specialize in fish and shellfish, but most offer meat choices as well. Traditional and/or contemporary takes on regional cuisine can be tried in Breton-themed restaurants. *Crêperies* serve both savoury and sweet filled pancakes, but most also prepare salads and grilled meats as well as jugs of cider.

The restaurants labeled as "DK Choice" have been highlighted for an exceptional feature – exquisite food or inviting atmosphere.

DIRECTORY

Types of Restaurants

Comité Régional du Tourisme
Tel (02) 99 28 44 30.
W tourismebretagne.com

Tables et Saveurs de Bretagne
W tablesetsaveursde bretagne.com

The Flavours of Brittany

Although the food most commonly associated with this part of France is the simple but scrumptious *crêpe*, visitors will easily find a good range of far more gastronomic fare, much of it based around the region's top quality vegetables and seafood. Brittany has an extensive coastline – around 1,700 km (1,055 miles) long – and really fresh fish is readily available. Of particular note are the fine oysters, reared in penned-off areas close to the shore. Not surprisingly, given the region's many pig farms, charcuterie features strongly on the Breton menu. Hearty stews made with lamb and beef are also good, especially washed down with the local cider.

Globe artichokes

Mussel-cultivation beds in the Baie de Cancale

Meat and Charcuterie

Brittany is France's main pig-rearing region. Look out for *porc fermier*, meat from pigs raised in the open on a cereal-based diet, and for the region's superb charcuterie, which includes a variety of cooked and smoked hams, garlic sausage, *boudin noir* (black pudding), *pâté breton*, a coarsely textured pork terrine, and *andouille de*

Guémené, a smoked sausage made from pigs' intestines.

On the marshy fields just inland from the coast, *pré-salé* (salt-marsh) lamb is raised. Most Breton farms rear cows for dairying, especially the black and white *pie noire* breed, but there are some cattle, mostly Charolais or Charolais crosses, that are reared for their excellent beef.

Fish and Shellfish

The sea off Brittany is rich in fish. Loctudy is a major port for mackerel, while Audierne is noted for langoustines, as Erquy and Loguivy-de-la-Mer are for scallops. Lobsters, crabs, prawns (shrimp), mussels, clams, whelks, cockles and oysters are also found in abundance. Huge platters of seafood are served at restaurants all along the coast.

Oysters   Prawns   Lobster   Mackerel   Sardines
          (shrimp)   Mussels

Selection of typical Breton fish and seafood

Local Dishes and Specialities

Meals often start with fish or shellfish. Fish soups, *moules marinières* and stuffed clams or scallops are popular, as are oysters, especially when served with rye bread spread with Breton salted butter. A lobster or crab with mayonnaise, or one of the massive platters of mixed seafood, make a meal in themselves. The main course may be fresh fish baked in sea salt, braised in cider or *à l'armoricaine* (in a herby tomato sauce).

Salted butter

Meat dishes include hearty stews, roast pork and lamb *à la bretonne* (with haricot beans, garlic, shallots and tomatoes). Prawns (shrimp) may come with cauliflower and *boudin noir* (black pudding) with slices of apple. Favoured desserts include *crêpes, far aux pruneaux* (a prune and batter pudding) and Plougastel strawberries.

Homard à l'armoricaine Fresh lobster pieces are cooked in a sauce of tomato, garlic and herbs, enriched with cognac.

Display of vegetables at a market stall in Vannes

Breton oysters are highly prized. Two basic types are on offer: the more common, crinkled *creuse* variety and the flat, rounded *belons*, reared at Riec-sur-Belon in the south and at Cancale on the north coast. The mussels that are cultivated in the Vilaine estuary and the Baie de Cancale, are also popular.

Butter and Dairy Produce

Salted butter is a Breton speciality and is excellent on rye bread to accompany oysters. It is also used in regional delicacies such as salt butter caramels and ice cream.

Brittany also produces much of France's fresh milk. Curiously, though, cheese production is only on a small scale. Local offerings include several fine goat cheeses as well as the mild, semi-soft cheeses, Campénéac, Timadeuc and St-Paulin.

Fruit and Vegetables

Brittany's mild winters make it an important area for winter and early spring vegetables. Globe artichokes fill local market stalls from October to May and most of France's

Sign outside a *crêperie* in the medieval village of Locronan

cauliflowers come from northern Finistère. Other important crops include onions, shallots, haricot beans, asparagus, broccoli, potatoes and tomatoes. Plougastel is famous for its sweet succulent strawberries.

Baked Goods

An array of delicious baked goods can be found in Brittany including *Kouign-amann* (a sweet bread), *sablé* (shortbread) biscuits, *quatre-quarts* (a rich buttery cake), and *crêpes dentelles* (thin, sugary pancakes, rolled up and baked until crispy).

ON THE MENU

Crêpes Both savoury and sweet, with fillings such as cheese, ham, honey and jam

Bisque de homard A smooth creamy lobster soup

Feuilleté aux fruits de mer Shellfish in puff pastry

Fricassée de pétoncles Clams and leeks fricasséed with white wine and cream

Gigot à la bretonne Leg of lamb with white haricot beans, tomatoes and garlic

Kig ha fars Meat and vegetable hotpot with buckwheat dumpling

Roulade sévigné A roulade of guinea fowl, apples and ham

Moules marinières Mussels are steamed with dry white wine, shallots, parsley and butter until their shells open.

Cotriade This traditional stew of fish, cooked with potato and onion, is often poured over with slices of toast.

Far aux pruneaux Prunes, first soaked in tea, rum or apple *eau-de-vie*, are baked in a thick sweetened batter.

Where to Eat and Drink

Ille-et-Vilaine

BILLE: Ferme de Mésauboin €
Breton   Map F2
*On the D23, 2 km (1 mile) west
of Bille, 35133*
Tel *(02) 99 97 61 57*
Charming 17th-century manor
offering authentic farmhouse
cooking. Home-made pâté, duck
in cider and *gratin fougerais* are
specialties. Book in advance.

CANCALE: Le Surcouf €€
Seafood   Map E1
7 Quai Gambetta, 35260
Tel *(02) 99 89 61 75*
Unpretentious spot on the port,
known for its excellent shellfish
platters, whole fish *à la plancha*
(grilled) and a formidable wine list.

DK Choice

CANCALE: Le Coquillage €€€
Fine Dining   Map E1
*Le Buot, St-Méloir-les-Ondes, 6 km
(3.7 miles) S of Cancale, 35350*
Tel *(02) 99 89 64 76*   **Closed** *mid-
Jan–mid-Feb; 2 weeks in Mar;
Jul & Aug*
Set in a peaceful seafront setting,
famous chef Olivier Roellinger's
restaurant takes diners on a
culinary adventure. The dishes
combine local seafood with
exotic spices and flavours
from around the world to per-
fection – think chocolate with
chilli, Asian lime or lemon confit.
There is a special tasting menu
and an amazing dessert trolley.

CHATEAUBOURG: Ar Milin €€
Fine Dining   Map F3
30 Rue de Paris, 35221
Tel *(02) 99 00 30 91*   **Closed** *Jan 1–7*
Interestingly planned around a
flour mill, with lovely views of the
Vilaine river. The menu includes lots
of seafood. There is also a bistro.

**DINARD: La Passerelle du Clair
de Lune** €€
Seafood   Map E1
3 Ave George V, 35800
Tel *(02) 99 16 96 37*   **Closed** *Tue & Wed*
Serves innovative dishes that do
justice to the day's catch and
exotic spices. Decadent desserts.
Stunning views of the port.

DINARD: Didier Méril €€
Fine Dining   Map E1
1 Place Général-de-Gaulle, 35800
Tel *(02) 99 46 95 74*
Known for its unabashed luxury,
Didier Méril features dishes

ranging from lobster, *foie
gras* and grilled monkfish to
sea bass, all prepared by a
dynamic young chef.

**FOUGÈRES:
Galon ar Breizh** €€
French   Map F2
10 Place Gambetta, 35300
Tel *(02) 99 99 14 17*   **Closed** *Oct–
Apr: Fri, Sat lunch*
The menu at Galon ar Breizh is
a combination of Breton seafood
and southwest *foie gras* and
goose. The inventive dishes are
satisfying as well. Try the superb
eggs-in-snow for dessert.

FOUGÈRES: Le Haute-Sève €€
Fine Dining   Map F2
37 Blvd Jean-Jaurès, 35300
Tel *(02) 99 94 23 39*   **Closed** *Sun
& Mon; 3 weeks in Aug*
Housed in an elegant Art Deco
room, this longtime local favour-
ite serves beautifully presented
dishes with flavours that surprise.
Book ahead.

**HÉDÉ: L'Hostellerie de
Vieux Moulin** €
French   Map E2
Ancienne Rue de St-Malo, 35630
Tel *(02) 99 45 45 70*   **Closed** *Sun
dinner, Mon; 2 weeks in Oct, Jan*
Set in a charming old water mill
and popular for the excellent
innovative cuisine served by the
young chef. Try the wild boar.

HÉDÉ: La Vieille Auberge €€
Fine Dining   Map E2
La Vallée des Moulins, 35630
Tel *(02) 99 45 46 25*   **Closed** *Sun
dinner, Mon, 2 weeks in Mar*
Feast on generous portions of
exquisite venison, roast lamb
and *ris de veau* (sweetbread) at
this 17th-century inn with a
beautiful terrace.

Price Guide

Prices are based on a three-course meal
for one, including a half-bottle of house
wine, tax and service.

€	under €40
€€	€40 to €70
€€€	over €70

LIFFRÉ: L'Escu de Runfao €€
Fine Dining   Map F2
*La Quinte (Domaine de la Reposée),
35340*
Tel *(02) 99 68 31 51*   **Closed** *3
weeks in Aug*
The sumptuous cuisine at this
restaurant includes seafood
with truffles, partridge, venison
as well as extravagant desserts.
Dine outdoors on a terrace
facing the lovely garden.

MONT-ST-MICHEL: La Sirène €
Crêperie   Map F1
Grand Rue, 50170
Tel *(02) 33 60 08 60*   **Closed** *Jan*
Simple but pleasant choice in
touristy Mont-St-Michel. Serves
buckwheat *galettes*, savoury and
sweet crêpes, salads, and cider.

MONT-ST-MICHEL: Le Pré Salé €€
Breton   Map F1
Route de St-Michel BP8, 50170
Tel *(02) 33 60 24 17*
Situated outside the centre,
Le Pré Salé is known for the
exquisite local delicacy, the
"salt meadow" lamb.

**MONT-ST-MICHEL: Relais
St-Michel** €€
Breton   Map F1
*On the causeway 2 km (1 mile) from
the mount, 35260*
Tel *(02) 33 89 32 00*
Dine with superb views of Mont-
St-Michel at this restaurant. Serves
mostly traditional dishes, inclu-
ding roast lamb and omelettes
flambéed with Calvados.

Peaceful seafront setting at Le Coquillage in Cancale

NOYAL-SUR-VILLAINE: Auberge du Pont d'Acigné €€€
Fine Dining   Map F3
Rue d'Acigné, 35530
Tel *(02) 99 62 52 55* **Closed** *Mon & Tue; 1 week in May; 3 weeks in Aug*
This Michelin-starred restaurant boasts a lovely dining room and a rising chef who has a way with seafood. The menu features creative dishes with lots of truffles.

DK Choice

PAIMPONT: Les Forges de Paimpont €€
Breton   Map E3
Rue des Forges (Plélan-le-Grand), 35380
Tel *(02) 99 06 81 07* **Closed** *Mon & Sun dinner*
An old stone forge in a magical location in the Forêt de Brocéliande; run by the fourth generation of owners, this historic inn serves traditional Breton cuisine as well as local products. Game dishes, terrines and home-smoked salmon and duck are the house specialities. Great atmosphere.

REDON: Le Moulin de Via €€
Fine Dining   Map E3
Route de la Gacilly, 35600
Tel *(02) 99 71 05 16* **Closed** *Mon, Tue & Sun dinner; 2 weeks in Mar*
Charming Breton farmhouse in a pretty garden. The menu includes roast pigeon, rack of lamb *en croute* and dishes made with fresh, locally caught seafood. Excellent desserts.

RENNES: Léon Le Cochon €
Breton   Map E3
Rue du Pré Botté, 35000
Tel *(02) 99 79 37 54*
A convivial city-centre institution, this bistro offers a variety of pork and tasty egg preparations. Good-value lunch menus. Book ahead.

RENNES: Le Cour des Lices €€
French   Map E3
18 Place des Lices, 35000
Tel *(02) 99 30 25 25* **Closed** *Sun & Mon; 2 weeks in May, first 2 weeks in Aug*
One of Rennes' best eateries, Le Cour des Lices serves delicious food in a 17th-century building. Make reservations for the special Saturday market lunch.

RENNES: La Fontaine aux Perles €€€
Fine Dining   Map E3
96 Rue de la Poterie, 35200
Tel *(02) 99 53 90 90* **Closed** *Sun dinner, Mon; Tue in Aug*
Set in a beautiful garden, La

Outside seating at the charming Crêperie Ahna in Dinan, Côtes d'Armor

Fontaine aux Perles is worth seeking out for the exceptional quality of its cooking. Every dish, especially the decadent desserts, pleases the taste buds.

ST-JOUAN DES GUERETS: Ferme de la Porte €
Breton   Map E1
Centre-ville, 35430
Tel *(02) 99 81 10 76* **Closed** *Mon*
Farmhouse with views of the Rance estuary. Known for its hearty traditional food: home-made *charcuterie*, suckling pig, duck and lamb. Bookings essential.

ST-LUNAIRE: Le Décollé €€
Seafood   Map E1
1 Pointe de Décollé, 35800
Tel *(02) 99 46 01 70* **Closed** *Mon; mid-Nov-Jan*
Local favourite reconstructed with a touch of the exotic. Offers deftly prepared seafood and idyllic views of the St-Malo bay.

ST-MALO: Au Coin Malouin €
Grilled meats   Map E1
22 Rue de la Herse, 35400
Tel *09 54 41 02 25* **Closed** *Sun & Mon*
Good option for grilled meats, salads and enormous hamburgers. Try the cheesecake for dessert. Quirky decor and fun vibe.

ST-MALO: Le Tournesol €
Crêperie   Map E1
4 Rue des Marins, 35400
Tel *(02) 99 40 36 23*
Bright *crêperie* near the port, with outdoor tables and a wide choice of crêpes and *galettes*. Vegetarian options also available.

ST-MALO: A La Duchesse Anne €€
Fine Dining   Map E1
5 Place Guy-la-Chambre, 35400
Tel *(02) 99 40 85 33* **Closed** *Dec-mid-Feb*
Long-established restaurant with a sweetly nostalgic dining

room as well as outdoor seating. Serves delicious classic French cuisine – Chateaubriand and lobster *à l'amoricaine*.

ST-MALO: La Coquille d'Œuf €€
Fine Dining   Map E1
Rue de la Corne-de-Cerf, 35400
Tel *(02) 99 40 92 62* **Closed** *Oct-Mar: dinner only*
Popular for its intimate atmosphere and the excellent cooking. The menu features highly original dishes at moderate prices. Only 18 covers, so book in advance.

ST-MALO: Le Chalut €€
Seafood   Map E1
8 Rue de la Corne-de-Cerf, 35400
Tel *(02) 99 56 71 58* **Closed** *Mon & Tue*
The dining room may be unimpressive, but this is one of the best places in St-Malo for scallops, lobster and grills.

ST-MÉLOIR-DES-ONDES: Tirel Guérin €€€
Fine Dining   Map E2
Gare de la Gouesnière, 35350
Tel *(02) 99 89 10 46* **Closed** *mid-Dec-mid-Jan*
Michelin-starred for over 30 years; serves exceptional seafood creations with hints of spices, saffron and truffles. Also offers seating in a garden terrace.

Côtes d'Armor

DINAN: Crêperie Ahna €
Crêperie   Map E2
7 Rue de la Poissonnerie, 22100
Tel *(02) 96 39 09 13* **Closed** *Sun; Mar, Nov*
A charming little *crêperie* in the heart of the city, offering a good choice of grilled meats, salads and baked potatoes.

For more information on types of restaurants *see page 230*

Les Filets Bleus in Lannion is the ideal place for seafood lovers

DINAN: La Mère Pourcel €
Seafood **Map** E2
3 Place des Merciers, 22100
Tel *(02) 96 39 03 80* **Closed** *Wed, Sun & Tue dinner*
A half-timbered Dinan landmark serving lots of delicious shellfish and oysters, grilled steaks as well as duck. Good bargain menus.

DINAN: Le Bistrot de Viaduc €€
Fine Dining **Map** E2
22 Rue du Lion-d'Or, Lanvallay, 22100
Tel *(02) 96 85 95 00* **Closed** *Mon; mid-Dec–mid-Jan*
Refined cuisine served in a bright dining room with views over Dinan. Favourites include *ris de veau*, grilled sea bass and *foie gras*.

ERQUY: Relais St-Aubin €
Breton **Map** D1
Lieu Dit St-Aubin, 22430
Tel *(02) 96 72 13 22* **Closed** *Sep–Jun: Mon & Tue; Jul–Aug: Mon; mid-Jan–mid-Feb; mid-Nov–mid-Dec*
Atmospheric restaurant in a 17th-century granite priory; dishes made with scallops and other seafood, escargots and lamb are very popular.

ERQUY: Restaurant l'Escurial €€
Fine Dining **Map** D1
21 Blvd de la Mer, 22430
Tel (02) 96 72 31 56 **Closed** *Winter: Mon, Thu & Sun dinner; Jan*
Chic dining room with panoramic views of the port. The innovative menu includes dishes such as lobster salad and lamb confit.

FRÉHEL: Le Victorine €€
Seafood **Map** E1
Place de Chambly, 22240
Tel *(02) 96 41 55 55* **Closed** *Sep–Jun: Sun dinner, Mon; mid-Oct–mid-Nov; mid-Feb–Mar*
This popular village restaurant boasts great cooking, generous seafood platter, and interesting local cheeses. Book ahead.

ÎLE DE BRÉHAT: Le Jardin des Coquettes €€
Breton **Map** D1
Le Bourg, 22870
Tel *(02) 96 20 02 19* **Closed** *Jan–Feb*
Has a wide choice of crêpes and traditional dishes, including *kig ha farz* (a traditional Breton beef stew) and sautéed peat-smoked lamb. Exotic teas and cakes are served in the afternoon.

DK Choice

LANNION: Les Filets Bleus €€
Seafood **Map** C1
Port de Loquémeau, Trezd, 23000
Tel *(02) 96 35 22 26* **Closed** *Mon & Sun dinner; Nov–Mar*
Just the place for seafood lovers. Two breezy terraces with sea views, and a skilled chef who cooks the local catch with herbs from the garden. Also has meat options, along with a range of exquisite desserts. Book ahead.

LANNION: La Ville Blanche €€€
Fine Dining **Map** C1
Lieu-dit Ville-Blanche
Tel *(02) 96 37 04 28* **Closed** *Sep–Jun: Sun dinner, Mon, Wed; Jul–Aug: Sun dinner, Mon; Jan*
Friendly Michelin-starred restaurant renowned for its subtle, artistic way of preparing seafood dishes. Good Loire wines.

LOGUIVY-DE-LA-MER: Au Grand Large €€
Seafood **Map** D1
5 Rue de la Jetée, 22620
Tel *(02) 96 20 90 12* **Closed** *Mon; Jan; mid-Nov–mid-Dec*
A local favourite for its no-frills seafood dishes served in a charming setting overlooking the fishing boats.

DK Choice

MÛR DE BRETAGNE: L'Auberge Grand Maison €€€
French **Map** D2
1 Rue Léon-Le- Cerf, 22530
Tel *(02) 96 28 51 10* **Closed** *Mon & Sun dinner; 2 weeks in Oct; 2 weeks in Feb*
The buzz at L'Auberge Grand Maison is solely due to chef Christophe Le Fur, and his creation of innovative dishes that explore tastes and textures. The menu inclds pigeon and *foie gras* cannelloni and Breton pork slow-cooked for eight hours. The chef offers cooking classes on Thursdays and Saturdays.

PAIMPOL: Crêperie de l'Abbaye de Beauport €
Crêperie **Map** D1
32 Rue du Beauport, 22500
Tel *(02) 96 20 80 21* **Closed** *Mon*
Unassuming little *crêperie* serving delicious food. Relish savoury *galettes* with smoked trout, sausages or scallops.

PAIMPOL: Le Riva €
Italian **Map** D1
33 Quai Morand, 22500
Tel *(02) 96 20 43 08* **Closed** *Wed*
Lovely views of the bay to accompany delicious pizza and pasta. There is also a special mussels menu. Excellent value weekday lunch *formule*.

PAIMPOL: La Vieille Tour €€
Breton **Map** D1
13 Rue de l'Eglise, 22500
Tel *(02) 96 20 83 18* **Closed** *Sep–Jun: Mon, Wed & Sun dinner; mid-Jun–early Jul; mid-Nov–early Dec*
Bright and welcoming eatery with good-value lunch menus.

Sophisticated local cuisine, featuring hearty beef and lamb dishes, and plenty of seafood.

PENVÉNAN: Le Crustacé €
Seafood **Map** C1
2 Rue de la Poste, 22710
Tel *(02) 96 92 67 46* **Closed** *Wed, Sun dinner*
Located in a pretty fishing village, this unpretentious restaurant is popular for its new twists on traditional favourites. Save room for the mouth-watering desserts.

PERROS-GUIREC: La Crémaillère €€
Breton **Map** C1
13 Place de l'Eglise, 22700
Tel *(02) 96 23 22 08* **Closed** *Mon lunch, Wed*
Set in an intimate 17th-century building with a convivial atmosphere. Go for the *bouillabaisse* (a traditional Provençal fish stew) starter or the salad of prawns and smoked *magret* (duck breast).

PERROS-GUIREC: Le Suroît €€
Seafood **Map** C1
81 Rue Ernest-Renan, 22700
Tel *(02) 96 23 23 83* **Closed** *Mon*
Visit this harbourfront eatery for delicious fish dishes. The seafood couscous and pasta, skate, as well as the *foie gras* and crayfish salad are house favorites.

DK Choice

PLÉLO: Au Char à Bancs €
Breton **Map** D2
Moulin de la Ville-Geffroy, 22170
Tel *(02) 96 74 13 63* **Closed** *Tue*
Welcoming family farmhouse inn with a restaurant in an ancient mill. The traditional *potée* (smoked pork and vegetable stew) is simmered on an open fireplace, and is made with ingredients from the farm or sourced locally. There are also delicious crêpes and *galettes* on the menu. Has pony rides and a playground for the kids. Reserve a table in advance.

PLÉNEUF VAL-ANDRÉ: Au Biniou €€
French **Map** D1
121 Rue Clémenceau, 22370
Tel *(02) 96 72 24 35* **Closed** *Tue & Wed (except Jul–Aug); Feb*
Near a casino and the beach, this restaurant honours local seafood with a delightful, modern blending of flavours.

PLÉRIN: La Vieille Tour €€€
Fine Dining **Map** D2
75 Rue de la Tour, Port du Légué, 22190
Tel *(02) 96 33 10 30* **Closed** *Mon, Sun, Sat lunch; mid-Aug–mid-Sep; 2 weeks in Feb*
Stylish restaurant with imaginative dishes such as prawns with mango and pomegranate seeds and *foie gras* with sweet potato. Good value set menus.

ST-BRIEUC: Crêperie des Promenades €
Crêperie **Map** D2
18 Rue des Promenades, 22000
Tel *(02) 96 33 23 65* **Closed** *Mon–Sat dinner, Fri & Sat lunch*
Gourmet *crêperie* specializing in local and organic products. Serves both savoury and sweet crêpes. Book ahead for the *kig ha farz*.

ST-BRIEUC: Bistrot du Port €€
Seafood **Map** D2
15 Rue des Trois-Frères-Le-Goff, 22000
Tel *(02) 96 33 83 03* **Closed** *Sun*
A long-established local favourite, with a 1970's decor. Savour dishes of fresh lobster and scallops. Don't miss the tasty fish soup.

ST-BRIEUC: La Croix Blanche €€
Fine Dining **Map** D2
61 Rue de Genève-Cesson, 22000
Tel *(02) 96 33 16 97* **Closed** *Sun dinner, Mon; 3 weeks in Aug*
Elegant house in a pretty garden setting. Offers delectable dishes such as salt cod with gooseberries, duck confit lasagna. Lavish desserts.

ST-BRIEUC: Youpala Bistrot €€
French **Map** D2
5 Rue Palasne de Champeaux, 22000
Tel *(02) 96 94 50 74* **Closed** *Sun & Mon; 1 week in Mar & 2 weeks in Jul*
Michelin-starred cuisine prepared by innovative chef Jean-Marie Baudic. Dishes are based on fresh, seasonal ingredients.

ST-BRIEUC: Restaurant aux Pesked €€€
Fine Dining **Map** D2
59 Rue de Légué, 22000
Tel *(02) 96 33 34 65* **Closed** *Mon, Sat lunch, Sun dinner,*
Sit out on the terrace with lovely views over Gouët Valley and enjoy the highly reputed seafood in this Michelin-starred restaurant.

ST-QUAY-PORTRIEUX: Fleur de Blé Noir €
Crêperie **Map** D1
9 Rue du Commandant-Malbert, 22410
Tel *(02) 96 70 31 55* **Closed** *Sep–Jun: Wed & Thu; Jan*
Exotic savoury crêpes and *galettes* made with meat or seafood. Try the fried *andouillette* and ham, scallops or the smoked salmon.

TRÉBEURDEN: Le Manoir de Lan Kerellec €€€
Fine Dining **Map** C1
Allée Centrale de Lan Kerellec, 22560
Tel *(02) 96 15 00 00* **Closed** *lunch (except Thu–Sun)*
Dining room with a ship's hull ceiling and sea views. Enjoy Breton favourites made with a modern touch, such as the *foie gras* with coffee and dried fruit chutney.

TRÉGASTEL: Auberge de la Vieille Eglise €€
Breton **Map** D2
Place de l'Eglise, 22730
Tel *(02) 96 23 88 31* **Closed** *Sun dinner, Mon*
Located in a quiet village, Auberge de la Vieille Eglise offers superb steaks and seafood, including delicious lobster dishes.

TRÉGUIER: Des Trois Rivières €€€
Fine Dining **Map** C1
Port de Plaisance, 22220
Tel *(02) 96 92 97 00* **Closed** *Oct–May: Mon; Jan–mid-Feb*
Part of the Hôtel Aigue Marine, this Michelin-starred restaurant is known for its contemporary approach to Breton seafood.

Crêpes with raspberries and fresh fruit

For more information on types of restaurants *see page 231*

Northern Finistère

BREST: L'Imaginaire   €€
Contemporary Breton   **Map** B2
23 Rue Fautras, 29200
Tel *(02) 98 43 30 13*   **Closed** *Mon;*
2 weeks in Jan
A chic setting and an open kitchen, where you can watch the acclaimed chef cook up unusual takes on *foie gras*.

DK Choice

BREST: Le M   €€€
Fine Dining   **Map** B2
22 Rue Commandant-Drogou, 29200
Tel *(02) 98 47 90 00*   **Closed** *Mon, Sun*
Surrounded by flower-filled gardens, this elegant 1930s granite manor house serves refined and inventive cuisine. Try the tasty *tortellini* filled with smoked duck breast or the pigeon with *foie gras* and prunes. Decadent desserts and one of the best wine lists.

DK Choice

CARANTEC: Restaurant Patrick Jeffroy   €€€
French   **Map** B1
20 Rue Kélénn, 29660
Tel *(02) 98 67 00 47*   **Closed** *Mon*
Patrick Jeffroy, one of Brittany's top chefs, creates culinary marvels that match the magnificent bay views from the dining room of this excellent Michelin-starred restaurant. Expect the best Breton ingredients, notably shellfish, prepared with surprising flourishes from the Far East in highly original recipes. Complemented by a superb wine list. Reservations essential.

GUIMILIAU: Ar Chupen   €
Crêperie   **Map** B2
43 Rue de Calvaire, 29400
Tel *(02) 98 68 73 63*   **Closed** *Mon*
In a renovated farmhouse; serves traditional *galettes* as well as fish soup, salads and stuffed artichokes. Good choice for families and vegetarians.

ÎLE DE BATZ: Crêperie La Cassonade   €
Crêperie   **Map** B1
Le Débarcardère, 29253
Tel *(02) 98 61 75 25*   **Closed** *Oct–Mar*
Located on a pretty terrace, this *crêperie* serves a wide selection of dishes, from mussels and chips (made from organic potatoes) to buckwheat crêpes.

Key to Price Guide *see page 234*

ÎLE DE OUESSANT:
Ty Korn   €€
Seafood   **Map** A2
Lampaul village centre, 29217
Tel *(02) 98 48 87 33*   **Closed** *Sun & Mon; 2 weeks in Nov & Jan*
Cosy restaurant with delicious and fresh seafood on offer. Serves superb sea bass, langoustines and fish soup. Live music in the pub.

LAMPAUL-GUIMILIAU:
Hostellerie des Enclos   €
Breton   **Map** B2
Rue de Saint-Jacques, 29400
Tel *(02) 98 68 77 08*
Choose from a range of delectable regional dishes and fish specialties. Don't miss the lobster ravioli or go for the tasting menu to enjoy multiple dishes.

LAMPAUL-PLOUARZEL: Auberge de Vieux Puits   €
Breton   **Map** A2
Place de l'Eglise, 29810
Tel *(02) 98 84 09 13*   **Closed** *Sun dinner, Mon*
Elegant restaurant popular for the chef's delicious variations on Brittany's freshest scallops, oysters, strawberries and more.

LANNILIS: Les Oliviers   €€
Breton/Mediterranean   **Map** B1
6 Rue Carellou, 29870
Tel *(02) 98 04 19 94*   **Closed** *Tue, Sun & Mon dinner, Sat lunch*
Smart little restaurant run by a young couple. Features a mix of Breton cuisine and flavours of the Mediterranean.

LE CONQUET: Auberge de Kéringar   €
Breton   **Map** A2
Lochrist, 29217
Tel *(02) 98 89 09 59*   **Closed** *Sep– Jun: Mon–Thu*
Located in a Breton farmhouse, this eatery is popular for hearty traditional dishes. Try their *kig ha fars* on Wednesdays and Saturdays and *cotriade* (fish stew) on Fridays.

Catfish with crust of black bread and Yuzu Hollandaise at Patrick Jeffroy, Carantec

LOCQUIREC: Le Grand Hôtel des Bains   €€€
Fine Dining   **Map** C1
15 bis Rue de l'Eglise, 29241
Tel *(02) 98 67 41 02*   **Closed** *Jan*
Early 20th-century building with modern decor and views of the gardens and the sea. Sophisticated cuisine focusing on seafood and organic vegetables.

MORLAIX: Atipik Bilig   €
Crêperie   **Map** C1
1 Rue Ange-de-Guernisac, 29600
Tel *(02) 98 63 38 63*   **Closed** *Sep– mid-Jul: Sun & Mon*
Set in a 16th-century house, this eatery serves inventive crêpes filled with *foie gras*, pinenuts, crushed pistachios and even a pepper jam.

MORLAIX: Le Viaduc   €
Seafood   **Map** C1
3 Rampe St-Mélaine, 29600
Tel *(02) 98 63 24 21*   **Closed** *Sep– Jun: Sun dinner, Mon*
Charming restaurant in one of Morlaix's oldest houses where locals feast on superb traditional seafood as well as meat dishes.

Le Grand Hôtel des Bains in Locquirec is set in a 20th-century building

PLOUDALMÉZEAU-PORTSALL:
Le Caïman €
Seafood Map A1
44 Rue du Port, 29830
Tel *(02) 98 48 69 77* **Closed** *Mon; 2 weeks in Mar*
Tropical decor, a lively atmosphere and a terrace on the water's edge make this a great place to enjoy grilled seafood or stuffed mussels.

PLOUGASTEL-DAOULAS:
Le Chevalier de l'Auberlac'h €
Breton Map B2
5 Rue Mathurin-Thomas, 29470
Tel (02) 98 40 54 56 **Closed** *Mon*
Dine on tasty traditional meat and fish dishes, such as salmon in puff pastry and pan-fried scallops, indoors or out on the pretty terrace at this restaurant.

PLOUIDER: La Butte €€
Breton Map B1
10 Rue de la Mer, 29260
Tel *(02) 98 25 40 54* **Closed** *Mon*
La Butte offers stunning sea views and fresh, imaginative Breton fare. The pan-fried *foie gras* with Couchen jelly is exquisite. Vegetarian food on request.

ROSCOFF: Le Surcouf €
Seafood Map B1
14 Rue Amiral-Révellière, 29680
Tel *(02) 98 69 71 89* **Closed** *Wed*
Fixed-price menu features well-prepared food made using local coastal produce as well as Roscoff's famous pink onions.

ROSCOFF:
L'Ecume des Jours €€
Seafood Map B1
Quai d'Auxerre, 29680
Tel *(02) 98 61 22 83* **Closed** *Wed; mid-Dec–Jan*
Regional dishes prepared with an exotic touch – try the roast monkfish with coriander pesto and risotto. One of the two dining rooms has very nice sea views.

ROSCOFF: Le Yachtman €€€
Fine Dining Map B1
Blvd Ste-Barbe, 29680
Tel *(02) 98 69 70 78* **Closed** *Mon; mid-Nov–mid-Mar*
Seasonal cuisine served in an elegant setting. Dishes such as the Roscoff crab and Jerusalem arti-chokes are a must try. Impressive desserts and an excellent wine list.

ST-POL-DE-LÉON: La Pomme d'Api €€
Fine Dining Map B1
49 Rue Verderel, 29250
Tel (02) 98 69 04 36 **Closed** *Sep–Jun: Mon*
Gastronomic cuisine prepared with a Mediterranean touch in this mid-16th-century house.

The contemporary dining area at La Butte

The turbot *gratinée* with black sesame and yuzu is superb. Good-value lunch menus available.

ST-THÉGONNEC: Auberge de St-Thégonnec €€
Breton Map B1
6 Place de la Mairie, 29410
Tel *(02) 98 79 61 18* **Closed** *Sun, Mon & Sat lunch*
Chic dining room offering original takes on Brittany's classic dishes such as red salmon crumble and Wagyu rumpsteak. Great desserts.

ST-VOUGAY: Crêperie du Château €
Crêperie Map B1
Kerfao, 29440
Tel (02) 98 69 93 09 **Closed** *Sep–Jun: Mon–Thu*
Set in a farmhouse surrounded by gardens, this *crêperie* is popular for its range of *galettes* and crêpes, pizzas, salads, fish, grilled meats and seafood platters.

Southern Finistère

AUDIERNE:
Le Goyen €€
Seafood Map A2
Place Jean-Simon, 29770
Tel *(02) 98 70 08 88* **Closed** *Jan–Mar*
Cheerful dining room facing the sea. Serves lobster and seafood prepared in exotic ways. Save room for the delicious desserts.

CARHAIX-PLOUGUER: Auberge de Poher €
Breton Map C2
Port de Carhaix, 29270
Tel *(02) 98 99 51 18*
Simple hearty cuisine including many traditional Breton dishes rarely seen on restaurant menus. Old fashioned country decor.

CLÉDEN-CAP SIZUN: L'Etrave €€
Seafood Map A2
Route de la Pointe-du-Van, 29770
Tel *(02) 98 70 66 87* **Closed** *Tue & Wed; Oct–Apr*
Gorgeous sea views and a short menu of simple, favourful food to remember. The creamy lobsters are a must try.

CONCARNEAU: Le Petit Chaperon Rouge €
Crêperie Map B3
7 Place Du Guesclin, 29900
Tel *(02) 98 60 53 32* **Closed** *Sun & Mon*
Themed on the story of *Little Red Riding Hood*, this place has been decorated with wicker baskets and checked tablecloths. Don't miss the *la Blandette* (goat's cheese, spinach and ham).

CONCARNEAU: Le Buccin €€
Seafood Map B3
1 Rue Duguay-Trouin, 29900
Tel *(02) 98 50 54 22* **Closed** *Mon*
Enjoy seafood specialities and meat dishes in this family-friendly place with a relaxed ambience. Good-value fixed-price menus.

CROZON: Le Mutin Gourmand €€
Breton Map B2
Place de l'Eglise, 29160
Tel *(02) 98 27 06 51* **Closed** *Mon & Tue lunch; 2 weeks in Mar*
Popular eatery serving beautifully cooked Breton seafood, lamb and artichokes with spices and cocoa from San Tomé in Africa.

DOUARNENEZ: Au Gouter Breton €
Crêperie Map B2
36 Rue Jean-Jaurès, 29100
Tel *(02) 98 92 02 74* **Closed** *Sun & Mon*
In business since 1951, Au Gouter Breton offers superb crêpes with both sweet and savoury fillings, and a range of ciders.

For more information on types of restaurants *see page 230*

DOUARNENEZ: Clos de Vallombeuse €€
Fine Dining Map B2
7 Rue d'Estienne-d'Orves, 29100
Tel *(02) 98 92 63 64* **Closed** *Mon*
Elegant restaurant with wood-panelled walls, parquet floors and a pretty garden. Serves classic gourmet cuisine. Good-value set menus.

FOUESNANT: Belle Vue €€
Breton Map B3
30 Descente de Belle-Vue, 29170
Tel *(02) 98 56 00 33* **Closed** *Mon & Tue; Nov–Mar*
Lovely sea views with great food to match. The menu features dishes made with the region's beef, pork, seafood, potatoes and cider. Try the gourmet salad with smoked duck breast and *foie gras*.

FOUESNANT: La Pointe-du-Cap-Coz €€
Seafood Map B3
153 Ave de la Pointe-du-Cap-Coz, 29170
Tel *(02) 98 56 01 63* **Closed** *Mon & Tue lunch, Wed; Jan–mid-Feb; 1 week in Nov*
The kitchen at this restaurant is led by a third-generation family chef who prepares tasty seafood dishes with extreme care. Don't miss the langoustine salad or warm spider crab with bearnaise sauce.

LA FÔRET FOUESNANT: Auberge St-Laurent €€
Breton Map B3
6 Rue Beg Ménez, 29940
Tel *(02) 98 56 98 07* **Closed** *Mon*
Traditional Breton *auberge* in the countryside offering delicious roast Guilvinec langoustines with citrus. Sit out in the lovely garden or on the terrace.

DK Choice

MOËLAN-SUR-MER: Le Raphaël €€€
Seafood Map C3
Rue des Moulins, 29350
Tel *(02) 98 96 52 52* **Closed** *Dec–Feb*
A pretty place to enjoy lunch in summer. This hotel-restaurant combines an enchanting, pastoral setting in a former mill and park with refined contemporary cuisine. There are special lobster, langoustine and shellfish menus; others are more varied. Go for the rack of piglet with a pepper curry and the Briton pudding with layers of chocolate and mascarpone for dessert.

The stylish dining room at L'Ambroisie in Quimper

DK Choice

PLEYBEN: Crêperie de l'Enclos €
Crêperie Map B2
52 Place Charles-de-Gaulle, 29190
Tel *(02) 98 26 38 68* **Closed** *2 weeks in Mar, May & Jun; mid-Nov–early Jan*
Frontrunner for Brittany's finest gourmet *crêperie*, offering gastronomic options diners would not find elsewhere -- scrambled eggs with truffles, Breton tripe and cider vinegar, and a sweet filling of warm apple and honey. Come on Thursday nights in July and August for the *fest-noz*.

PLOMODIERN: Auberge des Glazicks €€€
Contemporary French Map B2
7 Rue de la Plage, 29550
Tel *(02) 98 81 52 32* **Closed** *Mon & Tue; 2 weeks in Mar & Nov*
Original culinary creations that pick the finest local ingredients. The young chef Olivier Bellin, who has been called one of Brittany's best, has been awarded two Michelin stars.

PONT-AVEN: La Talisman €
Crêperie Map B3
4 Rue Paul-Sérusier, 29930
Tel *(02) 98 06 02 58* **Closed** *Mon*
An old local favourite, La Talisman has been using the same recipes since 1920. Try the four cheeses or *Galette* Talisman with onions and buckwheat.

PONT-AVEN: La Taupinière €€€
Seafood Map B3
Croissant Saint-André, 29930
Tel *(02) 98 06 03 12* **Closed** *Mon & Tue; mid-Sep–mid-Oct*
Housed in a charming thatched cottage, this restaurant has several ways of preparing the speciality, Concarneau langoustines. Great seasonal desserts. Offers cookery courses.

PONT-AVEN: Le Moulin de Rosmadec €€€
Fine Dining Map B3
Venelle de Rosmadec, 29930
Tel *(02) 98 06 00 22* **Closed** *Sun dinner, Mon; mid-Nov–mid-Dec, 3 weeks Feb*
Delightful, restored 15th-century mill serving Frédéric Sébilleau's gourmet classics with a focus on seafood. The grilled lobster with two butters is wonderful.

QUIMPER: La Nova €
Breton Map B3
33 Rue Aristide-Briand, 29000
Tel *(02) 98 64 42 58* **Closed** *Sun*
Chic decor and outdoor seating on a terrace. Serves Breton and traditional French dishes. Delightful home-made desserts.

QUIMPER: Erwan €€
Breton Map B3
3 Rue Aristide-Briand, 29000
Tel *(02) 98 90 14 14* **Closed** *Sat & Sun*
Relish traditional Breton cuisine in this cheerful, orange dining room. Don't miss the excellent *cassoulet Saint-Jacques* (large scallops in sauce).

QUIMPER: L'Ambroisie €€
Breton Map B3
49 Rue Elie-Fréron, 29000
Tel *(02) 98 95 00 02* **Closed** *un dinner, Mon*
Contemporary Breton cuisine served in a stylish dining room. The menu changes regularly but expect dishes such as tartare sea bass and scallops in spicy crust. Scrumptious desserts.

QUIMPERLÉ: Ty Gwechall €
Crêperie Map C3
4 Rue Mellec, 29300
Tel *(02) 98 96 30 63* **Closed** *Sun dinner, Mon, 2 weeks in Jan & Feb*
Atmospheric *crêperie* in a 1670's stone house. The menu features 150 choices of crêpes, to be enjoyed with local beers and ciders and live Celtic music.

**QUIMPERLÉ: Le Bistrot
de la Tour** €€€
French Map C3
2 Rue Domaine-Morice, 29300
Tel (02) 98 39 29 58 **Closed** *Sun
& Mon*
This restaurant is known for
quality seasonal cuisine and
a choice of over 600 wines
from Loire and Rhône Valley.

**RIEC-SUR-BÉLON:
Chez Jacky** €€
Seafood Map C3
Port du Bélon, 29340
Tel (02) 98 06 90 32 **Closed** *Mon;
Oct–Easter*
Part of an oyster farm, this
cheerful eatery is full of nautical
decor. Serves tasty hot and
cold crustaceans, from oysters
to lobster.

**ROSNOEN: Ferme Auberge du
Seillou** €
Breton Map A2
*On the D791, 5 km (3 miles) from
Faou, 29580*
Tel (02) 98 81 92 21 **Closed** *Mon;
mid-Sep–mid-Oct*
Delightful farm restaurant serving
dishes made with home-grown
beef, chicken and pork. Their *kig
ha fars* is famous. The cider is also
home-made. Book ahead.

**STE-ANNE-DE-LA-PALUD: Hôtel
de la Plage** €€€
Fine Dining Map B2
Beach road, 29550
Tel (02) 98 92 50 12 **Closed** *Nov–
Easter*
Excellent choice for colourful,
refined culinary combinations.
There is plenty of seafood,
Limousin beef and vegetables.
Lovely sea views.

Morbihan

ARRADON: Les Vénètes €€€
Seafood Map D3
9 Rue Carrière, 56610
Tel (02) 97 44 85 85
Soak in splendid views of
the Golfe du Morbihan while
feasting on delectable dishes
of freshly caught seafood as
well as other local ingredients.

**AURAY: La Closerie
de Kerdrain** €€
Fine Dining Map D3
20 Rue Louis-Billet, 56400
Tel (02) 97 56 61 27 **Closed** *Mon*
Eat at any of the four elegant
dining rooms at this restaurant
led by an enthusiastic and
expert chef. Mouth-watering
delicacies are flavoured with
home-grown herbs and flowers.

**BADEN: Hôtel Restaurant
Gavrinis** €€
Breton Map D3
1 Rue de l'Île-Gavrinis, 56870
Tel (02) 97 57 00 82 **Closed** *Sat
lunch, Sun dinner, Mon; a week in Nov*
Comfortable hotel-restaurant
featuring gourmet Breton cuisine.
The best locally sourced ingredients, from blue lobster to spinach
is what the menu is based on. The
bread is home-made.

BELLE-ÎLE-EN-MER: Roz Avel €€
Seafood Map C4
Rue du Lt Riou, Sauzon, 56630
Tel (02) 97 31 61 48 **Closed** *Wed;
mid-Nov–mid-Dec, Jan–mid-Mar*
Intimate restaurant with excellent
value menus. The set menus
feature dishes such as lobster
medallion with raspberry
vinaigrette and veal tongue
with *foie gras* and vegetables.

**BELLE-ÎLE-EN-MER:
Castel Clara** €€€
Fine Dining Map C4
Port-Goulphar, Bangor, 56360
Tel (02) 97 31 84 21 **Closed** *mid-
Nov–mid-Dec*
Contemporary design, impressive
views of the cliffs and beautifully
prepared meeals are the main
draws here. The menu focuses on
locally-sourced seafood, Breton
lamb and organic produce.

**BIGNAN: Auberge La
Chouannière** €€
Breton Map D3
6 Rue Georges-Cadoudal, 56500
Tel (02) 97 60 00 96 **Closed** *Tue–
Thu, Sun dinner*
Authentic *auberge* serving
exquisite takes on Breton classics
such as sole served with Tonka
bean and wild garlic sauce, in a
Louis XVI-style dining room.

The lovely Hôtel de la Plage in
Ste-Anne-de-la-Palud

DK Choice

**BILLIERS: Domaine de
Rochevilaine** €€€
Seafood Map D4
*On the Pointe de Pen-Lan-Sud,
56190*
Tel (02) 97 41 61 61
Seafood lovers across France
arrive at this rocky promontory
to indulge in chef Patrice
Caillault's luxurious, imaginative
and carefully prepared seafood
dishes. His *pièce de résistance*
is the Breton lobster in four
different courses, but he also
offers a Brittany-based land
menu for those who don't like
fish. Superb desserts and wines.

CARNAC: Chez Marie €
Crêperie Map C4
3 Place de l'Eglise, 56340
Tel (02) 97 52 07 93 **Closed** *Mon
& Tue*
Founded in 1959, this is Carnac's
oldest *crêperie*. Exceptional
crêpes, including the smoked
salmon "Nordique"' are served
in a welcoming wood and
stone dining room'.

CARNAC: La Calypso €€
Seafood Map C4
Anse du Pô, 56340
Tel (02) 97 52 06 14 **Closed** *Mon;
Dec–Jan*
Simple, delectable seafood starters,
followed by fish, lobster or steaks
grilled over an open fire is the
irresistable attraction. Book ahead.

CARNAC: La Côte €€
French Map C4
Kermario, 56340
Tel (02) 97 52 02 80 **Closed** *Mon,
Tue lunch; Jan*
Diners flock to this charming
old farmhouse in a garden to
savour seasonal dishes prepared
with flair and imagination. The
weekday menu is good value.

DK Choice

**HENNEBONT: Château de
Locguénolé** €€€
Fine Dining Map C3
Route de Port-Louis, 56700
Tel (02) 97 76 76 76
This 19th-century château
features an elegant, classic
dining room complete with
tapestries and chandeliers. The
cuisine of Michelin-starred chef
Olivier Beurné is equally regal,
featuring the best seasonal
ingredients (seafood, veal, and
lamb), divine desserts and entic-
ing wines. There is also a terrace
in a wooded waterside park.

ÎLE AUX MOINES: Les Embruns €
Seafood **Map** D4
Rue Commerce, 56780
Tel *(02) 97 26 30 86* **Closed** *Wed
(except Sun and French school
holidays) first 2 weeks in Oct; Feb.*
A delightful bar-restaurant
known for unpretentious dishes
based on the island's oysters,
crabs and fish. The menu
includes meat dishes too.

ÎLE DE GROIX: Les Alizés €
Seafood **Map** C3
8 Rue du Géneral-de-Gaulle, 56590
Tel *(02) 97 86 89 64* **Closed** *Mon;
last week of Jun*
Les Alizés features simple decor
and dishes written up on a chalk-
board menu, which reflects the
primary focus on the day's catch.

JOSSELIN: La Marine €
Crêperie **Map** D3
8 Rue du Canal, 56120
Tel *(02) 97 22 21 98* **Closed** *Mon*
Located on a canal, this restaurant
has a pretty terrace with chateau
vistas. Serves delicious crêpes
with a choice of seasonal fillings.

JOSSELIN: La Table d'O €€
Breton **Map** D3
9 Rue Glatinier, 56120
Tel *(02) 97 70 61 39* **Closed** *Sep–Jun:
Wed; 1 week in Jun; 2 weeks in Nov*
Enjoy superb valley views from
the windows and terrace while
you dine at this eatery. The menu
is limitied but the dishes are well
prepared. Excellent desserts.

LORIENT: La Rozelle €
Crêperie **Map** C3
7 Rue du Maréchal-Foch, 56100
Tel *(02) 97 64 41 74* **Closed** *Sep–
Jun: Sun*
Named after the wooden tool
used to spread the crêpe batter,
this little restaurant serves
superb light buckwheat
crêpes accompanied by cider.

LORIENT: L'Amphitryon €€€
Fine Dining **Map** C3
127 Rue du Colonel-Müller, 56100
Tel *(02) 97 83 34 04* **Closed** *Sun;
Mon; first 2 weeks in May, Nov*
Led by the master-chef Jean-Paul
Abadie, L'Amphitryon offers delect-
able dishes that retain a purity of
flavour. Specialties include slow-
cooked bass with vanilla.

PONTIVY: La Pommeraie €€
French **Map** D3
17 Quai du Couvent, 56300
Tel *(02) 97 25 60 09* **Closed** *Sun,
Mon & Tue dinner, Sat lunch*
The talented chef uses locally
sourced seasonal ingredients
to create delicious dishes. Try
the roast lamb with roquefort.

PORT-LOUIS: Avel Vor €€€
Seafood **Map** C3
25 Rue de Locmalo, 56290
Tel *(02) 97 82 47 59* **Closed** *Mon
& Tue, Sun dinner*
Delicious, ambitious cuisine
based on local produce and the
freshest ingredients from the
port – which is where the contemporary dining room is located.

QUESTEMBERT: La Bretagne €€€
Fine Dining **Map** D3
13 Rue St-Michel, 56230
Tel *(02) 97 26 11 12* **Closed** *Mon; 3
weeks in Jan; 1 week in Mar*
A charming winter garden serving
classic French cuisine. The menu
includes dishes such as saddle of
rabbit stuffed with morels and red
mullet fillet with quinoa. Excellent
value weekday lunch menu.

QUIBERON: Le Ty Retro €
Crêperie **Map** C4
12 Place du Repos, 56170
Tel *(02) 97 59 25 43* **Closed** *Wed*
Friendly, pretty dining room and
terrace offering Quiberon's finest
crêpes and *galettes*, stuffed with
homemade fillings.

QUIBERON: La Chaumine €€
Seafood **Map** C4
79 Rue de Port Haliguen, 56170
Tel *(02) 97 50 17 67* **Closed** *Sun
dinner, Mon, Tue lunch; mid-Nov–
mid-Mar*
Convivial, family-run inn featuring
the catch of the day and seafood
platters. The set menus are great
value. Booking essential.

**QUIBERON: Le Verger de
la Mer** €€
Breton **Map** C4
Boulevard Goulvars, 56170
Tel *(02) 97 50 29 12* **Closed** *Tue
& Wed; Feb*
The seasonal menu at this eatery
is inspired by the cuisine of the
Armor and Argoat regions. Try the
terrine of *foie gras*, lobster and fig.

**LA ROCHE-BERNARD: L'Auberge
Bretonne** €€
Fine Dining **Map** E4
2 Place Du Guesclin, 56130
Tel *(02) 99 90 60 28* **Closed** *Sun
dinner, Mon, Tue lunch; mid-Nov–
mid-Jan*
Sit at a garden patio and savour a
seafood platter or dishes such as
roasted prawns with saffron.

ST-PHILIBERT: Chez Jaouen €
Seafood **Map** D3
Jaouen Antoine, 56470
Tel *(02) 97 55 06 43* **Closed** *Nov–Mar*
Situated at an aquaculture
station, this place serves shellfish
at communal tables in a converted boat shed. There is also
an all-you-can-eat lunch buffet.

ST-AVÉ: Le Pressoir €€€
French **Map** D3
7 Rue de l'Hôpital, 56890
Tel *(02) 97 60 87 63* **Closed** *Mon*
Seasonal, Michelin-starred
cuisine full of delicious flavours

Pretty garden terrace at the delightful Le Jardin Gourmand, Lorient

with a touch of the exotic. Interesting wine list. Reservations are essential.

TRINITÉ-SUR-MER: L'Azimut €€
French   Map C4
1 Rue du Men-Du, 56470
Tel *(02) 97 55 71 88* **Closed** *Mon lunch; 2 weeks in Mar*
The port-facing L'Azimut serves lovely gourmet fare featuring a mix of both traditional and modern dishes. Good value lunch *formule*. Try the crab ravioli with vegetables bathed in a wild mushroom broth.

VANNES: Karpa €
Italian   Map D3
28 Rue du Port, 56000
Tel *(02) 97 47 48 34*
In an old-timbered house with chic and casual decor, Karpa offers a wide variety of pizza, pasta, salads and burgers.

VANNES: Les Remparts €
Breton   Map D3
6 Rue Alexandre-le-Pontois, 56000
Tel *(02) 97 47 52 44* **Closed** *Sun & Mon*
This bistrot has seasonal menus based on fresh regional ingredients, including organic produce. Wines are served by the glass.

VANNES: Le Roscanvec €€
French   Map D3
17 Rue des Halles, 56000
Tel *(02) 97 47 15 96* **Closed** *Sun dinner, Mon & Tue*
Enjoy some of Vannes' best gourmet food prepared by a young, dynamic team of chefs. Try the *foie gras* with fried cream marzipan or choose from the lobster menu.

Loire-Atlantique

ANCENIS:
La Charbonnière €€
Seafood   Map F4
La Charbonnière, 44150
Tel *(02) 40 83 25 17* **Closed** *Jun–Sep: Mon; Oct–May: Sun dinner, Mon*
Feast on gourmet specialities such as pike-perch with butter sauce and Gascon pig confit on a sheltered veranda overlooking the Loire.

CLISSON: La Bonne Auberge €€
Fine Dining   Map F5
1 Rue Olivier-de-Clisson, 44190
Tel *(02) 40 54 01 90* **Closed** *Mon, Tue, Wed & Sun dinner; 2 weeks in Aug*
Warm, inviting *auberge* with a pretty garden, offering superb, delicious takes on classics such as turbo with langoustines. Great desserts.

The elegant dining area at Manoir de la Boulaie, set in a historic Breton manor

GUÉRANDE: Roc-Maria €
Crêperie   Map D4
1 Rue Vieux-Marché-aux-Grains, 44350
Tel *(02) 40 24 90 51* **Closed** *3 weeks in Nov; 2 weeks in Jan*
Friendly *crêperie* in a 15th-century building with an open fireplace. Renowned for its savoury buckwheat *galettes* filled with seafood.

DK Choice

HAUTE-GOULAINE: Manoir de la Boulaie €€€
Fine Dining   Map F4
33 Rue de la Chapelle Saint-Martin, 44115
Tel *(02) 40 06 15 91* **Closed** *Mon, Wed & Sun dinner; 2 weeks in Aug*
Wonderful combination of chef Laurent Suaudeau's exquisite, inventive cuisine, served in an elegant, historic Breton manor. The finest local ingredients are artistically transformed into delectable dishes, from duck in a miso crust to sea bass and shellfish, with *pak choi*, coconut and galangal broth. Great wines to match. Book well in advance.

LA BAULE: Le Billot €€
Grilled meats   Map D4
17 Allée des Pétrels, 44500
Tel *(02) 40 60 00 00* **Closed** *Sun & Mon; 2 weeks in Aug*
Lively bistro offering a wide-ranging menu specializing in succulent grilled meats. Excellent wine list to accompany the dishes.

LE CROISIC: Le Neptune €€
Seafood   Map D4
11 Ave de Port-Val
Tel *(02) 40 23 02 59* **Closed** *Mon & Tue; Jan–Mar*
Classic seafood restaurant with a nautical decor and lovely ocean views. Seafood platters, fish soup, and traditional Nantais desserts are the house specialties.

NANTES: Crêperie Heb Ken €
Crêperie   Map F4
5 Rue de Guérande, 44000
Tel *(02) 40 48 79 03* **Closed** *Sun; 2 weeks in Aug*
A popular eatery ever since it opened way back in 1976; serves a wide choice of mouth-watering crêpes and savoury *gallettes* in a cheerful setting.

NANTES: La Cocotte €€
French   Map F4
27 Rue Foure, 44000
Tel *(02) 40 84 12 44* **Closed** *Mon & Sun*
An attractive conversion of a former butcher's shop, with a menu devoted to gourmet dishes based on organic-reared poultry, such as chicken, duck, pigeon and quail, as well as eggs.

NANTES: L'Atlantide €€€
Fine Dining   Map F4
16 Quai Ernest-Renaud, 44000
Tel *(02) 40 73 23 23* **Closed** *Sun*
Dining room with superb vistas of the river and port. The Michelin-starred cuisine by chef Jean-Yves Guého never fails to impress. Remarkable wine list.

PORNIC: Beau Rivage €€€
Seafood   Map E5
Plage de la Birochère, 44210
Tel *(02) 40 82 03 08* **Closed** *Mon & Tue*
Seafront restaurant serving the best of each season and region – seafood from Guilvinec and Croisic, Challans ducklings and Noirmoutier potatoes.

ST-JOACHIM: La Mare aux Oiseaux €€€
Fine Dining   Map E4
223 Rue du Chef-de-Île-de-Fédrun
Tel *(02) 40 88 53 01* **Closed** *3 weeks in Jan*
Imaginative cuisine based on marshland and sea ingredients such as eel, duck, sardines, crab, wild mint and edible seaweed.

SHOPS AND MARKETS

From the stalls laid out on a Saturday in Vitré to the great covered market in Plouescat, Brittany's weekly food markets are key events in the region's gastronomic life. It is here that the best and freshest local produce – crisp young vegetables, glistening seafood, farm-produced cheeses, cider and charcuterie – is to be found. There are also many fascinating shops to be explored, offering other Breton goods, among the most distinctive being striped sailors' sweaters, Quimper faience and craft items, such as ship models, with a marine theme.

Artichokes, sold in every market in Brittany

Markets

The regular weekly markets are the major outlet for local produce and local, or even family, specialities. But they are not the only choice. To promote their own produce, certain growers have set up small farmers' markets on their own farm premises, where they sell goat's cheese, buttermilk and other produce from local farms.

There are farmers' markets in Planguenoual, Milizac, Plouzélambre and Notre-Dame-du-Guildo. *Circuits gourmands* (gastronomic tours) are organized by local producers in an initiative to promote local delicacies. Organic food markets are also becoming popular. A list of all these markets and the addresses of the relevant producers are available from tourist offices.

Local Drinks

Thanks to a small group of cider-makers, such as **Éric Baron**, who use traditional methods, cider has undergone a revival in popularity since the 1980s. The Cornouaille region produces an excellent cider, which has an AOP classification. Robust and with an orange hue, it goes very well with seafood.

Some producers, such as **Fisselier** and **Dassonville**, also offer a wide range of liqueurs made from strawberries and other suitable kinds of fruit, as well as coffee liqueurs made with cider brandy, *chouchenn*, a mead made with cider and honey, *pommeaux* (sparkling apple wines) and Breton whisky. There is also *lambig*, made by distilling cider brandy and ideal for lobster flambé.

There were once 75 breweries in Brittany, and, following a decline, there has been a resurgence of small independent breweries since 1985. The beers that they produce – such as Coreff, a pale ale, Blanche Hermine and Telenn Du, a wheat beer – easily equal more famous brands.

Produce of the Sea

Fresh fish auctions are held in many harbours all along the coast of Brittany. If the idea of attending one does not appeal, there are alternatives. Oysters can be bought at oyster farms, such as that at the **Château de Belon**. Fish and seafood can also be bought from wholesalers and from fish farms *(viviers)*, such as those in Audierne, Camaret and **Roscoff**. Although wholesale prices fluctuate, they are always sure to be lower than retail prices.

The best kinds of oysters are Nacre des Abers and Morlaix-Penzé, which have a sweet taste; Aven-Belon, which are crisp and sweet; Cancale, firm with a nutty aftertaste; Paimpolaise, salty with a flavour of the sea; and the plump Ria d'Étel.

Easier to take home are sardines, mackerel fillets, slices of tuna and traditionally cured sprats, which are canned in factories, such as **Gonidec**, on the south coast of Brittany. Guérande salt, jars of samphire and seaweed products are also good buys. With 800 different varieties, the coast of Finistère is one of the largest seaweed-growing areas in the world. The benefits of seaweed are many and varied. **Thalado**, for example, makes seaweed bath salts, soap, tonic lotions and nutritional supplements.

Coreff beer

Oysters on a stall in Vivier-sur-Mer

Sailors' Clothing

In most harbours there is a fishermen's cooperative where traditional sailors' clothing, labelled "Made in Breizh" is on sale. This ranges from thick pullovers, indigo-and-cream striped sweaters and smocks, to waxed jackets and seamen's watch jackets with double waterproof collars. Perfectly suited for sailing and for fishing trips, these tough, weatherproof clothes are derived from traditional Breton clothing. The *kabig*, a jacket made of heavy cloth, evolved from the *kab an aod* that Breton seaweed-gatherers once wore.

The best-known brands of seamen's clothing are Captain Corsaire, **Bonneterie d'Armor** and **Guy Cotten**, the leading manufacturer of clothes for professional seamen.

Stall selling *Kouign amann*, the traditional Breton cake

Retail outlet of the Faïencerie Henriot in Quimper

Handicrafts

Colourful Quimper Faience *(see pp170–1)*, particularly that produced by the Faïencerie Henriot, is without doubt Brittany's best known hand-crafted product. The Île de Bréhat is also renowned for its glassware and Pont-l'Abbé for its embroidered linen, such as that offered for sale in **Le Minor**.

There are also craftsmen's workshops that are open to the public in Brasparts *(see p147)*, in Locronan *(see p158)*, in Guérande *(see p206)*, in the villages around Pont-Scorff, 7 km (4 miles) from Lorient, and in St-Méloir, 17 km (10 miles) from Dol-de-Bretagne.

Browsing in shops selling marine antiques may also turn up some interesting finds, as may a visit to woodworkers such as **Thierry Morel** in Plouvien, **Frères Douirin** in Plozévet, and Francis Tirot in Fougères, all of whom make wooden ship models.

Most shops are open from 9am to 12:30pm and 2:30 to 7pm, Monday to Saturday.

DIRECTORY

Regional Specialities

FINISTÈRE

Fédération Régionale des Pays Touristiques de Bretagne
Rue Jean-Claude-Jégat, Pontivy. **Tel** (02) 97 51 46 16. Provides booklets of recommended cafés, crêperies and restaurants.

Château de Belon
On the right bank of the river, Riec-sur-Bélon. **Tel** (02) 98 06 90 58. Oysters.

Dassonville
Pen-ar-Ros, Plouegat-Moysan. **Tel** (02) 98 79 21 25. Chouchenn (mead) & honey.

Éric Baron
Kervéguen, Guimaec. **Tel** (02) 98 67 50 02. Cider made by traditional methods.

Gonidec
2 Rue Henri-Fabre, Concarneau. **Tel** (02) 98 97 07 09. Canned fish.

Thalado
Quai d'Auxerre 29680, Roscoff. **Tel** (02) 98 61 28 83. Edible seaweed and seaweed for use in thalassotherapy.

Viviers de Roscoff
Pointe Ste-Barbe, Roscoff. **Tel** (02) 98 61 19 61. Crustacean farms.

Ille-et-Vilaine

Fisselier
56 Rue du Verger, Rennes-Chantepie. **Tel** (02) 99 41 00 00. Liqueurs made by traditional methods.

Clothes & Handicrafts

FINISTÈRE

Bonneterie d'Armor
21–3 Rue Louison-Bobet, Quimper. **Tel** (02) 98 90 05 29. Head office of Armor Lux (for sailors' clothing).

Faïencerie H-B Henriot
16 Rue Haute, Quartier de Locmaria, Quimper. **Tel** (02) 98 52 22 52. Quimper faience.

Frères Douirin
9 Impasse de la Poste, Plozevet. **Tel** (02) 98 91 42 04. Miniature Breton furniture.

Guy Cotten
Pont Minaouët, Trégunc. **Tel** (02) 98 97 66 79. 🖳 guycotten. com Sailors' clothing.

Le Minor
3 Quai St-Laurent, Pont-l'Abbé. **Tel** (02) 98 87 07 22. Embroidery, lace & tulle.

Thierry Morel
183 Rue Emile-Salaun, Plouvien. **Tel** (02) 98 40 99 24. Model ships.

What to Buy in Brittany

Brittany projects a distinctive image. This is reflected in the seamen's striped sweaters and yellow oilskins and the pretty Quimper faience that are the staple of so many souvenir shops. But there is, in fact, far more to Breton craftsmanship than this. Not only are there countless delicacies – butter made in the churn, local pâtisserie, cooked meats and traditionally made cider – but also many high-quality items with a marine theme. Ranging from seaweed balm to antique sextants and sailors' chests, these are redolent of the high seas and, of course, of Brittany itself.

Handmade toy boat

Souvenirs

In the most popular coastal resorts, a little discrimination is sometimes needed to distinguish good-quality pieces from cheap souvenirs. It is best to choose locally made items, or to look round old chandlers' shops. CDs of traditional Breton songs are another reliable buy.

The sailor's almanac, giving the times of tides, is an essential accessory for anglers and yachting enthusiasts.

Pipe

Nautilus shells make attractive ornaments and, like other souvenirs with a marine theme, they bring a taste of the sea to any décor.

Plaster figures of a Breton couple, sold in many local shops.

Lighthouse

Bowl

Breton pennant

Faience

Continuing a tradition established in the 17th century (*see pp170–1*), Quimper's faience factories produce wares in a range of shapes, decorated with patterns such as *petit breton* and *à bords jaune*, painted in various colours.

Quimper faience tray

Quimper faience salt cellar and pepper pot

Faience pitcher decorated with a classic Quimper floral pattern.

Quimper faience, like this colourful plate with floral border, is decorated entirely freehand, without the use of transfers. Good-quality pieces are signed by the decorator.

Clothes

Sturdy and weather-resistant, traditional sailors' clothing conjures up images of the open sea and ocean spray. With the rise in popularity of sailing and water sports, it has become essential wear both for yachting enthusiasts and for casually chic town-dwellers.

Seaman's woolly hat, ideal for keeping out a sea fret.

Sailors' sweaters

Kabig, a hooded jacket made of heavy waterproofed cloth.

Sweets and Biscuits

Among Breton specialities are many kinds of sweets and biscuits, some owing their distinctive taste to Brittany's excellent butter. These treats include pancakes (packaged in foil), butter toffees, butter biscuits, especially *petits-beurre* made in Nantes, and *berlingots*, handmade sweets also from Nantes.

Butter toffees

Traou Mad, butter biscuits, made in Pont-Aven

Berlingots are twisted sweets made by traditional methods.

Tins of coloured *berlingots*, made in Nantes

Box of Leroux toffees

Alcoholic Drinks

Brittany is renowned for its ciders and liqueurs, including *fleur de caramel* liqueur and *fraise de Plougastel*, a strawberry liqueur.

Skincare Products

A wide range of skincare products, including seaweed-based cosmetics and creams made with extracts of oyster, are on sale in thalassotherapy centres all along the coasts of Brittany.

Phytomer for skincare

Bath salts

Traditional Breton cider

Fleur de caramel

Fraise de Plougastel

ENTERTAINMENT

Bretons are fond of festivals and celebrations, and they are also enthusiastic communicators. Music, film and cartoon festivals, as well as live performances, take place all over Brittany throughout the year. The region also has a great variety of museums, art galleries and other cultural centres. Those who do not wish to spend all their time on the beach will find more than enough to entertain them. For details of local festivals, see Brittany Through the Year (see pp34–7).

General Information

The regional newspapers and magazines (see p263) are the best source of information regarding festivals and other events (see pp34–7). Lists of upcoming events are also available from the Comité Régional du Tourisme, for the whole of Brittany, and the relevant Comité Départemental, for each region of Brittany. Local tourist offices are another convenient source of information.

Buying Tickets

Tickets for shows and festivals for which there is an admission charge are usually available direct from the organizers. Shops run by FNAC (Fédération Nationale d'Art et de Culture), which can be found in large towns, also have ticket offices.

It is worth bearing in mind that most major events usually draw very large crowds, and it may be necessary to book tickets several months in advance.

Music

The passionate enthusiasm that Bretons have for music (see pp28–9) goes back to their ancient roots. Many solo musicians and groups who began their careers in Brittany have gone on to achieve much wider fame. In this respect, **Ubu**, the arts centre in Rennes, stands out for its policy of promoting avant-garde musicians.

Brittany also hosts many major music festivals. Among the greatest is the Festival des Vieilles Charrues in Carhaix (see p35), the Route du Rock in St-Malo (see p35), the Rencontres Trans Musicales in Rennes (see p37), the Flambée Musicales in Fougères (see p37), and the Festival Art Rock in St-Brieuc (see p34). For jazz enthusiasts there is the Festival du Jazz in Vannes (see p35).

Traditional Breton music is celebrated at the Festival Interceltique in Lorient (see p35), which draws 4,500 performers and 450,000 spectators each year. The focus of the Festival de Cornouaille in Quimper is world music.

Theatre

Besides the high-quality programme of plays performed by the **Théâtre National de Bretagne** in Rennes, theatre in Brittany comes to the fore at the annual Festival Tombées de la Nuit (see p34), which takes place in the city in July. Other theatres with dynamic programmes are in Nantes and Brest.

Cinema

Several annual film festivals take place in Brittany. Established over ten years ago, the **Festival du Film Britannique** in Dinard (see p36) shows feature films and organizes retrospectives. Prominent people from the world of film, including actors, directors, producers and distributors, attend.

Travelling, a week-long film festival that takes place in Rennes in early February, highlights the work of filmmakers from a particular city, such as London, Berlin or Istanbul. This is an opportunity to see some unusual productions.

Dancers at the Rencontres Transmusicales in Rennes

The **Festival du Cinéma des Minorités Nationales**, meanwhile, shows films on the theme of various civilizations.

Exhibitions

Brittany has a wealth of museums and art galleries, with interesting or unusual permanent collections and temporary exhibitions.

Some of the best temporary exhibitions can be seen at two venues in Rennes – the Musée des Beaux-Arts *(see p65)* and **La Criée**, a centre for modern art. There are also the **Centre d'Art Passerelle** in Brest, the Musée des Jacobins in Morlaix *(see p123)*, the contemporary art centre in Kerguehennec, the **Galerie Dourven** in Trédrez-Locquémeau, the Musée de La Cohue in Vannes *(see pp193–4)* and the Musée des Beaux-Arts in Quimper *(see pp164 and 167)*.

Participants in the Festival Interceltique in Lorient

DIRECTORY

Venues

CÔTES D'ARMOR

Le Masque en Mouvement
(theatre)
13 Rue de la Gare, 22250 Broons. **Tel** (02) 96 84 75 19.

La Passerelle *(theatre)*
Place de la Résistance, 22000 St-Brieuc.
Tel (02) 96 68 18 40.

Théâtre des Jacobins
Rue de l'Horloge, 22100 Dinan.
Tel (02) 96 87 03 11.

FINISTÈRE

Le Quartz de Brest
(theatre, music and dance)
Square Beethoven, 60 Rue du Château, 29200 Brest.
Tel (02) 98 33 70 70.

Théâtre de Cornouaille *(regional theatre in Quimper)*
Esplanade François-Mitterand, 29000 Quimper.
Tel (02) 98 55 98 55.

ILLE-ET-VILAINE

Opera
Place de l'Hôtel-de-Ville, 35000 Rennes.
Tel (02) 23 62 28 28.

Salle de la Cité *(music and dance)*
10 Rue St-Louis, 35000 Rennes.
Tel (02) 99 79 10 66.

Théâtre National de Bretagne
1 Rue St-Hélier, 35000 Rennes. **Tel** (02) 99 31 12 31.

Théâtre de la Parcheminerie
23 Rue de la Parcheminerie, 35000 Rennes.
Tel (02) 99 79 47 63.

Le Triangle
(music and dance)
30 Boulevard de Yougoslavie, 35000 Rennes. **Tel** 02 99 22 27 00.

Ubu *(music and dance)*
1 Rue St-Hélier, 35000 Rennes. **Tel** (02) 99 30 31 68.

LOIRE- ATLANTIQUE

Cité International des Congrès de Nantes-Atlantique
(theatre, music and dance)
5 Rue Valmy, 44000 Nantes. **Tel** (02) 51 88 20 00.

Le Grand T *(theatre, music and dance)*
84 Rue du Général-Buat, 44000 Nantes.
Tel (02) 28 24 28 00.
🌐 legrandt.fr

Lieu Unique *(theatre, music and dance)*
Quai Ferdinand-Favre, 44000 Nantes.**Tel** (02) 40 12 14 34.
🌐 lelieuunique.com

Théâtre Graslin
(Opera)
1 Rue Molière, 44000 Nantes. **Tel** (02) 40 41 90 77.

MORBIHAN

Le Grand Théâtre
Place de l'Hôtel-de-Ville, 56100 Lorient. **Tel** (02) 97 02 22 77.

Plateau des 4 Vents
(theatre)
2 Rue du Professeur-Mazé, 56100 Lorient.
Tel (02) 97 37 53 05.

Art Galleries

CÔTES D'ARMOR

Galerie Dourven
Domaine Départemental du Dourven, 22300 Trédez-Locquémeau.
Tel (02) 96 35 21 42.

FINISTÈRE

Centre d'Art Passerelle
41 bis Rue Charles-Berthelot, 29200 Brest.
Tel (02) 98 43 34 95.

ILLE-ET-VILAINE

La Criée
Halles Centrales, Place Honoré-Commeureuc, 35000 Rennes.
Tel (02) 23 62 25 10.

MORBIHAN

Domaine de Kerguehennec
Centre d'Art Contemporain Bignan, 56500 Locmine.
Tel (02) 97 60 31 84.
🌐 art-kerguehennec.fr

LOIRE-ATLANTIQUE

Le Grand T
10 Passage Pommeraye, 44000 Nantes.
Tel (02) 51 88 25 25.

Cinema

Festival du Film Britannique
Organizer's office:
2 Blvd Féart, 35800 Dinard.
Tel (02) 99 88 19 04.
🌐 festivaldufilm-dinard.com

Festival Travelling de Rennes
5 Rue de Lorraine, 35000 Rennes.
Tel (02) 23 46 47 08.
🌐 clairobscur. info

Festival du Cinéma des Minorités Nationales
13 Rue Michel-Le-Nobletz, 29100 Douarnenez.
Tel (02) 98 92 09 21.
🌐 festival-douarnenez. com

OUTDOOR ACTIVITIES

With beautiful bays and beaches, dramatic promontories and cliffs, and picturesque islands, Brittany is well endowed with areas of natural beauty. The region's coast is its best-known feature, and many water sports are available *(see pp252–3)*.

Brittany's spectacular coastline should not, however, obscure the attractions of the interior. These include the Monts d'Arrée and the Montagnes Noires, as well as heathland, forests, lakes, rivers, canals, valleys and marshland. These landscapes can be explored on foot, by bicycle or on horseback. Brittany's nature reserves and coastal areas offer plenty of opportunities for birdwatching, and, with more than 30 fine golf courses, the region is also attractive to keen golfers.

Cyclists at Fort de La Latte, a 13th-century fortress on Cap Fréhel

Walking

Running both along coastlines and inland, France has over 60,000 km (37,000 miles) of long-distance footpaths (Sentiers de Grande Randonnée, or GR) and 80,000 km (50,000 miles) of Promenade et Randonnée (PR) routes. These are maintained and marked out by volunteers of the **Fédération Française de la Randonnée Pédestre**.

Most of the best footpaths in Brittany are mentioned in the appropriate entries in this guide. Various organizations, such as the Comité Régional du Tourisme, offer walking programmes with overnight stays in gîtes (some of which have received an award for their standards of comfort), or in *chambres d'hôtes* (guest rooms) or small, family-run hotels.

Cycling

The Blavet valley, the Cornouaille region and the Baie du Mont-St-Michel have all been identified by the **Ligue de Bretagne de Cyclotourisme** as prime areas for mountain biking (Sites VTT).

As with long-distance walking *(see above)*, gîte and other en-route accommodation can be arranged through local cycling organizations or the Comité Régional du Tourisme.

Walkers near the Phare du Paon, Isle de Bréhat

Horseback Riding

Those who prefer to explore Brittany on horseback will enjoy following Équibreizh, a long-distance bridleway that traverses Brittany. It is clearly marked and covers over 2,000 km (1,250 miles) of varied and scenic terrain. The *Topo-Guide Équibreizh*, published by **CRTEB** (Régionale Comité pour le Tourisme Équestre de Bretagne), includes detailed maps indicating routes, overnight stopping places, riding centres, farriers and horse transporters. Accommodation can also be arranged through the **Comité Régional** in the revelant area of Brittany.

Birdwatching

Brittany is one of the best places in Europe for birdwatching. The diversity of the region's landscapes attracts a great variety of birds *(see pp22–3)*, from the ubiquitous herring gull and crested cormorant, to the marsh harrier and ringed plover. There is much for nature lovers to see, and almost 20 bird sanctuaries and other protected areas to explore.

Bretagne Vivante-SEPNB (Société pour l'Étude et la Protection de la Nature en Bretagne) and **Vivarmor Nature** both organize a variety of birdwatching trips, in winter as well as in summer. Useful information is also available from **LPO (Ligue pour la Protection des Oiseaux)**.

Golf

There are 32 golf courses in Brittany, providing golfing enthusiasts with a wide choice. The **Ligue de Golf de Bretagne** and the Comité Régional du Tourisme publish a guide listing all the golf courses in the region. Many options, from a day's play to a full week, are available. **Golf Holidays** offers golf breaks and accommodation at some of Brittany's most prestigious golf courses.

Sport and Tourism for Disabled People

Brittany has several organizations that arrange holidays and sports activities for people with disabilites. Founded in 1982 by UFCV (Union Française des Centres de Vacances et de Loisirs), of which it is a member, the **Association EPAL** (Évasion en Pays d'Accueil et de Loisirs, organizes sightseeing and sporting

Golf course at Les Rochers-Sévigné in Vitré

holidays for disabled people. **Disability Rights UK**, based in London offers a very similar service.

Comprehensive information relevant to activities organized in Brittany is available from the **Comité Régional de Sport Adapté de Bretagne** and the **Comité Régional de Handisport de Bretagne**. The names and contact details of other organizations that arrange a variety of sports and holidays for people with disabilities is given on p257.

Birdwatching at Cap Sizun, in southern Finistère

DIRECTORY

Walking

Comité Regional du Tourisme de Bretagne
1 Rue Raoul-Ponchon, 35069 Rennes. **Tel** (02) 99 28 44 30. 🔲 **rando-tourismebretagne.com**

Fédération Française de la Randonnée Pédestre
64 Rue du Dessous des Berges, 75013 Paris. **Tel** (01) 44 89 93 93. 🔲 **ffrandonee.fr**

Cycling

Ligue de Bretagne de Cyclotourisme
BP 6, 22400 St-Alban. 🔲 **ffct-bretagne.org**

Horseback Riding

CRTEB
5 bis Rue Waldeck-Rousseau, BP 307, 56103 Lorient. **Tel** (02) 97 84 44 00. 🔲 **equibreizh.com**

Tourisme Équestre des Pays de la Loire
2 Impasse du Porche, 34150 Grignac. **Tel** 04 67 92 21 14. 🔲 **terre-equestre.com**

Birdwatching

Bretagne Vivante-SEPNB (Société pour l'Étude et la Protection de la Nature en Bretagne)
186 Rue Anatole-France, BP 32,29276, Brest cedex. **Tel** (02) 98 49 07 18. 🔲 **bretagne-vivante.org**

LPO (Ligue pour la Protection des Oiseaux)
8 Rue du Docteur-Pujos, 17300 Rochefort. **Tel** (05) 46 82 12 34. 🔲 **ipo.fr**

Vivarmor Nature
10 Boulevard Sévigné, 22000 St-Brieuc. **Tel** (02) 96 33 10 57. 🔲 **vivarmor.fr**

Golf

Golf Breaks
2, Windsor Dials, Arthur Road, Windsor SL4 1RS, UK. **Tel** 0808 278 6715 🔲 **golfbreaks.com**

Ligue de Golf de Bretagne
130 Rue Eugéne Pottier, 35000 Rennes. 🔲 **liguebretagnegolf. org**

Visitors with Disabilities

Comité Régional de Handisport de Bretagne
Rue Auguste-Fresnel, 29490 Guipavas. **Tel** (02) 98 42 61 05. 🔲 **handisport-bretagne.org**

Comité Régional de Sport Adapté de Bretagne
9 Rue Jean-Daudin, 75015 Paris. **Tel** (01) 42 73 90 00. 🔲 **ffsa.asso.fr.**

Disability Rights UK
Ground floor, CAN Mezzanine , 49–51 East Road, London N1 6AH. **Tel** (02) 72 50 81 81. 🔲 **disabilityrightsuk. org**

Watersports

From the illustrious seafaring traditions of the past to the prestigious regattas that take place in its major coastal harbours today, Brittany has a close association with the sea. This, together with a spectacular coastline, makes it an ideal environment in which to enjoy water sports. Of the variety of water sports practised in Brittany, yachting, canoeing, scuba-diving, sand-yachting and surfing are by far the most popular. For beginners and experienced alike, the opportunities for enjoying them are many, and each in its different ways reveals the power and beauty of the sea.

Sailing boat bear Phare de la Vieille, off southern Finistère

Sailing

With hundreds of sailboards, catamarans, dinghies and traditional sailing boats invading its coastal waters each summer, Brittany is one of the best places in the world for sailing. It has more than 70 marinas and mooring for a total of 22,120 pleasure boats. Sailing courses and cruises are also available.

Brittany's sailing schools, of which there are over 70, together with several dozen watersports associations, have high standards of tuition and safety. The only conditions for joining are the ability to swim 50 m (55 yds), which can be proved either by showing a certificate or by completing a test, and the production of a medical certificate of fitness.

The main sailing centres are St-Malo, St-Cast-Le Guildo, Pléneuf-Val-André, Perros-Guirec,

Rade de Brest, Crozon-Morgat and Lorient. Information on sailing schools is available from **Nautisme** or the Comité Départemental in the relevant area of Brittany.

For coastal and ocean sailing, there are schools that offer high standards of tuition in a friendly atmosphere. Groups are organized according to participants' ability, and the schools cater for all levels, including introductory tuition for children, and theory and competitions for more experienced sailors. Information is available from **Formules Nautiques Bretagne**. During school holidays, this organization also offers residential courses for children aged six to 17, running from six days to one month. Any parents wishing to accompany their children are able to stay in gîtes, apartments or hotels.

Surfing

Cap Fréhel, Le Dossen, Le Petit-Minou, La Palue, La Torche, Guidel, the Presqu'île de Quiberon and other places along the coasts of Brittany attract some 15,000 surfers each year.

Catering for all abilities, Brittany's eight surfing schools offer tuition in long-boarding, body-boarding, skim-boarding and body-surfing. They are located in Crozon-Morgat, Audierne, La Torche, Cahors Carnoët, Perros-Guirec, Pouldreuzic and Plouharnel. The **ESB (École de Surf de Bretagne)** and **WSA (West Surf Association)** jointly constitute the regional surfing federation.

Diving

About 220 diving clubs in Brittany and the Loire area are affiliated to the **Comité Inter-Régional de Plongée de Bretagne et des Pays de la Loire**.

The organisation Plongée Label Bretagne has eight diving centres. Catering for children, families, individuals and groups, they offer tuition for beginners as well as tailor-made dives, underwater photography sessions, and visits to local shipwrecks. These centres are based in St-Malo, Belle-Île, Crozon-Morgat, Larmor Plage, Plougasnou and St-Pabu. Their details are available from the Comité Inter-Régional de Plongée.

Kayaks around the Île de Batz, in northern Finistère

Sand yachts in Plestin-les-Grèves, on the Côtes d'Armor

Canoeing

Neither canoeing nor kayaking require a high degree of skill. The boats are ideal for exploring bays and inlets accessible only from the sea.

To ensure good standards of equipment and safety, the **Comité Régional de Bretagne** has set up Point Kayak de Mer, an affiliation with 6 centres. These are based in St-Cast-Le-Guildo, St-Lunaire, Plouneour-Trez, Perroc Guirec, Pluer-sur-Rance and Larmor Plage.

Brittany's canals and rivers are also worth exploring by canoe. Special kayaking and rafting centres have been set up in Lannion, Cesson-Sévigné, Pont-Réan, Quimper-Cornouaille, Inzinzac-Lochrist, Parc d'Eau Vive at Île de Locastel and the Pole Nautique Sud Goelo at Etables-sur-Mer.

The canoeing centres have been made a Point Canoë Nature, a mark of quality bestowed by the Comité Régional de Bretagne.

Sand-Yachting

Now an international sport, sand-yachting has several sub-disciplines, each using a different type of equipment.

There are over 15 sand-yachting clubs in Brittany. Most bear the name "École de Char à Voile", which means they are affiliated to the **Ligue de Char à Voile de Bretagne**. Full information on sand-yachting is available from this organization.

Safety at Sea

Sailing is not a sport for the uninitiated. Many accidents are caused by a lack of knowledge or by negligence.

Before setting out on a sailing trip, it is essential to obtain a local weather forecast, as weather conditions can change rapidly. Novice sailors must be supervised by professionals at all times.

The *Almanach du Marin Breton*, an annual navigational handbook, is available from all good newsagents. Published by **Œuvre du Marin Breton**, a non-profit-making association, it contains information aiding the safety of vessels, a map of local currents, tidetables, astral and radio navigation, details of lighthouses and beacons, administrative information, maps of harbours and nautical instructions. In case of difficulties at sea, contact **CROSS** (Centre Régional Opérationnel de Surveillance et de Sauvetage), a coastguard and sea-rescue organization.

DIRECTORY

Sailing

Formules Nautiques Bretagne
1 Rue de Kerbriant, BP 39, 29281 Brest cedex.
Tel (02) 98 02 80 44.
🔲 nautismebretagne.fr

Nautisme en Ille et Vilaine
Maison Départementale des Sports,
13B Avenue de Cucillé.
35065 Rennes cedex.
Tel (02) 99 54 67 69.
🔲 voile35.com.

Nautisme en Finistère
11 Rue Théodore-le-Hars, BP 1334,
29103 Quimper cedex.
Tel (02) 98 76 21 31.
🔲 nautisme-finistere.com

Nautisme en Morbihan
Centre Nautique de Kerguélen, 56260 Larmor Plage. **Tel** (02) 97 33 77 78.
🔲 sellor–nautisme.fr

Surfing

Ecole de Surf de Bretagne
6 Ave de l'Océan, 56400 Plouharnel. **Tel** (02) 97 52 41 18. 🔲 ecole-surf.com

Ligue de Bretagne de Surf
5 Rue René-Madec, 29000 Quimper.
Tel (02) 98 95 23 31.

West Surf Association
Centre Nautique, 56520 Guidel-Plages.
Tel (02) 97 32 70 37.
🔲 w.s.a.free.fr

Diving

Comité Inter-Régional de Plongée de Bretagne et des Pays de la Loire
39 Rue de Villeneuve, 56100 Lorient. **Tel** (02) 97 37 51 51. 🔲 ctrbpl.fr

Canoeing

Comité Régional de Bretagne
Base Nautique, Plaine de Baud, 35 Rue Jean-Marie-Huchet, 35000 Rennes.
🔲 crck.org/bretagne

Comité Régional Pays de la Loire
Rte Angers, 49080 Bouchemaine. **Tel** (02) 41 73 86 10.
🔲 canoekayak paysdelaloire.fr

Sand-Yachting

Ligue de Char à Voile de Bretagne
1 Rue de la Plage, 35120 Cherrueix.
Tel (02) 99 48 83 01.
🔲 noroitclub.fr

Useful Numbers

CROSS Corsen (northern coast)
Tel (02) 98 89 31 31.

CROSS Étel (southern coast)
Tel (02) 97 55 35 35.

Œuvre du Marin Breton (publisher of Almanach du Marin Breton)
24, Quai de la Douane 29200, Brest
Tel (02) 98 44 06 00.

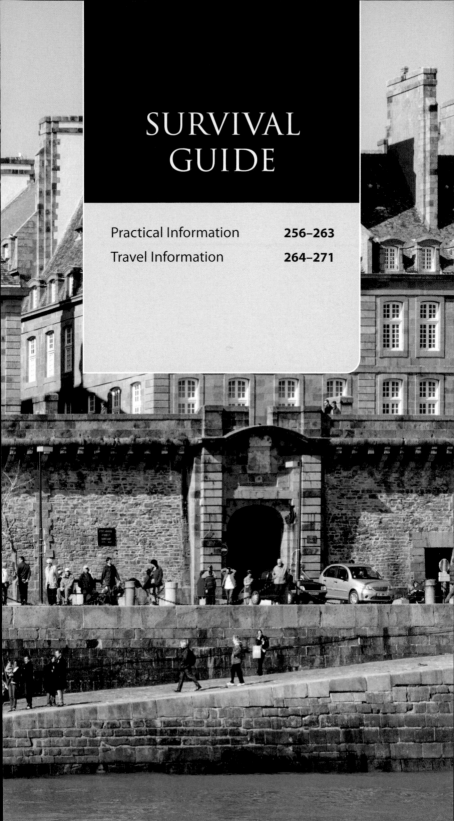

SURVIVAL
GUIDE

PRACTICAL INFORMATION

A prime tourist destination, Brittany attracts large numbers of visitors during the summer. At the height of the holiday season, which runs through most of July and August, the population of its coastal resorts can triple or even quadruple. This does not detract from the region's appeal, however, since Brittany has much to offer and is well geared to the needs of visitors.

Those who choose to visit at quieter times of the year will be able to experience a more intimate aspect of the region. Out of season, Brittany's beaches are almost deserted; its prehistoric monuments seem even more mysterious; and the region's towns and cities, with their fine architecture and strong historical associations, can more easily be appreciated.

Cycling near Mont-St-Michel, one of Brittany's most recognizable sights

When to Go

Some of the best times to visit Brittany are June, when the tourist season is just starting, and September, by which time many holiday-makers have gone home. At these times, Bretons have more time to welcome visitors, and historic monuments are open but not crowded; in September, in particular, the long autumn tides create sights of unforgettable beauty.

In high summer, Brittany offers the pleasures of the beach, a lush countryside and a lively restaurant, bar and entertainment scene.

Visas and Passports

EU nationals, apart from UK and Irish citizens who need a passport, can enter France for an unlimited period with an identity card. Visitors from the United States, Canada, Australia and New Zealand need a full passport for tourist stays of up to 90 days. Non-EU nationals who wish to work or study in France, or stay longer than 90 days, should obtain a visa from a French consulate in their home country before travelling. Check the website of the French embassy in your country and the Foreign Service travel advisories for more information.

Customs Information

EU residents travelling to France do not have to pay customs duties on any goods, so long as they are for their personal use. Among the limits generally accepted as being for personal use are 800 cigarettes, 90 litres of wine and 110 litres of beer.

Visitors from outside the EU can claim back the sales tax (*TVA*, currently 20%) on many goods in France if they have spent more than €175 in one single transaction. Obtain a *détaxe* receipt and take the goods (unopened) out of the country within three months. Present the form to customs when leaving the country; the refund will be sent on to you. For more information, contact the **Douanes** (customs) or see the *détaxe* leaflets available in many stores and at airports.

Tourist Information

All cities, towns and many villages in Brittany have *offices de tourisme* that provide information on nearby attractions and free maps. Most local offices can also help you find accommodation and offer useful guides and information on walking and cycling routes, bike-hire shops, traditional farm food producers that open for direct sales and so on. Some regional and *département* offices also have well-priced hotel and tour packages, and most city offices provide guided tours.

For basic orientation before travelling to France, visit the website of the **France Tourism Development Agency**; for more in-depth planning, contact **Brittany Tourism** or the individual tourist office of each of the five Breton *départements*. Their websites provide a huge range of detailed information, most of it available in English.

A tourist office in western Brittany displaying a bilingual sign

Visitors enjoying a stroll through the streets of a Breton village

Admission Prices

For public museums and historic monuments, entry fees generally range from around €3 to €8. Entry is free for small children and often for all under-18s (sometimes under-12s), and there are reduced prices for those aged 18–25; ID may be required. Privately owned houses may be a little more expensive. All EU residents under 26s get free entry to state museums.

Several areas offer local multi-entry schemes giving discounted or unlimited entry at nearby sights, such as the Pass des Mégalithes for the prehistoric sites around Carnac, or the Pass'Quimper and Rennes City Pass for those cities' attractions. The Rennes pass also includes discounts on local transport.

Opening Hours

Most municipal museums are closed on Mondays, and most national museums and sights on Tuesdays. Larger museums are usually open throughout the day, and many have a late-opening day each week (often on a Thursday); smaller museums often close at lunchtime. Churches are open daily, but they shut at lunchtime. Opening hours of private museums and chateaux may vary considerably from those of public attractions.

Opening days also vary by season. In July and August, most sites are open daily, while in spring and autumn they tend to close one day a week (usually Monday). In winter, many attractions are open only at weekends, or they are closed altogether except for a few days around Christmas. Many sights close on major public holidays (Christmas, New Year).

Shops are usually open 9am–noon and 3–7pm Monday to Saturday. Traditionally the only shops open on Sundays are bakers and patisseries, but this is becoming more flexible. Local markets generally have one set day a week and operate between 8am and noon.

Language

French is the main language in Brittany, and travellers will have a much better experience if they make an effort to speak it, particularly in basic courtesies such as greetings. For some useful expressions, see the phrase book on *pp287-8*.

In 1900, around 90 per cent of people in western Brittany spoke Breton, a Celtic language similar to Cornish. Today Breton can be seen in western Brittany in place names and beneath French on bilingual road signs, but rarely heard outside small villages and folk festivals.

Etiquette and Smoking

When entering a shop, museum or anywhere with an attendant, say *Bonjour Monsieur/Madame* before asking for what you want; say *Merci* when you are given your purchases and *Merci, au revoir* when you leave. Shake hands when introduced to someone, or any time a hand is proffered. In villages, locals may greet you with a *Bonjour Monsieur/Madame* in the street even if they have never seen you before.

Smoking is forbidden on public transport and in all enclosed public places, including bars, restaurants, cafés and museums.

Travellers with Special Needs

Disabled people should have no major problems travelling around France. For drivers, there are disabled parking spaces in many streets and all public car parks, which you can use for free with a European Blue Badge. **SNCF** (the French railways) provides the Accès Plus scheme, which allows people with mobility issues to book a space and free assistance on and off the train. Some radio-taxi firms have specially adapted cabs *(taxis aménagés)*.

Architecture and location might make access difficult at many historic houses and chateaux. The blue **Tourisme & Handicap** label is used to indicate attractions, hotels and restaurants that meet full access criteria. Many hotels and B&Bs *(chambres-d'hôtes)* have specially adapted rooms, and major booking agencies indicate this on their websites. The national tourist office's website has links to the Tourisme & Handicap scheme and other useful information on accessibility. The **Association des Paralysés de France** is also helpful.

Relaxing at the outdoor tables of a Breton restaurant

Travelling with Children

Families visiting Brittany benefit from a range of discounts. Admission to all national museums and monuments is free for EU residents aged under 25 and for all under-18s; most private attractions have reduced prices for the under-12s. Children under 12 travel for half the adult fare on most public transport, and children under 4 (or 6, in Rennes and some other towns) travel for free.

Many country hotels and B&Bs (*chambres-d'hôtes*) have family rooms with several beds (*chambres familiales*), which can be shared for a reasonable cost. Some hotel chains (notably Novotel and Ibis) specialize in family accommodation and often have good offers (check their websites for more information). If you are staying in one area, a self-contained *gîte* can be exceptional value.

Many restaurants offer a children's menu (*menu enfants*) for around €8–12. For children who won't eat more intricate French fare, there is the traditional Breton *crêperie*, offering a range of delicious sweet and savoury pancake fillings.

Travelling on a Budget

Costs in Brittany vary a great deal by season. Hotel rates and *gîte* rental prices as well as other costs, such as those for ferry crossings, are higher during the peak July–end of August holiday season. If you can choose when to travel, avoiding the summer season will work out cheaper and you'll miss the crowds.

Costs can also be cut by staying in *chambres-d'hôtes* rather than hotels. Prices are lower, they are often more attractive, and breakfast is included. Staying in a self-catering *gîte* can be more economical still, but most require a minimum stay of a weekend or a week. Camping is very popular in France. There are many sites offering mobile homes, pre-pitched tents, gypsy caravans and bungalows.

When dining, go for the set menus – ordering à la carte will be far more expensive – and take your main meal at midday, not in the evening, as the best-value *menus du jour*, or *formules*, are often only available for lunch. *Crêperies* are also great for a light, bargain meal.

Sightseeing can be made more cost effective with the use of multi-entry discount cards (*see p257*). If you rent a car, book it online to get the best rates.

Time

France is one hour ahead of Greenwich Mean Time (GMT) and six hours ahead of US Eastern Standard Time (EST) in winter, and moves another hour ahead to daylight saving time (DST) from late March to October. DST in Europe begins slightly later and ends earlier than in North America.

The French use the 24-hour clock; for example, 7pm is expressed as 19:00.

Electricity

The voltage in France is 220v-AC, and plugs are of the standard two-round-pin type used in most of Europe. Buy a plug adaptor (or a voltage transformer if coming from the US) prior to your trip.

Responsible Tourism

Facilities for environmentally-friendly travel are based on France's rural tourism network. Farmhouse accommodation is available through Gîtes de France (*see p222*). Visitors can find out about local green tourism (*tourisme vert* or *eco*) initiatives, activities and organic markets (*marchés bio*) through tourist offices. For green travel facilities, see p264.

DIRECTORY

Customs Information

Douanes
Tel 0811 204 444.
W douane.gouv.fr

Tourist Information

Brittany Tourism
1 Rue Raoul-Ponchon,
35069 Rennes Cedex.
Tel 02 99 28 44 30.
W brittanytourism.com

CDT Côtes d'Armor
7 Rue St-Benoît,
22046 St-Brieuc.
Tel 02 96 62 72 01.
W cotesdarmor.com

CDT Haute-Bretagne–Ille-et-Vilaine
5 Rue Pré Botté,
35101 Rennes.
Tel 02 99 78 47 46.
W bretagne35.com

CDT du Morbihan
PIBS Kerino, Allée
Nicolas-Le-Blanc,
56010 Vannes.
Tel 02 97 54 06 56.
W morbihan.com

Finistère Tourisme
4 Rue du 19 Mars 1962,
29018 Quimper.
Tel 02 98 76 25 64.
W finisteretourisme.com

France Tourism Development Agency
(US) W int.rendezvousenfrance.com

Loire-Atlantique Tourisme
11 Rue du Château-de-l'Eraudière, 44306 Nantes
Cedex. **Tel** (02) 51 95 30.
W ohlaloireatlantique.com

Tourisme en Pays de la Loire
7 Rue du Général-de-Bollardière, 44202
Nantes. **Tel** 02 40 89 89
89. W enpaysdelaloire.com

Travellers with Special Needs

Association des Paralysés de France
Tel 0800 500 487.
W apf.asso.fr (French only)

SNCF
W uk.voyages-sncf.com
For specific information on services for the disabled: **Tel** 0890 640 650. W accessibilite.sncf.com (French only)

Tourisme & Handicaps
Tel 01 44 11 10 41.
W tourisme-handicaps.org

Personal Security and Health

With low crime levels, competent local authorities and efficient public services, Brittany is a safe as well as a pleasant place to visit. However, as everywhere else, it's advisable to have some idea of how local services work in case the unexpected happens.

What to Be Aware of

Crime is not a major problem in Brittany, but it pays to follow a few precautions. Do not flaunt valuable items or leave them in full view in a parked car. Beware of pickpockets, especially in crowds. At cafés, keep your bag within reach and in sight, not on the ground or the back of a chair.

In an Emergency

The number 112 can be used to alert all emergency services, though calling each service direct can be quicker.

Report any incident as soon as possible. In cities, you can do so at the nearest police station (commissariat de police); in small towns and villages, go to the town hall (mairie) or the nearest station of the Gendarmerie, the force mainly responsible for rural policing. In an emergency, dial 17 for the police.

If you are the victim of a theft, you will have to go to a police station to make a statement (PV, or procès verbal) listing any stolen items. This is necessary for your insurance claim. If your passport is lost or stolen, notify your consulate immediately.

Lifeguards patrolling a sandy beach in Brittany

Hospitals and Pharmacies

In all towns and cities there are hospitals with emergency departments (service des urgences). If your hotel cannot direct you to one, call for an ambulance. Your consulate should be able to recommend an English-speaking doctor in the area.

Pharmacists can diagnose minor health problems or refer you to a doctor. When a pharmacy (identifiable by an illuminated green cross) is closed, a card in the window will give details of the nearest duty pharmacy (pharmacie de garde).

Travel and Health Insurance

It is wise to visit France with comprehensive travel insurance covering you for medical and legal expenses, theft, lost property, accidents and travel delays.

Although the European Health Insurance Card (EHIC) entitles EU citizens to use the French national health service, patients must pay for treatments, then claim most of the cost back from the health authorities. Be sure to keep the statement of costs (feuille de soins), including any stickers for prescription drugs. This is a time-consuming process, so it is simpler to have private health insurance. Non-EU nationals must have full travel and medical insurance.

By the Sea

Many of Brittany's beaches are patrolled by lifeguards. Flags indicate whether it is safe to swim – a green flag means that it is safe, orange that it is dangerous, and red that it is forbidden. A blue flag means that the water is clean.

Banking and Currency

As in most parts of the world, credit and debit cards are the most convenient way of paying for goods and services when travelling around France, and the best way of withdrawing local currency. You may bring any amount of currency into France, but anything over €10,000 must be declared on arrival. The same applies when you leave. Bureaux de change can usually be found at airports, large railway stations and ferry ports, and also in some hotels and shops.

Withdrawing cash at an ATM

Banks and Bureaux de Change

Larger bank branches in Brittany's cities and towns will exchange foreign currency and travellers' cheques for euros. However, many smaller and country branches no longer offer this service (especially not travellers' cheques), so be sure to have a card that you can use at an ATM cash dispenser. The commission rates charged by French banks vary, so check before changing money. If you use travellers' cheques, it will save money if you have them issued in euros.

Banks in Brittany are generally open from 8:30 or 9am to 5pm Tuesday to Saturday, closing for lunch from noon to 2pm. However, hours vary considerably between individual banks, and many close earlier on Saturdays. Banks usually close at noon on the day before a public holiday (see p37).

Independent bureaux de change are relatively rare in Brittany, except in airports, main railway stations and ferry ports. Rates are often less favourable than in banks.

ATMs

Virtually all bank branches, even those in more remote villages, have automated teller machines, or ATMs that are open 24 hours a day. ATM cash machines accept most major credit and debit cards, enabling you to withdraw money in euros directly from your own bank account. The international cards accepted by each ATM will be indicated by stickers on the machine itself, and most French ATMs give instructions in English.

Using an ATM is the quickest and most convenient way of obtaining cash in euros; however, it's advisable to be aware of charges that may be levied by your bank or card issuer for this service. One way to reduce such charges is to use a prepaid currency card, such as the Cash Passport issued by **Travelex**, which is loaded in advance with a set amount in euros. The **FairFX** is another prepaid card that can be used as a debit card without high commission charges.

It is also worth bearing in mind that cash machines in areas with heavy tourist passage may run out of banknotes over public holidays and during weekends. If an ATM is not working or has run out of cash, you can withdraw up to €300 per day on major credit cards at a bank. However, the bank may need to obtain telephone authorization for such a withdrawal first.

Avoid using cash machines in empty streets at night. Be aware of your surroundings and cover your PIN.

DIRECTORY

ATMs and Travel Currency Cards

FairFX
W fairfx.com

Travelex
W travelex.com

Credit and Debit Cards

American Express
Tel 01 47 77 70 00.

MasterCard
Tel 0800 90 13 87.

VISA
Tel 0800 90 11 79.

Credit and Debit Cards

Major credit cards such as **VISA** or **MasterCard** and debit cards such as Delta or Maestro are widely used all over France and are effectively essential for many larger transactions such as renting a car. However, because of the high commissions charged, many French businesses do not accept **American Express** cards.

French credit and debit cards operate on a chip-and-PIN system like that used in the UK; the two systems are compatible, so with a British card you will be asked to enter your PIN (code personnel) in the usual way. If you have a North American card that does not use chip-and-pin technology, you must ask that your card be swiped and then sign the receipt.

Logo for the Credit Mutual Bretagne (CMB) bank

The Euro

France is one of the 18 European Union countries that use the euro (€) as their common currency. Together they make up what is known as the Eurozone. Some EU member countries, notably Britain and Sweden, have opted out of joining this common currency, and Switzerland remains outside the EU completely, but otherwise the euro is used across the whole of western Europe. Euro notes are identical throughout the Eurozone countries, each one featuring designs of fictional architectural structures and monuments. The coins, however, have one side identical (the value side) and one side with an image specific to each individual European country.

Bank Notes

Euro bank notes have seven denominations. The €5 note (green in colour) is the smallest, followed by the €10 note (pink), €20 note (blue), €50 note (orange), €100 note (green), €200 note (yellow) and €500 note (purple). All notes show the European Union stars.

5 euros

10 euros

20 euros

50 euros

100 euros

200 euros

500 euros

2 euros   1 euro   50 cents   20 cents   10 cents

Coins

The euro has eight coin denominations: €1 and €2; and 50 cents, 20 cents, 10 cents, 5 cents, 2 cents and 1 cent. The €1 and €2 coins are silver and gold in colour. The 50-cent, 20-cent and 10-cent coins are gold. The 5-cent, 2-cent and 1-cent coins are bronze.

5 cents

2 cents

1 cent

Communications and Media

French telecommunications are reliable and efficient. Public telephones are located in most public places (frequently in the central squares of towns and villages), and post offices *(bureaux de poste)* are easily identified by the blue-on-yellow "La Poste" sign.

Foreign-language newspapers and magazines are available in most large towns and resorts in Brittany. Some television channels and radio stations broadcast foreign-language programmes.

Girl using a mobile phone

International and Local Telephone Calls

All French landline telephone numbers have 10 digits, and you must always key in all 10, even if the number you are calling from is in the same area as the number you are dialling. The first two digits indicate the region: 02 covers the whole of the northwest, including Brittany, while 01 is the code for Paris and Île de France. When you phone from outside France, you do not dial the initial zero. French mobile (cell) phone numbers begin with 06 or 07, while 08 indicates a special rate number, which in most cases cannot be called from outside France. All 0800 numbers are free; conversely, 0891 and 0892 are premium numbers and can be quite expensive. There are also 09 non-geographic numbers. For conventional landlines, cheap rates operate from 7pm to 8am Monday to Friday, from noon on Saturday and all day on Sunday and public holidays. Avoid making calls from your hotel, since it will likely incur a hefty surcharge.

If you are planning to make a large number of local calls, it could be worth buying a French prepaid SIM card *(carte prépayée sans engagement)* which costs around €10–20 and can be easily bought from the main service providers Bouygues, SFR, Orange and Free. Skype is another option for making calls at reduced rates. Once it has been downloaded, you can pay-as-you-go with Skype Credit.

Mobile Phones

Mobile (cell) phone coverage is generally good throughout Brittany, though signals may be weak in some rural areas, and local granite can interfere with signals inside buildings. Mobiles from other European countries and the rest of the world will work without problems here provided they have roaming enabled and a tri- or quad-band facility (now standard in most phones). However, before using your mobile phone abroad, check with your network service provider on the level of charges, which can be very high. The packages of foreign calls offered by many companies are one way to cut costs. With a smartphone, be sure to disable automatic data roaming or its equivalent before arrival, so that the phone only connects to the Internet when you want it to, or you can be liable for very high unexpected costs.

If you expect to use a phone frequently, you may find that purchasing a cheap pre-paid SIM card will work out cheaper. The three main service providers, **Orange**, **SFR** and **Bouygues**, all have a range of packages to choose from.

Internet

As elsewhere in France, the Internet is widely accessible in Brittany, and many hotels and *chambres-d'hôtes* now offer Wi-Fi connectivity. However, some places still charge for this, so ask if there are any fees and if there is a connection in all rooms. Many

Useful Dialling Codes

• **France's country code:** 33.

• **Calling France:** from the UK and US: 00 33; from Australia: 00 11 33. Omit the first 0 of the French area code.

• **International calls:** dial 00 + the country code + the area code (minus the initial 0) + the number. Country codes: Australia: 61; Canada & USA: 1; Eire: 353; New Zealand: 64; UK 44

Many central town squares in Brittany offer Wi-Fi connectivity

hotels use one of several subscription services (Orange France and Meteor are among the most common), with which you buy a certain amount of time credit (usually from 1 hour) and are then given an access code. If you have time remaining, you can use it up if you stay at another hotel using the same service. In addition, there are many Wi-Fi hotspots in hotels, airports, tourist offices, train stations and sometimes city squares. Note that French Wi-Fi servers often use different frequencies to those common in the UK and North America, so you may have to reconfigure your computer to get a signal.

Internet cafés have never been as commonplace in France as in most of Europe. In Brittany they may be found in main towns and resorts. In more remote areas you'll need a laptop or smartphone to check your email. Tourist offices often provide Internet access at low cost.

A distinctive bright-yellow French mail box

Postal Services

The postal service in France is fast and reliable. However, it is not cheap, especially when it comes to sending parcels abroad. There are post offices in most towns, and large main offices in all cities. Stamps (*timbres*) are sold at post offices singly or in books (*carnets*) of ten, but you will normally have to queue to get them, so the quickest and most convenient place to buy ordinary stamps is usually a tobacconist's shop (*tabac*). Letters are posted in yellow mail boxes, which often have separate slots for the town you are in, within the *département* and all other destinations (*autres destinations*).

Post offices usually open from 9am until 5pm Monday to Friday, often with a break for lunch, and from 9am until noon on Saturdays. However, the opening times of small-town post offices can vary considerably.

Newspapers, Magazines and Websites

The main national French dailies are, from right to left on the political spectrum: *Le Figaro*, *France Soir*, *Le Monde*, *Libération* and *L'Humanité*. Brittany also has several good local publications; among them, the daily *Ouest France* has the largest circulation, and comprehensive coverage of local affairs. The quarterly *Bretagne Magazine* also has attractive features on cultural and other events in Brittany.

The major British newspapers are frequently available on the day of publication in Brittany's resorts and main cities. The most widely available are *The Daily Telegraph* and *The Times*, but in larger towns you will have a broader choice, and you may also find US titles such as *USA Today* and the *International Herald Tribune*.

To find out what's on in terms of music, films, festivals, sport and every other area of culture, some of the best places to look – apart from local tourist offices, which provide a useful range of information – are listings websites, such as Cityvox (www.cityvox.fr) and Les Inrocks (www.lesinrocks.com). Although these cover the whole of France, they also have specific pages on different cities around the country. Cityvox has some content in English.

Television and Radio

Many hotels offer foreign digital and satellite channels (collectively known as *TPS*, or *télévision par satellite*), such as, in English, CNN,

CANAL+

Canal Plus logo

Sky and BBC World. In addition, in northeast Brittany it is very easy to get good reception of all the main UK TV channels from the Channel Islands. Of the French channels, Canal Plus (or Canal +) is a popular channel that is fully available only to subscribers, though a few programmes are shown uncoded (during coded programmes, if you do not have a subscription, picture and sound are distorted). Canal Plus frequently shows classic and modern films in English, with French subtitles.

It is easy to pick up UK radio stations in Brittany, particularly, as with TV, in the northeast of the region. BBC Radio 4 can be heard during the day (648 AM or 198 Long Wave) and BBC World Service broadcasts on the same wavelength through the night. Voice of America can be found at 90.5, 98.8 and 102.4 FM.

DIRECTORY

Useful Numbers

Directory enquiries
Tel 118 712.

International directory enquiries
Tel 118 700.

Mobile phones

Bouygues
Tel 3106 (free from a French landline).
W bouyguestelecom.fr

Orange
Tel 0800 100 740 (free from a French landline).
W orange.fr

SFR
Tel 1023 (free from a French landline).
W sfr.fr

TRAVEL INFORMATION

Brittany is easy to reach by air, train, road or ferry. The region's four main airports – at Brest, Dinard, Nantes and Rennes – receive direct flights from many parts of the UK and the rest of Europe. Long-haul travellers generally fly first to Paris and then catch a connecting flight or train from there; Brittany has fast rail links from Paris and the rest of France. If you choose to drive from Paris by *autoroute*, it takes around 3 to 6 hours. There are also frequent ferry services to Breton ports from the UK and Ireland.

Green Travel

Travelling without leaving a massive carbon footprint is easy in France thanks to the high quality of public transport, especially the SNCF rail network *(see pp266–7)*.

The French love to cycle, and there are spaces to carry bikes on most SNCF trains; information on cycle facilities on the railways can be found on the **Vélo SNCF** website. France has been a pioneer in the development of free-access cycle schemes, such as **Bicloo** in Nantes and **Vélo Star** in Rennes. Tourist offices will have information on all cycle hire facilities and bike routes.

Brittany has an exceptional network of long-distance footpaths, including the famous GR34, which goes all around the coast, and the **Voies Vertes** (green ways), a series of hiking, cycling and horse-riding trails that criss-cross the country, bypassing roads on long-distance routes such as from St-Malo to Rennes. For more information, visit **Rando Bretagne** or the Brittany Tourism website *(see p258)*.

If you don't hike or cycle, however, exploring the Breton countryside without a car can be difficult, and will take time, as local buses are often slow and infrequent.

Arriving by Air

Flights from the UK and the rest of Europe land at one of Brittany's four international airports: Brest, Dinard, Nantes and Rennes. Three more small airports, at Lannion, Quimper and Lorient, receive only domestic flights.

Travellers from outside Europe usually need to fly to Paris first, and get a domestic flight or train to Brittany from there. From North America there are frequent flights to Paris from about 20 cities, with **Air Canada**, **Air France**, **American Airlines**, **Delta** and other airlines. The only direct flights to Brittany are operated by **Air Transat** from Montreal to Nantes (May–October only). There are no direct flights to Paris from Australia or New Zealand, so changing in Singapore, London or another airport is necessary.

Airports

The airport of **Brest-Bretagne** is 10 km (6 miles) northeast of the city. From the UK there are regular flights with **Flybe** from Birmingham and Edinburgh, and with **CityJet** from London City. There are also flights from Barcelona and Paris, Marseille and other French airports. Brest is also the departure point for **Finist'Air** light-plane flights to Île d'Ouessant.

Dinard airport, 5 km (3 miles) south of Dinard, serves St-Malo and the north coast. It is chiefly used by **Ryanair**, with flights from London Stansted, East Midlands and Leeds-Bradford. There are also small-plane flights to Guernsey with **Air Aurigny**, but no domestic flights.

Nantes-Atlantique, 8 km (5 miles) southwest of Nantes, is the largest airport in Brittany and the west of France. A new airport, Aéroport du Grand Ouest, 30 km northwest of Nantes, is due to open in 2017. From the UK and Ireland there are flights with **Air France-Régional** (Southampton), Flybe (London Gatwick and Manchester), **easyJet** (London Gatwick), CityJet (London City) and Ryanair (Dublin). There are also flights with Air France, its budget airline **Hop!** and other airlines from many cities in France and the rest of Europe, and some long-haul services, including Air Transat flights from Montreal in summer.

Rennes-St-Jacques, 6 km (4 miles) southwest of Rennes, has many domestic services from Paris, Marseille and other cities. From the UK there are Flybe flights from Manchester, Southampton and Exeter (some summer-only); in summer **Aer Lingus** flies from Dublin and Cork.

Passengers disembarking from an Air France aircraft

Connections from Paris

Most long-haul flights land at Paris-Charles-de-Gaulle (CDG) airport, 30 km (18 miles) northeast of the French capital. There are some connections to Brittany from there, but most domestic flights operate from Paris-Orly (ORY) in southern Paris, so to get an ongoing connection you may well need to change airports. Take the RER suburban rail line (Line B) to Antony station; from there, take the special OrlyVal shuttle to Orly. This journey will take around two hours; there are also direct Air France buses, which are quicker. Note that there

Façade of the international airport of Rennes-St-Jacques

are two terminals at Orly Airport and three at CDG, so be sure to check which one you need.

Most internal flights are operated by Air France and Hop!, often through its subsidiaries Brit Air and Régional, but international low-cost airlines such as easyJet and Ryanair also offer some domestic routes.

Given the time it can take to change flights (and airports) in Paris, it's often easier to get to Brittany by high-speed train (see pp266–7).

Tickets and Fares

Air fares to Brittany tend to vary according to demand, so they are usually more expensive at peak times such as Easter and the July–August holiday season. However, bargains can be found even in peak seasons, so it's always worth checking around websites for the best deals. For transatlantic and long-haul flights, the best way to find low prices is to compare travel services online and book well in advance.

On domestic flights with Air France and its subsidiaries there are reduced fares for children under the age of 12; children under 2 travel free.

Transport from Airport to Town

None of Brittany's airports are far from the cities they serve. Brest and Nantes airports have frequent shuttle-bus services to their respective cities and main train and bus stations, and at Rennes city bus no. 57 runs from outside the terminal building. Details are on the airport websites. At Dinard, however, taxis are the only means of transport. It might be worth booking one in advance; taxi numbers are given on the airport website.

Taxis from the airports to the city centres will cost roughly €20 at Brest, €30 at Nantes and €20 at Rennes; from Dinard to St-Malo it will be around €25. However, taxi fares tend to vary depending on the time of day.

Airport Car Hire

Avis, Europcar, Hertz, National and other major international car rental companies have offices at all Brittany's main airports and in nearby towns. The contact details of car hire companies operating in Brittany are given on p269.

DIRECTORY

Green Travel

All in French only.

Rando Bretagne
w rando.tourismebretagne.com

Vélo SNCF
w velo.sncf.com

Voies Vertes
w voiesvertes.com

Airports

Aéroport Brest-Bretagne
Tel 02 98 32 86 00.
w brest.aeroport.fr

Aéroport Dinard
Tel 02 99 46 18 46.
w dinard.aeroport.fr

Aéroport Nantes-Atlantique
Tel 0892 568 800.
w nantes.aeroport.fr

Aéroports de Paris (for Charles de Gaulle and Orly)
Tel 3950.
w aeroportsdeparis.fr

Aéroport Rennes-St-Jacques
Tel 02 99 29 60 00.
w rennes.aeroport.fr

Airlines

Aer Lingus
Tel (France) 0821 230 267.
w aerlingus.com

Air Aurigny
Tel (UK) 01481 266 444.
w aurigny.com

Air Canada
Tel (France) 0825 880 881.
w aircanada.com

Air France (Brit Air and Régional)
Tel (France) 3272.
w airfrance.com
w britair.com
w regional.com

Air Transat
Tel (France) 0825 120 248.
w airtransat.com

American Airlines
Tel (France) 0821 980 999.
w aa.com

CityJet
Tel (France) 0892 012 013.
w cityjet.com

Delta
Tel (France) 0892 702 609.
w delta.com

easyJet
Tel (France) 0820 420 315.
w easyjet.com

Finist'Air
Tel 02 98 84 64 60.
w finistair.fr

Flybe
Tel (From outside UK) +44 1392 268 529.
w flybe.com

Hop!
Tel 0825 302 222.
w hop.com

Ryanair
Tel (France) 0892 562 150.
w ryanair.com

Travelling by Train

It is easy and enjoyable to travel to and around France by train, and this is also one of the best ways of reaching and travelling around Brittany. While both Nantes and Rennes are served by TGVs (high-speed trains) from Paris, comfortable *Intercité* trains link other main towns, and TER (local trains) provide connections to smaller towns and villages in the region. Some areas of Brittany cannot be reached by a rail service, but they can usually can be accessed by bus, some run by the SNCF railways.

The railway station at Brest

Arriving by Train

TGVs to Brest or Quimper via Rennes and to Nantes (and all other trains to Brittany) leave from Gare Montparnasse in south-central Paris. Journey time to Rennes or Nantes is about two hours; to Brest or Quimper, four hours. A LGV, serviced by TGV, between Connerré and Cesson Sévigné will start in 2017.

Travellers arriving from Britain on **Eurostar** trains can bypass Paris altogether by changing at Lille and catching a TGV to Brittany from there.

Unless they are on a direct Brittany train, travellers from Europe will arrive in Paris at Gare du Nord (from Holland, Belgium, north Germany), Gare de l'Est (most of Germany) or Gare de Lyon-Gare de Bercy (Italy, Switzerland). Metro line 4 runs from Gare du Nord and Gare de l'Est to Gare Montparnasse; from Gare de Lyon, take RER line A to Châtelet-Les Halles and change to Metro line 4. From Paris-Charles-de-Gaulle airport, there is a direct Air France bus to Gare Montparnasse (journey time about 1 hour), or you can take RER line B from the airport and change at Châtelet-Les Halles to Metro line 4, which will take longer.

All mainline trains and some buses in Brittany are operated by the French national railways, **SNCF**. Bookings can be made from France and (for long-distance trains only) from abroad through www.voyages-sncf.com. If you live outside France, however, the best service for information and bookings is generally **Rail Europe**. **The Man in Seat 61** website is a useful guide to the railways in France and other European countries.

Types of Train

SNCF offers several kinds of train. Luxury TGV (*train à grande vitesse*) trains travel at around 300 km/h (186 mph), making train journey times very competitive with flights. There are TGV lines from Paris to Nantes and Rennes, from where branch TGV lines run to St-Malo, Brest and Quimper. Some TGV trains from Bordeux also connect with Brittany, avoiding Paris altogether. Seat reservations are obligatory for TGVs; you can buy tickets at stations until shortly before departure time, but you will find better fares if you book online and well in advance.

Intercité trains are more traditional long-distance express trains, though they are still quite fast at a speed of around 200 km/h (125 mph). The main line in Brittany runs along the Atlantic coast from Bordeaux through Nantes and Vannes to Quimper. Reservations are required and can be made through Rail Europe or SNCF.

TER trains are regional services that stop (usually) at every station on the line. Some of these trains have been replaced by buses. Route maps and information are available (in French only) at stations and on www.ter-sncf.com (click on the map for Brittany). Reservations are not needed, and tickets cannot be bought much in advance, nor online or through Rail Europe. TER trains (and buses) are slow but provide an enjoyable way of exploring both the coast and small towns inland.

A TGV train, providing swift and comfortable passenger transport

Automatic ticket machine at
a train station

Booking Tickets

Train tickets can be bought at
any station and by phone or
online (through www.voyages-
sncf.com). At most stations
there are both staffed counters
and automatic ticket machines
(billetterie automatique) that
accept cash or credit cards and
have instructions in English.
Tickets for trains that require
reservations (TGVs, *Intercités*)
can be bought from 90 days in
advance and until 5 minutes
before departure. The Price
Calendar *(Calendrier des Prix)*
page on voyages-sncf.com is
useful for comparing prices
available at different times.

If you book by phone or
online, you can pick up the
ticket at the station. With
some online bookings you
need only print your email
confirmation. Travellers with
mobility problems can arrange
assistance through the SNCF
Accès Plus programme
(see p257).

There are no ticket controls
on station platforms. However,
you must validate your ticket
at one of the yellow or orange
composteur machines in station
lobbies and on platforms. Insert
your ticket and (if you have one)
separate seat reservation face
up into the machine, which
will date-stamp them. Tickets
are checked on the train, and
you are liable to a fine if they
have not been validated. The
only time this is not necessary is
with some online bookings,
which allow you to print out
your ticket.

Timetables

Schedules and other
information on TGV and
Intercité trains can be found
on www.voyages-sncf.com;
timings for TER services in
Brittany are available only
online through the Brittany
pages of www.ter-sncf.com.
All stations provide leaflets
with local timetables and
details of other SNCF services.

Tickets and Passes

Fares on French trains vary
according to the type of train.
For those that can be booked
online (TGVs, *Intercités*), there
are two or three basic fare rates
for each class, varying mainly
according to when you want
to travel and whether you can
change the ticket once booked.
When booking, check if there
are any reduced Prem's
advance fares available, which
often give great discounts.
The Kelbillet website (www.
kelbillet.com) also offers
bargain last-minute tickets.

The KorriGo is a credit
card-sized smart card that
you charge up with an amount
of credit and can then use on
all TER trains and buses and
nearly all other public transport
throughout Brittany, including
city buses. Fares work out a
little cheaper than if you buy
ordinary tickets or from www.
star.fr; KorriGo cards can be
bought from all SNCF stations
in Brittany. SNCF also offers
several discount cards that
give reductions of around 50
per cent to seniors, families

Validating a KorriGo smart card at one of the
station machines

DIRECTORY

Eurostar
Tel (UK) 08432 186 186.
W eurostar.com

The Man in Seat 61
W seat61.com

Rail Europe
Tel (UK) 0844 848 5848.
W uk.voyages-sncf.com
Tel (USA) 1-800 622 8600.
Tel (Canada) 1-800 361 7245.
W raileurope.com

SNCF
Tel (France) 3635.
W sncf.com

The modern train station in
Nantes

and other groups; however,
they are only really useful
to residents who use French
trains regularly. More
information can be found on
the SNCF website.

Foreign visitors intending
to make several train journeys
in France might find that it
is worth getting one of the
various multi-journey rail passes,
which can only be bought
outside the country. UK and
other European residents can
get an InterRail pass valid for
France or for several countries,
giving unlimited travel in that
area for 3, 4, 6 or 8 days (not
necessarily consecutively)
within one month. Visitors
from outside Europe can buy
a France Rail pass, for 3 to
10 days of unlimited travel
within one month, or a Eurail
pass, covering only France
or combining it with other
countries. Consider carefully
how much you expect to travel
by train before buying a rail
pass, because if you do only a
few trips it might be cheaper to
buy individual tickets. For more
information and to purchase rail
passes, contact Rail Europe.

Brittany by Road

Brittany has an excellent road network. Roads linking its major towns and cities include motorways, which are toll-free, and fast dual carriageways. By taking the region's minor roads, however, visitors will discover picturesque villages and remote places of interest. Many of the coastal roads command spectacular views.

A minor road in Brittany with a magnificent view of the sea

Arriving by Car or Coach

There are several motorways *(autoroutes)* leading into Brittany. The A10–A11 is the main highway from Paris to Nantes. Nantes is also the main junction point for motorways from southern France. At Le Mans, the A81 branches off the A10–A11 to Rennes. The A84 runs down to Rennes from Caen, where it connects with motorways from northern France. It takes 3–4 hours to drive from Paris to Rennes (350 km/217 miles). From there to western Brittany it takes another 2–3 hours.

There are quite a few car-ferry services to Brittany from several ports in the UK and Ireland *(see pp270–1)*. You can also take a car in the **Eurotunnel** between Folkestone and Sangatte, near Calais. The tunnel and the Dover–Calais ferries are cheaper than direct ferries to Brittany, but you will face a long drive to your destination.

Eurolines provides coach services to Rennes and Nantes direct from the UK and other countries, with more connections via Paris.

What You Need

All EU car insurance policies include minimum third-party cover. However, it is strongly advisable to have wider cover too. For holders of fully comprehensive car insurance, most companies provide full European cover for a small extra fee; some do not charge for this at all but still require you to notify them before travelling. An international Green Card confirming your car is insured is no longer a legal requirement, but it is still useful to have; most companies issue them when you obtain European cover.

It is also advisable to have breakdown cover with one of the Europe-wide networks. This can be arranged through a motoring organization such as the **AA** or **RAC** or via your insurance broker.

When driving in France, it is compulsory to have the original registration document for the car, a current insurance certificate and your driving licence. You should also carry a passport or ID card. The car's country of registration should be displayed on a sticker or as part of the licence plate.

Headlights of right-hand-drive cars should have deflectors fitted for driving on the right, and you must carry spare headlight bulbs, a red warning triangle, a high-visibility jacket to be worn in case of an accident or breakdown and a breathalyser kit. This equipment can be bought at all ferry ports and on board ferries.

Roads and Tolls

Most motorways in France charge tolls, but in Brittany all roads are toll-free, including highways that are motorway-standard (such as the N12 Rennes–Morlaix–Brest and the N165 Nantes–Vannes–Quimper–Brest). Heading into Brittany, tolls end at Caen, Laval and Nantes.

There is also an efficient network of major roads *(routes nationales)* between the main towns, as well as more scenic minor roads *(routes départementales)*. Roads from central France become congested on summer weekends and at the beginning and end of the summer holidays (around mid-July and towards the end of August). Inside Brittany, traffic also builds up in peak season around the most popular resorts, such as Carnac. For most of the year, though, road congestion is rare outside of a few cities, and even in summer country and coastal roads can be pretty quiet.

For more information on all aspects of driving in France, visit the website of **Bison Futé** or **Autoroute**.

One of several fast dual carriageways in Brittany

Rules of the Road

Unless road signs indicate otherwise, *priorité a droite* means that you must give way to vehicles joining the road from the right, except on roundabouts or from private property. This mainly applies in small towns and villages; most major roads outside built-up areas have the right of way indicated by a *passage protégé* sign. Contrary to UK convention, flashing headlights in France means that the driver is claiming the right of way.

D 50

CALLAC
KALLAG

D 31

MOUSTÉRU
MOUSTERUZ

Road signs in French and Breton

In addition to the requirements described in What You Need *(see opposite)*, it is compulsory to wear seat belts, and children under 10 are not allowed to travel in the front of the car and must have a booster seat. It is illegal to use a mobile phone (even a hands-free one) while driving. Dipped headlights (not just sidelights) must be used in poor visibility, and motorbikes must have dipped headlights lit at all times. If you have to stop by the roadside for a breakdown or other reason, you must put on your luminous jacket, and place your red warning triangle at least 100 m (328 ft) behind the car on motorways, 30 m (98 ft) on other roads.

For further information, visit the website of the AA or RAC motoring organizations.

Speed Limits and Fines

Speed limits on French *autoroutes* are as follows: 130 km/h (80 mph), 110 km/h (70 mph) when it rains; on dual carriageways: 110 km/h (70 mph), 90–100 km/h (55–60 mph) when it rains; on other roads: 90 km/h (55 mph), 80 km/h (50 mph) when it rains. In towns, the speed limit is 50 km/h (30 mph) unless otherwise marked.

On-the-spot fines of around €90 can be levied for speeding, not stopping at a Stop sign, overtaking where forbidden, and other driving offences. If you do not pay within three days, the fine will increase. Drink-driving can lead to confiscation of the vehicle or imprisonment. A level of 0.05 per cent alcohol in the blood is illegal.

Petrol

Virtually all fuel stations have two grades of unleaded petrol (95 and 98 octane) and diesel fuel (*gazole* or *gasoil*, and sometimes a higher-quality grade, *gasoil* +), which in France is cheaper than petrol. The cheapest places to buy fuel in France are the stations attached to big supermarkets and hyper-markets, which (like many rural petrol stations) are closed on Sundays. Filling up the tank is known as *faire le plein*.

Car Hire

All the main international car-hire companies operate in France. In Brittany, there are offices at the principal airports, main railway stations and in the centre of major towns. To get the best rates, it's advisable to book a car before you leave for France through the companies' international websites, via an Internet car rental booking service such as **Auto Europe** or in a package with your flight. Car rentals can also be booked in combination with train tickets through www. voyages-sncf.com or Rail Europe *(see p267)*.

Conditions vary, but in general to rent a car you must be over 21 and have had a driving licence for at least a year, and you must present your licence, passport and a credit card. The price quoted to you should include all taxes and unlimited mileage *(kilométrage illimité)*, which nowadays is usual practice.

Europcar

Logo of car hire company Europcar

Parking

Finding a parking space in coastal towns in summer can be difficult; however, most large towns have car parks with a pay-and-display system *(horodateur)*. Villages have free, and usually very central, parking areas.

DIRECTORY

Arriving by Car or Coach

Eurolines
Tel (France) 0892 899 091.
W eurolines.com

Eurotunnel
Tel (France) 0810 630 304;
(UK) 08443 35 35 35.
W eurotunnel.com

What You Need

AA
Tel (UK) 0800 085 2721;
(France) 0825 098 876.
W theaa.com

RAC
Tel (UK) 0800 015 6000.
W rac.co.uk

Roads and Tolls

Autoroute
W autoroutes.fr

Bison Futé
Tel 0800 100 200.
W bison-fute.gouv.fr

Car Hire

Auto Europe
Tel (UK) 0800 358 1229;
(USA) 1-888-223-5555.
W autoeurope.com

Avis
Tel (France) 3642.
W avis.com

Budget
Tel 0825 003 564.
W budget.com

Europcar
Tel 0825 358 358.
W europcar.com

Hertz
Tel 0825 861 861.
W hertz.com

Rentacar
Tel 0891 700 200.
W rentacar.fr

Brittany by Boat

With frequent ferry crossings from the UK and Ireland to Roscoff, St-Malo and Cherbourg, as well as to destinations further east along the French coast, Brittany is easy to reach by sea. Travelling by ferry allows you the convenience of bringing your own car, too.

With islands such as Belle-Île and Île d'Ouessant and coastal features like the Golfe du Morbihan among its most picturesque attractions, Brittany also invites exploration by boat; there is a wide range of trips out to sea on offer, and there are regular links to Brittany's many islands. Sailing along Brittany's rivers and canals, which are now reserved for pleasure boats, is a particularly attractive way of experiencing the riches and variety of Brittany's cultural heritage.

Passengers disembarking on Île de Sein

Arriving by Ferry

Direct ferries provide the most convenient means of travelling to Brittany from the UK or Ireland with your own vehicle. Prices vary greatly, so shop around when booking.

Brittany Ferries sails several times a week from Portsmouth to St-Malo (9 hrs, or 10–11 hrs overnight) and from Plymouth to Roscoff (6 hrs, or 8 hrs overnight), and weekly from Cork to Roscoff (14 hrs). The company also sails from Poole to Cherbourg, in nearby Normandy, and from Portsmouth to Cherbourg and Caen; these routes take 4–6 hours, but in summer, catamaran fast ferries to Cherbourg take only 2–3 hours. **Condor Ferries** has fast and conventional ferries from Poole to St-Malo and from Portsmouth to Cherbourg. Some are direct, while others require changing boats in Jersey or Guernsey. Condor also operates direct ferries from the Channel Islands to St-Malo. **Irish Ferries** operates ferries from Rosslare to Cherbourg (18 hours) and (May–Oct only) Roscoff.

DIRECTORY

Arriving by Ferry

Brittany Ferries
Tel (France) 0825 828 828.
W brittanyferries.com

Condor Ferries
Tel (UK) 0845 609 1024.
W condorferries.co.uk

DFDS Seaways
Tel (UK) 0871 574 7235.
W dfdsseaways.co.uk

Irish Ferries
Tel (IR) 0818 300 400.
(UK) 08717 300 400.
W irishferries.com

P&O Ferries
Tel (France) (0) 366 74 03 25.
W poferries.com

Boat and Canal Trips

Point Passion Plage
W pointplage.fr

Côtes d'Armor

Armor Navigation
Tel 02 96 91 10 00.
W armor-decouverte.fr

Vedette Jaman IV
Dinan.
Tel 02 96 39 28 41.
W vedettejamanIV.com

Vedettes de Guerlédan
Caurel.
Tel 02 96 28 52 64.
W guerledan.com

Finistère

Aulne Loisirs Plaisance
Châteauneuf-du-Faou.
Tel 02 98 73 28 63.
W aulneloisirs.com

Ille-et-Vilaine

Compagnie Corsaire
Tel 0825 138 100.
W compagniecorsaire.com

Cotre Corsaire Le Renard
St-Malo. Tel 02 99 40 53 10.
W cotre-corsaire-renard.com

Croisières Chateaubriand
Dinard. Tel 02 99 46 44 00.
W chateaubriand.com

Loire-Atlantique

Bateaux Nantais
Nantes. Tel 02 40 14 51 14.
W bateaux-nantais.fr

Morbihan

Izenah Croisières
Tel 02 97 26 31 45.
W izenah-croisieres.com

Island Links and Coastal Cruises

Armein (Île de Batz)
Tel 02 98 61 75 47.
W armein.fr

Compagnie Océane
Tel 0820 056 156.
W compagnie-oceane.fr

Navix-Compagnie des Iles
Tel 0825 132 100.
W navix.fr

Penn-Ar-Bed
Tel 02 98 80 80 80.
W pennarbed.fr

Vedettes Azenor
Tel 02 98 41 46 23.
W azenor.fr

Vedettes de Bréhat
Tel 02 96 55 79 50.
W vedettesdebrehat.com

Vedettes de l'Odet
Tel 02 98 57 00 58.
W vedettes-odet.com

The crossings from Dover to Calais or Dunkirk, operated by **P&O Ferries** and **DFDS Seaways**, take only about an hour and are cheaper than direct ferries. However, you will then have a drive of at least 5–6 hours to your destination in Brittany.

Boat and Canal Trips

There are many opportunities for visitors to take boat trips out to sea, often in old restored sailing boats. **Cotre Corsaire Le Renard** organizes trips of one or several days in the Baie de St-Malo. **Point Passion Plage** is a network of sailing centres all around the Breton coast that provide tuition, boat rentals and sometimes guided trips. Information on other boat trips and cruises is available from tourist offices.

Brittany has 600 km (375 miles) of canals and navigable rivers. There are several major routes, one of the most popular being the one along the exquisite Rance valley south of St-Malo, with the possibility of continuing down to Rennes and then following the Vilaine river all the way to the south coast. The Nantes–Brest canal (360 km/225 miles) goes through some of the most beautiful scenery in Brittany, and the Blavet valley goes from Lorient to Pontivy.

The small harbour at Dinan, on the Rance river

Sea Links to the Islands

Brittany's largest islands all have sea links with the nearest harbour on the mainland. The main departure points are Pointe de l'Arcouest for Île de Bréhat (15 mins); Roscoff, for Île de Batz (15 mins); Le Conquet and Brest for Île d'Ouessant (1 hr/2 hrs 30 mins) and Île Molène (30 mins/1 hr 45 mins); Audierne for Île de Sein (1 hr); Quiberon for Belle-Île (45 mins), Houat (45 mins) and Hoëdic (1 hr 10 mins); and Vannes, Larmor-Barden and Locmariaquer for Île d'Arz, Île aux Moines and other attractions around the Golfe du Morbihan. Other services run from St-Quay-Portrieux to Île de Bréhat, from Lorient to Belle-Île and Île de Groix (45 mins), and from Concarneau and Bénodet/Loctudy to Îles de Glénan (1 hr).

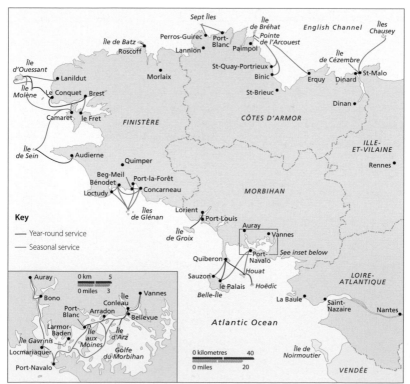

General Index

Page numbers in **bold** refer to main entries.

Acknowledgments

Dorling Kindersley would like to thank the following people and institutions whose contributions and assistance have made the preparation of this book possible.

Main Contributors
Gaëtan du Chatenet
Entomologist, ornitholist, corresponding member of the Muséum National d'Histoire Naturelle de Paris, draughtsman and miniature painter, Gaëtan du Chatenet is the author of many works published by Delachaux & Niestlé and Gallimard.

Jean-Philippe Follet
Jean-Philippe Follet, who was born and brought up in the Morlaix area, studied at the Faculté de Celtique in Rennes and at the Centre de Recherches Bretonnes et Celtiques in Brest. He works as a writer and translator.

Jean-Yves Gendillard
The son of Breton parents, Jean-Yves Gendillard is a teacher. He has a special interest in Brittany and in religious art. He has spent a considerable amount of time in southern Finistère, and has a particular knowledge of the chapels and calvaries of that area.

Éric Gibory
Born in St-Malo, Éric Gibory spent his childhood and adolescence there. He has helped to organize cultural events, is the author of four *Guides Bleus* published by Hachette and has contributed to several travel magazines.

Renée Grimaud
A specialist in tourism, Renée Grimaud has contrib-uted to many travel guides and has edited several illustrated books on the regions of France, notably on the Loire and its chateaux. A native of the Vendée, she has a detailed knowledge of the Loire region and of Brittany, which she visits regularly.

Georges Minois
A senior history teacher at the Lycée Renan in St-Brieuc and the holder of a doctorate, George Minois is also the author of 30 books, including several on Brittany, such as *Nouvelle Histoire de la Bretagne*, *Anne de Bretagne* and *Du Guesclin*, published by Fayard.

Other Contributors
Sophie Berger, Vanessa Besnard, Isabelle De Jaham, Marie-Christine Degos, Mathilde Huyghes-Despointes, Lyn Parry, Sonia Rocton, Sarah Thurin and Sébastien Tomasi.

Photography
Philippe Giraud.

Studio Photography and Additional Photography
Max Alexander, Anne Chopin, Andrew Holligan, Ian O'Leary, Rough Guides/Greg Ward.

Picture Research
Marie-Christine Petit.

Cartography
Fabrice Le Goff.

Additional Cartography
Quadrature Créations.

Illustrations
François Brosse
Architectural drawings, Street-by-Street maps and drawings pp 62–3, 84–5, 114–15, 122–3, 164–5, 172–3, 190–1, 192–3.

Anne Delaunay-Vernhes
Architectural drawings pp66–7, 110–11, 128–9, 168–9, 198–9, 214–15.

Éric Geoffroy
Illustrations on "Exploring" and "At a Glance" maps, on small town plans and tour maps pp56–7, 60–1, 65, 82, 87, 94–5, 104, 109, 120–1, 132–3, 139, 146–7, 150–1, 167, 178–9, 188–9, 189, 198–9, 202–3, 205.

Emmanuel Guillon
Façades, perspectives and artwork pp24–5, 26–7, 110–11, 128–9, 157, 198–9, 214–15.

Guénola de Sandol
Artwork pp66–7, 168–9.

Proofreaders
Cate Casey, Emily Hatchwell.

Index
Lucilla Watson.

Special Assistance
M. Alexandre and M. Tournaire at Service Départemental de l'Architecture et du Patrimoine du Finistère; Mme Delmotte, M. Charles-Tanguy Leroux and M. Christian Gerardot of DRAC de Bretagne; Marie Godicheau of the Service Météorologique de Rennes; M. Guillet, Château des Ducs de Bretagne; M. Job an Irien of Éditions Minihi-Levenez; M. le Curé Louis Le Bras and M. Paul Nemar of the church at Crozon; Henri Le Roux (butter toffees, Quiberon); Philippe Le Stum, curator at the Musée Départemental Breton in Quimper; Mathieu Lefèvre of the festival *Étonnants Voyageurs*, St-Malo; the mayor of St-Malo; Florent Patron of Éditions Coop Breizh; M. Alain-Charles Perrot (Parlement de Bretagne); Mme Marie-Suzanne de Ponthaud (head architect, Cathédrale St-Tugdual, Tréguier); Océanopolis, Brest; public relations department, Banque de France; information service, *Bretagne Magazine*; public relations department, La Poste; public relations department of the city of St-Malo for the *Quai des Bulles* festival; press office, Air France; press office, *Transmusicales*, Rennes; ADA; Musée des Vieux Outils, Tinténiac; Musée des Terre-Neuvas, Fécamp. Armor Lux (clothing, Quimper); Saint-James (clothing, Saint-James); Phytomer (beauty products, St-Malo); Thalado (beauty products, Roscoff); Verreries de Bréhat; the shop Quimper-Faïence de Paris; Fisselier (traditionally made liqueurs, Chantepie).

Revisions Team

Ashwin Adimari, Emma Anacootee, Claire Baranowski, Chris Barstow, Sonal Bhatt, Louise Cleghorn, Simon Davis, Surya Deogun, Dana Facaros, Rhiannon Furbear, Amanda Hodgkinson, Nicola Hodgson, Carly Madden, Tanya Mahendru, Alison McGill, Deepak Mittal, Casper Morris, Sangita Patel, Lyn Parry, Pollyanna Poulter, Nick Rider, Ellen Root, Sands Publishing Solutions, Azeem Siddiqui, Susana Smith, Anna Streiffert, Ajay Verma, Dora Whitaker.

Photography Permissions

The publisher would like to thank those individuals who gave permission to photograph on their premises:
Mme Martine Abgrall, for the alignments at Carnac; Mme Martine Becus, at the Château des Rochers Sévigné in Vitré; Florence and Marc Benoît, at the Hôtel La Reine Hortense in Dinard; Mme Burnot, curator at the Musée du Château de Dinan; M. de Calbiac, at the Manoir de Kerazan; Mme Caprini and Lan Mafart, at the Librairie Caplan in Guimaec; Mme Gaillot, at the Musée de la Pêche in Concarneau; M. and Mme Gautier, in Plouezoc'h; M. Bernard Guillet and Christelle Goldet, at the Château des Ducs de Bretagne in Nantes; M. Hommel, of the Musée de l'Automobile in Lohéac; M. Patrick Jourdan, curator at the Musée des Jacobins in Morlaix; M. Le Goff, of the Musée du Léon in Lesneven; M. Bernard Lefloc'h, of the Musée Bigouden in Pont-L'Abbé; Mme Lilia Millier, at the Hôtel Castel Marie Louise in La Baule; Mme Françoise Louis, for the Château de Suscinio; M. Mézin, curator at the Musée de la Compagnie des Indes in Port-Louis; Mme Quintin, at the Musée de la Fraise in Plougastel- Daoulas; Mme Riskine, curator at the Musée de la Préhistoire in Carnac; Mme de Rohan, at the Château de Josselin; Mme de Sagazan, at the Manoir de Traonjoly in Cléder; Mme Michèle Sallé, at the Château de la Hunaudaye; M. Sanchez, at the Parlement de Bretagne in Rennes; M. Jacques Thorel, at the Auberge Bretonne in Roche-Bernard; M. Bernard Verlingue, curator at the Musée de la Faïence in Quimper; Faïencerie H. B. Henriot in Quimper. The staff at the Château de Kerjean; the staff at the brasserie La Cigale in Nantes; the director at the Parc Animalier de Menez-Meur; Camac Harps in Mouzeil; the staff at the Maison de la Mariée on the Île de Fédrun; the owner of the Château de Goulaine; the shop L'Épée de Bois in Paris. The publisher would also like to thank all those who gave permission to photograph at various other shops, restaurants, cafés, hotels, churches and publics places too numerous to mention individually.

Picture Credits

a-above; b-below/bottom; c-centre; f-far; l-left; r-right; t-top.
The publisher would like to thank the following individuals, companies and picture libraries for permission to reproduce their photographs:

2-3: Robert Harding Picture Library: Tuul. 8–9: RMN/R.-G. Ojeda. *Port Breton*, Paul Bellanger-Adhémar. Château-Musée, Nemours. 10br: Dreamstime.com: Xantana. 11tr: Dreamstime.com: Prillfoto. 12bl: Alamy Images: David Bagnall. 12tr: Dreamstime. com: Elena Elisseeva. 13tr: Dreamstime.com: John Alphonse. 14tl: Dreamstime.com: Claudio Giovanni Colombo. 14br: Dreamstime.com: Lukasz Janyst. 15tl: Dreamstime.com: Nailia Schwarz. 20c: Béghin-Say. 22tr: Jacana/S. Cordier. 22cl: Jacana/C.

Bahr. 22cr: Jacana/M. and A. Boet. 22clb: Jacana/H. Brehm. 22crb: Jacana/M. and A. Boet. 22bl: Jacana/S. Cordier. 22br: Jacana/W. Wisniewski. 23tl: Jacana/G. Ziesler. 23cl: Jacana/B. Coster. 23cb: Jacana/P. Prigent. 23crb: Jacana/C. Nardin. 23cr: Jacana/S. Cordier. 23bl: Jacana/P. Prigent. 23br: Jacana/P. Prigent. 28tr: R. Viollet. 28bl: M. Thersiquel. 28br: R. Viollet/Viollet Collection. 28-29c: Darnis. 29b: Andia Presse/Betermin. 29t: Darnis. 30tr: Éditions Minihi Levenez/ Y. Le Berre, B. Tanguy, Y. P. Castel. 30c: Éditions Coop. Breizh. 30b: Keystone Illustration. 31tl: Corbis/Sygma/S. Bassouls. 31tr: Scope/B. Galeron. 31cb: J. L. Charmet. *La Revue Illustrée*. Bibliothèque des Arts Décoratifs, Paris. 31b: Rue des Archives. 32–33c: M. Thersiquel. Fête des Brodeuses, Pont-l'Abbé. 32tr: G. Dagli Orti. *Femmes de Plougastel au Pardon de Ste-Anne*, C. Cottet. Musée des Beaux-Arts, Rennes. 32cl: Michael Thersiquel, brooch by P. Toulhoat. 32crb: R. Viollet. 32bl: M. Thersiquel. 32bc: Éditions Jos Le Doaré. 32br: Éditions Jos Le Doaré. 33tl: Gernot. Brest. 33 tr: Éditions Jos Le Doaré. 33c: Musée Départemental Breton, Quimper. 33bl, bc, br: Éditions Jos Le Doaré. 34cr: Étonnants Voyageurs festival, Rennes. *Whales in the Ice in the Arctic*, William Bradford, Brandywine, Calgary, Canada. 35cra: A.-L. Gac. 36bl: G. Cazade, public relations, St-Malo. 37bl: A.-L. Gac. 38tr: Scope/B. Galeron. 38cla: R. Viollet. 38cl: Hachette/ C. Boulanger. 38bl: Scope/B. Galeron. 38br: Andia Presse/Le Coz. 39tr: Scope/B. Galeron. 39br: Y. Boëlle. 40: AKG Paris. *Chronique de Bretagne*, Pierre Le Beau. Bibliothèque Nationale, Paris. 43tl: Leemage/L. de Selva. Morlaix church. 43crb: Archbishopric of Rennes. Cartulaire de Redon No. 9, 11th century. 44t: *Josse. Capture of Dinan and Rendering the Keys*. Musée de la Tapisserie, Bayeux. 44br: Hachette. 45tr: Leemage/L. de Selva. 45crb: AKG Paris/J. P. Dumontier. Église St-Yves, La Roche Meurice. 45bc: RMN/J.G. Berizzi. Musée des Traditions Populaires, Paris. 46tl & 46crb: AKG Paris. *Chronique de Bretagne*, Pierre Le Beau. Bibliothèque Nationale, Paris. 47tc: G. Dagli Orti. *Chronique en Prose de Bertrand Du Guesclin*. Bibliothèque Municipale; Rouen. 47clb: Josse. *Procès de Gilles de Rais*. Bibliothèque Nationale, Paris. 47bl: G. Dagli Orti. Detail of Dance of Death fresco. La Ferté Loupière church. 47br: Hachette. 48tr: Leemage/ L. de Selva. Coat of arms of Anne of Brittany (1514). Bibliothèque Municipale, Rennes. 48–49c: G. Dagli Orti. *Marriage of Charles VIII and Anne of Brittany*, St-Èvre. Château de Versailles. 48cl: *Chroniques et Histoires de Bretons*, Pierre Le Beau, Bibliothèque Nationale, Paris. 49tl: Josse. *Louis XII and Anne of Brittany*. Musée Condé, Chantilly. 49tr: G. Dagli Orti. *Vie des Femmes Célèbres*, A. du Four. Musée Dobrée, Nantes. 49cr: Bridgeman/Giraudon. *Claude de France*. Pushkin Museum, Moscow. 49bl: G. Dagli Orti. Biblioteca Marciana, Venice. 49bc: Charles Hémon. Gold reliquary with the heart of Anne of Brittany. Musée Dobrée, Nantes. 50tl: Marine Nationale, Service Historique de la Marine, Brest. *Carte Britanniae*. 50cb: RMN/F. Raux. *François d'Argouges (1669)*, J. Frosne. Château de Versailles et Trianon. 50bl: Hachette. Engraving by the Rouargues brothers. 51tr: AKG Paris/S. Domingie. *Campaign of the Holy League in Brittany*. Uffizi, Florence. 51clb: G. Dagli Orti. Lollain, private collection, Paris. 51bc: Hachette. 52cla: AKG Paris. *Jean Cottereau*, A.F. Carrière. Bibliothèque Nationale, Paris. 52cb: G. Dagli Orti. Musée Dobrée, Nantes. 52bc: Hachette. Engraving by Berthault after Swebach-Desfontaines. 52br: Hachette. Lithograph by Bernard-Romain Julien. 53t: RMN/Arnaudet. Opening of the railway line from Paris to Brest. Musée de la Voiture, Château de Compiègne 53bl:

A. Chopin. 54-55: SuperStock: Photononstop. 57tr: Getty Images/Shaun Egan. 57br: Andia Presse/Diathem. 58: Robert Harding Picture Library: Gimmi. 59b: Getty Images: Frans Sellies. 63bl: Robien Collection. *Head of an Angel*, Botticelli. Musée des Beaux-Arts, Rennes. 64br: RMN. *Effet de Vagues*, Georges Lacombe. Musée des Beaux-Arts, Rennes. 67crb: Inventaire Général-ADAGP/C. Arthur/Lambart, 1998. *La Félicité Publique*. Centre de Documentation du Patrimoine, Rennes. 69cl: AKG Paris. *Histoire de Merlin*, R. de Boron. Bibliothèque Nationale, Paris. 69cr: Hachette. *The Holy Grail Appears before the Knights of the Round Table*. Bibliothèque Nationale, Paris. 69bl: J. L. Charmet. *King Arthur and the Knights of the Round Table*, fresco by Viollet-Le-Duc. Bibliothèque des Arts Décoratifs, Paris. 69br: J. L. Charmet. *Merlin and Vivien*, Gustave Doré. Bibliothèque des Arts Décoratifs, Paris. 73bc: Hachette. 74c: D. Provost. clogs, 1928. Musée de l'Outil et des Métiers, Tinténiac. 75bc: Hachette. Lithograph by Lardereau. 78bc: Hachette/Musée de Bayeux. 79tl: Getty Images/Shaun Egan. 83cra: Jacana/M. Willemeit. 88ca: Lee Miller. 90tl: Alamy Images/John Warbuton-Lee Photography/Calum Stirling. 92: SuperStock: age fotostock. 93b: Alamy Images: Hemis. 100br: Gaulish village, Pleumeur Bodou. 101br: Jacana/J. T. Guillots. 103clb: Bertrand Brelivet Collection/carte-postale.com. 105br: RMN/P. Bernard. *Rue à Bréhat*, Henri Dabadie. Musée des Beaux-Arts, Lille. 107tc: G. Dagli Orti. Engraving from *Petit Journal*. 108bl: Alain Grenier, private collection. 110bc: Quintin town hall. Musée-Atelier des Toiles de Lin. 111tr: Alamy Images: STOCKFOLIO®. 111cl: Musée Mathurin Méheut, Lamballe. 118: Robert Harding Picture Library: Guy Thouvenin. 123cr: Musée de Morlaix. 125tc: P. Seitz/Caplan and Co. café-bookshop, Morlaix. 127tl: Office Municipal de Tourisme, Roscoff. Musée des Johnnies. 128bl: Alamy Images: Mark Boulton. 133tc: Musée Départemental Breton/P. Sicard. *Le Miroir du Monde*, Michel le Nobletz. See of Quimper. 133crb: Écomusée des Goémoniers et de l'Algue/S. Allançon, Plouguer-neau. 135c: Jacana/B. Coster. 138cl: Getty Images: Fred Tanneau. 139tl: RMN/J. de la Baume. *La Mer Jaune*, Georges Lacombe. Musée des Beaux-Arts, Brest. 141tl: Le tour de monde 141tr: Océanopolis/T. Joyeux. 142tr: Alamy Images: LOOK Die Bildagentur der Fotografen GmbH. 148: Robert Harding Picture Library: Amanda Hall. 149b: Dreamstime.com: Saintho. 152br: Getty Images: Panoramic Images. 153br: Abbaye de Landevennec. Frontispiece of the Évangéliaire de Landevennec (c. 870). 154–155bc: Louis Le Bras, parish priest at Crozon. 159bl: SCOPE/B. Galeron. 161tr: Keystone. 163b: Alamy Images: Hemis. 164tr: Musée Départemental Breton, Quimper. 167tr: RMN/M. Bellot. *Le Génie à la Guirlande*, Charles Filiger. 170cl, cr, c: Musée Départemental Breton, Quimper. 173br: Josse. Musée du Château, Versailles. 174bc: Le Gonidec canning factory. 175br: Josse. *La Belle Angèle*, P. Gauguin. Musée d'Orsay, Paris. 176:

Robert Harding Picture Library: ICP. 183tl: Keystone Illustration. 187tl: Gamma/T. Rannou. 200br: Pontivy town hall. 202: Robert Harding Picture Library: Michael Busselle. 203b: Getty Images: Hiroshi Higuchi. 204tr: Alamy Images: Mick Flynn. 205crb: Chateau Clisson. 211tc: RMN/ M. Bellot. *Louis XII and Anne of Brittany at Prayer*. Musée Dobrée, Nantes. 212bc: G. Dagli Orti. Musée Dobrée, Nantes. 213br: Alamy Images: imageBROKER. 213tl: ADAGP, Paris 2002/RMN/C. Jean. *Le Gaulage des Pommes*, Émile Bernard. Musée des Beaux-Arts, Nantes. 213cra: Hachette. 215bc: Musée de Chantilly. *Duc de Mercoeur*. 217bl: Josse/Anonyme. *D'Elbée Libérant les Prisonniers Bleus*, Cholet. 218-219: Robert Harding Picture Library: SGM. 220bl: Castel Beau Site. 220cr: La Ferme Saint. 223tr: Fédération Unie des Auberges de Jeunesse – www.fuaj.org. 224bl: Alamy Images: David Burton. 225tl: Alamy Images: Hemis. 226bl: Manoir de Lan-Kerellec. 227tr: La Ferme Saint. 228br: Dihan. 229tc: Villa Kerasy. 230bl: Les Filets Bleus. 231bc: Le Jardin Gourmand. 231tr: Alamy Images/Stockfolio. 233c: Alamy Images/AA World Travel Library. 233tl: Authors Image/Christine Pinhera. 234br: Le Coquillage. 235tr: Crêperie Ahna. 236t: Les Filets Bleus. 237br: Alamy Images: Bon Appetit. 238tr Alamy Images: Hemis. 238br: Le Grand Hôtel des Bains. 239tr: La Butte. 240tr: L'Ambroisie. 241bc: Hôtel de la Plage. 242br: Le Jardin Gourmand. 243tr: Manoir de la Boulaie. 244cla: CRTB/ J.P.Gratien. 245tr: CRTB/Martin Schulte-Kellinghaus. 245cl: G. Fisher. 246: All Chopin except *Almanach du MarinBreton*: œuvre du Marin Breton, and nautilus shells: Verreries de Bréhat. 247: All Chopin. 248b: G. Saliou. 254-255: Robert Harding Picture Library: Guy Thouvenin 256cla: Corbis/Hemis/RIEGER Bertrand. 256br: Alamy Images/incamerastock. 259bl: Alamy Images/FORGET Patrick/SAGAPHOTO.COM. 260cla: Corbis/Xinhua Press/Gao Jing. 260br: Alamy Images: incamerastock/ICP-UK. 261: Banque de France. 262 cl: Alamy Images/STOCKFOLIO®. 262br: Getty Images/Gamma-Rapho/Alain DENANTES. 263cl: Alamy Images/a la poste. 263tr: Canal+. 264bl: Photothèque Rennes Dinard Aéroports Bretagne. 266br: Alamy Images/Gary Moseley. 267tl: Getty Images/Stringer/AFP. 267bc/cr: SNCF. 269crb Europcar .

FEP: Robert Harding Picture Library: Michael Busselle Rbl, Gimmi Rcr, Guy Thouvenin Lcl, Amanda Hall Lcb, ICP Lbr.
SuperStock: age fotostock Rtl

Jacket: Front main and Spine t: Alamy Images: Prisma Bildagentur AG

All other pictures Dorling Kindersley. See www.dkimages.com for further information

Special Editions of DK Travel Guides

DK Travel Guides can be purchased in bulk quantities at discounted prices for use in promotions or as premiums. We are also able to offer special editions and personalized jackets, corporate imprints, and excerpts from all of our books, tailored specifically to meet your own needs.

To find out more, please contact:
in the United States **SpecialSales@dk.com**
in the UK **travelspecialsales@uk.dk.com**
in Canada DK Special Sales at **general@tourmaline.ca**
in Australia **business.development@pearson.com.au**

Phrase Book

In Emergency

Help!	Au secours!	oh sekoor
Stop!	Arrêtez!	aret-ay
Call a doctor!	Appelez un médecin!	apuh-lay uñ medsañ
Call an ambulance!	Appelez une ambulance!	apuh-lay oon oñboo-loñs
Call the police!	Appelez la police!	apuh-lay lah poh-lees
Call the fire department!	Appelez les pompiers!	apuh-lay leh poñ-peeyay
Where is the nearest telephone?	Où est le téléphone le plus proche	oo ay luh tehlehfon luh ploo prosh
Where is the nearest hospital?	Où est l'hôpital le plus proche?	oo ay l'opeetal luh ploo prosh

Communication Essentials

Yes	Oui	wee
No	Non	noñ
Please	S'il vous plaît	seel voo play
Thank you	Merci	mer-see
Excuse me	Excusez-moi	exkoo-zay mwah
Hello	Bonjour	boñzhoor
Goodbye	Au revoir	oh ruh-vwar
Good night	Bonsoir	boñ-swar
Morning	Le matin	matañ
Afternoon	L'après-midi	l'apreh-meedee
Evening	Le soir	swar
Yesterday	Hier	eeyehr
Today	Aujourd'hui	oh-zhoor-dwee
Tomorrow	Demain	duhmañ
Here	Ici	ee-see
There	Là	lah
What?	Quel, quelle?	kel, kel
When?	Quand?	koñ
Why?	Pourquoi?	poor-kwah
Where?	Où?	oo

Useful Phrases

How are you?	Comment allez-vous?	kom-moñ talay voo
Very well, thank you.	Très bien, merci.	treh byañ, mer-see
Pleased to meet you.	Enchanté de faire votre connaissance.	oñshoñ-tay duh fehr votr kon-ay-sans
See you soon.	A bientôt.	byañ-toh
That's fine	Voilà qui est parfait	vwalah kee ay parfay
Where is/are…?	Où est/sont…?	oo ay/soñ
How far is it to…?	Combien de kilomètres d'ici à…?	kom-byañ duh keelo-metr d'ee-see ah
Which way to…?	Quelle est la direction pour…?	kel ay lah deer-ek-syoñ poor
Do you speak English?	Parlez-vous anglais?	par-lay voo oñg-lay
I don't understand.	Je ne comprends pas.	zhuh nuh kom-proñ pah
Could you speak slowly please?	Pouvez-vous parler moins vite s'il vous plaît?	poo-vay voo par-lay mwañ veet seel voo play
I'm sorry.	Excusez-moi.	exkoo-zay mwah

Useful Words

big	grand	groñ
small	petit	puh-tee
hot	chaud	show
cold	froid	frwah
good	bon	boñ
bad	mauvais	moh-veh
enough	assez	assay
well	bien	byañ
open	ouvert	oo-ver
closed	fermé	fer-meh
left	gauche	gohsh
right	droite	drwaht
straight ahead	tout droit	too drwah
near	près	preh
far	loin	lwañ
up	en haut	oñ oh
down	en bas	oñ bah
early	de bonne heure	duh bon urr
late	en retard	oñ ruh-tar
entrance	l'entrée	l'on-tray
exit	la sortie	sor-tee
toilet	les toilettes, les WC	twah-let, vay-see
free, unoccupied	libre	leebr
free, no charge	gratuit	grah-twee

Making a Telephone Call

I'd like to place a long-distance call.	Je voudrais faire un interurbain.	zhuh voo-dreh fehr uñ añter-oorbañ
I'd like to make a collect call.	Je voudrais faire une communication PCV.	zhuh voodreh fehr oon komoonikah-syoñ peh-seh-veh
I'll try again later.	Je rappelerai plus tard.	zhuh rapel-eray ploo tar
Can I leave a message?	Est-ce que je peux laisser un message?	es-keh zhuh puh leh-say uñ mehsazh
Hold on.	Ne quittez pas, s'il vous plaît.	nuh kee-tay pah seel voo play
Could you speak up a little please?	Pouvez-vous parler un peu plus fort?	poo-vay voo par-lay uñ puh ploo for
local call	la communication locale	komoonikah-syoñ low-kal

Shopping

How much does this cost?	C'est combien s'il vous plaît?	say kom-byañ seel voo play
I would like …	Je voudrais…	zhuh voo-dray
Do you have …?	Est-ce que vous avez…?	es-kuh voo zavay
I'm just looking.	Je regarde seulement.	zhuh ruhgar suhlmoñ
Do you take credit cards?	Est-ce que vous acceptez les cartes de crédit?	es-kuh voo zaksept-ay leh kart duh kreh-dee
Do you take traveller's checks?	Est-ce que vous acceptez les chèques de voyage?	es-kuh voo zaksept-ay leh shek duh vwayazh
What time do you open?	A quelle heure vous êtes ouvert?	ah kel urr voo zet oo-ver
What time do you close?	A quelle heure vous êtes fermé?	ah kel urr voo zet fer-may
This one	Celui-ci	suhl-wee-see
That one	Celui-là	suhl-wee-lah
expensive	cher	shehr
cheap	pas cher, bon marché	pah shehr, boñ mar-shay
size, clothes	la taille	tye
size, shoes	la pointure	pwañ-tur
white	blanc	bloñ
black	noir	nwahr
red	rouge	roozh
yellow	jaune	zhohwn
green	vert	vehr
blue	bleu	bluh

Types of Shops

antiques shop	le magasin d'antiquités	maga-zañ d'oñteekee-tay
bakery	la boulangerie	booloñ-zhuree
bank	la banque	boñk
book store	la librairie	lee-brehree
butcher	la boucherie	boo-shehree
cake shop	la pâtisserie	patee-sree
cheese shop	la fromagerie	fromazh-ree
dairy	la crémerie	krem-ree
department store	le grand magasin	groñ maga-zañ
delicatessen	la charcuterie	sharkoot-ree
drugstore	la pharmacie	farmah-see
fish seller	la poissonnerie	pwasson-ree
gift shop	le magasin de cadeaux	maga-zañ duh kadoh
greengrocer	le marchand de légumes	mar-shoñ duh lay-goom
grocery	l'alimentation	alee-moñta-syoñ
hairdresser	le coiffeur	kwafuhr
market	le marché	marsh-ay
newsstand	le magasin de journaux	maga-zañ duh zhoor-no
post office	la poste, le bureau de poste, le PTT	pohst, booroh duh pohst, peh-teh-teh
shoe store	le magasin de chaussures	maga-zañ duh show-soor
supermarket	le supermarché	soo pehr-marshay
tobacconist	le tabac	tabah
travel agent	l'agence de voyages	l'azhoñs duh vwayazh

Sightseeing

abbey	l'abbaye	l'abay-ee
art gallery	la galerie d'art	galer-ree dart
bus station	la gare routière	gahr roo-tee-yehr

cathedral	la cathédrale	katay-**dral**
church	l'église	l'ayg**leez**
garden	le jardin	zhar-**dañ**
library	la bibliothèque	beeb**leeo**-tek
museum	le musée	moo-**zay**
tourist information office	les renseignements touristiques, le syndicat d'initiative	roñsayn-**moñ** too- rees-**teek**, sandee- ka d'eenee-sya**teev**
town hall	l'hôtel de ville	l'oh**tel** duh veel
train station	la gare (SNCF)	gahr (es-en-say-ef)
private mansion	l'hôtel particulier	l'oh**tel** partikoo-**lyay**
closed for	fermeture	fehrmeh-**tur**
public holiday	jour férié	zhoor fehree-ay

Staying in a Hotel

Do you have a vacant room?	Est-ce que vous avez une chambre?	es-kuh voo-za**vay** oon shambr
double room, with double bed	la chambre à deux personnes, avec un grand lit	shambr ah duh pehr-**son** avek un groñf lee
twin room	la chambre à deux lits	shambr ah duh lee
single room	la chambre à une personne	shambr ah oon pehr-**son**
room with a bath, shower	la chambre avec salle de bains, une douche	shambr avek sal duh bañ, oon doosh
porter	le garçon	gar-**soñ**
key	la clef	klay
I have a reservation.	J'ai fait une réservation.	zhay fay oon rayzehrva-**syoñ**

Eating Out

Have you got a table?	Avez-vous une table libre?	avay-**voo** oon tahbl leebr
I want to reserve a table.	Je voudrais réserver une table.	zhuh voo-**dray** rayzehr-**vay** oon tahbl
The check please.	L'addition s'il vous plaît.	l'adee-**syoñ** seel voo **play**
I am a vegetarian.	Je suis végétarian.	zhuh swee vezhay-**tehryañ**
Waitress/ waiter	Madame, Mademoiselle/ Monsieur	mah-**dam**, mah-demwah**zel**/ muh-**syuh**
menu	le menu, la carte	men-**oo**, kart
fixed-price menu	le menu à prix fixe	men-**oo** ah pree feeks
cover charge	le couvert	koo-**vehr**
wine list	la carte des vins	**kart**-deh vañ
glass	le verre	vehr
bottle	la bouteille	boo-**tay**
knife	le couteau	koo-**toh**
fork	la fourchette	for-**shet**
spoon	la cuillère	kwee-**yehr**
breakfast	le petit déjeuner	puh-**tee** deh-**zhuh**-nay
lunch	le déjeuner	deh-**zhuh**-nay
dinner	le dîner	dee-**nay**
main course	le plat principal	plah prañsee-**pal**
appetizer, first course	l'entrée, le hors d'oeuvre	l'oñ-**tray**, or- duhvr
dish of the day	le plat du jour	plah doo zhoor
wine bar	le bar à vin	bar ah vañ
café	le café	ka-**fay**
rare	saignant	**say**-noñ
medium	à point	ah **pwañ**
well-done	bien cuit	byañ **kwee**

Menu Decoder

l'agneau	l'an**yoh**	lamb
l'ail	l'eye	garlic
la banane	ba**nan**	banana
le beurre	burr	butter
la bière, bière à la pression	bee-**yehr, bee**-yehr ah lah pres-**syoñ**	beer, draft beer
le bifteck, le steack	beef-**tek**, stek	steak
le boeuf	buhf	beef
bouilli	boo-**yee**	boiled
le café	kah-**fay**	coffee
le canard	kanar	duck
le chocolat	shoko-**lah**	chocolate
le citron	see-**troñ**	lemon
le citron pressé	see-**troñ** press-**eh**	fresh lemon juice
les crevettes	kruh-**vet**	prawns
les crustacés	kroos-ta-**say**	shellfish
cuit au four	kweet oh foor	baked
le dessert	deh-**ser**	dessert
l'eau minérale	l'oh **meeney**-ral	mineral water

les escargots	leh zes-kar-**goh**	snails
les frites	freet	chips
le fromage	from-**azh**	cheese
le fruit frais	frwee freh	fresh fruit
les fruits de mer	frwee duh mer	seafood
le gâteau	gah-**toh**	cake
la glace	glas	ice, ice cream
grillé	gree-**yay**	grilled
le homard	om**ahr**	lobster
l'huile	l'weel	oil
le jambon	zhoñ-**boñ**	ham
le lait	leh	milk
les légumes	lay-**goom**	vegetables
la moutarde	moo-**tard**	mustard
l'oeuf	l'uf	egg
les oignons	leh zonyoñ	onions
les olives	leh zoleev	olives
l'orange	l'oroñzh	orange
l'orange pressée	l'oroñzh press-**eh**	fresh orange juice
le pain	pan	bread
le petit pain	puh-**tee** pañ	roll
poché	posh-**ay**	poached
le poisson	pwah-**ssoñ**	fish
le poivre	pwavr	pepper
la pomme	pom	apple
les pommes de terre	pom-duh tehr	potatoes
le porc	por	pork
le potage	poh-**tazh**	soup
le poulet	poo-**lay**	chicken
le riz	ree	rice
rôti	row-**tee**	roast
la sauce	sohs	sauce
la saucisse	soh**sees**	sausage, fresh
sec	sek	dry
le sel	sel	salt
la soupe	soop	soup
le sucre	sookr	sugar
le thé	tay	tea
le toast	toast	toast
la viande	vee-**yand**	meat
le vin blanc	vañ bloñ	white wine
le vin rouge	vañ roozh	red wine
le vinaigre	vee**naygr**	vinegar

Numbers

0	zéro	zeh-**roh**
1	un, une	uñ, oon
2	deux	duh
3	trois	trwah
4	quatre	katr
5	cinq	sañk
6	six	sees
7	sept	set
8	huit	weet
9	neuf	nerf
10	dix	dees
11	onze	oñz
12	douze	dooz
13	treize	trehz
14	quatorze	ka**torz**
15	quinze	kañz
16	seize	sehz
17	dix-sept	dees-**set**
18	dix-huit	dees-**weet**
19	dix-neuf	dees-**nerf**
20	vingt	vañ
30	trente	tront
40	quarante	karoñt
50	cinquante	sañkoñt
60	soixante	swasoñt
70	soixante-dix	swasoñt-**dees**
80	quatre-vingts	katr-**vañ**
90	quatre-vingt-dix	katr-vañ-**dees**
100	cent	soñ
1,000	mille	meel

Time

one minute	une minute	oon mee-**noot**
one hour	une heure	oon urr
half an hour	une demi-heure	oon **duh-mee** urr
Monday	lundi	luñ-**dee**
Tuesday	mardi	mar-**dee**
Wednesday	mercredi	mehrkruh-**dee**
Thursday	jeudi	zhuh-**dee**
Friday	vendredi	voñdruh-**dee**
Saturday	samedi	sam-dee
Sunday	dimanche	dee-**moñsh**